One day
at a

Sus... ...ewis is the bestsell... ...She is al.. ...e author of *Just One More Day*, the moving memoir of her early childhood in Bristol. She lives in Gloucestershire. He website address is www.susanlewis.com

Susan is also a supporter of the childhood bereavement charity, Winston's Wish: www.winstonswish.org.uk and of the breast cancer charity, BUST: www.bustbristol.co.uk

Praise for Susan Lewis' novels

'Utterly compelling' *Sun*

'Expertly written to brew an atmosphere of foreboding, this story is an irresistible blend of intrigue and passion, and the consequences of secrets and betrayal' *Woman*

'Spellbinding! . . . you just keep turning the pages, with the atmosphere growing more and more intense as the story leads to its dramatic climax' *Daily Mail*

'A multi-faceted tear jerker' *heat*

'One of the best around' *Independent on Sunday*

'Sad, happy, sensual and intriguing' *Woman's Own*

Also by Susan Lewis

A Class Apart
Dance While You Can
Stolen Beginnings
Darkest Longings
Obsession
Vengeance
Summer Madness
Last Resort
Wildfire
Chasing Dreams
Taking Chances
Cruel Venus
Strange Allure
Silent Truths
Wicked Beauty
Intimate Strangers
The Hornbeam Tree
The Mill House
A French Affair
Missing
Out of the Shadows
Lost Innocence
The Choice
Forgotten
Stolen
No Turning Back

Just One More Day, A Memoir

Susan Lewis

One day
at a time

arrow books

Published by Arrow Books 2011

1 3 5 7 9 10 8 6 4 2

Author photograph on p. 429 © Colin Thomas

This book is a work of non-fiction based on the life, experiences and
recollections of the author. In some cases names of people have been changed
to protect the privacy of others. The author has stated to the publishers that,
except in such minor respects not affecting the substantial accuracy of the
work, the contents of this book are true.

First published in Great Britain in 2011 by
Arrow Books
Random House, 20 Vauxhall Bridge Road,
London SW1V 2SA

www.randomhouse.co.uk

Addresses for companies within The Random House Group Limited can be
found at: www.randomhouse.co.uk/offices.htm

The Random House Group Limited Reg. No. 954009

A CIP catalogue record for this book
is available from the British Library

ISBN 9780099560074

The Random House Group Limited supports The Forest Stewardship Council
(FSC®), the leading international forest certification organisation. Our books
carrying the FSC label are printed on FSC® certified paper. FSC is the only
forest certification scheme endorsed by the leading environmental
organisations, including Greenpeace. Our paper procurement policy can be
found at www.randomhouse.co.uk/environment

MIX
Paper from
responsible sources
FSC® C016897

Typeset by SX Composing DTP, Rayleigh, Essex
Printed and bound in Great Britain by
CPI Group (UK) Ltd, Croydon, CR0 4YY

For Eddie and Eddress's grandchildren
Grace and Tom

Acknowledgments

My warmest thanks got to ex-Red Maid and former partners-in-mischief Christl Hughes, Lindy Stacey and Sara Clark. They have different names in the book, but they'll know for sure who they are.

With love and many thanks to my cousin Alwyn Brabham.

A huge thank you and much love to my partner, James Grafton Garrett, for his invaluable support, interest and encouragement during the research and writing of this book. I know my dad would have loved him so I'm very sorry that they never met. A big thank you too to my agent Toby Eady and editor Susan Sandon. Nothing would ever get written without them, never mind published.

I'd also like to dedicate this book the the enormous number of readers who contacted me after reading *Just One More Day* to ask what happened to my father and brother. Herein lies the tale . . .

Chapter One

Susan

I saw a film once, or part of a film anyway, where two prison officers were walking a murderer along this creepy dark corridor to where he was going to have his head chopped off. Actually, they might have been going to hang him, or shoot him to bits, or fry him up in an electric chair. I never found out, because my mum caught me hiding behind her chair watching the film I was too young for, and packed me off to bed, lucky not to have a clip round the ear for sneaking downstairs.

Anyway, the point is, I'm that person now, being walked along a creepy corridor to the end of my life. I know they don't put eleven-year-olds to death, but they do lock them up, and that's definite, because it's happening to me right now. My dad and Auntie Nance are marching me along like prison warders, and I – even though I haven't done anything wrong – am going to be shut away in this stinky, horrible, really scary place that's full of ghosts and evil witches and probably has secret passageways all gummed up in spider's webs and rat nests that you can never find your way out of.

And you should see my shoes.

Even my gran wouldn't wear shoes like this. Well, actually she does, and that's my point. She's really old and I'm not, so it's just mean to make me wear these black lace-ups with a round toe and big thick heels like a man's. They even squeak, and they hurt, but no one cares, because no one asked me if I wanted to come here and I *don't*. I cried and cried and begged my dad not to make me, but he kept saying it would be for the best.

'You'll get a good education and go to university and I'll be very proud of you,' he said, over and over again.

'I don't want you to be proud of me,' I shouted, over and over again. 'It's stupid being proud. It's a sin, even, because it says so in the Bible.'

'She's got an answer for everything,' my auntie muttered. I could tell I was getting on her nerves and I was glad, because she was getting on mine. I wished she'd go home, and my mum would come back. Mum might have been strict, and it might have been her idea for me to go to this stupid school in the first place, but I knew she thought it was creepy too – and stuck-up and not somewhere she'd ever really want to send me. Would she? When I came to think of it, I decided that perhaps it was a good job she wasn't there to ask, just in case her mind was still made up, because there was never any getting round her. Not like Dad.

'Please Dad, I want to stay home with you and Gary and all my friends,' I begged. 'I'll be really good, I promise. I'll do all the housework and the washing, I'll make your tea every night and wash up all the dishes and dry them and I'll never answer back.'

'My love,' he said, in the voice he uses when he's sorry and upset, but he won't back down, 'you've won your place there now, which is marvellous, because it goes to show how clever you are. Not everyone can go to Red Maids . . . '

'I don't care. I don't want to go. I'm not clever, I'm really dumb and I want to stay here with you.'

He gave me a big hug, mainly because I was crying, and he never likes it when I cry. 'I can't let you stay here,' he told me (I think he was close to crying too, which just went to show that he didn't want me to go really). 'People might start saying things, because you're a girl and there's only me and Gary . . . '

'Then we'll bash them up. What sort of things?'

'Bad things, and if they do, someone might come and take you away and we don't want that, do we?'

'So you're sending me away instead?'

'To a place where you'll grow up to be a proper lady, the way your mum wanted.'

I didn't say anything else after that. I just put on my cross face and stormed off, because I didn't see why we had to do anything Mum wanted when she wasn't even there to tell us what she thought any more. I want her to come back, more than anything. Sometimes I feel as though all my skin is going to explode I want it so much. It makes me really mad that she's gone. I mean, some days it's all right, I just get on with things and it's like normal, but then it suddenly becomes all horrible and wrong, and I feel really afraid to think that I might never see her again. I hide under the sheets so no one can hear me crying – or stand by my bedroom window and look up at the sky in case she's there, looking down. 'Please come back,' I whisper. '*Please.*'

They keep saying she's dead, and I know it's true, but then suddenly I'm not all that sure. You see, I found a photo once, when I was about nine which was before she was dead. It was tucked inside her cookbook and it was of a man called Michael. He'd even signed it, *To Eddress, with love.* I remember feeling really scared and angry, like everything was going out of control. I ended up tearing it into little bits so she wouldn't be able to look at it any more. Because she had a wicked temper I expected her to go on the rampage after that, demanding to know what had happened to the photo, but she never said a word, which just goes to show it must have been a secret. Apart from once hearing her say to Mrs Williams – her best friend and our next door neighbour – that she had to see Michael, I never heard her mention him, and I never asked who he was in case she told me it was someone she loved more than Daddy.

The next time she went into hospital I asked her if it was where she was really going and she said, 'You're a dafty, aren't you? Where else would I be going?'

'I don't know,' I answered. 'When will you be coming back?'

'Soon, I hope, but you have to be brave for Daddy and Gary and keep your chin up while I'm gone, all right?'

'Are you taking your cookbook?'

She gave a cry of laughter. 'You do ask the funniest things at times,' she said. 'What am I going to be needing that for?'

I only shrugged, because I couldn't give her a proper answer, and because I felt glad she didn't need it I put my arms around her.

'Oh, what's all this nonsense now?' she said as I started to cry.

'I don't want you to go,' I told her.

'I know, my old love, and I don't want to go either, but it's the only way I'm going to get better.'

'But there's nothing wrong with you, not really.'

'Just a little bit, but we'll get it sorted out, and if it turns out to take a bit longer than we think it'll still be all right, because whatever happens you'll still be my best girl, and nothing's ever going to change that.'

I don't know if I'm still her best girl now, because I don't know if it counts when people are dead. Unless she's not really dead and she did go off with Michael. I hope she did in a way, because then she'd be able to come back. The trouble is, I saw them carrying a coffin out of our house just after Daddy told me the angels had come to take her to Jesus, and I think she must have been in it. I was next door when it happened, and I saw, because I peeped out of their landing window. They put the coffin in a big black car and drove off. It could have been a trick, of course, and if it was I don't know where she's living with her other family, I just think it's really mean to leave your husband and children, especially when they haven't done anything wrong.

It's worse for Gary, because he was only five when she went. (He's seven now.) Everyone felt really sorry for him. I heard my aunts and uncles talking and arguing about him one night. They all wanted him to go and live with them. No one wanted me, which was good, because I wouldn't go and live with any of them if they begged me. I just want to stay with my dad, because he's the best person in the whole wide world with loads of stories up his sleeve and great big hugs any time we want one. He's really clever and funny, and everyone likes him and says hello to him, and offers to do things to help him. The only thing he's not very good at is cooking, but that doesn't matter. We don't have to eat much, beans on toast will do, or fish-fingers and chips. I quite like corned-beef mash too, except when the potatoes are still hard. On Sundays we usually have a roast dinner with one of my aunties, followed by tinned peaches and condensed milk for afters – my favourite.

Wonder what poison we'll be served up here in this bloody school.

We've just reached a prison bed, which is the last but one in a row of about twelve going down one side of the dormitory. Opposite is another row of twelve and at the end are two private rooms where, apparently, sixth-form girls live. All the beds have blue iron frames (and snakes under, I expect), with a cubicle behind that has a curtain across the front so no one can see in. Inside the cubicle is a dressing table with two drawers for our brassieres and bags (that's what they call knickers here, or so it said in the information they sent – *bags*, what a stupid name), and a wardrobe to hang up all our uniforms. There are loads of them. One for school, in summer, another for winter, another for evenings, a different one for Saturdays, and one that's actually quite mod for Sundays. (The Sunday uniform is a bit like a Mary Quant dress, because it's straight with long sleeves, a zip up the front and a white collar that can be unbuttoned off the dress so we can put it in the wash. If it was short it would be really fab, like one I've seen my cousin Alwyn wearing, but it comes right down to the knee and we have to wear these thick granny stockings under it that are as old-fashioned and vile as our shoes. Honestly, I'm so glad no one can see me.)

There are lots of other girls arriving with their parents, and by the sound of it they all speak really posh. I'm not going to speak posh for anyone. The girls in the beds either side of mine are first-formers too, and the one whose name turns out to be Laura has a sister up the other end of the dormitory who's a year older. Her name's Cheryl.

'Are you all right then?' my dad asks in his best chirpy voice. He's trying to seem jolly and jokey, but I think he looks a bit worried and shabby in amongst all these tall, stuck-up people with their smart hairy overcoats and bri-nylon shirts. He's taken his cap off now and put it in his pocket, but Auntie Nance's scarf is still tied up under her chin like it's trying to stop her mouth falling open. No one else is wearing a scarf – or a cap.

'No,' I say.

'I know, why don't we put your things in your dressing table?' he suggests.

'No.'

'Come on, I'll do it,' Auntie Nance tells him.

So they open up the curtain behind my bed and start stuffing my smalls, socks and nighties into the drawers. Everything has a name tag on it – Susan Lewis RM 74. My dad sewed them in himself, so they're a bit wonky, but who cares? I was going to help, but then I thought, why should I when I don't even want to go there?

'We've put your nice writing pad in your top drawer,' Dad tells me. 'You'll be able to send us lots of letters telling us what's happening.'

My stomach's starting to go all funny now and I think I'm really scared. 'I'm not writing to you,' I tell him sharply.

'Well, that's a shame, because I'll be writing to you.'

'I won't read your stupid letters.'

Auntie Nance is taking something out of her handbag. 'Here's a couple of mint humbugs,' she says, passing them over. 'Don't tell anyone you've got them, because you're supposed to hand in your sweets.'

I look at my dad, but he's not looking at me. He's

watching what everyone else is doing. Some parents are starting to leave now, and some of the girls have already changed into their uniforms. Our own clothes have to be laid out on the end of our beds ready for collection, and we won't get them back again until the next time we're allowed home. 'Please don't make me stay,' I say, catching hold of Dad's hand.

He's starting to look all worried and ruffled.

'That's enough of that nonsense now,' Auntie Nance butts in. 'You're a lucky girl to be here, and don't you forget it.'

I don't think my mum liked Auntie Nance very much, and I can see why.

Suddenly an alarm starts shrieking around the walls like a witch's scream. Fab! There's a fire! Let's move! I start grabbing my things, but then I realise no one else is reacting the same way.

'That'll be it then,' my dad says. 'Time for us to go.'

I look at him again. He's not really going to leave me here. I know he won't, because he loves me, or he's always said he does, so he wouldn't be so mean as to go home without me. He can see how horrible this place is with its stink of BO and cabbage and great big windows that are too high to see out of, even if you stood on a chair. There are all sorts of rules and regulations we got sent that I still don't understand, and I'll only get to see him on Sundays after church, and that's not fair when all my friends are seeing their mums and dads every single day. I want to see my mum. Where is she? Why doesn't she come and save me?

Daddy won't leave me. I know he won't.

'All right then, my love,' he says, and puts his arms around me.

I turn away.

'I'll put your suitcase here, at the end of the bed,' Auntie Nance says. 'They'll probably tell you what to do with it later.'

'Dad,' I wail.

'Oh, come on now, you're a big girl,' he chides.

I don't want anyone to see me crying, but it's really hard to make myself stop. I steal a quick look round and see that the other girls are unpacking, or chatting to one another, or lying on their beds reading comics and magazines. I like *Dandy* and *Beano*, but *Jackie*'s the best, even though I'm not supposed to be old enough to read it. All I've got now is a copy of Lambs' *Tales From Shakespeare* which I don't like reading myself, because it's always better when Dad reads it out loud.

'Do I get a kiss then?' he asks.

I shake my head.

'That's not very nice now, is it?' Auntie Nance says.

I don't look at her, because I've really stopped liking her now. She used to be my favourite auntie once, but not any more.

'I'll be up next Sunday,' Dad tells me. 'I'll bring Gary to the church with me and we'll see you after.'

'I don't want to go to church,' I reply. 'I don't believe in God.'

'Now, now. You won't go to heaven if you say things like that.'

'I don't want to go to heaven, I want to go home.'

'Try to be a good girl,' Auntie Nance says.

I want to tell her to bugger off, the way my mum did once, but I don't have the guts. So I look at Daddy and say, 'Please let me come with you.'

He takes both my hands in his and says, 'All you have to do is take one day at a time and everything will be fine.'

He said that after Mummy died and it wasn't, and now it never will be again.

He plonks a kiss on my head and gives me a great big hug, then I stand next to my bed watching him walking away. I keep staring at his back, willing him to give in and come back to get me. I know he will. He won't be able to leave me on my own, because he's too kind and always gives me everything I want – well, most of the time anyway.

Anything could happen to me in a place like this, so he must be scared too. I wasn't supposed to be a boarder. I was supposed to be a day girl, and I would be if my mum hadn't died. It's all her fault really and now there's nothing I can do to change it.

Daddy goes out through the double doors at the end of the dormitory and disappears with Auntie Nance. I'm still standing next to my bed. I don't know what to do. I'm so full up with unhappiness that I can hardly move.

I clench my hands really tightly. I don't care that he doesn't love me. I always knew he was just pretending, like everyone else. I expect him and Gary would rather be on their own, without me. They might not even write me letters, or come to see me, or let me go home for holidays.

Why doesn't anyone want me?

I'm all on my own now, like an orphan in an orphanage.

I have to try and be brave, like Oliver Twist.

Keeping my head down, I go into my cubicle and close the curtain before anyone can tell I'm crying. I can hear them all talking out there, but I'm too afraid to go and join in. They all seem to know one another and no one's interested in me. Why would they be when they're all posh and I'm stupid and common?

I wish I was dead with Mummy, but knowing her she'd only send me back again and tell me to go and make Daddy proud.

I don't want to make anyone proud. I just want my mummy back so we can go home.

◆

Eddie

Dear oh dear oh dear, this hasn't been an easy day, getting our Susan out of the house and then having to leave her like that. I kept wondering if Eddress could see us, motoring along in our blue Ford Consul, chugging up the drive of that school to those gloomy old front doors. Our Susan was sitting in the back, hardly saying a word, which isn't like her at all, because she's always had a lot to say for herself. Too much, our Nance reckons. The cat definitely had her tongue today, though.

I'm back home again now, and I don't mind admitting it broke my heart leaving her there. I couldn't let it show, or it would have upset her even more, and she was already crying when Nance and I walked away. It must have been terrible for her, watching our backs. Maybe I should have turned around and given her a wave, but I was afraid it might make it harder for us both if I did.

It's a blinking irony, isn't it? Her mother dying goes and gets her a place as a boarder at the school. She passed the scholarship to become a day girl, but then I was told that the founder, John Whitson, set aside funds to educate two girls every year whose mothers have passed on. So we've got a boarding grant, which brings the fees down to two hundred and eighty-eight quid a year. Still a lot, but I'm going to do me best to manage it, because it's what her mother would want, and so do I.

Blimey, the house feels empty without my girl. I keep thinking she's going to come thundering up the stairs any minute and fly into my room the way she does. It still upsets me to think of it as my room, when it always used to be 'ours' – mine and Eddress's – Eddie and Ed get wed. Where are you, Eddress? Can you see us now? Do you know what I'm thinking? It's been over a year since you went, and I'm no closer to getting used to it now than I ever was. I miss you, my love, more and more as the days pass. The world's a colourless place now you've gone. My only joy is in our children, but watching them growing up without you is every bit as hard as losing you. Our Susan gets more like you every day, little minx that she is. They both look like you, with their red hair and fiery freckles. I didn't know love could be so fierce until we had them, and now it's fiercer than ever, because they're yours and I know how much you love them too.

Your wardrobe's still here, with most of your clothes in it, and your dressing table, full of all your petticoats and smalls, and our photograph albums and other knick-knacks you collected over the years. There's a book of Green Shield stamps that I keep meaning to give to your mam. I'll get round to clearing it all out sooner or later, no rush though, I don't need the space, and I like having your things around me.

Back to our Susan. I can hardly bear to picture her face when I left her today. You should have seen her, Ed. Maybe you did, because for all we know you were with us, in your own dimension, trying to guide us through the right thing to do. I know you agree with me that it'll be good for her to have women taking care of her now you can't be here any more. People like that lot up there, the teachers and matrons and whatnot, they know much more than I do about showing a girl how to get on in the world, and it's what we always wanted for our Susan, isn't it, that she should do well?

Dear little soul, she's had her mind set on being my housekeeper ever since you went, but between us, she's a bloody nuisance when she starts up with the vacuum and dusters. And as for cooking, she's worse than me and that's really saying something. Our poor Gary, no wonder he looks forward to going up your mother's or round our Nance's a couple of times a week, at least then he gets some decent food on his plate.

He'll be going to boarding school too when the time comes, if I can get him in, that is. It's only right that he should have a good start in life too. I might be earning a bit more by then, with any luck. Shan't like it much without either of them around, won't like it one bit, as a matter of fact, but I keep reminding myself it'll be for the best.

It's funny how things happen, isn't it. There we were, the four of us, happy as can be, like any normal family, then before we know it you've gone, leaving us all out of balance, like a table with three legs. We can't seem to hold on to anything now, and I feel as though it's my fault. I ought to be propping us up better than I am, and I try, but I'm not daft enough to think I can ever take your place. I just don't have the love and common sense and magic that was you.

Do you know, Ed, that we have a home help these days who comes in the morning to get the kids off to school, and again in the afternoons for when they come home? Our Susan didn't want to know about her at first. A right little madam she was, saying she was old enough to look after herself, but luckily she took to her all right in the end. Gary loves her to bits. Mrs Jewell's her name. She wants them to call her Auntie Kath, which I don't think is right, when she's not a relative, but they're doing it anyway. I can hear you telling me I'm too much of a stickler for using proper titles, but I suppose that's the way I am. I get the feeling she thinks I'm cruel for sending Susan to Red Maids, and you should have seen the state our Susan got herself into when she had to say cheerio to her last Friday. I had to practically drag her off, and poor Mrs Jewell was crying too. I offered her a lift home, but she said no, it was best she made her own way so I could stay and try to settle our Susan. She's a kind woman. The salt-of-the-earth type, with a fag always hanging out the corner of her mouth, and a laugh that could grate cheese. She does a good job with the kids, and around the house. She's keeping your front door knocker nice and polished, and the doorstep spotless too.

Oh, there's our Gary shouting for me downstairs, so watch me putting on a smile before I go to see what he wants. Can you see me in the mirror? I'm looking around the room. Where are you then, Ed? Where can we find you, my old love?

'Dad! *Dad*! Oh, there you are. Shall we have a fight?' Gary's dear little face with his cornflake freckles and missing front teeth is looking up at me with all the eagerness his seven-year-old heart can muster.

'But you always beat me up,' I complain.

He beams with delight. 'I know, that's because you're a weed, and I'm the champion. Come on, Dad, please, let's have a fight. You said we could when you got back.'

'All right then. You were a good boy for Mrs Williams, were you?'

'Yep.' He's already lunging at me, grabbing me round the middle and trying to force me to my knees.

Down I go, yielding to the champ.

'Yeah!' he cries, and next thing I'm in a headlock with his legs wrapped round my waist, and his growls filling up my ears.

Suddenly I wrench him over my shoulder and catch him just before he hits the floor.

He looks up at me with astonished eyes. 'Cor! That was a good move, Dad.'

'Submit?' I demand, holding him down.

'Never!' He can't move an inch.

'Submit?'

'No, cos you cheated so I'm the winner.'

'No, I'm the winner.'

'Grrmph!' and he's up. He's on my back and I'm in a headlock again.

'Submit?' he shouts.

'No!'

'Yeah, Dad, you've got to submit.'

'Oh. All right. I submit.'

'Hooray! I'm the champion of the world and you're my slave from now on. You have to do everything I say, and I say I want four pieces of beans on toast for tea please.'

'*Four*?'

'Yep, because I have to build up my muscles. You should have four too, then you might not be a weed any more.'

Laughing, I ruffle his ginger crew cut and haul myself up. Beans on toast it is – at least I can't go far wrong with that.

'Dad?' he says, following me into the kitchen a few minutes later. 'Where's our Susan?'

I look down at his puzzled face and want to scoop him up for a cuddle. He won't like it though, because he's a big boy now and cuddles have become soppy lately. 'Do you remember I told you, she's at school?'

'But it's Sunday.'

'I know, but she's going to be what's called a boarder,' I explain again. 'That means she'll be sleeping there as well as having lessons.'

This seems to be a problem his little brain's having some difficulty solving. 'She'll be coming back though, won't she?'

'Oh yes, on Sundays when they have exeats . . . '

'What's that?'

'An exeat is like a day off. So she'll be coming home then, and for school holidays. And we'll be able to see her *every* Sunday after church.'

He's starting to look increasingly worried. 'What about her bedroom? Won't she be sleeping there any more?'

'When she's here, of course she will.'

He falls quiet for a while. It seems all the explaining I've done up to now hasn't meant very much, but with Susan no longer here it's starting to sink in. 'Does that mean she'll be doing lessons every single day and never have any time off?' he asks, apparently appalled.

I give a little laugh. 'No. She'll do her lessons the same as you, but when she's finished she'll stay at school with the other girls.'

'What about her tea?'

'She'll have it there.'

He takes some more time to absorb this, while I open a large tin of beans and empty it into a pan. 'Doesn't she want to be with us any more?' he asks in the end.

Seeing how troubled he is, I hike him up on to the draining board so we're at the same level. 'It's not that she doesn't want to be with us,' I tell him gently, 'it's just not right for a girl to be in a house where there's only a daddy to look after her. That's why she's gone away to school, so

14

she can be with other girls and teachers who are women, not because she doesn't want to be with us – especially you, because you're the best brother in the whole wide world.'

His eyes grow round with amazement. 'Is that what she says?'

'Only to me, and it's supposed to be a secret, so don't tell her I told you.'

He's downcast again. 'I know she's really bossy,' he says dismally, 'but I wish she'd come back.'

I do too, but I can't tell him that, so I put him back on the floor, suggesting that he goes and lays the table. Funny how he never asks about his mother now. He used to, at first, always wanting to know when she was coming back, going to sit out on the doorstep to wait, asking if we could go to the hospital to pick her up. I suppose he must be getting used to her not being here now, which I'm glad about, but sorry too, because it's not right for a little boy to grow up without his mother. I expect he's starting to wonder why everyone seems to be leaving, but he'll come to understand one of these days that sometimes things happen that we can't do anything about.

Susan hardly ever mentions her mother either, and though that used to upset me at first, I've come to realise that I probably don't help matters because I don't know if I can talk about her without breaking down, and I wouldn't want our Susan seeing that. Besides, it doesn't do any good to dwell on these things. I know I do in my head, but all the talking in the world is never going to bring Eddress back, so best to do as I told our Susan, take one day at a time and sooner or later we'll get used to being without her.

I wonder what our Susan's doing now? Is she all right? Has she had her tea yet? I hope she's not crying.

Dear God in heaven, please bless her and keep her safe.

Have I done the right thing? I know I have, but it's breaking my heart all the same.

Susan

'Right, all of you first-formers come and stand in a line. Susan, you go in the middle. Laura and Glenys, either side of her. That's right. Stand up straight, you pathetic creatures. Don't slouch.'

Laura and Glenys are the other two new girls in our dorm. Our beds are the last three in the row on the right-hand side, with Laura's on the end, next to the piano, then mine, then Glenys's. Laura's about the same height as me, with mousy-coloured hair and glasses. Glenys is much taller, with dark hair that looks like it's been cut round a pudding bowl.

I don't know who the girl is who's bossing us around. Someone said she's third form which means whatever is about to happen is serious, because according to Laura only second form normally speak to new girls. (Laura would know from her sister, Cheryl.)

We finished our tea, downstairs in the dining hall, about an hour ago – cauliflower cheese and something black, or dark brown, and slimy, that I'd never seen before, so I didn't eat it. Someone said it was called orange bean, which I've never heard of and I hope we never get again. We had to say grace first, in Latin. I don't know what's wrong with English, especially when our Bibles are written in it. If you ask me it's just showing off, saying grace in another language.

Anyway, God doesn't listen to anything I say, because if He did I wouldn't be here, so who cares which language I speak to Him in? (I hope He didn't hear that thought, because it was a bit rude and if I make Him cross he might never do anything to get me out of here.)

We're standing in a line now, Laura, me and Glenys, at the foot of my bed. Our dormitory is called Speedwell, after one of John Whitson's ships (he's the school's founder and apparently he had a wooden leg). Everything in our dorm is dark blue, a bit like the sea I suppose. The beds, the walls, the hot-water pipes, the doors, everything. If you go through the bathrooms at the far end you get to the next dorm which is called Discoverer (another John Whitson ship), where everything's yellow, maybe like the sun coming out when he spotted dry land. On the floor below are two more dorms called Maryflowre, which is light blue, like the sky, and Seabreake, which is green, again like the sea. (I reckon one of them should be red, but I suppose they can't do that because that's the colour of our uniforms and the girls might blend in like cherries in a bowl of fresh blood.)

A group of older girls are staring at us. There are about six of them, and they're looking all snooty and menacing. I don't think I've done anything wrong, but they're making me feel as though I have. We only arrived a few hours ago, so how are we supposed to know all the rules yet? I wish my dad was here, because he knows everything, and he'd probably be able to stop them looking as though they want to hit me. I wonder what Gary's doing now. I bet he had something lush for tea, like fishcakes, peas and mash, or beans on toast.

'Susan, are you really going to sleep in *those* pyjamas?'

Everyone starts to laugh.

I feel my face go all hot and red and I want to hit Auntie Nance, because I hate these pyjamas and didn't want to bring them in the first place. They're all quilted like an anorak and covered in big yellow roses. She bought them in Jones's downtown, and made me pack them, because, she said, it's what posh people wear, so I should too, now I'm going to be posh. *I don't want to be posh. I want to be common and normal and get out of here!*

'Answer,' someone shouts at me.

I'm getting all flustered. I don't know what to say.

'My name is Nina Lowe,' she tells me.

My heart does a jump as I look at her. She's got black hair and a bit of a hairy face. She's definitely one of the third-

17

formers, because everyone else is too young to grow a moustache, whereas hers is coming along nicely.

'There are the written rules of the school,' Nina Lowe declares, 'and there are the unwritten. I'm here to tell you about the unwritten. Are you listening?'

I nod, very fast. *Yes, I'm definitely listening*.

I think Glenys and Laura must have nodded too, because Nina goes on. 'Years one to five *never* use the front stairs,' she informs us. 'There are back stairs which we all use, but whenever you see someone older than you coming, either from in front, or behind, you immediately stand back. Do you understand?'

We all nod.

I think it's raining outside. I'm tempted to look up at the window, but I don't expect they'll like me doing that.

'Susan, what did I just say?'

I think really fast. 'I have to stand back on the stairs,' I jabber.

Everyone starts sniggering, and I realise I must have got something wrong, but I'm sure she didn't say anything after telling us about the stairs.

'She's from Kingswood,' I hear someone whisper.

'Where's that?'

'The other side of Bristol. All council houses.'

'How did she get here?'

I can feel my face going beetroot again, and I wish I could call them stuck-up pigs and tell them to get lost, but I don't have the guts.

Nina carries on ranting about all kinds of rules that don't seem to make any sense to me, or I'm not really taking them in. I hear something about struck-ons, which is where a first-former can choose an older girl – second form up, any dormitory – to get *struck on*. The meaning of it seems to be that she would come and tuck you up at night, and maybe read you a story (if she feels like it) and you have to make her bed, sweep under it, write her poems and draw her pictures. I think there are other things too, but I missed them, because I'm watching another girl peeling an orange and throwing the skin on the floor.

'Are you listening to what's being said, Susan?' Nina Lowe asks.

I nod.

'Pick up that orange peel,' she barks.

Quickly I stoop to get it.

'Now eat it.'

I stare at her. Orange peel is the most disgusting thing in the world.

'Give it to me,' someone snaps, and grabs it out of my hand. For a minute I think she's going to shove it into my mouth, but luckily she walks over to the piano and drops it in a bin.

'So, Susan,' Nina says to me, 'you'll fill your struck-on's hot-water bottle, give her your tuck and buy her anything she wants with your pocket money?'

I go a bit still. I don't have any pocket money, and even if I did I don't want to spend it on someone else. I don't want to give anyone my tuck, either, in case I get hungry.

The girl with the orange passes a segment to Nina, and after chewing it up Nina spits a pip into my face.

It hits my cheek, just below my eye, and really stings. I don't know what to say.

'Sadie, tell them about Johnny,' Nina commands.

A pretty, dark-haired girl, with freckles on her nose and dimples, says, 'The school's haunted by our founder, John Whitson. There's never any knowing when he might come to visit, but it's always before Founder's Day which is in November. After that, he disappears until the start of a new school year.'

I'm beginning to shake. I knew this place was haunted, and without Daddy here to save me I don't know what I'm going to do – unless, if Mummy's a ghost now, maybe she can fight him off.

I don't want Mummy to be a ghost.

'Johnny is most interested in the youngest girl in each

dormitory,' Sadie goes on. 'Who's the youngest out of you three?'

It turns out to be me, because my birthday's in August. I'm only just eleven, whereas Glenys and Laura are nearly twelve. I think Johnny should haunt them, because it's mean to pick on the youngest.

'Flying angels,' someone else says. 'You have to do at least three before Founder's Day, or you'll be made to wash everyone's bags in your year for a week.'

'A flying angel,' Nina Lowe explains, 'is a jump from the top of your wardrobe on to your bed. If you break your leg it doesn't count, so you'll have to do it again.'

'Tomorrow morning you'll be given your offices,' Sadie continues. 'First bell will ring at ten to seven, second bell at ten past. That's when everyone who's on offices has to start sweeping the stairs, or laying tables for breakfast, or cleaning out the house maids.'

I wonder what house maids are, but don't dare to ask. I expect it's toilets or something, and if they think I'm cleaning them then they've got another think coming.

Nina spits another orange pip in my face and it comes really tight on my nose.

I give her one of my best dirty looks.

Her mouth falls open in shock. 'Don't you dare look at me like that,' she cries. 'As a first year you're not allowed to look at me at all. Now get down on your knees and say sorry this minute or I'll slap your face.'

I don't want to get down on my knees, but I don't want her to hit me either, so I do it. 'You shouldn't spit pips at me,' I tell her, 'it's not polite.'

She looks shocked all over again. 'Never speak until spoken to,' she rages at me. 'Now apologise for that look.'

I hang my head. 'I'm sorry,' I mumble.

'Now apologise for speaking without being spoken to.'

'I'm sorry.'

'As a punishment you'll do Sadie's offices for a week,' she tells me. 'She's on bog-cleaning duty.'

Everyone sniggers, even Laura and Glenys.

'What are you two laughing at?' Nina barks. 'You don't even know what's funny. Susan, don't look at them. You're supposed to be staring at the floor.'

'Get her to dance a jig,' someone says.

'Yeah, that should be a laugh. In those pyjamas.'

'Can you dance, Susan?'

'What about the slippers? Have you seen them? My grandma has slippers like that.'

I'm trying really hard not to cry, but I'm scared and I want to go home so much that I might start sobbing if I don't stop thinking about it. This is worse than being in prison, because at least there I might have a cell to myself, or my head chopped off and then it would all be over.

Suddenly the swing doors at the end fly open and someone dashes in. 'Cluttie's coming,' she hisses, and everyone instantly rushes to their beds.

'Come on,' Laura says, getting hold of my arm. 'Quick.'

I'm just climbing under the covers when a great big fat woman with flick-up glasses and curly silver hair stomps into the room.

'It's Miss Clutterbuck,' Laura whispers. 'The head matron.'

Miss Clutterbuck is glaring up and down the room like a dragon looking for a snack. I wouldn't be surprised if smoke started coming out of her nose, or a spiky tail came swishing in the door behind her. 'Where are the new girls?' she booms.

'At the end,' someone answers.

As Cluttie's fiery eyes find us we cower under our counterpanes.

When she reaches the foot of Glenys's bed she checks something on a list she's holding. 'Glenys Beach?' she barks.

I can hear Glenys swallow from where I am. 'Yes,' she whispers.

Cluttie moves on, checks her list again. 'Susan Lewis?'

'Yes,' I mutter.

She goes to Laura next, and once she's satisfied we're all there she says, 'The older girls will tell you a lot of nonsense about unwritten school rules. They are not to be obeyed. You will only adhere to the official rules which you'll find in your school manual. Any questions, bring them to me. Any sickness or other difficulties, bring them to me. My office is behind the nursery down on the next landing. Do any of you have sweets or chocolate in your cubicles?'

I've still got my mint humbugs, but I'm not telling her, because she'll probably take them away and I'm getting a bit hungry after that horrible tea.

'No,' Laura says.

'No what?'

Laura looks confused.

'No Miss Clutterbuck,' the matron explains. 'What about you two?'

I shake my head. So does Glenys. 'No Miss Clutterbuck,' we say together.

'If anything's found it'll be confiscated,' she warns us, 'and you'll find yourselves on report. Do you know what a report is?'

She's looking at me so I shake my head.

'Three reports lead to a punishment, and that wouldn't be a good start. Now, I'm glad to see you're all in bed. Seven thirty lights out, apart from Thursdays when you'll be allowed to stay up to watch *Top of the Pops*. Have you looked at your bath rota yet?'

I have, so I know I'm due to have one on Tuesday mornings and Friday evenings. Two a week seems a lot; I only used to have one on Sundays at home.

'In the morning,' Cluttie was saying, 'you'll get up at first bell if you're due for a bath, at second bell if you're on offices, which are duties that will be explained to you after school tomorrow. The third bell will ring at seven twenty, which is the last bell before breakfast which is at seven thirty sharp, except Sundays when it's at eight. Don't be late, or you'll receive a report. No getting out of bed during the night, unless you're ill, or can't wait for the toilet. And no talking after lights out. Welcome to Red Maids. Good night.'

With that she turns on her heel and squeaks off on her rubbery soles towards the door to the bathrooms, which is opposite our beds. I'm just starting to breathe when she suddenly turns back. 'Have you all handed your money in to Miss Sayward?'

'Yes, Miss Clutterbuck,' say Laura and Glenys.

I don't say anything, because I haven't got any money, but she doesn't seem to notice, thank goodness, and next thing she's gone stomping on through the bathrooms ready to invade Discoverer.

I stay where I am, watching the second- and third-form girls getting into bed, then Laura's sister, Cheryl, comes to tuck Laura in. Lucky Laura. I wish I had a sister. If I did I wouldn't have had to come here, because I wouldn't be the only girl at home. I wonder if Gary's missing me. I expect he'll have a story tonight. Dad's really good at reading stories. I hope they don't like it better without me, that would be so mean.

I watch Cheryl give Laura a kiss goodnight, and I feel really pleased when she says goodnight to me too. And to Glenys. At least not all the older girls are horrible.

After that the lights go out, and everything stays quiet for a while. I hear someone whispering a few beds away, and when I turn to look at Laura I can tell she's got a torch on under her blankets.

'What are you doing?' I whisper, wishing I had a torch too.

She peeps out. 'Writing a letter to my mum and dad.'

'Oh,' I say.

'I can give you some paper if you want to write to yours,' she offers. 'You can borrow the torch when I've finished.'

That's really nice of her, so I say thank you and tell her I've got a new pad and envelopes. 'How are you going to post it?' I whisper.

'We have to put stamps on and then we can drop them in a basket down in the front hall.'

I suddenly go all cold inside. I didn't think about stamps, and I haven't got any money to buy some, even if I could get out to the post office, which I can't. I'm really scared now, because if I can't send a letter to Daddy he might think I don't love him any more and then he won't come to see me after church next Sunday, which means I'll be left here all alone and I might never see anyone I love ever again.

Chapter Two

Eddie

Dear Susan, I hope you are all right at your new school. I'm sorry I went away like I did on Sunday night and I hope you forgive me if it upset you. Any partings are usually made worse by drawing them out.

It is dinnertime as I am writing, or should I say lunch? I thought there might have been a letter from you by now, but there isn't, so instead of reading a letter I am writing one. The sun is shining and the day is pleasant.

I'm sitting in Fishponds library where everything's quiet and familiar, and people speak in whispers, or go about on tiptoe. I appreciate the respect this shows for others and am careful to behave the same way. Being amongst so many books is, for me, like being surrounded by scores of old friends. I can feel their energy and nourishment sometimes without even opening the pages. What a blessing it is to be able to read and write. I think of all the great authors and poets who have shared their genius with us and feel linked to them through their words in a way that is both humbling and uplifting.

I often wonder how I'd have got through this past year without my books. Losing myself in history or science, mathematics, politics or the influence of Dostoevsky on the form of the novel has provided me with an escape from the grief like nothing else. Not that it ever goes away, but if I was to stay with it the whole time I dread to think how I'd be. I expect the neighbours thought I'd lost my mind the night before last, when I took myself down to the rhubarb patch at the end of the garden and started tearing it apart. Gary was already in bed, and it was dark out, so maybe no one saw me. I hope not, but they'd have seen the mess in the morning. It gets me like that sometimes, though. It's all bottling up inside me and suddenly I can't take any more and I have to hit out in a way that would be awful for Gary to see. I want to know what I did to deserve this. First my brother, Bob, then six months later my wife. What's God got against our little family that He'd punish us like this?

I don't like violence, I never have, but sometimes the confusion, the grief, gets me all riled up in a way that's not easy to hold in. It's not very Christian either and I feel bad about it after, but the rage I feel towards those people who make cigarettes, and towards Eddress for bloody well smoking the things . . . Well, it's better I get it out of my system by ripping up a rhubarb patch, or thumping a few pillows, than turning on someone at work as he lights up, or writing to the government and finding myself arrested for threatening behaviour.

I hope our Susan writes a letter soon.

I popped into a couple of shops on the way here to pick up some odds and ends we need at home, and a nice big orange and cream slice that Gary and I can share for afters tonight. I'm hoping it might cheer him up a bit, because he seems to be missing our Susan even more than I expected. He's slept in with me these past three nights, needing a cuddle with his dad, in spite of being a big boy now. I wonder if I should have taken him to the school with us last Sunday. If I had, he'd have been able to see for himself where she is, which might have helped him to understand that she hasn't gone to the same place as his mum and won't ever be coming back. I hope he doesn't think that, but if he does it should put his mind at rest when we go up to the church to see her on Sunday.

He's a good boy. I love him so much I've got to be careful

26

when I squeeze him not to make it too hard or I'll hurt him. He was his mother's pride and joy, and he's mine too, along with our Susan who I know is in good hands, but I can't stop worrying about her all the same. I'd really hoped to hear from her by now, even though she said she wouldn't write. I know her though, she says these things, but she doesn't mean them. I'm sure she's all right. I'm writing to her so she'll know we're thinking about her.

Gary and I are well. Gary went to his pony-riding lessons last night and Mrs White (the teacher) was very pleased with him and said he could go round on his own next time. He was overjoyed with himself, as I expect you can imagine. He's taking good care of Sixpence, remembering to feed him and play with him, and at the weekend he's going to help me clean out his cage.

That should please her, to know we're looking after her hamster.

I called in Auntie Nancy's as usual on the way home from work last night. She's making up a nice box for you which I'll bring with me on Sunday. There's the extra stockings you need and she's going to put in some fruit. I've added a copy of Black Beauty *in case you feel like having a read.*

When you write to me please tell me about your lessons and the other girls. I expect you're making lots of friends by now. Love and God bless, from Daddy and Gary. XXXXXXXXXXXXXX

I think she'll like lots of kisses at the bottom. It'll show how much we love her. I ought to get Gary to write too. That should help him to understand that she's not very far away, just the other side of Bristol in a school that's going to do her the world of good in the long run.

PS: Also in the box will be linen bags, two reels of cotton, a packet of needles, a tape measure and a thimble, which we forgot to pack. Auntie Nance has also added some cotton wool and two tins of talcum powder which she says is your favourite, Topaz by Avon.

That should cheer my girl up, knowing she's going to have some nice smelly stuff. She's like her mother in that way, always trying out new scents and soaps, and bubble baths. (She's like her mother in more ways than I can bear to think about at times.) I read in the school manual that she's going to be having two baths a week now, which is nice for a girl. We'll just have to hope she doesn't have a needlework lesson before I can get her parcel to her, or she won't have the right equipment. I wonder if I should ring the school to explain, just in case. I don't want her getting into trouble for something that's not her fault. I can imagine how much that would upset her, and she'll be angry with me, which isn't how we want to spend our time after church on Sunday.

Ah well, time's getting on, so I suppose I'd better be making my way back to work. If I'm late clocking in my pay'll be docked, and I can't afford for that to happen now I've got these fees to pay, even though they have been reduced. I'm hoping to be promoted to foreman of the tool shop when old Fred retires. It'll mean fifty bob or even a couple of quid extra a week, which'll come in very handy now we've got this added expense.

We make pneumatic drills at our factory on Lodge Causeway. I've been there for a good ten years now, since finishing up at the BAC (that's Bristol Aeroplane Company) just after Ed and I got married. The management were very good about letting me have time off when she was ill, but I tried not to take too much because I only get paid for the hours I work, and being short of money wouldn't have helped us at all.

Turned out nothing did in the end, but best not start feeling sorry for myself because that won't get us anywhere.

I found an old book on engineering in a second-hand shop last week by an American chap called William Barclay Parsons. Marvellous it is, and I only had to pay threepence for it. I got so engrossed reading it last night that I didn't notice the time going on, and that rascal Gary stayed out on the green playing football until gone seven, when he should have been in bed.

I'm halfway along the Fishponds Road now, nearly at the

Causeway where they're putting in some traffic lights – about time too – when who should I bump into but Mrs Beach. She's the mother of Glenys, who also started Red Maids this week. When we were leaving the school Mr Beach and I got chatting and he told me they lived around here. Mrs Beach talked about being able to help one another out with lifts and things if ever there was a need. Very nice woman. Her husband's a solicitor, I believe.

'Hello Mr Lewis,' she says in a friendly way, 'what a nice surprise.'

I can just imagine our Susan speaking like that when she grows up, and how thrilled Eddress would be to hear her. I wonder what she'll be, a doctor? The manager of a big office? A travel agent? She likes adventure, so I can see her going round the world in a fearless way, leaving me worried sick at home, with just the odd postcard from places like Guam, or Singapore, or Timbuktu to reassure me she's still alive.

It turns out Mrs Beach has just delivered a box of books to the War on Want shop we're standing outside. I give a quick glance in through the window and catch Mrs Patel's eye – she works in the shop Mondays, Wednesdays and Fridays, and when she gives me a nod I know she's keeping the books back for me to have a sift through first. Very kind of her, but no time today.

'Have you heard from Susan yet?' Mrs Beach asks.

I give a fatherly roll of my eyes. 'They're probably busy settling in,' I reply with a chuckle. 'You know what girls are like.'

She smiles indulgently. 'We've had two letters from Glenys.'

Already? It's only Wednesday.

'Between us, I think she's a little homesick, but she doesn't want to worry us so she won't actually come out and say so. Very stoic. The best way to be, don't you think?'

'Oh, indeed,' I reply. I'm being a jolly, polite sort of chap, while feeling a bit miffed that our Susan hasn't written yet, especially when she picked out the writing pad and pens herself. And hey ho to Mrs Beach that Glenys is so dutiful and stoic. Good old stiff upper lip, can't beat it.

Time's running on, so I have to hurry. One minute past the clocking-in time and I'll lose a full half-hour's pay. Which reminds me, I've got a union meeting tonight, so I'd better get my papers ready, because I might have to stand up and speak. I wonder if being deputy shop steward will stop them giving me a promotion?

Lucky our Nance and Doreen come every Wednesday to help with the washing and make the tea, or I wouldn't be able to go up the union any more. Gary'll be pleased it's Wednesday, some nice tasty food to eat, thanks to his aunties, followed by one of his favourites, an orange and cream slice. Better make sure they don't let him stay out too late playing football again, because the nights are drawing in now and he's got school tomorrow.

I wonder how stoic our Susan's being? I decide I rather like that word: stoic. I don't get to use it very often, but here is a good opportunity: Wonder how stoic our Susan's being?

Susan

I hate it here more than anything else in the entire world, and when Daddy finds out how horrid it is I just know he'll let me go home. I've written it all in a letter, explaining how horrible and mean and stuck-up everyone is, but I don't have any stamps, so I can't send it. He'd better come to church on Sunday so I can tell him and then we can pack my bags and leave. I'm really worried that he might not come, because if he doesn't I'll be all on my own with no one on my side when the older girls poke fun at the way I speak, or the colour of my hair. I'd rather call it auburn than ginger, but they seem to think it's really funny to call me names like carrot top, or rusty head, or gingey. It's lucky I don't wear glasses any more, because they'd probably take the mickey out of me for them too, calling me four-eyes and stuff like that. I'll never forget the day the optician told me I didn't have to wear them any more. I jumped up and down, clapping my hands with joy, and said to Daddy, 'Come on, let's go and tell Mum.'

Then I remembered she wasn't there any more, so we went to get a cup of tea in the caff near Gran's instead and didn't speak very much at all.

I wonder if Mummy's looking down and can see that I don't wear glasses now. I remember the way we giggled when I first tried them on, especially the round National Health ones, which they gave us for free in case my others got broken. I always loved it when Mummy laughed. I don't suppose I'll ever hear her laugh again, unless she has gone off to be with another family and decides to come back to us in a few years.

We might not want her then, but I expect we will.

I've decided that if Daddy tries to make me stay here any longer then I'm going to run away to New Zealand to be with my cousin Jacqueline and Uncle Maurice. Or I'll go up to London to live with Auntie Kathleen who's quite rich and always brings me a costume doll whenever she comes to see us. (Gary and I checked under the costumes once to see what they were wearing and found that lots of them didn't have any knickers on. We couldn't stop laughing for ages and Mummy kept laughing too, even though she didn't know what we were finding so funny. We couldn't tell her because it was rude and she never allowed us to be rude.)

I'm in the first-year classroom now, which is over the stable block. I suppose they must have kept horses here once, but now it's showers and a cloakroom on the ground floor, with two classrooms full of prisoners on the first. We're having a scripture lesson at the moment, which is called religious instruction here. Miss Dakin – or Dotty – who's actually the headmistress, is teaching us. Everyone says she's a man, and I think they're right, because her voice is deeper than Harry Secombe's, and she wears men's lace-up shoes. She also wears a black cape like a magician's that flutters behind her when she walks, so if she's not a man she's definitely a witch. I'm not listening to what she's saying about Jesus, because it's not true that He loves children, or He wouldn't be doing this to me.

There are twenty of us in our class, twelve boarders and eight day girls. It turns out that I've met one of the day girls before. Her name's Susan Cruse, which is funny, because we met on a school cruise that I went on with everyone from High Street about five months ago, just before I left. Our ship was called the *Devonia* and it sailed us to Olden and Bergen in Norway and Copenhagen in Denmark. I was seasick most of the way there, but it got better after a while and when I saw a glacier and the fjords I sent Daddy a postcard straight away to tell him that Norway was the most beautiful place I'd ever seen in my entire life. I didn't know sea could be that blue – it's not at all like that down Weston-super-Mare or Weymouth, and fancy there being a mountain made entirely of ice.

Susan Cruse and the girls from her school were in the same cabin as those of us from High Street, while boys from two different schools were in a cabin across the corridor. They were always taking the mickey out of us for something or other, but they weren't nearly as funny as they seemed to think. In fact they were really smelly, and thought it was hilarious when they farted, so none of us ever went over to their side of the ship.

I don't think me and Susan are going to become friends particularly – the day girls and boarders don't mix very much, mainly because they, lucky things, get to go home after school while we're stuck here. When lessons are over at half past three we have an hour's free time before tea – unless, like me, you're on offices, which means that when the bell rings at ten past four I have to go and lay the tables before everyone comes charging in for their chocolate-spread sandwiches and Typhoo tea. After we've finished we have some more free time until prep at six, when we have to do homework, yuk, then we have supper before going to bed.

I'm sitting next to Laura in class, which is nice, because I like her and I think she's probably going to be my best friend. She doesn't seem to mind that I don't talk in the same upper-class accent as her and Cheryl, and she shared some of her tuck with me during break today. That was probably because I gave her one of my mint humbugs on the first night. If we'd got caught by Cluttie we'd have been sent down on the landing and put on report, because food isn't allowed in the dorm, but everyone has some. I think I'll ask Dad to bring me some Marmite, because everyone seems to like that and if I share mine with Nina Lowe and her friends they might not be so mean to me.

'Susan Lewis, are you paying attention?'

'Yes, miss,' I say quickly, even though I wasn't.

'Then please read to us. The Gospel according to Matthew, Chapter Five, verses one to sixteen.'

I can feel myself starting to shake a bit as I open my Bible. Why did she pick on me to read out loud? It's not fair, they'll all start laughing at my accent and I can't help the way I speak. Anyway, I don't want to be posh and snooty like them – except maybe I wouldn't mind being a bit more like Laura and Cheryl, but only because they're nice, not because they're a better class. I can feel Peggy Lamont-Jones watching me. She's from Seabreake dorm, which is the one under ours. With a double-barrel name like that her dad's bound to be stinking rich, he might even be a duke or a lord. She calls herself Peg Jones, and she's got long dark hair that she wears in a single plait right down her back, and she's so full of herself you'd think she was six feet tall instead of the little squirt that she really is. I've watched her quite a bit, but I'd never let on that I think she's cool and really pretty because she's *not*.

I find the right place in the Bible and using my finger to

follow the words I start to read: '*When he saw the crowds he went up the mountain. After he sat down his disciples came to him. Then he began to teach them by saying, Blessed are the poor in spirit . . .*'

I stop as someone behind starts to snigger. I keep my head down so no one can see how red I've gone.

'Carry on,' Dotty barks.

Why doesn't she make someone else do it, the horrible witch? '*. . . for the Kingdom of Heaven belongs to them. Blessed are those who mourn . . .*'

I hear someone mimic the way I said mourn and I have to swallow really hard before I can read on. '*. . . for they will be comforted.*'

'Do you see a T in comforted, Susan?' Miss Dakin asks.

I feel really fed up as I nod, because I know I shouldn't have dropped it, but it's too late now, she's told me off, and lots of girls are laughing behind their hands.

'Then pronounce it when you say the word, please,' Miss Dakin tells me. 'Let me hear it.'

'Comforted,' I say, making sure to use the T.

'Very good, and if I hear the rest of you laugh again, you'll all find yourselves on report.'

Good, that told them!

I read on to the end, knowing they're all still snickering and sniggering and getting ready to mock me as soon as the lesson's over, but if I don't keep going she'll probably give me a report and Daddy'll be cross about that. He'll say, 'That's not a very good start, Susan. I'm disappointed in you, because you can do better than that.'

He doesn't have to put up with all these horrible snobs though, does he? Or stay locked up here while all his friends go to another school, or play out in the street, or have a cuddle with their mums when they're feeling upset.

He'd also say, '*. . . let your light shine before people, so that they can see your good deeds, and honour your Father in heaven.*' That's verse sixteen, so I've finished now. Let someone else have a turn.

'Well done, Susan, you're a good reader,' Miss Dakin tells me. 'Now, let's discuss the meaning of Jesus's message to His disciples.'

Luckily, she doesn't pick on me again, so I don't have to join in. I try to listen though, because she's bound to ask questions later and I don't want people thinking I'm dumb as well as common.

At last the lesson's over, and it's the end of school. The jammy day girls pack up their satchels and go downstairs to the cloakrooms to get their coats. They have the same winter uniform as us, a dark red kilt, same colour V-neck jumper, white V-neck shirt and fawn socks, ugh! Why do the socks have to be fawn? I'd rather wear the thick granny stockings that are part of the uniform too, at least they look more grown up. My suspender belt's been digging in me a bit today so I think I'll have to put it on a looser notch tomorrow.

Me and Laura are on our way across the stable yard with the other first-form boarders when word starts going round that there are some third-form girls in the bootroom, which we have to go past. I know this means trouble, because I've already been told that the bootroom is where the serious blowing ups happen. I go all hot and wobbly inside, and quickly start saying sorry to Jesus for not paying attention all the way through RI, hoping that He'll make sure it's not me who's in for it.

It is me though, because I can already hear my name bouncing in whispers from one girl to the next, until it reaches me and covers me in guilt for something I haven't even done. *Please God don't let me be the only one to get blown up.*

He's still not listening, because a couple of minutes later I'm standing on my own in the middle of the bootroom with Nina Lowe and her crowd perched on top of the racks, looking down at me, or sitting astride the pipes, or slouching against the windowsill.

'Don't look at me,' Nina snaps. 'I've told you about that before.'

I put my head down and wish Mummy was here to make them leave me alone, or better still to put them all in their place, because she would, she was like that.

'We've been wondering,' Nina says, 'why you haven't got struck on anyone yet.'

I don't answer.

'Is it because you think you're too good for us?' she asks in a way that sounds surprised, but I know is sarcastic.

The others seem to find that funny, and I can see why, because they're all much better than me.

'Is it?' she shouts.

I jump and shake my head. 'No,' I reply.

'Then why?'

'I – well, I didn't think anyone would want me struck on them.' I can feel my face going a deep, ugly, beetroot red.

Nina seems intrigued. 'And why would you think that?' she prompts.

I shrug. I don't want to say because I'm common, but I know that's what they all think of me.

'You're a strange thing,' Nina tells me. 'We don't really want you in Speedwell, but I suppose, since we're stuck with you, we'd better try to make something of you. Let's begin with your failure to stand back for a fifth-former on the stairs this morning. I thought we made it abundantly clear the other night that you *do not* keep walking if an older girl is either coming towards you, or needs to get past. So why did Judith Harris have to tell you to stand aside?'

My heart's beating really fast now. 'Because . . . Well, Miss . . . Cluttie said that we have to obey only the written rules, or we'll get into trouble.'

Nina's hairy lip curls up like she's been caught on a fishhook. 'Are you completely *stupid*,' she snarls. 'You don't do what Cluttie tells you. She's a *matron* for God's sake. You do as *we* tell you, and when we say stand back on the stairs, you stand back on the stairs. All right? Have you got that?'

I nod quickly and add, 'I'm sorry,' hoping it might help her to forgive me quicker.

'Good. Now put your bag down and jump up and down on the spot ten times saying, "I'm an ugly ginger nut."'

The others laugh, but someone says, 'Oh come on, that's a bit mean.'

'Do it!' Nina tells me.

I don't want to, but I'm too afraid to say no, so I put my bag on the floor and start to jump. 'I'm an ugly ginger nut. I'm an . . .'

'Louder. I can't hear you.'

'I'm an ugly ginger nut. I'm an ugly ginger nut.'

When I've done ten I stop and pick up my bag.

'All right, you can go.' I don't think it was Nina who spoke, but I don't care.

I'm halfway out of the door when Nina says, 'What are you?'

I turn back. 'An ugly ginger nut,' I whisper.

'And don't you forget it.'

Laura's waiting for me out in the corridor. 'Are you all right?' she asks. 'What did they say? Oh don't cry,' she wails, and puts an arm around me as we walk on towards the main hall.

'I'm all right,' I tell her, shrugging her off. 'I don't care what they say. I don't want to be here, anyway, and my dad's going to take me home on Sunday.' He will, I know he will, once I tell him what it's really like here.

As we walk into the recreation part of the hall Peg Jones and her friends come speeding over to us. 'What did they say?' Peg wants to know. 'Was it a really bad blowing up?'

'She's crying, it must have been terrible.'

'I'm not *crying*,' I inform them. 'I'm just angry because they're stupid.'

'Ssh, don't let them hear,' Laura warns. 'You don't want to be in trouble again.'

'Come on, what did they say?' Peg urges.

I toss one of my bunches back over my shoulder. 'Not very much,' I reply, wondering if everyone really does think

I'm ugly. I expect so, because I am. 'They were annoyed that I didn't stand back on the stairs this morning.'

'On the stairs this morning,' someone mimics, like a yokel.

I wish people wouldn't do that.

'Did they give you a punishment?' Peg asks.

'I had to jump up and down, which is really stupid. Anyway, I'm not scared of them, and I'm going to get my own back on them one of these days, then they'll be sorry.'

'You're not going to split, are you?' Laura gasps. 'You can't do that, or everyone'll hate you.'

'I'm not a splitter.'

'We've been told,' someone says, 'that we've got to be especially nice to you because your mum died, is that true?'

I can feel my throat going tight as I look at her. I don't think she's laughing, but it's hard to tell.

'What did she die of?' Peg Jones asks. She looks a bit sad, and not at all mean, so maybe they aren't trying to trick me. I want to tell them that Mummy's really a famous actress who has to spend a lot of time in Hollywood, but they'll only want to know her name and then they'll say they've never heard of her. I could always make out she's an air hostess or a doctor who helps people in Africa. They wouldn't look down their noses so much if they thought I was the daughter of someone important instead of someone who's dead.

'Ssh, here's Seaweed!' Laura hisses.

We all fall back, like petals falling off a flower, and try to look innocent as the senior housemistress comes towards us. She's as thin as a stick and has short bobbed grey hair, big glasses and a reedy voice. 'What are you girls doing there?' she wants to know. 'Come along, shoo, shoo, time you were in your evening uniforms, especially those who have offices. Does anyone here?'

Along with three others I put up my hand.

'Off you go then,' she says, 'and *don't* run.'

After skirting round the dining hall and cutting across

the end of the sixth-form corridor to the back stairs, we all go thundering up to our dorms to change into another one of the five uniforms we have to wear. This one is a dark red shirtwaister dress with a white detachable collar that has to go in the laundry once a week (the dress itself only gets washed at the end of term). It comes right down to the knee, which is miles too long, and there's no way to tuck it up the way we can with our kilts so everyone hates it. We're not allowed miniskirts in this school, even though the whole world is wearing them now. Goes to show what a horrible place it is, all Victorian and old-fashioned and revoltingly smelly.

I'm just about ready for duty when the office bell rings at ten past four, but when I reach the nursery landing I see my name chalked up on the matron's blackboard. What have I done now?

'Yes, miss?' I say to Cluttie, who's in the nursery.

She looks up from what she's doing. 'Who are you?' she asks.

'Susan Lewis. My name's on the board.'

'Ah, yes. You had a letter in the second post,' she says, and taking it down from the shelf she hands it over.

I recognise Daddy's handwriting straight away and I can hardly wait to tear it open, but if I don't hurry up I'll be late for laying the tables and then I'll be in trouble again.

Actually, I don't care if I am, because I definitely think I'll be leaving here on Sunday.

But I go and lay the tables anyway, and wait till I'm in bed later to read Dad's letter which I just manage to finish before lights out.

Daft old thing, he doesn't realise I don't have any stamps, so he thinks I'm not bothering to write. I feel a bit upset about that, because I don't want him to think I don't love him or he might not take me home with him on Sunday. *Please God, please, please make Daddy take me away from here.* The box Auntie Nance is sending sounds nice, and I like all the kisses at the end of the letter and the fact that they're taking care of Sixpence. As I tuck the letter under my pillow I feel as if I've heard Daddy's voice and I wish harder than ever that I was all tucked up in my own bed with him next door in his, and Sixpence running round on her wheel downstairs, and Gary in his boxroom with his Beatles wallpaper and *Thunderbirds* posters, and his little voice calling out to ask if he can come in with me so I can tell him a story.

Chapter Three

Eddie

I'm enjoying sitting here in this church, knowing our Susan's up the front amongst all the Red Maids in their smart black hats and claret-coloured capes. I calculated that it probably took them about a quarter of an hour to walk here from the school, whereas it took Gary and me an hour and twenty minutes on two buses. Lucky the Consul broke down yesterday and not today, or we might not have got here at all.

We're standing up now to sing 'All Things Bright and Beautiful'. I like to have a good sing, and it seems lots of the other parents do too, because they're putting their hearts and souls into it, the same way I am. It's lovely knowing Susan's amongst good Christian people who take their faith and church-going seriously. Not that they don't at Holy Trinity in Kingswood, because they do, but since my girl developed a mind of her own I haven't been able to get her through the door very often, I'm afraid. Luckily she doesn't have a lot of choice in the matter now. She'll be glad of it in the years to come, and to tell the truth, she's a long way short of being heathen, because she didn't mind joining the Salvation Army about a year back when I decided to give it a go. Turned out she was a bit of a dab hand with the tambourine, all happy bangs and flying ribbons, which, fortunately, drowned out her singing, because, love her as I do, it makes me wince when she strikes up a song.

I shall miss Holy Trinity and Canon Radford. He married

me and Eddress and christened both the children. He buried our mam too, and our Bob, my brother, and he says as soon as I'm ready to bury Ed's ashes I only have to let him know. One of these days I'll have to pluck up the courage to admit that I had them scattered at Arnos Vale. Can't think what got into me now, doing that, but I suppose I wasn't thinking straight at all at the time. I'm still not sure I always do now, but I'm trying me best with things, and as long as I don't dwell too much on how much I miss her I seem to get by. I reckon it would be a good deal easier if I had our Bob to chat to, but I haven't.

Funny how you spend your whole life growing up with someone, hardly ever apart (our Bob was only a year older than me), and then suddenly one day they're not there any more. It was a terrible shock him dying like that, about eight months before Eddress went. I suppose with her being ill I didn't have much time for it to sink in that he'd actually gone, but it seems to be hitting me a lot lately. I miss him almost as much as I do Eddress and I can't stop asking myself why they both had to die so young, and if I'm being punished in the worst possible way for the sins I've never confessed. We're not Catholics any more – our mam never was, only our dad went in for it, and since we moved up from Wales, over twenty-five years ago, he's hardly set foot in a church of any sort. He didn't mind about burying our mam at Holy Trinity when a heart attack took her about six months before our Susan was born, because it was where she used to go of a Sunday, while he waited for her up the Legion. I don't know if he ever goes to see the grave – having lost my own wife now I understand how difficult that can be, so I'm not so hard on him any more. Our Nance takes care of things though – she takes flowers every week to our mam and our Bob, and if she had somewhere to put them for Eddress I expect she'd do that too.

Thirty-seven our Bob was when he died, four years older than Eddress was when she went. He was a driver on the buses, a really popular bloke, more outgoing than me, the life and soul was what they always said about him, and he was. He left two little ones behind, our Julie and Karen, the dearest, prettiest little girls, and his wife, of course, Flo. She has a real struggle making ends meet now. I wish I earned more so I could help her with the bills, but I can barely pay my own these days, never mind anyone else's. I try to help out in other ways though, like the odd repair job, or clearing the garden, but I don't want to overdo it in case she gets the wrong end of the stick and thinks I'm trying to take our Bob's place.

I don't ever want to get married again, I know that, and I don't think Flo does either. I told the doctor after Eddress went that I'd live long enough to make sure my children were all right, and then I'd go to join her. I'm still of that mind and I can't see it changing.

We're just sitting down for the sermon to begin when I catch our Susan turning round to make sure I'm here. I give her a wave and feel very pleased when I see her eyes light up. Then Gary says, 'Who are you waving at, Dad?'

'Ssh,' I say. 'Sit down, there's a good boy.'

'Have you seen our Susan? Is she wearing one of those funny hats? Can I have one?'

The people around us have a little chuckle, and I put a finger over his lips before he can disgrace us even more. Lucky we left his trumpet on the bus, I'm thinking. Luckier still that he doesn't seem to have noticed yet.

I'm interested in the sermon, not only for its subject, which is all about gratitude, but because the vicar will have written it himself, and I'm intrigued – and impressed – by the words he's chosen and how cleverly he uses them. Language is the most fascinating tool of communication. It can be shattered by incorrect usage, moulded into all kinds of shapes by imaginative minds, drilled into listeners with utmost precision, or painted every conceivable colour by our celebrated poets and authors. I'm fascinated by the vicar's vocabulary, and wish I could take out my notebook to jot down some of the words that seem to be rising up from all the others like the tallest flowers in a field of green. Joyous. Clarity. Newness. Honourable. Robust. I particularly like words that I've never heard before, but he hasn't used any yet. I found a few in the books I brought home from War on Want the other day. Logorrhoea – uncontrollable flow of words. I especially liked that one and could imagine Eddress teasing me with it. Barbula – a small tuft of hair below the lower lip. Paedotrophy – art of rearing children. Ha, ha! A good one for me. There was only one book amongst those Mrs Beach donated that I decided to buy – *Astrophel and Other Poems by* Algernon Swinburne. I haven't started it yet, but a quick glance through suggested I'm in for a treat.

I used to write poetry myself, but not any more. They called me a pansy when I was young and working down the mines in Wales. Poets were queers, not real men. What did I want to be getting involved with all that nancy stuff for? It turned out to be a good question, because nothing ever came of it, and it won't now because I burned it all just after Eddress went.

It shames me now to think of the state I got into that day. The anger was terrible, the frustration and grief. I don't know who I was trying to get back at – myself, I suppose, for not being able to keep her alive. And God for taking her. And the publishers who'd rejected the novel I wrote in secret while she was ill. *Dear Mr Lewis, thank you for sending us your manuscript* Onward Socialist Soldiers, *which we are returning. Unfortunately it does not conform to the type of novel we are interested in publishing.* So curt and pompous, or that was how it read to me. 'Bloody capitalists the lot of 'em,' I could hear Eddress saying. 'They'll regret it one day when you're top of the best-sellers. They'll come grovelling to you then.' Except she wasn't there to say it any more, and because she was the only one who'd ever really believed in me, I'd burned the lot. All I had left was the publisher's letter as a reminder for me not to get too above myself again.

There's lovely. We've now sung the last hymn, said a final prayer and the girls with their bonny smiles and mischievous twinkles are following the vicar down the aisle, taking crafty peeks at their parents, while the organist excels himself with something jolly I've not heard before, and the campanologists ring all the bats from the belfry.

When I walk outside, holding tight to Gary's hand to stop him getting carried off in the jostle, I search around for Susan, and there she is, over by a lopsided gravestone, waving out so I can see her. I make my way through the crowd, careful to be friendly and polite as I go, and . . . Oh, it does my heart good to see her, in spite of her frown.

'I was afraid you weren't coming,' she tells me, as I give her one of my biggest hugs. 'When I got to church I couldn't see you . . .'

'The car broke down,' Gary interrupts. 'We had to get the bus.'

Susan looks panicked. 'You've got to have the car. Oh Dad, please! You have to take me home. I can't stay here any more. Please don't make me.'

'Oh dear, oh dear,' I say as tears roll down her cheeks. 'Come on now, you don't want to be making a spectacle of yourself with all these people around.'

'I don't care,' she mutters, but I'm sure she does or knowing her as I do, she'd have shouted it. 'That blinking car,' she seethes. 'I hate it, and I hate you for making me come here.'

'Ssh,' I say, putting an arm round her.

'Don't do that, I'm not a baby.'

'Yes you are, you're crying,' Gary helpfully informs her.

Catching her hand before she belts him, I say, in my best jolly voice, 'Wasn't that a lovely sermon the vicar gave? I hope you were listening and taking it in.'

'Dad, please, you've got to take me home,' she begs. 'I'll kill myself if you make me stay here.'

'Don't talk silly, there's a good girl. Shall we start walking back now?'

'No! I'm not going. If you make me I'll run away.'

I look at her mutinous face and have to stop myself trying to hug her again, because seeing her unhappy like this is upsetting me too. Quite a lot, in fact, and while I dare not let it show I'm trying desperately to think what her mother would do in my shoes. Eddress was always so much better at handling the kids than I am. I don't understand why God didn't take me. If He had to take someone, and I still don't know why He did, it would have been better all round if it had been me.

'Don't just stand there,' Susan mutters. 'Everyone's looking.'

Not sure what I'm supposed to do now, I watch her turn and start towards the gates where some of the other girls are milling about with their parents. 'I think we're supposed to follow,' I whisper to Gary.

Apparently thinking a whisper calls for tiptoe, he starts after her. She turns round suddenly and almost bumps into him.

'Don't let anyone hear you speak,' she growls.

'What?' he says.

'Just don't.'

He looks up at me.

Susan looks at me too, and realising what must be happening I put on my best posh voice and say, 'Righty-oh young lady, I'd like to know why we haven't had a letter from you, telling us all you've been up to.'

'Dad, don't,' she pleads, looking as though she might cry again.

'I'm sorry,' I say quickly. 'I don't think anyone heard and I was only trying to make you laugh.'

'Well you're not very funny.'

'All right, but I'd still like to know why we haven't had a letter from you.'

'I don't have any stamps,' she cries. 'Or any money.'

I give a groan of dismay. What a chump I am, why didn't I think of that? 'I'll send you some first thing tomorrow,' I promise, 'and I didn't know you were allowed to have money.'

'Well we are, but Seaweed has to keep it and she gives it out every Saturday morning, but we have to tell her what we want it for, and if she doesn't think we're spending it right she won't let us have it, which everyone thinks is really mean, because it's our money and she shouldn't have a say.'

'What would you spend it on? Is there a shop at school?'

'No, silly. The shops are down in the village. We're not allowed out of the grounds, *ever*, but the sixth form can go down on Saturday mornings and they'll bring stuff back for us if we ask them.'

'What kind of stuff?'

'All kinds. Yoghurts . . . '

'What's that?' Gary chips in.

Susan's cheeks go pink, showing that she's not too sure either. 'It's like a cream with fruit in,' she says, waiting for me to correct her.

'Yum, yum,' from Gary.

'Anyway, yoghurts and liquorice and writing paper and records,' she goes on. 'Sadie, who's in our dormitory – she's second form, so a year above me – well, she let me have a dip of her bilberry yoghurt yesterday, and it's the best thing I ever tasted, and she bought "All You Need is Love" by The Beatles and . . . '

'That's really good,' Gary informs me.

'. . . Cheryl, she's Laura's sister, she's in the second form too, and Sadie's best friend, she bought "The Day I Met Marie" because she's got a crush on Cliff. And we all danced to the records yesterday afternoon in the hall, because it's allowed on Saturdays. I want to get "Flowers in the Rain", by the Move, but I can't because I don't have any money, and everyone said they'd really like it if I did get it, so can I have ten shillings, please Dad?'

I try not to gulp. 'Records only cost sixpence,' I remind her, taking a moment to realise that this desire to please everyone must mean that she's not as convinced I'll take her home as she'd like to be.

This could be what they call a small mercy. *Ten bob!*

'Yeah, but it has to last me all term,' she says, apparently forgetting she's giving herself away.

'Well, how about half a crown to be going on with?'

'All right. Did you bring the parcel from Auntie Nance?'

'I gave it to Mr and Mrs Beach when we got here. They're going to take it over to school in their car.'

She looks downcast again and I can tell her mind's not on the parcel, or records, any more. 'When will the car be mended?' she asks miserably.

'I'm not sure yet,' I answer.

'We came on two buses,' Gary tells her. 'Are we going back on two, Dad?'

Sorry that he's mentioned our return journey, I'm still fishing about for an answer when Susan exclaims, 'I know! We can carry all my stuff between us so I can come on the bus too.' Apparently pleased with the solution, she says, 'Shall we go now? The way back to school's dead easy, and other people are walking, so we won't look silly being the only ones.'

She links my arm and takes hold of Gary's hand, while I give a little wave to Mr and Mrs Beach who are getting into their car with Glenys. 'So let's hear all about the friends you've made,' I say encouragingly, as we leave the churchyard to start the walk back. We should have about an hour together, before she has to go in for dinner – lunch – and I've already got an uneasy feeling about how the time's going to pass.

'Well, there's only Laura really,' she says. 'She's in the bed next to me and we sit together in class. The others are all stinky and horrible, so that's why I don't want to stay any longer.' She glances up at me. 'I won't need any pocket money if you let me come home, or the parcel, but we'd better take it with us, so it doesn't go to waste.'

'Mm,' I say, hoping she doesn't read the wrong thing into it.

She does. 'I've already folded everything up ready to put in my suitcase,' she tells me eagerly. 'I asked Cluttie for it last night, but she wouldn't let me have it. She is so horrible, Dad. Everyone is. If you knew what it was like, you wouldn't make me stay. Honestly, you wouldn't. You want me to come home, Gary, don't you?'

He gives an energetic nod. 'Definitely,' he says.

'So you see, Dad, it's for the best if I come back with you today. I promise I'll be really good. I'll do all the washing up, and I'll make the beds, and I'll work really hard at school. I don't mind which one I go to, but I think The Grange would be best, because that's where most of my friends have gone, and I expect they're really missing me.'

She looks and sounds so earnest, so rational, that it's the hardest thing in the world to say, 'I expect they are, my love, but you go to this school now, and it's not . . .'

'Only because you say so. If you tell Miss Dakin that you want me to come home she'll have to let me. Please tell her you want me to, please Dad.'

Her eyes are filling up again, and I've rarely felt so wretched. 'You'll be home next Sunday,' I remind her. 'It's an exeat, so we'll pick you . . .'

'It's not the same!' she shouts. 'I want to be with you and Gary all the time, like I used to. Everyone's mean to me here. They take the mickey out of the way I speak, and they say I'm ugly.'

'You are,' Gary joyfully interjects.

'You're the most beautiful girl in the world,' I tell her.

'Don't say that,' she cries savagely. 'It's not true.'

'Well I think it is.'

'You would, because you're my dad, but that doesn't make it true. And if you really loved me you'd let me come home. Wouldn't he?' she says to Gary.

'Yes, Dad, you would,' young Solomon informs me.

I'm starting to wish I'd left him on the bus with his trumpet. 'Now, you know it's silly talking like that,' I tell them both. 'Of course I love you, Susan. That's why you're here, because you're so important to me that I want the very best for you, and you're a very clever girl to have passed the exam.'

'No! I was stupid to pass that exam. I wish I'd messed it up now, and I would have if I'd known I was going to be locked away with a load of nasty, stuck-up pigs who make me do things I don't want to do and spit orange pips in my face.'

'Who did that?' I ask, alarmed, but half suspecting she might be exaggerating.

She's about to answer, but seems to think better of it. I realise someone's walking close behind, so probably she doesn't want to be overheard telling tales. I let it drop for now, curious to see if she brings it up again later.

By the time we start walking up the drive to the school I can sense her becoming more and more agitated. She can be a devil when she doesn't get her own way, but I keep reminding myself that she's barely eleven, so it's natural for her to be homesick, and besides, she's only been here a week. Of course this is hard for her, but it'll get easier once she's more used to it. I wouldn't dream of telling her I'd give all the tea in China to be able to take her home with me, because that wouldn't help one bit.

'What's that over there?' I ask, pointing to a high stone wall with an arched gate in it.

'It's the walled garden,' she says sulkily.

'Oh, that sounds interesting, shall we go and have a look?' This is as much to get her away from the other girls and their parents as to try and distract her, because if she does end up losing her temper with me we won't want witnesses.

'Is this like the book, *The Secret Garden*?' Gary asks, going to press his face to the gate.

Mindful of the time he got his head stuck in the bars of the bear pit at the zoo, I hike him back to safety and ask Susan to tell us what happens in the garden.

She tilts her face up to look at me and her chin's wobbling

so fast she can hardly speak. '*Please*, Dad,' she begs. 'I hate it here and I don't like being on my own without you.'

Wrapping her up in my arms I say, 'I know it's hard, my darling, but I want you to do your best to get on here. It's . . .'

'Can I be a day girl then?' she asks. 'I'd be able to come home every night and . . .'

'I want her to come home,' Gary says, starting to cry too.

I gather him into the embrace, and putting my face between both of theirs I blow a raspberry on their cheeks. This usually makes them laugh, but today it only works on Gary.

'Dad, you're not listening to me,' Susan cries. 'It's really mean making me stay here. No one else has to go to this vile school, so why should I?'

Vile. Never heard her use that word before. 'Because you're clever and this is . . .'

'I am *not* clever. I'm dumb and I hate it here, and I hate you for sending me.'

'Now, now, you know what Jesus says, you must honour your mother and father, and look at our Gary. He's all upset seeing you like this, and it's making me unhappy too.'

'Why can't I be a day girl?' she rages.

'Because I want you to be a boarder where you'll be properly taken care of and grow up to be a lady.'

'Ugh! I don't want to be a lady.'

I catch her hands as she tries to punch me. 'This isn't the way to behave,' I tell her, trying to sound cross. 'You're a big girl now, and I want you to stop being rude and defiant.'

'Is that a football pitch?' Gary suddenly cries, wide-eyed with glee.

Susan looks round. 'No, it's for hockey, stupid,' she retorts. She turns back to me.

'Come on, my love,' I say, giving her a smile. 'It'll be all right, I promise. You'll be home next Sunday . . .'

'Yes, but only for the day.'

'I know, but we'll have a nice time, all of us. You'll be able to see your friends, and I expect Auntie Nance will make us some dinner.' I cup her face in my hands. 'Be a good girl for me,' I say softly. 'I want you to be a boarder because I know you'll make a very good one once you've settled in.'

She drops her head and pushes it against me, so I stroke her hair and only allow myself to think of how lovely and rich it is. Just like her mother's, only longer.

'What's that noise?' Gary asks, looking towards the school.

Susan's face is very pale now. 'It's the bell for lunch,' she answers, her voice sounding as broken as her little heart. 'You won't forget to come next week, will you?' she says, her eyes once again awash with tears as she looks up at me.

'Of course not,' I assure her. The worst part of this now is the suddenness with which she's accepting I'm going to leave her. Does it mean she's lost what little faith she has left in me? Why shouldn't she when she's right, I am going to leave her here? Am I getting everything wrong? *Eddress, what shall I do?*

'And you'll write to me?' she says. 'I've got loads of letters to send to everyone, so don't forget the stamps.'

'I won't. Do you have a letter for me?'

She shakes her head. 'I did,' she says, 'but I've seen you now, so it doesn't count any more.'

'You'll write me another?'

She shrugs. 'I suppose so.' Then clasping her arms around me, she starts to sob. 'Please Dad, take me home.'

'Oh Susan, Susan, Susan,' I say, 'what am I going to do with you? Come on now, give Gary a kiss.'

'I don't want a kiss from her,' he protests, backing away.

She gives a bubble of laughter and pretends to go after him.

'Ugh, Dad, save me,' he cries.

Turning back to me, she takes hold of my hand to make sure I walk over to the school with her.

I wonder if Eddress is watching us, and what she might be making of it all. I know she'd be much stricter than I am, but she had her soft side too, and I know it would upset her a lot to see our Susan like this.

We have to give it time, Eddie, I can hear her saying, *it's only been a week*, and I know she's right.

Susan

It's Sunday afternoon now and we're lying on our beds having quiet time. This means we're not allowed to talk even though it's the middle of the day, and no one's tired, so no one wants to go to sleep. We just read, or lie there trying not to be bored, when really it's more boring than anything I've ever done in my whole life. Dad put a copy of *Black Beauty* in the parcel from Auntie Nance, which is one of my favourite books, but I'm too angry with him for leaving me here to read it. Serve him right!

We've changed out of our Sunday uniforms now, and are wearing our pyjamas, in the middle of the day! Really stupid, especially when we have to get dressed again to go down for tea.

I can hear Glenys crying in the next bed. She's missing her mum and dad. I wonder if she asked them to take her home and they said no too. When I was little I used to dream about living on an island where there were no parents at all, only children – I think I might start dreaming about that again now. There won't be any boarding schools or foul girls like Nina Lowe, there will just be nice people and lots of freedom to do as we want.

I wonder if Mummy will be able to see the island. Maybe she's on an island somewhere now.

Actually, I'm feeling a bit nervous at the moment, because after lunch today Laura decided I should get struck on Nina Lowe.

'That way she won't be horrible to you any more,' Laura said.

Even though I'd rather have Dracula coming to tuck me

up at night I've agreed to let Laura ask her, because I wouldn't mind it if the nasty old cow stopped being so horrid to me. We can't do it now, while we're being nuns – all silent and godly – so Laura's going to wait until the bell rings to signal the end of quiet time, before going to talk to Nina. I wonder if I'll be able to tell Nina I'm homesick when she comes to say goodnight to me. She'll probably think I'm a great big baby and tell me to grow up. I'll want to smash her face in if she does, but she might smash me back and she's bigger than me.

Really, I want to get struck on Sadie who's about five beds along from me. She let me join in the dancing to her record yesterday afternoon, and she even said that I was quite good. She also said I can sit next to her for *Top of the Pops* next Thursday, if I want to, which is a great big honour, because first formers don't usually get invited to sit with second-formers.

I wonder if Dad and Gary are home yet. Every time I think of them I feel all choked up again, and really guilty for upsetting them while they were here. I didn't mean to, I just couldn't help it. Daddy doesn't understand what it's like being locked away, because it's never happened to him. If it had, I know he wouldn't make me stay here, but I know he's still unhappy about Mum not being with us any more, so I mustn't make him feel bad about me as well.

I think I'll write him a letter.

Dear Dad, It's Sunday afternoon now and I'm lying on my bed having quiet time. As God says obey your parents I'm trying to obey you and be happy. I'm getting on quite well with it I think, (I'm not, but it might make him feel better if I say I am), *but it's hard. Please don't be unhappy, and on Sundays when I see you I'm going to try and be good. I still want to be a day girl, but if it is your wish I should be a boarder I'm going to try and be happy as a boarder. I'm looking forward to half-term when I can come home for a week.*

I feel terrible when I go to bed at night and get up in the morning. But now you've told me not to be unhappy I won't be.

Well, I must close now, so cheerio.
All my love, Susan
PS: Please don't forget the stamps.
PPS: Please make sure Gary goes on taking care of Sixpence.
Time to read my book now. I wish I was a horse.

There is no religion without love, people may talk all they like about their religion, but if it does not teach them to be good and kind to other animals as well as humans, it is all a sham.

I'm just thinking that I might give this book to Nina Lowe as a present, when the bell blasts through the dormitory, putting a very noisy end to quiet time.

'I'll go and ask her now, shall I?' Laura whispers.

Feeling a bit sick, I look over to where Nina is going into her cubicle and pulling the curtain. I'm really not at all sure about this. I hate her and she hates me, and I definitely don't want her moustache coming anywhere near me. 'Give her a chance to get dressed,' I say.

Laura and I go into our cubicles to change into our uniforms. My laundry bag is full, so I'll have to go to the house maids later to do some washing. I think I've got some Omo left. I've got some pictures of Davy Jones next to my mirror that I cut out of one of Laura's magazines. I love the Monkees. Some of the older girls have pictures of their boyfriends in their cubicles. I wish I had a boyfriend. I was thinking about writing to Davy Jones, because everyone would be dead jealous if I had a famous boyfriend. Nina Lowe wouldn't be mean to me then. She'd be dripping all over me trying to be my friend, and I might say yes, but there again, I might not.

I hear a knock on the side of my wardrobe. Guessing it's Laura, I tell her to come in.

'I'm going over to ask her,' she says. 'Cheryl thinks this is a good idea too, so here goes.'

I want to tell her to go to Sadie's cubicle instead, but it's too late, she's already gone. And then I think of how nice it would be if Nina Lowe didn't blow me up any more, or make people laugh at me when I'm dancing. Or make fun of me when I speak. I can buy her presents with the half-crown Dad gave me before he left, and then she'll really like me and I expect I'll become quite popular, and instead of me trying to talk like everyone else, they'll want to talk like me.

I don't have the guts to go out of my cubicle so I stay where I am until Laura comes back. The second I see her face my insides go all tight.

'She said no,' Laura whispers, and she looks really upset. 'I asked her – I said, can Susan be struck on you, and she said . . . Well, she said . . . She doesn't want anyone to be struck on her.'

I think she probably said something really nasty about me that Laura doesn't want to repeat. I give a shrug to show I don't care.

Laura stands there, not sure what to do.

I turn away and catch a glimpse of myself in the mirror. I'm an ugly ginger nut, so it's no wonder Nina Lowe doesn't want me struck on her.

I won't ask Laura to go to Sadie instead, because she won't want an ugly ginger nut struck on her either.

It's night-time now. We're all back in our beds and supposed to go to sleep, because the lights are out. Tea was all right, because we had chocolate-spread sandwiches and apple pie, then we were allowed to go for a walk in the grounds. I didn't have anyone to go with, because Laura's gone down with a cold so she's in the nursery, and Glenys has made friends with some girls from Discoverer who don't want me in their gang. I don't care. I don't want to be in their stupid gang anyway, and if any of them poke fun at me again for having ginger hair and white eyebrows I'm going to smash their faces in.

Someone said that there's a secret cellar under Dotty's study that you can get to through the bush that's in front of her window. We're not really supposed to walk round that way, but I did, earlier, just to show everyone that I'm not scared of anything or anyone. (Mummy was never scared of anyone and I think I'm like her.) I couldn't see the entrance to the cellar, but apparently one of these days we first-formers have to go down there amongst all the spiders and rats to steal a bottle of Dotty's wine. There are all these scary and dangerous things we have to do and I'm not looking forward to them one bit.

I did some washing before getting into bed, cleaning my bags with the special soap Auntie Nance gave me, and scrubbing the feet of my socks with a nailbrush. I rubbed a ladder into one of my stockings, so I'll have to darn it when it's dry, and the elastic has broken in my new suspender belt, but I don't know what to do about that. When I'd finished I carried everything down to the laundry room, leaving a trail of water behind me that bossy old Cluttie made me mop up when I came back. I could hear the other girls sniggering at the top of the landing, but I didn't care. At least my clothes are clean, when I expect theirs are all foul and smelly.

Everything's gone quiet in the dorm. There are only first- and second-formers here; the third and fourth forms are allowed to come to bed later, when they put on the lights and wake us all up again. The fifth and sixth form have separate rooms, apart from the two girls at the end of the dorm. They're both in Lower Sixth and they're really fab, like models they're so lovely-looking, especially Paula Gates. Whenever I watch her striding up and down the dorm, or laughing at a joke during break-fast or tea, I wish I could be like her, flicking back my hair – hers is lovely and dark and crinkly – and looking glamorous like a movie star. I don't have the guts to ask to get struck on her, even though she's always nice to people, and she even smiled at me once when I stood back on the stairs to let her go by. Sadie's struck on her actually, lucky thing, because Paula always comes to tuck her up at night, and says something to make Sadie laugh. I wish I could be friends with them. If I was struck on Sadie they might include me.

'Sue, Sue,' Glenys whispers from the next bed. 'Are you awake?'

'Yes,' I whisper back.

'Guess what, everyone's saying Johnny's coming tonight.'

I go very still. *Johnny the ghost who picks on the youngest.*

'There's no moon,' Glenys gabs on, 'and apparently he always comes then.'

My heart's starting to beat quite hard now. 'There's no such thing as ghosts,' I say weakly.

'I hope you're right,' she says back, but I don't think she means it, because she sounded quite excited just now. It's all right for her, she's not the one he'll be coming for.

I'm feeling terrified now, because if there is such a thing as ghosts then my mum might be one, and I don't want her going around frightening people, especially not me. She did that enough when she was alive, so it would be really mean if she carried on doing it now.

Anyway, if she's not really dead, she can't be a ghost. And she's not mean either, she's lovely and kind and makes people laugh – when she's not being cross and ill. She definitely wouldn't frighten children – unless it was someone like Nina Lowe. Then she would.

It's so black in the dorm that I can't even see the opposite beds. I can hear some whispering and moving around along by the door though, then suddenly it crashes open and a great big white thing billows up out of nowhere.

I nearly scream, and dive under the covers. I'm shaking really hard and my heart's beating so loudly I can't hear anything else. But then there's the sound of someone walking, and he's definitely got a wooden leg, because I can hear the soft squidge of a shoe, followed by the clop of a stick. He's going 'woo, woo' and I'm so frightened I think I'm going to be sick.

Suddenly the piano next to Laura's bed starts playing. I peek out and nearly scream again when I see that the lid is down and no one's there, but it's still playing. And the one-legged man that must be Johnny is still coming down the dorm. He's really close now, so close that he stumbles into the end of my bed.

'Are you the youngest one here?' he asks in a thunderous voice.

I don't say anything. I just keep myself buried under the sheets.

'Are you the youngest one here?' he asks again.

I know I am, but I don't want to admit it in case of what he might do. I want my mum. She wouldn't be afraid of ghosts and if she is one she'd know how to make him shrivel up and go back to his grave.

Mummy. Mummy. Mummy.

'Susan Lewis,' he booms, 'are you the youngest one here?'

He knows my name! Who told him? I'm so scared I feel as though my head's going to burst. I might even wet myself. *Please, please God make him go away. I promise I'll be good and never say anything bad about anyone ever again.*

Someone tries to drag back my covers and I start to fight.

'Ssh, ssh,' someone whispers, 'it's all right. He won't hurt you. You just have to say yes. That's all.'

Sadie's kneeling next to my bed – her face is very close to mine. I'm too afraid to look at the end of my bed so I keep staring at her as I say, 'Y-ye-es.'

Suddenly the piano starts playing again, all dark, deep notes, and I dive back under the covers. How can the piano play when no one's there? Why does Johnny have to pick on me just because I'm the youngest? It's not fair.

I can hear him walking away.

The piano stops.

I stay where I am.

After a long time Glenys says, 'Are you all right?'

I don't answer. I want my dad and my mum. I wish we could all be together again the way we used to be. God's mean and cruel to make me come here. How can I make Him tell Mummy that I'll go to bed without arguing every night if she'll come back? I won't ever cheek her again, or hit Gary or pick the scabs on my legs when I fall down. I'll be good for the rest of my life. I'll go to church every Sunday and say my prayers every night. *Our Father who art in heaven, hallowed be thy name* . . .

Dancing to *Top of the Pops* is fabsville. Everyone's grooving to 'Flowers in the Rain', which is one of my favourites. It's Sadie's too, so I might buy it for her instead of for myself when the sixth-formers go down to the village on Saturday. She was really nice to me the night Johnny and his wooden leg came and frightened the living daylights out of me, so maybe, if I ask to get struck on her, she'll say yes. I won't do it yet though, because she might say no.

The Move aren't actually on the programme tonight, which is a shame, because Sadie's got a crush on one of them. I can't remember his name, but I expect I can find it out. We're all hoping the Bee Gees are going to be on, and the Herd. We reckon Engelbert's probably still at number one with 'The Last Waltz', but we won't know till the end of the programme.

I love having someone to dance with. It's the best thing about being here. Mummy used to dance to *Top of the Pops* before she got ill. Even when she was ill she'd sometimes get up, or click her fingers from a chair and tell me I was doing a good twist. I think she'd like the way I'm dancing now. I wish she could see it.

Peg's a fab dancer. I wish I could waggle my shoulders back and forth the way she does. I keep my nose in the air, because I don't want her to know I think she's good, but I'm watching her out of the corner of my eye, and trying to copy. Laura's got her own way of dancing which is a bit odd, but that's her. Sadie and Cheryl are brilliant. I expect Paula Gates is fantastic, but she's in the sixth-form common room with her friends. They don't rough it out here in the main hall with us.

Oh, bloody hell, the telly's gone all fuzzy and flickery,

and Procol Harum was about to come on. To be honest I think he's a bit creepy, so I don't mind missing him, but lots of the others seem seriously fed up. One of the fourth form is banging the top of the set, and someone else is sitting on the stage with her head in her hands, sobbing out loud. She must be really mad about Procol Harum to get that upset.

Ah ha! The picture's back again, and as soon as Procol Harum's finished we carry on doing the hippy hippy shake. Actually that's an old one, but it's a good name for a dance and Mum showed me how to do it, so that's more or less what I'm doing. The Box Tops are on now. This is my very, very favourite, ever. I wish someone would get me a ticket for an aeroplane. I'd love to be the girl who Alex comes running home for. (I think that's the lead singer's name. He's lush.) Everyone would think I was really special then, and no one would make fun of my eyebrows and eyelashes, or my ginger hair or the way I speak. They'd all be really jealous of me, because my boyfriend was the lead singer of a famous pop band.

But what if it was Davy Jones! That would be really *really* fab.

The Monkees don't have a new record out, so he's not on *Top of the Pops* this week.

I'd probably faint if he was.

We're all out of breath when we finally go up the stairs to bed. Fussy old Cluttie is on the landing, making sure we haven't got radios, or food, or anything that might seem like fun. Then we see that she's chalked a row of RM numbers on the blackboard (big offenders), followed by a notice saying *Fluff under bed*, and I can't stop laughing.

Laura wants to know what's so funny, but I'm splitting my sides so much it's ages before I can tell her that my brother says fluff instead of blow off, so all the girls who haven't swept under their beds are now being told to fart under them.

Word soon gets round, and before we know it everyone in all four dormitories is screaming with laughter, and no one can stop. Cluttie doesn't have a clue what's going on, so she keeps shouting at us all to shut up and get into bed, or we'll be sent on the landing.

At first I hope that everyone knows it's me who made them laugh, because it might make them like me. But then I think of Dad and Gary, and I start to feel guilty about having a nice time when they might be missing me. I know I'm missing them, and I wish I was in my own bed at home now, but if I was no one here would be laughing.

Chapter Four

Eddie

I'm having a bit of a chuckle to myself, watching our Susan out in the street with her friends, putting on her new, posh voice and making them all wonder what the dickens she's on about. She's home on an exeat after two weeks of being locked up in prison, as she likes to put it. I picked her up after church today – lucky the car's back on the road – and took her to our Nancy's for a lovely roast dinner. I had to sit her down in the front room first though, to tell her the bad news about Sixpence, and there was a heck of a to-do when she found out the poor little creature had popped its clogs.

'Why does everyone have to die?' she shouted as though it was all my fault. 'It's not fair. I really loved him and he was mine. I don't want him to be dead.'

'I know, I know,' I said, trying to comfort her. 'But hamsters don't live very long and he's in heaven now, so he'll be all right. Jesus will take care of him.' I was in half a mind to add that her mother would too, but we don't tend to mention Eddress all that often and it's probably best that way, or we'd only both end up in a sorry state.

I told her how Gary and I had buried Sixpence in a shoebox next to the cabbages and said a prayer for him, and she seemed to cheer up a bit after. By the time our Nance put the dinner on the table she was full of it, making us all say grace in Latin, which befuddled our Nance good and proper and got right on our Gary's nerves. Stan never says much anyway, so he only grunted when she finished, and got stuck into his roasters, barely even batting an eye when a fight suddenly erupted across the table between his nephew and niece. Fists flying, tempers raging and old Stan helps himself to more greens boiled with bicarb, while Nance gamely helps to try and bring things under control. And all over the way to say grace.

Watching our Susan now, skipping in the middle of a rope being turned by two of her friends, I start my usual wondering whether Eddress can see her too. And if she can, is she feeling as proud of her as I do, and as happy to see her home? Or is she worrying about what it's going to be like at five o'clock when it's time to take her back to school?

'Dad! Dad! Can I go over the bluebell field with Rodney and Stuart?'

I can't see Gary yet, but I can hear his feet thundering past the kitchen window, and an instant later he charges in through the door, all demerara freckles and bright blue eyes – plus the beginnings of a bruise where our Susan clocked him one earlier. All forgotten now, tears wiped away, cuddles and a kiss to make it better, and a grudging apology from his sister with a warning that he was going to grow up to be stupid and common if he didn't learn to speak Latin. 'Here's some Latin for you,' he'd said, and treated her to a great big raspberry.

'We're going to collect caterpillars and ladybirds and see if we can catch some mice,' he tells me, in his best budding zookeeper voice.

'All right,' I say, 'but don't be gone long, and remember to look both ways before you cross the road.'

'I will,' he promises, and off he zooms, yelling to his friends that he can come.

I watch them take off up the street, three important little souls on a vital mission, in much the same way as me and our Bob used to go off with our mates when we were seven and eight, down Abertridw. The games we played, and the fights we got into, was nobody's business – and the way our dear mam used to cluck and tut when we came back with split lips and sleeves torn off. I wonder what she'd make of our Susan and Gary. She'd love them to bits, of course, because she was like that with kids. She'd be just the same with our Julie and Karen. It must be breaking her heart to see her little granddaughters trying to get on without their dad. I can just imagine Eddress giving our Bob a piece of her mind when she saw him up there, about going off so suddenly the way he did. I wonder what it's like where they are, what kind of form they take, if they really can see what we're doing back here.

Noticing our Susan waving at me, I start to wave back until I realise she's telling me to go away and stop watching her. Obediently, I take myself off into the dining room where I put some more coal on the fire and sit down in one of the brown leather chairs with my notebook and pen. It's not all that cold today, but if I don't keep the fire going we won't have any hot water for Gary's bath tonight. I'll boil up a drop of water in the kettle for me to have a shave and quick lick and promise before taking Susan back to school. I'll leave Gary at his gran's, where we're going for a spot of tea. She'll be looking forward to seeing our Susan, because I know she worries about her, especially since Susan wrote her a letter saying how unhappy she is at Red Maids.

'Please Gran will you tell Daddy to let me come home. You're older than him so he has to do what you say, and I really hate it here. Everyone thinks I'm ugly and common and the lessons are really hard. The teachers are dead strict and creepy and none of them like me.'

I can still see the concern in Florrie's eyes when she handed me the letter to read. She's not at all sure how to deal with this, because, like the rest of us, she's keen for Susan to have a good education, and to be properly taken care of, but she doesn't want her to be unhappy along the way. It's a pity Florrie hadn't been there to see her after church today, surrounded by other girls and looking very much as though she was finding a place at the centre of things.

'Yeah, well, some of the girls are all right,' she grudgingly admitted when we were on the way home, 'like Laura and Cheryl, and Sadie – and a couple more girls in my year, oh, and a few others too, but mostly everyone is vile and I hate them all.'

Picking up my pen I start to write. Often it doesn't matter what words I use, or even what I'm trying to say, the simple act of writing is as soothing to me as a hot bath on a wintry day. It's like a flow of yarn unravelling from all the knots inside me, spilling on to the page in random, occasionally gentle verse, or even in ordered, strident prose. I document thoughts, feelings, actions, observations, spreading them over page after page, until all the tension inside me has melted away.

By the time I look up again the world seems different, or dislodged, or the same but with a new sort of hue. I wonder where I've been and what's been happening while I was away. How long has Gary been gone? Is Susan still outside playing?

Ah, here she is by the sound of it.

'Dad! Where are you?'

'In here.'

The door bangs the back of my chair as she comes into the room.

'What are you doing?' she asks.

'Just sitting here quietly,' I tell her. 'Has everyone gone in?'

'Most of them, yes.' She flumps down on the opposite chair and stares moodily into the fire. 'I'm not stuck-up, am I?' she growls. 'It gets right on my nerves when they keep saying that, just because I talk posher than them.'

'I think you're starting to speak very nicely,' I tell her, in spite of how comical her efforts are. What's important is that she's trying, though a new worry starts up inside me, that I could be turning her into someone who won't fit in at home or at school.

Her eyes flash. 'You think everything I do is nice,' she snaps, 'so it doesn't count.'

I give one of my sage, fatherly nods, and feel a bit like my own dad who we won't be going to see today, because there isn't time. Next exeat, we'll make a point of going over there. I'll give Beattie, his wife, a bit of warning, so she can try to sober the old man up before we arrive. On second thoughts, he's usually much jollier in his cups than when hung-over. 'We've got about an hour before we're due up Gran's,' I say, 'so what would you like to do?'

She shrugs, impatiently. 'Nothing. Everything's boring. Are we going over Auntie Doreen's today?' Doreen's my other sister who we don't see quite so often as Nance because she and her husband Alf live over Wick, which is about five miles away, and in the opposite direction to Bristol, so we're never passing. We make special journeys out there from time to time though, and we always see them at Christmas and on birthdays. My two are very fond of Doreen and Alf's children, young Doreen and Robert, who are eighteen and sixteen and tend to make a bit of a fuss of Susan and Gary.

'No,' I answer. 'Remember, I told you, they've gone down the Forest of Dean to see Uncle Alf's relatives today. Auntie Doreen's hoping to come to church with me next Sunday though.'

Unfortunately her scowl doesn't disappear, and I suspect this is because the person she'd really like to see is her cousin Robert. She's always had a bit of a crush on him, and he's very good with her, going for walks and playing chess or dominoes with her, and I believe he's promised her a ride on his motorbike one of these days. We'll have to see about that.

'I think we should go to live in the front room,' she suddenly announces. 'It's boring in here, and stupid that we don't ever go in there.'

Catching a sense of her despair, I say, carefully, 'That's your mother's best room.'

Her face looks pinched all of a sudden, and I tense, certain she's going to explode in a rage, or maybe into tears, but then the moment seems to pass and a new, but awkward, silence falls over the room. It happens like this whenever we mention Eddress, which is probably why it's best that we don't.

As I watch her, I'm anxious about what she's thinking, and wondering if she feels the same sense of incompleteness that I do. Is that why she wants us to move rooms? She knows the front room is her mother's, but so is this one, and they are each as empty as the other, whether we're in them or not. Time ticks on as though we're waiting for someone to join us, and my heart grows heavier knowing that the one person we want to see won't ever come.

'I know,' she says, her eyes surprisingly bright as she looks at me, 'why don't you tell me a story?'

Pleased with the suggestion, I reply, 'Good idea. What shall it be?'

'I don't know. Ummm.' After some time her mind has obviously wandered elsewhere, as she asks, 'Dad, do you think my eyebrows and eyelashes will always be white? Will they ever turn black, like everyone else's?'

'Well, my love,' I say, 'being the colouring you are makes you very special, because not many people . . . '

'But I hate it. And I'm not special. And I don't want them to be this colour. I'm going to dye them.'

'Don't be silly. Now, we were about to have a story, so what would you like?'

She thinks about it again, then says, 'I know, tell me about when you were little, down Wales. Not the soup kitchen, because we've had that before, or the mines . . . What about when Auntie Nance had scarlet fever so she was at home when you were born, and when it came time for her to go back to school you were three, and you'd got so attached to her that you wouldn't let her go so you went with her.' She starts to laugh. 'Do you remember, you said your feet didn't touch the floor when you sat down at the desk, and all the other children made a big fuss of you because you were so little. And then at the end of the year you came top of the class.'

With a shout of laughter I say, 'I think you made the last bit up.'

'No I didn't, that's what you said. Anyway, tell me about when you all moved up to Bristol. It was because Auntie Nance got a job here, wasn't it, when she was fourteen, and Granny Lewis missed her so much that she made you all move up, and Grampy could hardly speak English. Which school did you go to?'

'Ah, now there's an interesting story,' I tell her, 'because I was ten when we came to Bristol, and Uncle Bob was eleven, which meant we had to go to different schools. He was enrolled at Hanham Road, and I was supposed to go to High Street . . . '

'Which is where I went before you sent me to prison.'

I waggle my eyebrows in a way that tugs a smile out of her. 'Exactly,' I say. 'We were living in Northend Avenue, which is a long way from either of the schools, and your gran was worried about me having to go off on my own when I was still so young, and in a foreign country too, so she decided I should go to Hanham Road with Uncle Bob in spite of my age.'

Susan's eyes grow wide. 'Was she allowed to do that?' she asked.

'Not really,' I admit, 'but she'd made up her mind, so the weekend before we were due to start Grampy walked all the way to the school with us, and back again, to make sure we knew the way. Then, on our first day, he took us in and left us in the playground along with the other boys. Within ten minutes Uncle Bob and I were in a fight, because someone called us Taffies. We were giving them what for, when the teachers broke it up and sent us into the classroom. I squeezed in next to Uncle Bob, sharing his chair, because, of course, there wasn't one for me. When the teacher spotted the two of us at one desk he came to find out what was going on, and the next thing I knew one of the dinner ladies was marching me off to High Street School to join my class there.

'Well, this was fine, until it came time to go home at the end of the day. The bell rang and all the children poured out of the gates, including me. Everyone started off in different directions, but I didn't know which one to take, because I had no idea where I was. I couldn't even remember the way back to Hanham Road, except I was sure we'd come through Kingswood Park which, as you know, is right next to High Street School. So I set off that way, and had a go on the swings when I got there because one of them was empty and usually you had to wait a long time for a turn. After a while I realised everyone else had gone, and it was starting to get dark. I felt quite scared then. I wanted to find Uncle Bob, or Granny, but I still didn't know which way to go. I set off again, trundling on through the park and out the other side, trying to keep warm because it was starting to get cold. I walked and walked but there was no sign of Uncle Bob's school, or of our house, or anyone I knew because we didn't know anyone yet.'

I'm getting so carried away with the story that it takes me a moment to realise our Susan is crying.

'Oh dear, what is it, my love?' I say, opening my arms for her to come and sit on my lap.

'I don't want you to be lost,' she sobs, snuggling up to me. 'Please don't be lost, Dad.'

'Oh you daft old thing,' I chuckle as I wrap her up tight.

'I don't want to think of you being on your own without Granny or Grampy, not knowing where to go. Were you crying?'

'No,' I lie, realising it'll upset her even more if she thinks I was. 'I was a big brave boy, and when a policeman found me – they were out looking for me, you see – he let me ride home on the crossbar of his bike and then he told Granny and Grampy how proud they should be of me for being so brave.'

She gives a little splutter of laughter, but she's still clinging on to me. 'You won't ever get lost again, will you?' she says. 'You know your way everywhere now, don't you?'

'Everywhere,' I assure her, glancing up as the back door bangs open. 'Aha, that'll be my boy. I was wondering where you were,' I tell him as he surges into the room.

Gary screws up his face in disgust. 'What are you doing on Dad's lap?' he demands of Susan. 'You're such a baby.'

'Shut up, or I'll smash your face in,' she warns.

'Yeah, you and whose army?'

'That's enough,' I gasp, holding her back. 'Where are your caterpillars?' I ask Gary.

'In a box out by the door. We got loads. And I even got a mouse,' he adds in triumph.

'You caught a mouse!' I say, duly, and genuinely, impressed.

He nods happily, then scowls at Susan. 'And I'll set it on you if you don't shut up.'

'I'm not scared of mice,' she informs him. 'So go and get it.'

By the time he comes back she's sitting on one of her play chairs in front of the fireguard, and I'm winding up the clock.

'It's in there, hiding in the grass,' Gary says, handing me an old shoebox with no lid. There's a veritable caterpillar convention going on inside, but no sign of a mouse.

'Oh dear, he must have escaped,' I say, bracing for the storm.

'No, he can't,' Gary protests. 'He's definitely there,' and yanking the box back he fishes around and a moment later he has a mouse dangling by its tail.

Susan's scoff says it all. 'It's dead,' she snorts.

Gary looks angry. 'So what, it's still a mouse,' he snarls.

'Anyone can catch a dead mouse,' she sneers. 'What did you bring it home for?'

Gary looks at me. 'I thought we could bury it,' he says, 'the way we did with Sixpence.'

'Sixpence was a pet,' she tells him. 'That thing there is a wild animal. And Sixpence would still be alive if you'd remembered to feed him.'

'I did feed him, didn't I, Dad?'

'Yes, you did,' I assure him.

'And I said a prayer for him,' Gary told her earnestly. 'So I think you should let my mouse go and keep him company.'

Susan pulls a face, but I can see the idea has some appeal. 'All right,' she agrees. 'We ought to give it a name first though.'

Gary wastes not a second. 'Mickey?'

'No, that's too obvious.'

'What's that?'

'It means everyone would call a mouse Mickey, so we have to think of something else.'

'I know, what about Rodney? He was with me when I found it.'

'All right, Rodney. Unless it's a girl. Can you check please, Dad?'

Determining the sex of a dead mouse is a skill I've yet to acquire, whereas exercising the parental licence to lie I'm already getting quite good at. 'It's definitely male,' I declare, after swinging it back and forth a couple of times.

'How do you know?' Gary asks.

'If it was a girl it would swing the other way,' I tell him. I don't know, but I'm sure I can hear Eddress laughing.

'Aren't you supposed to find out if it has a dicky-dye-doh?'

Susan's watching me, and I could swear there's a devilish little gleam in her eyes.

'He has one,' I insist, 'but it wouldn't be polite to stare at it, especially now he's dead. So who's going to help dig the hole?'

'Me!' Gary cheers.

'Me too,' Susan echoes.

I glance at the clock and feel her eyes lancing me as I say, 'You ought to be getting yourself ready to go back now, my love. We have to pop in and see Gran on the way.'

The look on her face throws me back all those years to the

time I was lost, when I thought everyone had returned to Wales and left me. Never had the world seemed so lonely, or frightening. I'll never forget it. It's not like that for Susan, though. She's well taken care of at school and though she might not know her way home, I don't have to worry, because she's as safe as safe could be behind those walls, and much as she might talk about running away, I know that deep down inside she doesn't mean it.

Susan

I love Granny Price more than anyone else in the world, except Dad and Gary who I love the same. She's really old and has bad legs that have to be bandaged every day, and whiskers on her chin that some of my older cousins pluck out with tweezers. She doesn't like that much, but she lets them do it anyway, because she lets everyone do everything they like. Apart from Reggie, her lodger. She's really mean to him, and so is everyone else, except Dad, because he's never mean to anyone. He talks to Reggie, and never seems to mind about the dewdrop at the end of Reggie's nose, or the stumpy little fag poking out of the corner of Reggie's mouth. Reggie is very poor, and scruffy, and can hardly walk, or talk. He doesn't have any family, or a job, or anything at all. Gran's always saying she doesn't know why she puts up with him, the lazy good-for-nothing that he is, but she never throws him out. I think this must mean that she's got a bit of a soft spot for him really, but she'd never let it show.

Dad's out in the garden now, having a look at the potatoes Reggie's planted. Gary's next door at Uncle Graham's and Auntie Ivy's, playing with our cousins Geoffrey and Deborah. So it's just me and Gran, buttering some toast while the tea brews in a big brown china pot under a cosy that I knitted, with Mummy's help, for her eighty-first birthday.

'You see, Gran,' I'm telling her, 'it's horrible being there. Everyone's really stuck-up and snobby and they hardly give us anything to eat. They treat us like slaves, too, because we have to get up before it gets light in the morning to sweep the stairs, or lay the tables, or wash up, or wait on the staff and sixth form hand, foot and finger. They're really lazy and mean and wicked. You can see it in their eyes. I'm really scared of them, and that's not right, is it? I shouldn't be in a place where people are evil and tell me off all the time, even though I haven't done anything wrong, should I?'

'Well, no, my old love, but . . .'

'Oh Gran, I knew you'd agree with me,' and I throw my arms around her for a great big hug, forgetting about my buttery knife that goes all down her back and in her hair. She won't mind though, because she never minds about anything. 'So you'll talk to Dad and tell him that I don't need to go back today?' I urge.

'Susan, my old love, you can't leave school just like that,' she says, 'and being up the Red Maids means you're going to go far one of these days . . .'

'But I want to stay here,' I shout, 'with you, and Dad and Gary, and all my friends.'

'I know you do,' she says, putting one of her trembly old hands on my head, 'but I expect you're making new friends already . . .'

'No, I'm not! I hate everyone and they hate me.'

She gives me one of her Granny Price looks. 'Are you sure you're telling the truth?' she asks.

I start to nod, but I shouldn't lie, really, so I tell her about Laura and Cheryl, and a couple of other girls who I suppose are all right, in their way.

'There you are, you see, you've got some lovely friends . . .'

'But I don't want them, Granny. I want to go to school with all my proper friends and come home every night the way they do. It's not fair that I have to stay in that horrible place. You should see it. There are ghosts and spiders and rats . . . '

'I think we're exaggerating, aren't we?' she chides. 'There's no such thing as ghosts . . . '

'Yes there is! His name's Johnny and he has a wooden leg and it's always me he picks on. And the piano plays all on its own. I promise, I'm not lying. There's no one there, but the keys go up and down, like there's fingers on them. It's a really spooky place, Gran. I think everyone's a witch in disguise, and they're going to turn me into one too.'

'The things that go on in that head of yourn,' she sighs. 'I wonder what you're going to come out with next.'

'It's true, Gran, honest. All of it. If you had to stay there, you'd see what I mean.'

'It's got a very good reputation,' she tells me. 'The girls who come out of there go on to places like Oxford and Cambridge.'

'*I don't want to go there*,' I rage. Why won't anyone listen to me?

'What's all this, shouting at your grandmother?' Daddy demands, coming into the room. 'You'll say you're sorry now, or there won't be any tea for you.'

'Oh, don't go getting on at her,' Granny tells him. 'She's a good girl really, aren't you, my old babby?'

'Yes,' I agree, with a scowl at Daddy.

'If the wind changes you'll stay like that,' he warns.

'Well, I can't be any uglier than I already am.'

'Stop talking nonsense now, and go next door to get Gary.'

I find him in Uncle Graham's shed making a den with Geoffrey. I want to make a den too, because I love dens, but there isn't time. We have to eat our toast and drink our tea before I have to go back to school.

'So what's it like up that posh place?' Geoffrey asks. He's nearly a year older than me, and is one of the fastest runners in the world. 'Bet you're a right old babby-ass always crying to come home.'

I glare at Gary. He's really in for it now. To Geoffrey I say, 'It's a very nice school, h'actu-ally, much too good for the likes of you,' and snatching Gary's hand I drag him after me, back over to Gran's, where I'd have given him a good thumping if Dad hadn't been on his way out to find us.

Here I am, back in the haunted castle. Actually, it's quite nice to see Laura, who hates it here as much as I do. She's been with her parents for the day – Cheryl too, naturally – and her eyes are still quite red from how much she cried when they brought her back. I saw some other first-formers on our way up to bed, and they all looked miserable too. None of us wants to be here. If I pay more attention in science I might learn how to blow the place up, and then we'd all be free.

I found out the other day about a girl who got expelled. Her name was Caroline Gooding, and apparently she was thrown out when she was in the fifth form for sneaking out to go with boys. It must be really terrible to be expelled. I expect her whole life is ruined, and her name's not even written in gold on the old girls' board in the dining room. It's like she never existed, but everyone knows she did.

I wonder how I can get a boyfriend. Not to sneak out and see or I might end up expelled too, but to write to the way some of the older girls do. They even get visits from them at the weekends. It would definitely shut everyone up if I had someone like Davy Jones or George Harrison visiting me. It makes me go all lush and giggly inside just to think of it. I love imagining what it might be like kissing them. I do that for ages sometimes; it's loads better than doing prep or listening to some boring lesson. I think about having all their records, and everyone knowing their songs are written about me. I've been thinking about sending them a letter to ask if they'll come. You never know, they might. It would be a bit embarrassing if they both turned up at the same time though, so if I do write, I'll send a letter to Davy first because he's my favourite. George is my second.

I wonder if my cousin Robert would come to see me? He's really, *really* good-looking, *and* he's got a motorbike. I'd like to marry him when I'm old enough. I think it's allowed between first cousins. He's got a girlfriend at the moment, but that's only because I'm too young for him now, and he's always finishing with girls. He's promised to let me have a ride on his motorbike one day. It would be dead cool if he came to church next Sunday and we zoomed off together with everyone watching. They'd all wish he was their boyfriend, and they'd be ganging round me the minute I came back, dead keen to hear all about him.

I wonder what Paula Gates's boyfriend is like?

Or Sadie's?

'*Susan Lewis*. Get out of bed!'

My heart stops beating and I go icy cold. They're going to give me a blowing up, and I was nearly asleep.

'Go in the bathrooms,' someone hisses. I think it's Nina, but it might be Sonya, who sleeps in the next bed to Glenys.

I don't know whether or not to get my dressing gown. It's cold and my new brushed nylon pyjamas aren't all that warm.

'Hurry up,' Nina growls.

Forgetting my dressing gown I run over to the bathrooms, scared and angry and wishing they'd leave me alone.

Two more third-formers, from Discoverer, are waiting in one of the bath cubicles, where a single light is on. Sonya closes the door behind me and Nina orders me to stand in the bath.

I do as I'm told, and struggle not to gasp and cry as they turn on the cold tap, covering my feet and the bottoms of my pyjamas with freezing water.

'Do you know why you're here?' Nina barks.

I shake my head, and try not to shiver, but I can't help it.

'It's because you're sullen and lazy and you don't listen to what you're told,' she informs me.

'I-I'm sorry,' I tell her. My feet are turning numb and the water's going up around my ankles.

'So you should be,' she snarls. 'Do you realise you pushed in front of Felicity in the house maids tonight?'

I look at Felicity. She's fair-haired and stick-thin and has even more freckles than I do. She's looking as though she wants to slap me. If she does I'd love to slap her back, but I'd be too scared. 'I didn't see you,' I tell her truthfully. 'I thought I was in there on my own.' I know I was, because it's a really big room with a huge sink at one end and two wooden draining boards and nothing else at all, so if someone else was there I'd have been bound to see them.

'That's because,' she hisses, 'you only ever think about yourself. I had to wait for you to finish your disgusting washing with all your scummy filth stinking the place out.'

'You never, *ever*, do your washing before us older girls have done ours,' Nina spits. She's poking me in the shoulder, which hurts, and I'm afraid I might lose my balance and fall down in the water.

'Tomorrow morning you'll get up at first bell,' Nina tells me, 'and while Felicity's downstairs doing her offices you will go to the house maids and do her washing. What's more, you'll use your own washing powder and soap. Have you got that?'

I nod, and sniff and shiver and try not to sob.

Eventually they say I can go back to bed, but they won't let me dry my feet, or change my pyjamas, so I can't get to sleep because I'm too wet and cold. I hope I catch flu and die. They'll be sorry then, because they'll be arrested for murder and put in an even worse prison than the one we're in now, and it'll serve them right!

Chapter Five

Eddie

Oh blimey, here comes Mrs Baines from over the back. They don't call her Flirty Gertie for nothing. Quick as I can I drop what I'm doing and duck out of the kitchen into the passage to tuck myself out of view.

'Eddie!' she shouts, giving a manly rap on the door. 'Are you in there, my old love?'

I've never been one for saying bad things about people, but there's no getting away from the fact that Gertie's voice is as shrill as a parrot's, and her make-up's as colourful. She's been after me ever since Eddress passed, inviting me for a drink over the Anchor, or down to Made for Ever for a game of bingo, or round her house for a cup of char, as she calls it, with a wink and a nudge that never fails to make me blush. I really don't want to hurt her feelings, but even if I was interested in meeting someone else, which I'm not, she's not my type at all. I don't want to say she's a bit of a hussy, because that's a dreadful thing to say about anyone, but she has a reputation with the blokes that, frankly, makes me slightly scared of her.

'Eddie! Eddie!' she squawks.

Oh my goodness, she's banging on the kitchen window now. What am I going to do if she opens the door and comes in? She's going to think I'm off my rocker if she finds me lurking about behind the door without answering. I look at the cupboard under the stairs. It's where we keep the boots and shoes, some coats and the vacuum cleaner. It's not big enough to stand up in, but if I get down on my hands and knees and close the door behind me . . .

I'm in here now, skulking in the pitch dark and praying she doesn't come any further, because she's only gone and let herself into the kitchen and if she finds me like this . . .

I swear I can hear Eddress laughing.

'Eddie! Is everything all right?' Gertie shouts. She's standing at the bottom of the blooming stairs now, right outside my cupboard. I can smell her cigarette smoke, see it even, curling in through the cracks in the door like a detection device. 'I saw your car outside. How come you'm not at work?'

She's not really going to go up looking for me, is she? The answer's yes, because I can hear the stairs creaking as she starts to climb.

I break out in a bit of a sweat, thankful I'm not in bed, or she'd likely jump right in with me.

'Are you in there?' she calls out from the landing.

It goes quiet then, and I can't imagine what she's doing – until it suddenly hits me and I start to panic. Please God she's not undressing herself and getting into bed to wait for me to come back.

'Everything all right, Gert?'

Blimey, Betty Williams has turned up from next door now.

'I saw you come in. Where's Eddie?'

'I don't know,' Gertie answers, coming down the stairs. 'I saw his car outside and wondered if he might be ill, but he's not up there. Thought I'd make the bed for him while I was here, poor love. Can't be easy having to manage on his own, can it, without a woman around the place?'

'No,' Betty agrees, 'but he seems to be doing all right. And he knows he can always knock on our door if there's anything he needs.'

'So how come his car's out there?' Gert goes on. 'Didn't he go to work today?'

'They'm on strike,' Betty tells her. 'I saw him come back

from taking Gary to school, so I expect he's popped round the shop, or summat . . . Or he's out in the shed.'

'I'll go and have a look,' Gertie decides, and off she trundles, stuck on her mission to find me, while I sit cooped up here like a flaming troglodyte, getting cramp in my backside and hardly daring to breathe.

'No, no sign of him,' Gertie confirms a couple of minutes later. 'You're right, he must have gone round the shop. I'll put the kettle on, shall I, have a nice cup of tea waiting for when he comes back.'

Please don't let me have heard that right!

'Yeah, you do that, and I'll make a start on this washing up,' Betty says. 'The home help's on holiday this week, so he's having to do it all himself.'

'There we are, gas all lit,' Gertie declares. 'I'll do the drying up, then I might have a quick go round with the vacuum. Do you know where he keeps it?'

Bugger!

'It used to be under the stairs,' Betty helpfully informs her.

Bugger! Bugger!

'There's no hot water so we'll have to use that kettle for the washing up,' Betty says.

'What's this?' Gertie asks.

'God knows,' Betty answers.

What are they looking at?

'It's got a shoe on it,' Gertie says. 'One of Gary's, by the look of it.'

'Oh, that's one of them mending things, what the cobbler uses,' Betty realises. 'He must be trying to repair Gary's shoes. He can be quite handy sometimes, can Eddie. Eddress always used to say that about him. Whatever needed doing, he'd get a book on it and find out how to do it.'

'Him and his books. If you ask me, it's not doing him any good, burying himself away the way he does, always reading and doing all that writing. You should see how many books he's got up there in the bedroom. I bet Eddress wouldn't have allowed it, taking up all that room and gathering dust the way they do.'

'Oh, she never minded about his books. I think she used to like how well read he was, made him seem a cut above most of the blokes round here.'

'Oh, he's that all right,' Gertie agrees. 'A proper gentleman, is what I always say about him. He needs a good woman though, if you ask me. It's not right him living on his own, the way he does, trying to bring up a boy of Gary's age without a mother. I hear Susan's not very happy at her school. Poor love, locked away like that. What good's an education if it's making you miserable, is what I want to know?'

'She's at her dad all the time to let her come home,' Betty says, 'but it's better for her, where she is. He can't manage a girl her age on his own, and I can't see him getting married again, not for a long time yet.'

'It's going to be two years come next May since Eddress went,' Gertie sighs, 'and it's not right for a man to, you know, be without a woman, the way he is. It's not natural.'

'I reckon that's for him to decide, and he was very close with Eddress, you have to remember that.'

I feel a surge of affection towards Betty for that.

'Oh, there's the kettle whistling,' Gertie says, 'stand back while I pour some hot water over those dishes.'

I'm not a bit comfortable, on any level. My legs have gone dead, and I've got an itch in the middle of my back that's getting more urgent by the minute. Ten times worse though is listening to myself being talked about. I'm dreading what they're going to say next, but they'll think I've gone completely cuckoo if I come out of the cupboard now. And what am I going to tell them I've been doing in here?

'So did Susan come home for half-term?' Gertie chatters on. 'I can't say I saw her.'

'She was up her gran's every day, with Gary, while Eddie was at work.'

'How is Florrie, these days? Haven't seen her down the bingo lately.'

'I think her legs is playing her up again, so she's not getting out all that much. I popped in to see her when I was up our Elsie's the other day. We had a nice cup of tea and a chat. She told me Susan's been writing to all her relations begging them to ask her father to bring her home. Poor Eddie, it can't be easy for him knowing she's unhappy, but I still say the same as he does, she'll be glad of it in the long run.'

'Let's hope you're right. Do you know what he's intending to do with Gary? Will he go to a boarding school too? I don't know how Eddie affords it, meself. They can't be cheap, those places.'

'Between us, I think he is feeling the pinch, especially with all these strikes they keep going on. They loses their pay if they don't go in, and my Don says the management down where Eddie works isn't very likely to give them the rise they'm after.'

'Eddie's always been a bit of a union man, hasn't he? My Pete was like that. Still is, I s'pose, wherever he is with his little tart.'

Gertie's husband, Pete, got a seventeen-year-old girl pregnant back around the time Eddress went, and ended up running off with her. I don't know if Gertie's divorced now, but from the sound of it, she doesn't ever see him.

'These days it'd be legal for that kid to have an abortion,' Betty points out. 'Makes you wonder what the world's coming to, doesn't it? Never mind abortion, they shouldn't be having sex before marriage in the first place, is what I say. We never did.'

'Speak for yourself,' Gertie tells her. 'And I think it's a good thing they've legalised abortion. It was terrible, the way all those poor girls was having to go to backstreet butchers. Some of them actually died.'

'It wouldn't have happened if they hadn't had sex,' Betty snaps, and gives a sigh. 'I don't know, all this free love and flower-power stuff going on these days . . . It's not right, I'm telling you. And the length the young girls are wearing their skirts, it's not decent. I saw that Linda Watkins over on Dawn Rise the other day with a hemline right up around her backside. I swear you could see next week's washing when she walked. Makes me thankful I've got boys, it does.'

'Mm, me too,' Gertie agrees. 'Girls is a lot of work, God bless 'em.'

'And it's only going to get worse now there's all this women's lib and burning your brassieres coming in. Not that I'm against women having rights, mind you, but I wouldn't want to be seeing youngsters going on this pill they'm all talking about. It should be for women who are married and don't want to have any more kids. Or girls over twenty-one who'm going steady. It'll all end in tears if they don't keep a rein on it, you mark my words.'

It's interesting what you can learn when you're in a cupboard under the stairs. I wish I had my notebook with me, and a spot of light so I could jot it all down. Turns out Gertie Baines, who everyone says has had more blokes than hot dinners, might be a bit more conservative than I thought – or responsible, is probably a better word. I'm not all that surprised by Betty's views though, because she's always been a decent, God-fearing sort of woman who keeps herself to herself and does what she can to make a good home for Don and the boys. Pity Gertie's husband left her the way he did, must have been hard for her, poor soul, and I expect she gets lonely, so that's why she goes with other men. It's still not right though, because marriage is the only proper place for sex, and listening to them now makes me doubly grateful that our Susan's where she is, out of harm's way. No birth pills, no miniskirts, no flower power, and thank goodness, no boys. She's already well developed for her age compared to some of the girls round here, with her bust starting to show quite a lot now, and talk about having a mind of her own! I wonder how many letters she's going to write to Eddress's family this week, asking them to persuade me to let her come home. She's even written to Canon Radford, up Kingswood church, the little madam. It's a good job I see for myself how well she gets on with her friends when I'm at the school on Sundays, or I'd still be worried out of my mind.

'Look at this tea towel,' Gertie remarks. 'It could do with a blooming good wash. I'll take it home with me and give it a boil along with mine.'

'Eddie's got a washing machine,' Betty reminds her. 'They bought it when Eddress was ill, to help her out.'

'Oh yeah, I forgot about that. So where does he keep it?'

'That's it there, in the corner,' Betty tells her. 'Makes a heck of a racket when it's going, but it seems to do a good job.'

'Not if this tea towel's anything to go by,' Gertie retorts. 'I've never wanted one of those new-fangled machines meself, I don't trust 'em. Much better to give everything a bloody good scrub with a bit of soap and elbow grease, then put it through the mangle. You know where you are then.'

'Eddie's sister, Nance, says the same. Her and Doreen come here every Wednesday to change the beds and do the washing, but they'd rather do it by hand too. Meself, I wouldn't mind giving it a go, because Eddress got on all right with it. Put the willies up her sometimes though, the way it shudders and jumps about. I was in here once when it was going, and we ended up running out the back door it scared us so much. We had a good laugh about it after, but at the time it was like the whole bloody house was going off into space.'

Gertie gives one of her raucous chuckles, and I have a smile too. I remember the day that happened, and how Eddress declared she wouldn't have any more to do with the bloody thing after that. 'It's going to finish me off quicker than anything else,' she told me when I got home that night. So we dug out the instruction book again, read it from cover to cover and realised she was putting too much in, and not spreading it around enough to even out the load. After that, it was fine.

'Ah, there's the kettle boiling again,' Betty says. 'I wonder what's keeping Eddie. He must have run into someone round Lloyds. Or he might have gone up the union.'

'But his car's out there.'

'It might not be working, because he walked to school with Gary, so maybe he's walked up the road to the union offices.'

'Mm,' Gertie grunts. 'He won't be back for ages if he has, so maybe there's no point making him a cup of tea.'

'We can still have one though. He won't mind, and if we give the place a bit of a clean-up before we go, I expect he'll be really pleased to find it all spick and span when he comes back.'

Oh no!

'All right, if you brew the tea, I'll go and find the vac. Where did you say it was, under the stairs?'

'That's right. We should probably give this floor a bit of a wash too. Dearie me, when I think of how spotless Eddress always used to keep the place . . . Like you said, it's too much for a man. They'm better off going out earning the money and leaving the housework to us women. It gets done proper then. The home help does her best, but you never used to see fingerprints on the door knocker when Eddress was alive.'

God save me from well-meaning housewives, is what I'm thinking when the cupboard door opens and Gertie's face looms into view. I hardly have a chance to say boo before she screams.

'It's all right. It's only me,' I tell her, as she looks about to faint.

'Bloody hell, Eddie. What the dickens are you doing in there? You gave me the fright of my life. Oh, gorblimey, I think I'll have to sit down.'

'What's going on?' Betty demands, squeezing round the cupboard door to come and join us. She does a double take. 'Eddie? Is that you under there?'

'Yes, it's me,' I say cheerily. Always best to put a smile on things. 'I was, er, putting a couple of bob in the gas meter when I dropped it. Funny, I thought I heard voices. It must have been you two.'

'How long have you been under there?' Gertie asks.

She and Betty are on their knees now, affording me no dignified way out of here – were such a thing possible, which, in the circumstances, I have to accept it isn't.

'Oh, not long,' I assure her. 'I had a job to see what I was doing . . . And it's that dark, I must have nodded off for a couple of minutes.' Probably better not to let them know I heard what they were saying, it'll only make things more complicated than they already are.

'Are you feeling all right?' Betty asks.

'Can we get you something?' Gertie offers.

'No need to bother,' I smile. 'I'll just pop out to the shed for a torch, then I should be able to find the two-bob bit.'

Realising they're blocking my exit, they start to get up and I look away so I can't see up their skirts.

'The kettle's just boiled,' Betty says. 'Shall I make a cuppa?'

'Oh, you can go on home now, if you like,' Gertie tells her. 'I'll look after the tea, and the hoovering.'

'No, no, don't you go worrying about all that,' I try to insist. 'I can manage. I've got the day off, so there's plenty of time.'

She gives me one of her saucy winks. 'Why don't I stay and give you a hand?' she offers.

Feeling the colour rush to my cheeks, I say, 'No need. I can manage, honest, and our Nance'll be here any minute.' It's not true, but I have to say something to try and make her leave.

'Oh, is that right,' Gertie replies, either not sure whether to believe me, or not keen to see our Nance. Probably a bit of both, because they've never got on.

'Any minute,' I repeat. 'She's going to do the hoovering, and put the washing machine on.'

Gertie pats her hair, trying not to look defeated. I can't say I like seeing her embarrassed and hurt, but better that than let her stay. Heaven only knows how embarrassed and hurt we'd both end up then.

'Well, I s'pose I'd better be getting home,' Betty says. 'I'm going up the road later, if there's anything you want.'

'Thank you,' I say, 'but I expect I'll go up myself, with our Nance. Nice to see you, Gertie. Hair's looking smart. Say hello to your Bert for me. Tell him if he wants to borrow my bike again, the puncture's mended now.' Bert's her brother, who's lodging with her while his house is being redecorated after a fire.

'That's kind of you, I'll pass it on.' She takes out her cigarettes and offers them round. Betty takes one, but I don't. 'I'd best be on my way then,' Gertie says, shaking out the match and blowing two streams of smoke from her nostrils. 'Me and our Bert'll be over the Anchor tonight, if you wants to join us.'

'Thanks,' I say, hating and loving the smell of the smoke. It reminds me of Eddress in a way that seems to make all the clouds in the world gather at once. She'd probably still be here if she hadn't become addicted to that evil weed. 'If there's time,' I add. I'm not a drinker, and I'll have my hands full with cooking our Gary's tea and putting him to bed, but I don't have to tell Gertie that.

When finally they go, I wait in the kitchen, willing them not to stand out by the gate gossiping, or they'll start to wonder where our Nance is.

This time, fortune's on my side, because after a couple of minutes they tread on their fag ends and go their separate ways.

Now, where was I, before I made a great big chump of myself? Oh, that's right, trying to mend our Gary's shoes. He's gone to school in his daps today, or plimsolls as his teacher calls them, but they won't do now it's getting cold, nor with all the rain we've been having lately. I'll have to get him a new pair of shoes soon, because the ones I'm repairing are starting to pinch, but we'll have to stretch it out as long as we can. Money's going to be tight now we're having these strikes, and it won't be long before I have to find the fees for Susan's next term.

It'd cheer her up no end to think we can't afford to send her there any longer, but I'm not going to let that happen. Come what may, I'll find the wherewithal and she can holler and shout all she likes when I take her back after Christmas, I won't be listening, because I know she's a lot more settled there than she's letting on to us all.

I'm not sure about the black eyebrow pencil she asked for in her latest letter though. I can't imagine those girls are allowed to have make-up, especially not at her age. And black, when she's got red hair? That can't be right, but I can already see the face on her if I turn up on Sunday without this pencil. If I do give in, though, I'll probably end up getting her into trouble for having something that's banned.

Dearie me, what to do for the best?

Susan

'Are you ready? Get steady. Go!'

Everyone shrieks and screams as we launch ourselves off the top of our wardrobes to plunge, kilts round our ears, stockings twisted round our thighs, on to our beds below.

Five flying angels. And it didn't hurt a bit, unlike when we had to jump off the piano in the classroom and I nearly broke my back. That was how it felt, anyway. It was *agony*. I screamed and screamed, so did everyone else because they were really scared. They were grouped around me, jumping up and down, not knowing what to do, while I writhed and sobbed and yelled for my dad. It turned out I'd landed on my cockish, or something like that (it sounds a bit rude, anyway), and Cluttie went on and on making a huge fuss about the dangerous things we do, and if there's any more of it, she'll send us to Miss Dakin. If that happens we might have to sign the black book, and anyone whose name goes in three times gets expelled.

I'd love to be expelled.

So would everyone else. We all agree it's absolutely foul here, and we absolutely detest it, and if the only way out is to get chucked out, then that's what we'll have to do. I don't want to hurt my back again though, so I'll have to find another way to get my name in the black book.

I wish they'd expel Nina Lowe. I hate her, but at least she's leaving me alone more now, since Sadie told Paula Gates about the way I was made to sleep in wet pyjamas. When she heard about it Paula walked straight up to Nina's bed, ordered Nina out of her cubicle and right in front of everyone, she told Nina that if she ever did it again she'd report her. Nina went so red in the face I thought she was going to catch fire. I even thought she was going to do something horrible to Paula, but she can't, because Paula's Upper Sixth which means she's in charge. I know Nina wants to kill me now, but if she comes near me Laura has promised to go straight to Sadie or Paula.

'OK. Well done, everyone!' Cheryl shouts. 'Five more fully-fledged angels.' Everyone's saying 'OK' now, so I am too. Mum always said I shouldn't, because it's American slang, but she was just being old-fashioned. I don't expect she'd mind so much if she heard the Red Maids saying it.

I'm still feeling all breathless and excited from my jump, and as though I want to do it again, but I'm secretly quite glad when no one suggests it.

We're in Speedwell dorm with two girls from Discoverer who came to join us because the other first-formers in their dorm are too chicken to fly, and are getting a blowing up now from Discoverer second form. Glad it's not me. If I find one of them crying later I'll tell her to ignore them, they're just bullies and it's all right if you're too scared to risk your life trying to fly. (It's not, but I don't want to make them feel any worse than they already do.)

'Now, tonight is the last night Johnny's going to visit,' Sadie tells us.

I feel myself going cold, but I don't want everyone to

know I'm a coward so I keep my head up and carry on looking at Sadie. She's got lovely dimples in her cheeks and her eyes shine like sparklers when she's in a good mood, which is most of the time. I still haven't plucked up the courage to ask if I can get struck on her yet, but I'm trying. At the moment I'm struck on Claire Radley who's in second form Seabreake. I chose her because she's quite ugly, so I thought she wouldn't mind that I'm ugly too. She's a bit boring though, because she's not very mod, or anything, and she's got loads of spots which makes me wish she wouldn't kiss me goodnight. I'm afraid one of them might burst in my face. I only got struck on her because everyone said I had to be struck on someone, and I didn't want Nina Lowe blowing me up again for thinking I'm better than everyone else.

'And how do I know it's Johnny's last night?' Sadie's asking.

'Because tomorrow is Founder's Day,' Laura answers, 'and he never comes after that.'

'Correct.' Sadie claps her hands. She's always really enthusiastic about everything, especially pop music, like me.

I still haven't heard back from Davy Jones who I wrote to over a month ago. I sent it to *Top of the Pops* so they might be waiting for the next time he's on the programme to give it to him. I wonder where he actually lives.

Here's what I said,

Dear Davy, my name is Susan and I think you're really fab and groovy. I have lots of pictures of you in my cubicle at school and I kiss them all goodnight before I go to bed. I'm going to be fourteen on my next birthday (everyone says I look much older than my real age so I reckon it was all right to put that – he'll be more interested if he thinks I'm grown up). *I would love to meet you and if you're looking for a girlfriend I think you'd like me. I'm not sending a photograph, because I haven't got any* (I don't want him to know I've got ginger hair or he might be put off!) *but if you can send one of you, signed to Su Lu, because that's what all my friends at school call me, then that would be great.*

I love watching you on Top of the Pops, *and on* The Monkees. *You are the greatest, the grooviest, the coolest and the most lush. I love you, Su Lu* (and then I filled up the rest of the page with kisses).

'So, Su Lu,' Sadie is saying, 'as the youngest in our dorm it'll be you who Johnny leaves a letter for. In it he's going to tell you how well you're doing at school and whether or not everyone likes you.'

Though I do my best to keep smiling, I'm not finding it very easy, because I'm very nervous and worried. It's true, people have been a bit nicer to me lately, and since I started to realise that everyone else hates it here I haven't felt quite so much of an odd one out. Apart from when they're taking the mickey out of my hair, or my eyebrows, or my accent, that is. They're not doing it so much any more, though. I wonder if it's because everyone knows Paula Gates is on my side. It was her idea for me to get an eyebrow pencil. She said it one day when I was in her private room with Laura, watching her putting make-up on Sadie and Cheryl. She's really good at it and they'd looked really super when she'd finished. Then, when Dad brought me an eyebrow pencil, like I asked, I took it to her and she showed me how to put it on. I think I looked a bit stupid actually, with thick black lines over the tops of my eyes, but everyone said it was really cool.

I hope they weren't laughing at me behind my back.

If only I was in second form already. If I was then Johnny wouldn't be visiting me *again* tonight to deliver a letter. I know the youngest in every dorm is getting one, and we're all dreading it. He should stay away from us, the revolting monster. Anyway, I know he's really someone from second or third form hiding under a sheet with a broom handle to make the sound of his wooden leg. I haven't let on to anyone that I know that, just in case I'm not right and they all start laughing at me, but I'm sure I am. It doesn't stop me being scared, though.

Anyway, apparently he's going to leave a parchment letter under my bed, and I'm not allowed to look at it until tomorrow morning when I'll probably get to find out that everyone in the entire school hates me.

I wonder who's really going to write it. (I don't care what anyone says, I know there's no such thing as ghosts really, so it can't be him.) I even know how the piano plays on its own now. Someone from second or third form Sellotapes cotton to the keys, then they hide under Laura's bed when no one's looking and after lights out they pull the cotton and because no one else can see it, it looks like the piano's playing itself. Laura told me, because Cheryl told her.

It must be lovely having a sister.

I wonder what Gary's doing today. He hasn't written to me lately. I've had loads of letters from my aunties and uncles though – on my mum's side I've got more than ten aunties and uncles and on my dad's side I've got three. I used my best handwriting when I wrote to them, and double-checked my spelling – I even remembered to ask how all my cousins are. They all wrote back saying more or less the same thing, that they're sorry I don't like my school, but they're sure I'll grow to in no time at all. Not one of them said they'd talk to Dad to persuade him to let me go home, like I asked, so it just goes to show that none of them care about me really. In fact, no one in the world does, not even Dad, or he'd have given in by now and taken me home – and if Mum's watching I don't think she cares much any more, because she never does anything to help me.

I wonder if she can, where she is.

Anyway, I definitely feel like an orphan.

Gary can't come to the cathedral tomorrow for the Founder's Day service because he has to go to school, but Dad promised to take a day off so he could be there. It's really dumb what we have to do. Everyone's in a bad mood about it, because we have to walk all the way from school, across the Downs and down over Park Street to the cathedral wearing our dark red capes and straw bonnets.

I hope Davy Jones never sees me like that.

Or George Harrison.

Or anyone else I know.

'Su Lu, are you paying attention?'

It's Sadie who's asked and I feel really soft for having been caught out. I hate it when I feel soft, it makes me angry and like I want to start shouting at someone, maybe myself.

'Do you have something to say?' Sadie asks me.

I can feel my face starting to burn as I shake my head. I expect my freckles look like stupid specks of sick on a piece of red paper now.

'Are you scared about the letter?' Sadie says.

I shake my head again, but I am.

'There's nothing to be afraid of,' she tells me.

Everyone's looking at me.

'I know,' I say.

She looks a bit surprised, then she says to Cheryl, 'Do you think we should let them go now?'

Cheryl nods. 'They've done their angels and . . . Oh, wait a minute, we've forgotten the most important thing. The cellar.'

'Oh bloody hell,' Sadie says. She likes swearing. Everyone does, and we'd do it a lot more if we didn't keep forgetting to. I know loads of words, but I don't have the guts to use them yet. I want to hear someone else say them first. Or I suppose I could always teach them if they haven't heard them themselves.

'OK,' Sadie says. (It sounds really good when she says it.) 'One of you has to go down into the cellar under Dotty's study and bring back a bottle of wine to prove you went. So who's it going to be?'

I can feel my mouth turning dry. I don't want it to be me, but somehow I already know that it's going to be. I can feel Laura and the others looking at me.

'What happens if we get caught?' Laura thinks to ask.

Sadie and Cheryl shrug. 'No one ever has been,' Sadie

answers, 'but I expect you'd have to sign the black book.'

If I signed that book it would make me famous and take me one step closer to being expelled. I'm terrified of being expelled really, but it's definitely what we all want. I think some girls are just saying it to try and look big and actually I might be one of them, but there again, I might not, because at least it would get me out of here. 'I'll go,' I say.

Sadie looks impressed and really pleased. So do Cheryl and the others. By tonight they'll have told everyone else about how quick I was to offer, and they'll all think how cool I am, and fearless and much more grown up than the rest of the immature first form who don't have the guts to smuggle a jar of Marmite into the dorm, much less to sneak down a tunnel for a bottle of wine.

'When does she have to do it?' Laura asks.

Sadie looks at the clock. It's five past four. We have to change into our evening uniforms by ten past, ready for tea, then we've got some free time until prep at five.

I shiver and hope she's not going to say now, because it's freezing outside and starting to get dark.

'If you want to come to our midnight feast,' Sadie says to me, 'you can, but only if you bring some of Dotty's wine. So it's up to you when you go. Before or after tea.'

My heart's doing some big thuds now. No first-formers ever get invited to an older girls' midnight feast. It would make me a legend if I went, but the thought of going down that tunnel in the dark and not knowing what I might find waiting for me at the bottom – dead bodies, vampires, skeletons – is sucking out all my courage.

Everyone else is looking excited and eager and ready to go. It's all right for them, they only have to keep watch.

'When you get the wine,' Sadie says, 'take it to Paula's room. She'll keep it with the food we've already smuggled up here.'

That's another thought, how am I going to get a bottle of wine past Cluttie? Even when she's in the nursery, her spies are out on the landing because she's like a Hydra. The other matrons aren't much better, Miss Daisy and Miss Hunter. (Miss Hunter looks exactly like Harry Worth, which is hilarious and definitely true, because even Dad says he can see the resemblance.) A bottle of wine isn't something I can stick up my jumper or down a stocking top without it being noticed.

I wish I hadn't said I'd do it now, because even though I want my name in the black book, and I'm dying to go to the midnight feast, I definitely don't want to go down that cellar.

As it turns out God's on my side, because while we're having our peanut butter and lemon curd sandwiches for tea (which, for the first time ever I couldn't eat because I was so nervous) a humungous storm breaks out with thunder and lightning howling round the school, and even some hail, so there's no way anyone can go outside.

It's the nicest thing God's ever done for me, because normally He just ignores everything I ask Him.

We're in prep now and I'm having to write my history as though I'm a river. So this is what I write:

At first I started out as a very small stream and little children often used to paddle through my cool waters. They had several names for me. They called me either Lilly Brooke, or Buttercup Stream, or Pebbles Puddle or just the brook. I got used to the children and came to know their names. There was Sheila, Paul, Lynn, Susan, Nicola and John. I was in the middle of the country and there was just one big house where all the children lived with their mum and dad. I was there, just behind the wall in the children's garden, for more years than I can remember. It was only about fifty years ago when it all happened. It was a stormy day, the wind was howling and the rain was coming down in buckets. There was so much of it that I turned into a river.

I'm hoping I might get a Commended for that. I've had quite a few already for maths and English and French, so I'm not anywhere near the bottom of the class the way I expected to be. I keep wondering if it might be better if I was, because if I'm not doing well with my lessons there wouldn't be any point to sending me here, would there?

We've got half an hour now before supper, then it's bedtime. I'm trying not to think about the letter Johnny's going to bring, but I can't think about anything else.

'Su Lu, do you want to come and play some records?'

It's Peg and her gang asking, which is very nice of them because they don't normally include me. 'All right,' I say, 'but only if Laura can come too.'

When we get to the recreation area at the back of the hall some of the second and third form are already there, and because they're older they get first turn with the record player. It's OK, though. (I said OK! – I know it's only in my head, but it came all on its own!) Most of them have really cool records that we can all dance to, and they like the ones we have too, so everything usually gets played. The Dave Clark Five were number one last week, but none of us has been able to get it yet, because most of us have run out of money.

'You're a really good dancer, Su,' Peg tells me, as I try to copy her shoulder shakes to 'Let's Spend the Night Together'.

'So are you,' I say.

The record's all scratched and bumpy, because it's been played so many times, but we don't care, we all love it. It's coming to the slow bit now, where Mick Jagger really gets worked up and Peg jumps right up in the air, so I do too. We love the Rolling Stones. Then suddenly there's a big fuss going on, and someone hisses 'Seaweed' and like magic the record disappears just before Miss Sayward, the house-mistress, comes striding into the hall.

'Whoever has it, hand it over,' she commands in her reedy little voice. 'You know very well that record is banned from this school. The lyrics are disgusting and you are most certainly too young to be listening to them.'

No one moves. I don't know who has the record behind their back, I'm just glad it's not me. I'm not even sure who it belongs to, but even if I knew, I'd never split. It's one of the worst things anyone can ever do, is split on someone else, especially to the teachers.

'I'm waiting,' Seaweed says, her hands on her hips, and her funny round face looking like a lollipop with glasses on top of her long thin neck.

There are about twenty of us in the rec area and no one says a word.

'You won't be going anywhere until the owner of that record steps forward and hands it over,' she tells us.

I'm dying to look round to see who's going red, but I just keep staring straight ahead.

'Do I have to put you all in detention?' Seaweed asks.

A few girls start murmuring and I know why. When a day girl gets detention she has to stay behind for an hour on Wednesday. When a boarder gets one she has to miss an exeat *and* do a punishment. I can't imagine anyone's going to split, though.

Seaweed looks at her watch. 'Right you are,' she says, 'go and form a line outside my office so I can take down all your names.'

'Please miss,' Nina Lowe says, stepping forward.

Seaweed glares at her. 'So you're the culprit. I had . . . '

'No miss,' Nina interrupts. 'It's not mine, and actually, miss, I don't think it's anyone's.'

'Don't be absurd, girl. It has to belong to someone.'

'It's an old record,' Nina tells her. 'It was number one last January, and it's now November . . . '

'I don't need its history, thank you very much. I simply want to know its ownership.'

'That's just it, nobody knows,' Nina says. 'It's one of the general pile . . . '

'Enough of this. Start filing up to my office, all of you. There will be no exeat for you next Sunday, and you can be assured Miss Dakin will hear of this.'

'Please miss,' I say, putting my hand up, 'the record's mine.'

Everyone gulps.

98

Seaweed glares at me. '*Yours,*' she says acidly.

I nod, but it's a bit wobbly because I'm starting to shake.

'How did you get it?' she wants to know.

'I bought it,' I lie.

'When? How? I'm sure your father doesn't approve of this kind of filth, so I'd like to know who bought it for you.'

I'm trying to think what to say. She knows very well that the sixth form buy all our records, plus, like Nina said, the record came out last January, before I even started at the school, so you probably can't get it now.

I've walked myself on to a tightrope.

'My cousin bought it for me before she went to New Zealand,' I blurt. 'I've kept it because it reminds me of her.'

I don't think she believes me, but for ages all she does is glare at me. 'Well, it's a very odd choice of record to give to a girl as young as you,' she informs me tartly. 'I'll be writing to your father about it. Is he coming to the cathedral tomorrow?'

I nod. I wish I hadn't done this now, but I don't know how to get out of it.

'Then I shall seek him out after the service. The record please.'

I look around to see who has it. In the end, Angela Lyall from second form pulls it out from under a chair. I suppose she must have chucked it there before Seaweed came in.

'Thank you,' Seaweed says, snatching it from her. 'You won't be seeing it again, any of you. And you, young lady,' she says to me, 'are in detention. Now, off to bed . . .'

'But miss, it's not time,' someone complains.

'Do as you're told. Up to bed and no more backchat. We've got a big day ahead of us tomorrow, so an early night won't do any harm.'

As she ushers us all past the dining hall, towards the back stairs, Laura presses herself in next to me.

'Why did you do that?' she whispers. 'It's not yours.'

'I know. Shut up.' I'm too angry with myself to talk to anyone.

'You're mad,' Peg hisses as we reach Maryflowre and

Seabreake landing. 'You'll miss your exeat now.'

'Get lost,' I snap at her. I don't need reminding, thank you very much.

Cluttie's on the upper landing with Harry Worth. 'No talking!' she bellows as those of us from Discoverer and Speedwell swarm past. 'Caroline Phelps! Why are you wearing those stockings?'

'They're all I have, miss,' Caroline wails.

We all look. There's so much darning in them they might have been knitted.

'Report to me in the morning, we'll sort you something out. I want you all looking your best for Founder's Day.'

'I heard we're going to be on the news,' Glenys whispers to me and Laura as we stomp past the doors to Discoverer and along the corridor to our dorm.

'Red Maids always are on Founder's Day,' Laura tells her. 'We actually saw Cheryl last year. We could make her out, going into the cathedral.'

'Su Lu, it's my turn for a bath tonight,' Sadie says, coming up behind us, 'but you can have it if you like.'

I don't want to have a bath. All I want is to get into bed and pretend I'm not here, because only someone really stupid like me would try to rescue everyone from a detention.

'I've got some Marmite left, if you want some,' Sarah McGinty offers. 'You can have the rest of it, if you like.'

I know she's being kind, but I shake my head, even though I normally love burrowing down under my blankets to dip my finger into the jar and then lick it till every last trace is gone. I wonder what's happening about the midnight feast. They won't let me come now I'm not bringing any wine. I don't care. I don't want to go anyway. I just want everyone to leave me alone, but they won't because bloody stupid Johnny's supposed to be bringing me a letter. Everyone says it's an honour to have one, provided he says something nice, but I know he won't, so as far as I'm concerned he can stay in his grave, or wherever he lives, and bloody well rot.

After washing my face and brushing my teeth, I change into my pyjamas and get into bed. By the time Cluttie turns up for lights out I'm already asleep. It's how I'm supposed to be when Johnny comes, so I stay that way for hours and hours and in the end I pretend not to know when someone (not under a white sheet, or with a wooden leg) turns up at the end of my bed to slide something underneath.

Chapter Six

Eddie

I had to push the flipping car this morning to get it going. The starting handle let me down, and with no one else about to lend a hand, I had to put Gary in the driver's seat to steer. He was thrilled. Little monkey, he had us swerving around all over the place, like he was in a bumper car up the fair. Good job there were no other cars in the street or I could be in a lot of trouble today.

What a job it was, huffing and puffing and shoving it up the hill so I could let it run down again. By the time the engine caught I was all hot and sweaty, and I'd managed to get grease on my only clean white shirt. Luckily, my suit jacket is covering most of it up, and at least Gary was only a few minutes late for school. I had to give him a note to explain why he was still wearing his daps, though I didn't tell the whole truth, because I don't want people knowing that we can't afford a new pair of shoes yet. I said his old ones were still up the menders and I'm hoping to get them back at the weekend. The truth is, they really are too small for him now so there's no point wasting money getting them repaired, having failed to do it myself, and what with strikes and having to take a day off for our Susan's Founder's Day today, heaven only knows when I'm going to be able to afford some new ones.

I'll have to make some economies somewhere though, because what a fuss the school is making about a simple pair of daps, sending me a letter telling me that 'plimsolls are only for gym' and they hope to see Gary wearing his proper shoes in the future. I can just imagine what Eddress would have had to say about that. Knowing her, she'd have marched up the school and given them a piece of her mind and a wave of a fist. I felt like doing it myself, but it wouldn't do any good. And I have to admit they had a point when he came home soaked to his skin last night. You should have seen the state of him. Our Nance had had the brainwave of using shoe polish to turn his white daps black, in the hope it would make them look more like shoes. It wasn't too bad an idea, as it turned out, until it started to rain. I don't know how long it took me to get his feet clean, and though I boiled his socks in bleach and detergent for over an hour, I had to throw them out in the end.

Poor chap. I feel terrible about him not having any shoes. We'll get it sorted out soon though. Our Nance has offered to lend me the money, but like I tell the kids, 'Neither a borrower, nor a lender be.'

'You'm going to struggle to afford them principles if you go on like that,' our Nance's husband, Stan, told me last night in a rare spurt of communication.

He's right, I suppose. I don't expect I'll get much more than ten quid in my wage packet this week, and how on earth I'm going to make that last till next Friday heaven only knows. It'll be a lot of beans on toast for a while, or egg and chips, which'll please our Gary no end. I'll have to ask the milkman if I can pay him next week, the same for the baker, but I'll have to find the rent because we're already a couple of weeks behind with that. At least if our Susan asks for something today there's the half-crown Nance and Stan gave me for her last night, because all I've got in my pocket is enough for the bus fare back to work in case the car decides to conk out on me again.

This is a special day for the Red Maids, so I couldn't let our Susan down. I just hope I manage to get there on time, because I've still got to pick up her gran, and all the coughing and spluttering going on under the bonnet isn't sounding at all promising to me.

Susan

Everyone's been going on and on since we got up this morning about my letter from Johnny. They all crowded round when I pulled it out from under my bed, and I could hardly believe my eyes when I saw it. It's much bigger than I expected, and all crumbly and ancient with really old-fashioned handwriting, and a wax seal with the image of a three-masted ship on it, like on the back of a halfpenny. (That's the emblem of our school.)

Here's what it said:

Susan Lewis, RM 74, Speedwell House.

Susan, I have been watching you since you arrived at the school and I am pleased to say that you are a good friend to the other girls, who all like you, and I believe you will set a good example to those younger than you when the time comes. Congratulations.

It's signed John Whitson.

I couldn't stop smiling and laughing after I read it. I'd been so nervous about what it was going to say, and then it turned out that I needn't have worried at all. He says everyone likes me. I thought they might, but I was never really sure. I'm going to keep this letter for ever.

I wish I could take it to the cathedral to show Dad.

Remembering what else has happened I feel my heart starting to sink. I'll have to tell him about the detention Seaweed gave me, which is something else everyone is talking about today. I'm a real heroine now, because I saved everyone from missing an exeat, which I'm glad about, I just wish I wasn't going to miss mine. Dad's going to be really cross, and I'll have to stay here all on my own on Sunday when I could have been at home with him and my friends and Gary. It wouldn't be so bad if the record really had been mine and I still had it, but I don't. Seaweed's probably smashed it up by now, which is what most of us feel like doing to her.

At nine o'clock sharp all us boarders gather on the forecourt outside the school's front doors. Under our big red capes we're wearing our best Sunday frocks with zips up the front, and our thick granny stockings with black lace-up shoes. We're also wearing straw bonnets that tie in bows under our chins and make us look like Quakers off the porridge box. We're all complaining about how dumb we look, but I don't think any of us mind all that much really, apart from the older girls, because they do look a bit stupid dressed up like Easter dollies at their age. The day girls are just wearing their red gaberdines and normal black hats, and they have to walk behind all of us. Dot and Celery (that's Miss Dakin and Miss Ellery the history teacher) will lead in Dot's car, and the rest of the teachers will follow behind in a bus.

It's a bit mean that we've got to walk while they're allowed to ride in the warm.

I hope everyone I know is watching the news tonight so they can see me.

We start off down the drive, doing our best to match our steps. Girls from Upper Sixth are keeping their eyes on us young ones, making sure we don't lag behind which would make the second form trip over us, because we're right at the front. As we turn out on to the main road lots of people are standing on the pavement waiting to watch us go by and wave.

I feel all proud and tall and I'm loving walking along with all my friends. I know everyone likes me now because Johnny's letter said so. I'm not taking any notice of Nina Lowe and the snide little remark she made earlier about me only getting a nice letter because I saved everyone from detention last night. She's only saying that because no one's on her side any more, so she won't be able to be mean to me in future. And because she's a nasty, fat, ugly pig.

We march across the Downs, keeping our eyes straight ahead as we've been told to do. I think it's a bit rude not to wave back to those watching and driving past. The television camera's going to be in Clifton, outside the university, apparently, and then it's going to follow us down the hill to College Green, which is in front of the Council House, and into the cathedral. These are the most important places in Bristol, Dad says, so I'm very lucky to be a part of all this. I expect my friends in Greenways will be really jealous if they see me on the news, because none of them have ever been on telly.

I hope Gran manages to come, but if she does I hope she doesn't talk too loud. She's a bit deaf, so she tends to shout, and the way she speaks is all slang and common. I don't want anyone looking down their nose at her, or making fun of her, because that would be horrible when she's really lovely and wouldn't hurt a fly – apart from Reggie, but he's not a fly so he doesn't count.

As we go down over Blackboy Hill it starts to rain so we pick up our step. Luckily it's not very heavy, but it could turn into a downpour and if our bonnets start to wilt we'll look really stupid for the news. If that happens I'll just keep my head down and pretend to everyone later that I wasn't there. My hands are freezing inside my cape and one of my suspenders has come undone. My brassiere's a bit tight, but I'm too embarrassed to ask Dad for a new one. It makes me feel all strange and sick inside to think of him knowing that my bosoms are growing.

We're going past the university now, but I can't see a camera. There are lots of people around, though. This is a bit like the Whitsun parade up Kingswood, when everyone puts on their best clothes to go and watch all the marchers and bands. I rode on the Salvation Army lorry last year, playing my tambourine. It was nice, but this is much more important.

By the time we get to the cathedral the rain has gone off, but there's a bitter wind and most of us have got mud splashed up the backs of our legs. Some of my friends are using their hankies to try to wipe it off, but I don't have one, so I can't. I'm much more worried about the stocking that's hanging on to one suspender. It's already bagging round my ankle and if it comes down altogether I'll feel so soft I'll want to die.

The cathedral is massive and cold and dismal. I can't see Dad and Gran anywhere as we start filing in. Visitors are supposed to be here first, but we pass by the people at the back so quickly that I don't have time to get a good look at who's there. We take up all the front rows. I'm right on the end of one, next to the aisle, with Laura next to me and Sadie and Cheryl behind. Everyone's whispering and the organ's playing, great big fierce chords that rattle the stained-glass windows and send shivers down the spines of the saints. Someone said the Pope was taking the service, but that can't be right because he's Catholic and we're Church of England. Dad was a Catholic when he was little, in Wales. He's the same as us now, though.

I'd love to meet some Jewish people. They had a terrible time in the war, Hitler killed millions of them. Makes you wonder if there are any left. If there are, I think I'll say one of my special prayers for them today, because we all believe in the same God. I learned that in RI this week, and that Jesus was a Jew. I couldn't believe that at first, but after Dot explained it, it started to make sense. I wonder why Hitler killed Jesus's people, if he was Christian. I'm glad he's dead now. We don't want people like him in the world, they make it too dangerous to go out anywhere, and if he kills you just because you're Jewish then there's no knowing where he might stop. I hope all the Jews he murdered are getting their own back on him in heaven now, except he'll definitely have gone to hell. I wonder if the little Jewish children are mixing with the ones who died in Aberfan. We had a special memorial service for them at St Peter's last month. Lots of us cried, even though it's been a year now since the coal pile collapsed and crushed them all to death. Dad didn't have any relatives who perished, which was lucky because many of them live close to where it happened.

I went to Wales once when I was really small to see Granny Morton, that's Daddy's gran. I can't remember much about it now, except that there was coal everywhere, and I couldn't understand anything anyone said.

The head of the cathedral is coming now, with the choir, so we all stand and start to sing the hymn 'At the Name of Jesus'.

Just like the ones at St Peter's the service goes on and on, especially the sermon, which I don't bother listening to. I've got other things on my mind, like being hungry and freezing and afraid to let go of my stocking top under my cloak. I wonder if Dad's here. I hope so. I wish I could go home with him after and snuggle up in front of the fire with a cup of Bournville and a piece of toast. I could ask him about the Jewish people, and his family in Wales, and why God lets bad things happen to innocent people. He knows practically everything, because he's read tons of books on all kinds of subjects like religion, politics, engineering, history, astronomy, Greek myths, and art. He's interested in everything. He even likes the Beatles, which is really good for someone his age, but I think he prefers classical music really, or the old songs he used to dance to with Mum.

I don't want to think about what Mum might say if she could see me today, so I try not to. I reckon she's around somewhere though, so I say hello to her in my heart and tell her I miss her. I feel some tears stinging my eyes, so I make myself think about Davy Jones.

It's time now for the sixth form to go down to the crypt where Johnny's buried. Rather them than me, even though he did write me a nice letter. We stay in the cathedral with the organ playing and candles burning, getting colder and colder and hungrier and hungrier. The ceiling's so high you can hardly even see it, and the stained-glass windows are massive. I look at Jesus on the Cross and Mary at His feet. I still don't really understand why He died to save us. I mean, if He's not around any more, what can He do? And when you look at all the terrible things that happen, earthquakes, volcanoes, shipwrecks, car crashes, murders, Aberfan, the Jews, slaves, beheadings, the Spanish Inquisition, well you have to say it didn't work, did it?

Realising what a bad thought that is I quickly put my head down and start to pray.

'Have you seen your dad yet?' Laura whispers in my ear.

I open my eyes. 'No. Have you seen your mum?'

'Yes, she's right at the back with my dad. I'm dying for the loo and I'm starving. Did you bring any sweets?'

I shake my head. My box in the tuck cupboard is empty, so I won't have anything until the weekend, providing Dad gives me some money today. I hope he's here. If that stupid car's broken down again I'll go mad.

Eddie

We managed to get here just in the nick of time. With Florrie not being able to walk very far, I dropped her outside the cathedral then drove round the back of the Council House to park. By the time I got back the Dean was leading everyone outside, so we missed the service, which is a great shame, but at least we're here on the green where the other parents are gathering, ready for when the girls come out.

'Glad I put my big coat on,' Florrie murmurs as I join her. 'Flipping cold out this morning, and it won't be doing me chilblains any good, standing here in all this damp grass.'

'Move over there,' I say, edging her towards the pavement. 'It'll help keep your feet dry.' I recognise her boots with their fur trim and zip top. They used to belong to Eddress. I think her gloves did too, and her burgundy handbag. They still look smart, so they're probably the best ones she has. She could do with a new coat though, because in all the winters I've known her I've never seen her in anything but the brown mohair one she has on now.

Still, at least the rain's gone off, and the wind's dying down a bit. I wish we'd been here in time to see them arriving in their Founder's Day uniforms. Bloody car. I'll have to stop relying on it in future and catch the bus. The main thing is though that it got us here, in the end. We broke down twice on the way, so heaven only knows how we'll manage to get back, but I'll worry about that when the time comes.

The cathedral green is starting to fill up with Red Maids now, swarming all over and looking as pretty as pictures in their sprightly straw bonnets and capes. I spotted a TWW van further down the road, so the television people must be around somewhere. Our Gary's so excited about seeing Susan on telly that I'm not sure what I'll do with him if we don't. Something else I'll worry about later.

'There she is,' Florrie cries, pointing through the crowd. 'Yoohoo! Susan! Here we are, over here!'

A few heads turn to see who's shouting. I can see they don't approve, so I give them a cheery smile and open my arms to welcome my girl.

'No, don't do that,' Susan whispers, keeping her head down and pushing my arms away. 'Everyone's looking.'

'Oh, don't be daft,' Florrie tells her. 'Everyone's giving their mums and dads a kiss. Come on now, let's be having you.'

'Ssh,' Susan says through her teeth. 'Don't talk so loud.'

'What? What did she say, Eddie?'

'Nothing. It's all right. Doesn't she look lovely?'

Florrie gets our Susan's face between her hands and tilts it up. 'Oh, I'm so proud of you,' she beams. 'I wish your mother could see you all grown up and a proper lady.'

'*Gran*,' Susan hisses. This is all much too embarrassing for her, and I'm not at all sure what to make of it. I suppose it's a part of growing up, and only to be expected, but I can see that Florrie's baffled and starting to feel a bit hurt.

'Isn't it lovely that your gran made it today?' I say cheerily. 'This is the furthest she's been in months, and all to see you.'

As intended, my remark hooks into Susan's conscience, because she looks a bit sheepish as she says, 'Yes, it's cool,' then to my relief I see her hand snake into Florrie's. 'Are you coming back to school?' she asks.

'What?' Florrie shouts.

Susan looks at me helplessly. She's obviously torn between loving her gran and feeling shown up by her, though I can't see anyone taking any notice myself. I give her a wink that makes her roll her eyes and smile. 'What's that about going back to school?' I ask.

'All the parents are invited straight after the cathedral,' she answers. 'I told you, Dad. There's tea and cakes and everything.'

Oh dear, this isn't good news. I have to get back to work, or I'm going to lose even more money, but the look on her face has me saying, 'Of course we're coming back, aren't we, Gran? We're looking forward to it.' I smile encouragingly. *Tea and cakes,*' I shout, so Florrie's got some idea of what's going on.

'Oh, yes please to a cuppa,' she answers. 'Look at all these people, Ed. They're proper upper class, with all their fur coats and smart suits, aren't they? One woman over there's even got a fur hat. You don't see many of them round our way, do you?'

Sensing our Susan cringing again I keep my voice down as I say to her, 'Your gran's having the time of her life being here. It meant the world that you asked her to come.'

'I wish she'd keep her voice down a bit,' Susan complains.

'I know, but she's not doing any harm. Now, what happened about the letter from Johnny? You were all worked up about it when I saw you last Sunday . . . '

'It came!' she cries, her eyes sparkling with delight. 'And he says that I'm a good friend to all the girls and that everyone likes me.'

'Aha!' I laugh, wanting to hug her, but managing not to. 'Wait till I tell Gary. He's been going on about that letter all week. You'll have to bring it home with you on Sunday so we can put it somewhere safe.'

Her face falls.

'What is it?' I ask.

She shakes her head. 'Nothing,' she mumbles. 'Only that . . .'

I miss what she says next because someone's making an announcement, telling us all that it's time to start back to the school.

'Girls whose parents aren't here go to the bus, please,' the teacher shouts, clapping her hands to scurry them along. 'The rest of you count yourselves lucky and be back in thirty minutes.'

'Where's the car?' Susan asks.

'Just round the corner,' I tell her. 'Gran's wrapped up some sandwiches for us, so we can have a bit of a picnic on the way. Are you ready, Florrie?'

'Bloody right I am,' she grumbles. 'I'm catching me death here in this cold. Fancy making us stand outside in November. You'd think they'd know better.'

'I couldn't agree more,' a very chilly-looking woman pipes up. 'My hands are turning blue and I can't even feel my feet.'

Startled to find such a posh-sounding person addressing her, Florrie's lost for words.

'I'm Eddie Lewis,' I say, holding out a hand to shake. 'Susan's dad.'

'Oh, hello Mr Lewis,' the woman says charmingly as she takes my hand. 'Rita Barker-North. My husband's around somewhere, Tom. Julia Barker-North's ours. Fifth form. Seabreake.'

'I don't think h'ive met 'er,' I say, tripping over my words and sounding just like our Susan. 'Susan's only in first year. Speedwell.'

Mrs Barker-North looks down at Susan, who's gone as red as a beetroot. 'Hello dear,' she says, giving her a chuck under the chin. 'I suppose this is your first Founder's bash.

Hope you're enjoying it in spite of the cold. Ah, there's Julia. Do excuse me,' and she was gone.

'What a *lovely* woman,' Florrie gushes. 'So polite, talking to us. Oh, Susan, you're in the right place here, my girl. Your mother knew what she was doing when she got you to sit those exams.'

'Can we go now?' Susan begs. 'I'm starving, and if you've got some sandwiches . . . '

It takes a while to reach the car, with Florrie not being too steady on her legs, but the rain keeps off and when we get there we find I'm parked next to a hot-air grille so she hikes up her dress to catch some warmth while I get the starting handle out. Now she's out of sight of her friends Susan seems much less self-conscious, and dives into the car to tuck into the fish-paste sandwiches dear old Florrie had thought to make for my dinner.

Inky, pinky, plonkey, Daddy bought a donkey. I don't half wish I had, because I reckon it'd be a darned sight more reliable than this temperamental rust heap I've got here. I can see our Susan's face through the window, starting to look worried, and Florrie's staring off into space either pretending she's not with us, or that everything's normal and all right.

I give another turn of the handle, and another and another. Then, lo and behold, the blessed thing catches.

'Quick,' I say to Florrie, 'jump in before it stops again.'

Susan's already in the back seat, so fast as she can Florrie piles herself into the front, and with some grinding and whirring I force the old girl into gear and start to ease forward. This wouldn't be the time to lose the clutch.

Well, what do you know, here we are, chugging in through the school gates having made it all the way up Park Street and across the Downs. I have to admit I don't like the noise she's making much, and I can see that our poor Susan's mortified, but at least we're here.

'We're like the Beverly Hillbillies,' Susan grumbles, as I pull up alongside a spanking new S-type Jaguar that must

113

have cost upwards of a thousand quid. Better not get too close. I can already hear my old Betsy hissing and popping with envy! Don't want her going into the attack and landing us all in debt, or jail.

'Well, I'm damned if they haven't got us all standing around outside again,' Florrie protests.

The engine's still running. I'm afraid to turn it off, certain if I do that it'll never start again, and the way I'm parked now the Jaguar's well and truly boxed in. Knowing our Susan'll never forgive me if one of her friends' dads has to help me push our old banger, I drive on towards the stall they've set up to serve tea.

'I'll wait in the car while you go and get a cuppa, if that's all right, Ed,' Florrie says. 'I can't take any more of the cold.'

'Where are you going to stop, Dad?' Susan asks, sounding anxious. 'You're too close, Dad. *Dad, stop!*'

'It's all right, don't worry,' I tell her. 'I'm just parking here so your gran doesn't have too far to walk.'

Susan

I have never, ever, *ever*, felt so embarrassed in all my life.

Gran's still in our car which is the oldest and scruffiest one here, and parked halfway up a bank right next to where everyone's having tea. No one can miss it, especially as the engine's still grinding and coughing. Gran's sitting in the passenger seat with her feet on the grass, waiting patiently while Dad and I go to get her some tea. I'm so upset that I can't look anyone in the face. I know they're all laughing their heads off, or sneering, or deliberately turning their backs, and I don't blame them, even though I hate them.

I don't want to be here.

I wish I was dead.

What makes it worse is that Dad's embarrassed too and keeps apologising.

'I don't mean to let you down, my love,' he says, 'but

we're not doing any harm where we are. No one's asked us to move.'

'You didn't have to come so close,' I mutter through my teeth. 'You nearly knocked Miss Hunter over, and Dotty's giving you really dirty looks.' I don't know if she is, because I can't bear to look up, but she definitely might be.

'Su Lu, Su Lu!'

It's Sadie coming our way. I want to feel pleased, but I think I'm going to cry.

'Hi,' she says, bouncing up to us and amazing me as she holds out a hand to shake Dad's. 'I'm Sadie Hicks,' she informs him. 'Second form, same dorm as Su. Did she tell you about the really cool letter she had from Johnny last night?'

'Yes, she did,' Dad answers, shaking Sadie's hand as though she's an adult.

'We all think she's amazing,' Sadie bubbles on. 'And we love your car. I wish my dad had one like that.'

No, you don't, I'm thinking. Why is she saying that? She's just mocking, and that's horrible.

'Tell him he's more than welcome to that old pile of trouble,' Dad says, turning round to have a look at it.

I sneak a quick look myself, and it's so embarrassing that I want the ground to suck me up and shoot me straight to Australia. No one else's car is hanging off the edge of the hockey field, and no one else's gran has got their false teeth out so they can give their gums a bit of a smack.

'Su Lu!' Cheryl cries, coming to join us. 'Hello Mr Lewis. It's very nice to see you.' There's a small gang of other girls with her, first and second form.

'And to see you, Cheryl,' he smiles, pleasing me that he remembers her name.

'Have you seen Su's letter?' Cheryl asks. 'It's one of the nicest ones Johnny's ever sent.'

'No, but I'm looking forward to it,' he tells her. 'And how's Cliff these days? I haven't seen him on *Top of the Pops* lately.'

My mouth nearly drops open. How did he remember that she loves Cliff?

Cheryl's cheeks turn rosy. 'He hasn't had a new record out for a while,' she explains, 'but he's still my favourite. We all love him, don't we?' she says to the others.

'No!' most of them shout.

'The Beatles.'

'The Stones.'

'Manfred Mann.'

'Davy Jones.'

'The Box Tops.'

Everyone's shouting at once, and they're all shouting at my dad! He's right in the middle of everything, and he looks quite small in some ways, because he's not very tall, but really tall in others. I don't quite understand what's happening, but then he says, 'I have to take a cup of tea to Susan's gran.'

'I can do it,' Cheryl offers.

'I can,' Sadie says.

'No, me.'

'Where is she?'

'Over there, in the car,' and everyone turns to look.

Gran's putting her teeth back in, and I'm suddenly afraid that someone's going to say something mean about her, so I quickly find Dad's hand and give it a tug. I don't mind if I think he and Gran are embarrassing, but if anyone thinks they can get away with mocking them I'll punch them so hard they'll fly straight down the tunnel under Dot's study and won't be able to get back up again.

'Mr Lewis.'

This is a different voice, and one I know even before I turn round. I've gone all stiff now, because Seaweed's on the rampage and I know what she wants.

All the girls step aside to let her through, some of them poking out their tongues behind her back, others holding up crossed fingers to show they're wishing me good luck.

'Mr Lewis, can I have a word, please?' Seaweed asks.

She's like Uriah Heep, all smiley and slithery and pretending to be nice when she's absolutely foul.

'Yes, of course, Miss Sayward,' he replies. 'Susan, take Gran a cup of tea, there's a good girl. Two sugars, and if there's a biscuit I expect she'd like one or two.'

I go off, leaving them to talk, feeling miserable and stupid and wishing I could hide myself away somewhere, but pleased too by the way everyone's grouping around me.

'Do you think your dad's going to be angry?' Laura whispers.

'I expect so,' I say.

'You'll have to tell him it wasn't your fault,' Sadie advises. 'We'll all back you up.'

'Definitely,' everyone agrees.

'Does anyone know who the record actually belongs to?' Peg asks.

One by one they all shake their heads.

'I think it just got left behind by one of last year's sixth form,' Cheryl says. 'It's so scratched, they probably didn't want it any more.'

We're at the tea stall now, so I order a cup for Gran, pop a couple of biscuits on the saucer and start back to the car. I haven't got very far when I realise Seaweed and Dad are already there. I wish I could disappear, but I'll have to face it some time, so on I go.

Dad's face is pale and grim as I come up to him.

'Here we are, Gran,' I say, passing her tea.

'Oh thanks, my old love, just what I need.'

'Where did you get the record?' Dad asks deeply.

'It's not mine,' I tell him.

Seaweed gives a horrible frown. 'That's not what you said last night,' she reminds me. 'You told me your cousin gave it to you.'

'I know, but it's not true. I was only trying to stop everyone getting into trouble.'

Seaweed looks at Dad. 'We don't encourage lies at the school,' she informs him. 'As I've already explained, Susan will remain here on Sunday to serve her detention. Now, if you'll excuse me . . . ' She looks at Gran, gives a withery sort of smile and takes off.

'Stuck-up old bitch,' Gran mutters under her breath.

'Susan, Susan, Susan,' Dad sighs in his biggest disappointed way. 'What on earth is going on? This isn't what I expect of you.'

'It's not my fault,' I cry. 'I was just trying to make everyone like me, so I took the blame, and it worked because I got a nice letter from Johnny. It would probably have been horrible otherwise, because I know no one likes me really, not even you.'

'I'm not arguing about that again, I'm simply going to hope that you've learned your lesson. By taking the blame you've let the guilty person go free, and now you won't be able to come home on Sunday, which is a great pity, because Auntie Doreen's invited us over for tea and Robert's going to be there. He specially wanted to see you, but now he won't be able to.'

My eyes are swimming in tears. I feel so unhappy and lonely that I don't know what to do. I wonder what Robert's going to think when he finds out I'm in detention. Probably that I'm a stupid, snotty little schoolgirl with plaits and freckles and long white socks, and I'm not. I'm growing up really fast now. I wear stockings and eyebrow pencil and I'm starting to speak posh. I want him to see what I'm like, because I know he'll write to me then, and if I can get a photo of him everyone will see how good-looking he is and be really jealous and wish they knew him too.

'Well, if you've learned anything from this,' Gran says, 'it's that you have to look out for number one in this life. You do that, and you'll go far.'

I look at Dad who doesn't seem particularly convinced by that, but he doesn't argue with it either. 'I'm very disappointed in you,' he tells me. 'I don't know how you got hold of that record . . . '

'I told you, it's not mine!' I shout.

my bike to work now, and we go everywhere else on
or by bus.
ert Pitman's due tonight. He comes every other
day to bring the *Soviet Weekly* and have a chat about
world and politics. I look forward to our couple of hours
her, dealing with the issues of the day and how this
ry's going to the dogs. We usually go in the front room
nk our tea, but it's much too cold in there tonight, so
oked up the fire in the dining room, and the kettle's
y on a low light, close to the boil to make a nice fresh
hen he gets here. We'll have a lot to talk about tonight,
with that old busybody de Gaulle vetoing Britain's
into the EEC the week before last. Not that I'm pro-
e myself, but the way that Frenchie carries on, anyone
think he'd won the flipping war, when everyone
he probably wouldn't have a country to run now if it
't for us.
ușescu's become president of Romania, so it's going
nteresting to see what happens there. There's a lot of
hat goes on behind that Iron Curtain that no one ever
hear about over here. I often think back to the time
s and I went to Poland, the year before our Susan
rn, when we were able to devote more time to our
t beliefs. Ed used to call me a commie sometimes and
to admit the ideology is one I could subscribe to in
and maybe even in practice if I was free to. Freedom,
ere's a subject to warm up the frozen cockles of the
n a winter's night with spirited debate. I think I
ar Ed groaning with despair and heading off to
ion Street.
rip to Poland was the first and only time either of us
ent abroad, and the welcome we received, the
lity and offers to show us round, were over-
ng. I can't imagine the English being as friendly as
h foreigners, or the Welsh, it has to be said. We
ave a socialist government in power, but that
mean we're not on our way to becoming a capitalist

'Then I hope that's the truth, because you're far too
young to be listening to that sort of muck, and if it's the kind
of thing you've been spending your pocket money on, I'll be
putting a stop to it.'

'No! It's not fair. I have to have some money or I'll starve,
and I won't have any records, or stamps, or writing
paper . . .'

He holds up his hand. 'Here's half a crown from Auntie
Nance and Uncle Stan,' he says, handing it over. 'You'll
write and thank them, and then you'll send a letter to
Auntie Doreen explaining why you can't come for tea.'

Chapter Seven

Eddie

What with Christmas coming and winter settling in, time's flying by and I still haven't repaired the paraffin stove to help warm up the house. Generally I put it at the bottom of the stairs to take the chill off for when Gary goes up to bed, but to my shame he's having to go up in the cold for now.

Poor mite, he comes home from school with his legs all chapped from the wind, and his lips turning blue, but at least we've got him some new shoes at last. I managed to put in some extra overtime to help get us past the worst of the rough patch, but I'm sensing some more tricky times ahead down the factory.

I don't think the bosses are very happy with me, because I got the inspectors in to run a check on all the grinding dust. I swear, they'd have let us suffocate to death before they'd done anything about it, so someone had to take some action. Our Nance and Doreen keep warning me not to upset the management. 'Remember how they sacked you from the BAC,' Doreen said. 'You got above yourself then, getting involved in the unions and what have you. They always find a way to push you out when you start rocking the boat.'

I didn't argue with her, because I'm afraid she's right, but if we all stood back and did nothing, letting management run roughshod over our rights, we'd end up back in the flaming nineteenth century, tipping our hats to the rich, and sending our children down the mines.

Gary and I had fish fingers, peas and chips for tea tonight.

As usual Gary wolfed his down, making covered in Daddies Sauce and chasing plate till every last one was gone. Then h the little rascal. I don't know where h Still, it's good for him to have a bit of have to be coated in breadcrumbs befor

I'm getting more and more worried at teaching him at school. They've got thi on that's supposed to help the kids lea faster, but for the life of me I can't se work. This is what it says on the front *Mie Wurk Bwk*. And inside he's writter *zw. Mis Ritchie will bee our teecher* comment from the teacher: *Gwd boi*.

It's supposed to be some sort of ph how the heck are they ever going to le want to know. I can just hear what Ed say about it. She wouldn't be doing that, and I'm damned if I can see any se up there to investigate. There must be as worried as I am. I suppose not eve store by learning proper English as I d boy growing up to look like a dunce from it.

We had a nice story tonight. I read then we had a look through his fo a good collection now that includ Geoff Hurst, his heroes, so we're g scrapbook at the weekend. He's bee elevens down at Made for Ever thi chuffed to bits with himself tonight. out how to get him from the match, change, and up to the church in tim be easier if we still had a car, but ou ghost in the middle of Kingswood and got carted off to the scrapyard for her, and said they were bein

state, because it's happening all around us. And if we don't put a stop to it, mark my words, the rich'll get richer, the poor'll get poorer and in years to come we're going to find ourselves embroiled in so much greed and corruption that we'll probably end up in as bloody a revolution as the Russians went through in 1917, or the French back in 1792.

There's still a few minutes before Albert's due to arrive – he's always regular as clockwork – so I think I'll finish off the letter I started to our Susan in Fishponds library today. I'll have to make sure to post it tomorrow, or she might not get it before she comes home for Christmas. I received a list as long as her arm a few days ago, of all the presents she wants: a Mary Quant top, a psychedelic dress, Twiggy's magazine, *Her Mod, Mod Teen World* (this is American, she wrote, *so you might not be able to get it, but please try*). She wants some scent called Fidji, a long pencil with a tassel on the end, a polka-dot pencil case, a page-a-day diary that locks, a white Bible, a dressing-table set with flowers on the back, some Avon Topaz talcum powder, and plenty of record and book tokens. I don't know where she thinks we're going to get the money for all this, but at least I've been able to give her aunts and her grandmother some idea of what she wants.

I write:

I was very pleased to hear about your Commended for History. Well done. I know English can be a little difficult at times, and when to use 'I' and 'me' isn't very straightforward, but here's something that might make it easier for you. All you have to do is take the other person away in your head, like this: 1) Dad and I go up Gran's, would become I go up Gran's if you take Dad away, which is correct (you wouldn't say me go up Gran's, so it can't be Dad and me – or me and Dad). 2) Can Gary come up Gran's with Dad and I? would be wrong, because that would be like saying can Gary come up Gran's with I? So you should say Can Gary come up Gran's with Dad and me? I hope that helps. It's a little trick I learned when I was at school, which seems a very long time ago now.

Ah, there's Albert knocking on the door. He'll have

ridden his bike, as usual, and it's perishing out there, so I'm quick to go and let him in.

'Hello,' he says, stomping his feet on the front doormat and stooping to snap off his bicycle clips. 'It's turning arctic out there. They say there's going to be snow next week.'

I take his coat and drape it over the bottom of the stairs, then usher him along the passage into the kitchen, where the gas oven's on with the door open to make it nice and warm. 'What are you doing for Christmas?' I ask, turning up the heat under the kettle.

'Oh, the same as always,' he answers, 'going over my sister's for dinner, then up to Frank and Vi's for tea. How about you?'

'The same as last year. Our Doreen's for dinner, then Flo's for tea.'

'Ah yes, Flo,' he says, perching on the edge of a stool where the Flatley used to be. It's upstairs on the landing now, with a long cable running into my bedroom so we can plug it in to dry the clothes. Eddress would never have allowed that, but it was taking up too much space in the kitchen, half blocking the doors into the passage and dining room, and it was the only other place I could find to put it. 'How's she getting on with her little kiddies?' he asks.

'As best as can be expected,' I tell him.

We go on chatting as the tea brews, and I wonder, the way I do sometimes when I'm with him, how he manages without a woman. He's never been married, so I don't suppose he can miss what he never had, but all the same he's a normal red-blooded bloke, so he must have his needs. I don't ever think about my own, it's best not to when no one will ever be able to take Eddress's place.

We're facing our second Christmas without her, and remembering what it was like last year is making me dread this one. She always knew exactly how to make everything sparkle for the kids, what presents to get, how to wrap them up, what time they should go to bed the night before. I remember how we used to listen for them in the morning, shuffling about between one another's rooms, opening their stockings . . . *Look what I've got! A yo-yo. Cor, look at this! Pretend nail varnish and a doll's brush and comb. I've got an orange. Me too. And some nuts. Oh look, Gary, chocolate pennies!*

They brought everything in to me last Christmas morning. Nance and Doreen had done their stockings, so they didn't go short of anything. We sat there in bed, the three of us, looking through everything they had, and when it was over we didn't know what to do with ourselves. We just sat there, staring at it all, listening to the clock ticking and not saying a word.

It was our Susan, bless her, who thought of getting breakfast.

'I'll make you something to eat,' I heard her telling Gary as she took him downstairs, 'and then we'll bring some upstairs for Dad, all right? What do you think he'd like?'

'Um, cornflakes and porridge and four pieces of toast with jam on.'

'He can't eat all that.'

'Why not? I can.'

He can, as well.

I made myself get up then, because I didn't want her trying to make a cup of tea. She was too young to be messing about with boiling water, and knowing her she'd probably have a go at lighting the fire too. I wasn't wrong, because by the time I got downstairs the kettle was on, and she was about to light the gas on the back burner. The way it was hissing out, if she'd put a match to it, it would have probably blown her to kingdom come, so lucky I was there in time to grab the matches and start everything over again, showing her what to do in case she ever tried it another time. I could see she was upset, because she wanted to take charge and prove she was capable of looking after us all, but she was only ten, and I should have known better than to lie around in bed feeling sorry for myself when my kids were trying to make something of their Christmas.

I shall have to make sure that doesn't happen again this

year, because it's not fair on them, and if Eddress is looking down on us all she'll be mad as heck and thoroughly ashamed of me.

Susan

Everyone's in a fantastic mood, because it's the end of term and we can't wait to go home tomorrow. We'd give anything not to have to come back again after Christmas, mainly because it's so *freezing* here that there's ice on the insides of the windows, and half the time we can't get any hot water in the morning because it's frozen up inside the tap.

I think it's cruel making people sleep in a great big dormitory with only one measly pipe going round the skirting board to keep it warm. Half the time we pretend we're ill so we can go down to the nursery where Cluttie's always got the gas fire on. Because I'm the youngest, I always have to go to the end of the queue in the house maids to fill my hot-water bottle, so by the time I get to the tap the hot water's all gone cold.

Being the youngest doesn't get any easier, and now everyone's forgotten how I saved them from a detention, I'm back to being a nobody again. The only time I enjoy myself is when I go home on an exeat. I see all my proper friends then, and we play skipping and Simon Says, and The Big Ship Sails through the Alley Alley Oh. They tell me about their school and I can't help feeling jealous of all the freedom they have, like being able to come home every night, watch telly when they want to, go up Kingswood with their mums, or down Made for Ever to the youth club. Plus, no one ever blows them up, and they don't have to do dangerous things because of tradition.

The last time I was at home (after the exeat I had to miss, which I spent scooping up leaves from the hockey field and lying on my bed doing nothing) I told my friends that I hadn't been able to come the time before because I had gone to spend the day with my boyfriend who lives over by my school. They immediately wanted to know his name, so I said it was Steve, which is what Paula Gates's boyfriend is called.

She's got a photograph of him next to her bed. He's really dishy with quite long curly hair, a moustache and these tiny little glasses like John Lennon wears. She sees him at weekends when she's allowed out of bounds, and he writes to her all the time. Sadie's got a boyfriend too, and so has Cheryl. They're always getting letters, or writing to them. Even Peg's got one, so it's only me and Laura who don't have anyone, but I don't think Laura's as bothered as I am. I'd love to have one more than anything else in the world. I'm sure it would make me miss Mummy a bit less, because it'd show I'm growing up and getting on with things.

I wish she was going to be there at Christmas. I had a dream about her last night. We were over the bluebell field, running and twirling through the long grass like aeroplanes. Gary was there too, zooming around with his arms stuck out behind him and rolling over on his back. Mummy kept running and running. She never seemed to stop and then I realised she was getting further and further away. I kept calling out to her to wait, but she couldn't hear me. Gary started to cry so I held his hand and shouted again for Mummy to wait, but I couldn't make my voice loud enough. Then someone else was with her, a man and some children, and they walked out of the other side of the field. When Mummy turned round I couldn't see her face, and it frightened me so much that I woke up.

'What are you doing for Christmas, Su Lu?' Paula Gates asks me.

We're in her room watching her brush her lovely long crinkly hair and put on make-up ready for when she sneaks out to meet Steve on his motorbike. Sadie's lying on the bed with Cheryl curled up at the end, and Laura and I are sitting on cushions on the floor.

'Um, I'm going to my auntie's, I expect,' I say, wishing I

had something more exciting to tell them. Then I suddenly remember that I do. 'My cousin Robert will be there. He's really dishy and sexy, you should see him.' (Sexy is our new word, and everyone's saying it.) 'I'll bring some photos back with me if you like.' (I'm still not too sure what sexy means, but I expect I'll find out soon enough.)

'How old is he?' Laura asks.

'Sixteen. He's got a motorbike, and he's always asking me if I want to go on it.'

'Wow. Are you going to?'

I nod. 'Definitely.' I've sat on it before, with him in front of me, and I felt all tingly and funny when I put my arms round him to hold on. We didn't go anywhere, it was just so I could find out what it was like to get on it. 'We're probably going to get married when I'm older,' I tell them.

Sadie wrinkles up her nose. 'Are you allowed to marry your cousin?' she says.

'Oh yes,' Paula answers. 'It's not against the law.' She goes on applying her eyeliner, all thick and black like Twiggy's. I'm going to buy some with my Christmas money, if I get any.

'Do you miss your mum?' Paula suddenly asks.

I think she's talking to Sadie and Cheryl so I look at them, waiting for one of them to answer. Then I realise she means me, and I suddenly feel all strange and afraid as I remember the dream I had last night. I don't want to talk about my mum, but I don't want to be rude either.

'Of course you do,' Paula says, watching me in the mirror. 'It must be horrible without her.'

I don't know what to say, so I don't say anything.

'What did she die of?' Cheryl asks.

I take a breath and it catches in my throat. I want to tell them that she's not really dead, but they know that she is. I'm thinking about the way she went off with a strange man in the dream.

I wish she had. She might come back then.

'It was, um, something called cancer,' I say.

'I've heard of that,' Sadie tells me. 'Lots of people die from it, apparently.'

'How did she catch it?' Cheryl asks.

'I don't know. She just did.'

'Do you remember her?' Paula wants to know.

I look away. 'No, not very well,' I lie.

'I bet your dad misses her. I know mine would if my mum died. He can't do anything without her.'

'My dad can do most things,' I tell her.

'Do you think he'll ever get married again?' Laura asks.

I'm starting to feel like I want to run away. 'No,' I reply.

'Would you mind if he did?'

I wish I knew what they wanted me to say, but I don't, so I don't say anything, because it might seem selfish if I say I don't want my dad to get married again, but I don't, not ever. No one can take Mummy's place.

Except me, if Dad would just let me live at home.

'Of course she'd mind, wouldn't you?' Paula says. 'Who wants a stepmother, for heaven's sake?'

'They're not all wicked,' Cheryl tells her.

'Most of them are,' Sadie insists.

'Has your dad got a girlfriend?' Paula asks.

I'm really hating this now. It's horrible to think of my dad with a girlfriend, it's making me feel sick and like I want to hit someone. He's too old for things like that. I wish they'd stop.

'What if she was beautiful and mod and let you do everything you wanted?' Paula says. 'Wouldn't that be great?'

'Oh God, just imagine a mother who let you wear minidresses and black patent boots,' Sadie swoons.

'And false eyelashes and lipstick,' Cheryl adds.

'And a fringe right down to your eyes,' I laugh, wanting to join in. I'm always being told off because my fringe is too long, but it hides my eyebrows so what choice do I have? I can just hear what Mummy would have to say about it though, so maybe it's just as well she can't see it.

If cutting it would make her come back I'd get the scissors out and do it right now. She'd be there on Christmas morning then to jump into bed with and watch us unwrap our presents. She'd make our breakfasts and put a turkey in the oven so that the whole house smelled of Christmas. Later, after the Queen's speech, she and Dad would play our games with us, and we'd all dance to our new records. I wouldn't be the only girl in the house the way I was last year, because she'd be there and everything would be all right.

I didn't like Christmas very much last year. I don't think Dad did either, but he didn't say anything. Admittedly, it got better when we went over to Auntie Doreen's for dinner and played Monopoly in the afternoon. Robert was there, so was young Doreen, my other cousin who's his older sister. I always wanted to be like her when I grow up, but now I'd rather be like Paula. What would be really cool would be having Paula for a sister, but I don't say so, or she'll think I'm a loony.

'What's your cousin's name again?' Cheryl asks. 'The one with the motorbike.'

'Robert.'

'Have you ever kissed him?' Sadie wants to know.

My cheeks go beet red. 'Only once,' I mumble.

Cheryl's eyes pop out. 'What, on the mouth?'

I swallow hard and give a little nod.

Paula's watching me in the mirror again. I can tell she thinks I'm lying.

'What was it like?' Cheryl asks.

'It was nice.'

'How long did it last?'

I shrug. 'About a minute,' I lie.

Sadie shrieks and kicks her legs in the air. 'That is a really long time. You're so sexy, Su Lu. I've never kissed a boy for that long. Have you, Paula?'

Paula rolls her eyes and carries on making them up.

'I'd kiss Cliff for hours and hours if I could,' Cheryl swoons.

'Oh no, give me Mick Jagger any day,' Sadie protests.

'What about your boyfriends?' I ask. 'Don't you want to kiss them?'

'Oh yeah,' Sadie answers, 'but they're really immature in comparison to Mick Jagger and Steve, Paula's boyfriend. Aren't they, Paula?'

'How old is Steve?' Cheryl wants to know.

'Nineteen,' Paula replies. 'A year older than me.'

'I think we should have a dare for the Christmas hols,' Sadie declares. 'I think we should all kiss someone for at least a minute, and when we come back if anyone hasn't she's a baby and has to walk the plank.' The plank is a piece of wood that we place on the fire escape to jut out into mid-air for about ten feet, and if anyone does something hideously wrong, or is cheeky to sixth form, they're made to walk it. I've never known anyone to do it, but I've been threatened with it lots of times. As we're four storeys up, if I have to walk it I know I'll fall off and die.

Paula's not looking very pleased, and I hope it's because she doesn't approve of the plank. 'I'm not part of your gang,' she tells Sadie.

'No, I don't mean you,' Sadie says hastily. 'I mean the rest of us. We should get Peg and some of the others to come in on it too.'

I want to object to that, because knowing Peg she'll have loads of boys to choose from and if there's anyone who should be made to walk the plank, just because she's so full of herself, it's her, but Cheryl's saying, 'Fab, fab, fab idea. I wish I had your guts, Su Lu, to kiss someone for a whole minute, but I'm definitely going to give it a try.' She lets out a squeal of excitement. 'This is so sexy and groovy. I can hardly wait. Happy Christmas everyone, roll on going home and then coming back next term to tell all our secrets.'

I join in with what they're saying, but if I get my way I won't be coming back. I'm still not sure how I'm going to prevent it yet, but I'll have a lot more time to talk to Dad during the break and make him see things my way. What would also be really fab and groovy would be for Robert to scoop me up on the back of his motorbike and whisk me off to Gretna Green so we could get married. Then I really wouldn't have to come back here any more.

If only I was (were) sixteen. Everything would be different then.

I wonder what time Dad's picking me up tomorrow. I hope he hasn't forgotten.

I think the man I saw in the bluebell field with Mum might have been Dad. I wonder why they didn't wait for us.

This is going to be the best Christmas Day we've ever had. Last night, about six o'clock, Robert came over on his motorbike and while he was here he whispered to me that he has a secret that he's going to share with me when I go to his house today. It was really fab the way he pulled up outside on his motorbike. His hair's quite long now and he walks like a pop star. All the neighbours were watching him and Gary raced down the garden path to jump on him. He'd brought a sack full of presents from his mum and dad, which we spread out under the tree, and when Dad went to make a cup of tea, after ordering Gary up to the toilet before he wet himself, Robert said to me, 'You've got taller since I last saw you.'

I felt myself blush as I nodded. I wished I'd known he was coming, because I'd have put on my eyebrow pencil and turned over the waist-band of my skirt to make myself look more mod. I did manage to do my posh voice though, and he seemed to like it, though I'm not sure he really understood it at first. He did in the end though, because he said, 'You're growing into a proper young lady sounding all your Ts and Hs. I hope you're not becoming too good for us.'

It worried me that he might think that, until I saw him laughing, so I laughed too.

'I'm going to tell you a secret tomorrow,' he said. 'Do you promise to keep it?'

'Of course,' I assured him, feeling as though I was already his girlfriend.

He gave me a wink. 'I don't think it'll be much longer before you have all the boys after you,' he teased.

I felt really beautiful then, and I'm glad he thinks that, because it might make him jealous and want me himself. I think he does anyway, but just in case, I was about to tell him that I'm writing to Davy Jones, when Gary zoomed back into the room with a Thunderbirds kit that he'd won from one of his comics. Little brothers can be really annoying at times, especially mine, but this morning I love him because he's so happy opening his presents, and he keeps showing them to me, the way he used to show them to Mummy. I still wish she was here, because everything would be much better if she was. I'm sure Dad thinks so too, because his eyes are all sad and if I look at him it makes me want to cry, so I only look at Gary. I'm starting to realise how much he misses me when I'm not here, so I really must have another talk with Dad about how important it is for me to be at home with Gary, and not locked away in that stupid school.

Although Dad's watching us, he's also listening to the carols on TV. 'O Come All Ye Faithful'. 'Hark the Herald Angels Sing'. 'O Little Town of Bethlehem'. Gary and I sang them all when we went round the street carol singing two nights ago. Dad doesn't like us to go any further than he can see us, so he stands at the kitchen window and watches as we knock on everyone's front door. (Sometimes he comes with us, which is embarrassing because he's too old to go carol singing, but at least he's a good singer. Lots of Welsh people are. I remember Mum telling me that.) Hardly anyone ever says no, whether he's with us or not, so we ended up with a lot of singing to do, but we came home with three and six between us, which makes one and ninepence each, so we're quite rich now. We always give tuppence to the carol singers who come to our door, which is only fair when that's what we usually get. When Gary's older we'll be able to go over Pound Road and Champion Lane to sing our carols, but he's still too young to go that far yet, and I have to take care of him, which is why I stay in Greenways when some of my friends go along the lane to Holly Green and even Holly Hill.

There's a church service on the telly now, which Dad keeps telling us to take notice of. He's reminding us that it's Jesus's birthday, so all our presents are presents for Jesus really, and not for us.

'But Jesus would look silly in a dress,' I tell him, cheekily. 'This is for me.' I picked it out of the John Myers catalogue when I was last up Auntie Nance's, and Dad actually said I could have it, even though it's above the knee. It's not a proper mini, because it's too long for that, but I love it anyway. It's turquoise with a white polka-dot collar and cuffs and white buttons down the front. I'm so happy to have it. I can't wait to show Paula Gates when I go back to school, if I go, which I probably won't once I've talked to Dad.

I could wear it on a Sunday if I go to visit them all at church.

'Dad, do you think Jesus likes the Beatles?' Gary asks.

I'm not sure if Dad has heard until he says, 'Jesus loves all His children, and no matter who we are, we are Jesus's children.'

Gary looks at me. I can see he hasn't understood the answer properly, so I say, 'You are Dad's child and Dad is one of Jesus's children, and so are you.'

Gary, because he's annoying, seems more puzzled than ever. 'What about Grampy?' he asks. 'I thought he was Dad's dad.'

'He is,' I confirm, 'but he's also Jesus's son. Or I think he is, but it doesn't really matter, because what does is that we understand who was born today, and if He hadn't been born then nor would we.' (I don't think that's quite right, but neither Dad nor Gary argue, so I don't say any more. Phew! Children! Honestly! You never know what they're going to ask next.)

When all our presents are open Dad goes to do some washing up and Gary skids out into the snow to play with his friends. I'm staying by the fire to look through my new Monkees Annual that Gran gave me. (I expect Dad got it for her.) It's really fab, with a purple cover that has *The Monkees* printed in the shape of a guitar across the top, and the group pictured inside a big keyhole, but I only look at Davy. Inside there are loads of groovy photos in black and white *and* colour.

Suddenly I start feeling restless and angry and I don't know why. I wish Dad would stop calling out for me to come and wipe up – it's Christmas Day so I shouldn't have to do any chores. I start picking up all the wrapping paper and stuffing it into a sack, then I have a go on Gary's new machine gun which makes a heck of a racket. It's a bit boring, so I have a look at the King Kong which he's left on the floor along with his new vests and underpants. I wish it was time to go to Auntie Doreen's already. I think about going out to play in the snow, and taking some of my presents to show my friends, but they were quite mean to me yesterday, calling me a snob and saying I was stuck-up so they didn't want to be my friend any more. It's not my fault that I go to a better school than they do. I don't want to be there, and now they're blaming me and sending me to Coventry so I don't have anyone to talk to.

Anyway, they're just immature and stupid. I'd much rather be in here with Dad, so I think I'll go and wipe up.

'Did you like your book token?' I ask him as I take the tea towel from the rail on the back door. It's what I bought for him with the money he gave me to go Christmas shopping.

'Oh yes, very much,' he answers.

'What are you going to get with it?'

'Dad! Dad!' Gary shouts, bursting in through the door. 'I fell over in the snow and cut my knee. Look, it's bleeding.'

'Oh dear,' Dad says. 'Let's give it a wash. How did you do it?'

135

'I was skidding down the pavement with Gordon, but then I hit a bump.'

'You're as cold as ice,' Dad tells him. 'It's time you came in now and got yourself warmed up.'

'All right. What time are we going over Auntie Doreen's?'

'Uncle Alf's picking us up at twelve . . . '

'Ow, ow, ow, ow,' Gary squeals, as Dad dabs some water on his knee. 'Can I have a plaster?'

'If we've got some.'

'You can put the dishes away,' I tell him.

'No!' he shouts.

'Yes!' I shout back. 'I'm wiping up, so you have to do something too.'

'Oh, Dad,' he says sulkily.

'It won't take long,' Dad tells him. 'Then we'll all have a nice cup of cocoa. How does that sound?'

'Yes,' Gary cheers, 'and can I eat some chocolate from one of my selection boxes?'

'No, or you won't want your dinner.'

Dad sounds quite tired, I think, and a bit fed up, and we're not supposed to be fed up on Christmas Day. To try and cheer him up I remind him of his book token and ask again what he's going to spend it on.

'Well,' he says, sounding slightly jollier, 'it's not very often that I can treat myself to a brand-new book, so I thought I might put a little bit extra to my token and buy a very important book that's just come out called *The Naked Ape*.'

Gary snorts. 'That's rude,' he sniggers.

'No it isn't,' I say. 'When did you ever see an ape with clothes on?'

'My Jacko monkey's got shorts,' he reminds me.

'That's not the same thing, is it, Dad?'

'Not at all,' Dad answers.

'You're such a show-off,' Gary tells me. 'Everyone hates you now because you're all brainy and stuck up.'

'No they don't.'

'Yes they do.'

'All right, that's enough,' Dad intervenes. 'Why don't you go and choose a game from Gary's new compendium while I go up and make the beds?'

'Tiddlywinks,' Gary shouts, charging into the dining room.

I look at Dad.

'Go on,' he says, giving me a little push, 'I'll come and play when I've finished upstairs.'

We're at Auntie Doreen's now, eating our Christmas dinner of cockerel, roasters, cabbage, carrots, peas and lovely runny Bisto. (I don't like it thick, because it's usually got lumps in, or it has when Dad makes it.) It's much better than the food we're served up at school, which isn't fit for pigs, and here we can wipe up our gravy with a lovely chunk of bread and dripping.

Auntie Nance and Uncle Stan look really funny in their paper hats. Gary's is too big and keeps slipping down over his eyes. He got told off just now for belting me across the back, so his eyes are all red from crying. I think Dad's quite fed up with him today, because he doesn't look very happy, and when Gary threw a Christmas cracker across the table at me I thought Dad was going to smack him. Dad almost never smacks us, so if he does we know we've done something very wrong indeed.

I'm sitting next to Robert who keeps nudging me and mucking about. He's in a really good mood, so I am too. I'm wearing my new turquoise dress, which young Doreen (we call her that because she's younger than her mum who has the same name) said was the nicest dress she'd ever seen, and she'd like one too. She's wearing a really short skirt, at least halfway up her thighs, and no one's getting on at her, but I suppose that's because she's eighteen. I can't wait till I'm sixteen, I'll be able to do just as I want then without having to listen to anyone.

I'm dying to know what Robert's secret is, but after

dinner we *have* to watch *Top of the Pops*. I'd rather die than miss it. It's fab, because they play all the number ones from the year, and the Monkees are on first with 'I'm a Believer'. Doreen and I get straight up to dance, and I think she's quite impressed with the way I can groove. Gary jumps about being his usual stupid self, and Robert sits watching us, pretending to play a guitar. There are lots of other great songs on too, like 'Puppet on a String', by Sandie Shaw, and 'Silence is Golden', by the Tremeloes, which is the first record I ever bought with my own money. 'Baby Now That I've Found You' is Doreen's favourite, and 'Something Stupid' is Auntie Nance and Auntie Doreen's. Number one this week is 'Hello Goodbye' by the Beatles, which we all love and sing along to. I had two record tokens for Christmas so I think I might use one of them to get it.

When the programme's over we sit and watch the Queen's speech, which is really boring, then Gary wants to go outside to build a snowman, so young Doreen, Robert and I take him. I'm starting to get worried now that there might not be time for Robert to tell me his secret, because we're leaving soon to go to Auntie Flo's for tea. I keep going all funny inside every time I think about Sadie's dare to kiss someone for a whole minute. I know I said I kissed Robert once for that long, but I didn't really. It was just a peck, but it was on the lips and I don't think it was an accident, so it must count as a proper kiss. I don't think I've got the guts to try and do it for longer, but you never know. His secret might be that he wants to kiss me.

I go all tingly in private places when I think that.

Robert gives Gary a piggyback into the outhouse, where we take off our wet coats and boots and rush into the kitchen before our feet get too cold. Auntie Doreen's making a cup of tea while Auntie Nance dries the dishes from dinner, and Uncle Alf and Uncle Stan are in the dining room snoozing in front of the telly.

'Where's Dad?' I ask straight away.

'He's in the front room, my love,' Auntie Doreen answers.

'I'll go and get him,' Gary says.

Auntie Doreen catches him. 'No, let him be for a while,' she tells him. 'He's not feeling all that well, so he's after a bit of peace and quiet.'

I start to feel strange and panicky inside. 'What's wrong with him?' I ask.

'Just a headache,' she answers. 'He'll be right as rain in an hour.'

It would be rude to ask if she's telling the truth, but I want to, because I'm afraid he might be really ill and if he is he might die if we don't go to check on him.

'Oh come on, now,' Auntie Doreen says, giving me a hug, 'there's no need to cry. Like I said, it's just a headache.'

'I want to go and see him,' I tell her.

'So do I,' Gary says, starting to cry too.

'You heard Auntie Doreen,' Auntie Nance says, 'leave him be now. He works hard down that factory and looking after you two, so he needs a rest. Go and play with some of your games, there's a good boy and girl.'

Gary looks at me and I feel his hand slip into mine. I want to charge past my aunties into the front room, but I'm afraid Dad'll be angry if we do, so I keep hold of Gary's hand and take him into the dining room to wait for Dad to join us.

'How about some snakes and ladders?' young Doreen suggests, coming to give Gary a cuddle.

'All right,' he agrees, 'but you have to let me win, because I'm smaller than you.'

What's funny about that is that he means it.

'Fancy a game of chess?' Robert asks me.

My chest goes all tight. We have to play in his bedroom where the pieces are set up on a table next to his bed. I'm not very good at the game, although I have managed to beat him a couple of times when we played before. I always beat Dad, but I know he lets me.

As Robert and I go along the passage I stop outside the

front-room door, wondering what Dad's doing. Everything's very quiet, making me afraid that he might not be in there at all. What if he's gone off and left us? But he wouldn't do that. Auntie Doreen wouldn't let him. I want to check he's put the electric fire on to keep himself warm, especially if he's not very well.

'He's probably having a nap,' Robert says.

I feel better then, because Robert's usually right. Dad often likes to have a nap, so I'm sure that's what he's doing.

Upstairs in Robert's room he closes the door and invites me to sit on the bed one side of the chessboard, while he pulls up a chair to sit the other. There are lots of posters on his walls of motorbikes and flower-power people, and some girls with nearly nothing on. It makes me feel all embarrassed when I notice them. I want to stare at them, but I turn away quickly in case he catches me looking. I don't want him to think I'm a lezzie, or anything. (I think that's what they call a girl who likes other girls, anyway, that's what they say about Trudie Fox and Annette Ryder at school, who are always in Trudie's sixth-form room together.)

'Do you like them?' he says.

For one horrible minute I think he's talking about the pictures, and then I realise he is! I go blood red as I say, 'They're OK. I wouldn't want them on my wall though.'

He laughs. 'I'd be worried if you did.' He leans back in his chair and stretches out his legs. He reminds me of Billy Fury when he does that. 'Do you want to listen to some music?' he asks.

I glance at his record player.

'Choose what you want,' he offers.

After going through his collection I pick 'Dedicated to the One I Love' by the Mamas and Papas, because I know he likes it. I do too. I've put 'A Little Bit Me, A Little Bit You' second in the pile, and 'Penny Lane' third. It's fantastic the way the records drop down to play on their own without you having to get up to change them. The sixth form at school have a record player like that in their common room.

'Do you ever listen to Radio Caroline?' he asks, tapping his feet to the music.

I catch my breath. 'It's not allowed,' I remind him.

He gives me a wink. 'I bet you do though.'

Actually, I've never been able to find the pirate station on the little transistor Uncle Stan gave me, but I've definitely tried. 'Some of the girls at my school do,' I admit. 'Do you?'

'All the time. It's fab.'

We go on listening to the music, and I can feel him watching me as I stare down at the floor. I'm thinking how lush it would be if he leaned over and kissed me, but I don't expect he will.

'You seem to have gone all shy on me,' he teases.

I give a laugh and blush at the same time. 'What's your secret?' I ask.

He tilts his head to one side. 'I'm not sure I should tell you now.'

'You have to,' I protest. 'You promised.'

'No, it was you who promised not to tell.'

'I won't. I swear it.'

His eyes are narrowing as he watches me. 'How old are you now?' he asks.

'Nearly twelve,' I lie. I've got another eight months to go, worse luck.

He shakes his head. 'You look closer to fourteen,' he tells me.

I'm very pleased by that and feel myself sit up a little straighter. 'Lots of people say that,' I boast.

'Do you have a boyfriend yet?'

My throat starts to feel tight. 'Sort of,' I reply, thinking of him. Then out of nowhere I say, 'What about you? Have you got a girlfriend?'

Because he looks at me for quite a while before he nods I start to wonder if it's me. But then he says, 'Her name's Jenny.'

Suddenly I want to go. I shouldn't be here anyway, I

should be downstairs with my dad making sure he's all right. He's the only one who matters.

'I've told her all about you,' he says.

I'm finding it hard not to sound miserable as I ask, 'What did you say?'

He gives a big smile and leans forward to tweak my nose. 'Wouldn't you like to know?' he teases.

'I'm not a child,' I snap, pulling back angrily. 'And I don't care that you've got a girlfriend, because I've got a boyfriend. I just didn't want to tell you in case you . . . In case you thought I was too young.' I don't know if he believes me and I don't care. 'I'm going down now,' I say, getting to my feet.

'What about our game of chess?'

I look at the board and feel tempted to sweep all the pieces to the floor. 'I'm not in the mood any more.'

He catches hold of my hand. 'Why are you so cross?' he says, looking up at me.

'I'm not.'

'You look it.'

I shrug.

He keeps hold of my hand. 'Are we still friends?'

I want to say no, but I can't.

'I'm not letting you go until you say we're friends.'

I turn my head away. 'OK, we're friends,' I say sulkily.

He gets to his feet and draws me into a great big hug. 'That's better,' he says, dropping a kiss on the top of my head. 'I'll write to you when you're back at school, if you like.'

I would like him to, but Christmas is still ruined for me now I know he's got a girlfriend. Except I expect he only told me that to make me jealous. I bet she doesn't exist really, and even if she does, he's had loads of girlfriends before who he's always finished with sooner or later, so I'm sure he'll do the same to her. What's more, getting a letter from him will be almost as good as getting one from Davy Jones. So really, everything's all right.

When I go downstairs I find Dad playing ludo with young Doreen and Gary, his headache all gone.

One by one the clouds are lifting.

I wonder if we've got any photos of Robert in our albums. When we get home I go upstairs to have a look, but when I take them out of Dad's dressing-table drawer, I remember who else is in them and I decide to put them away again. I don't really want to see any pictures of Mummy.

I can always ask Robert to send one of him when I write back to his letter.

Chapter Eight

Eddie

I've finally managed to afford a new car. It's been a hard winter without one, grinding back and forth to work on my pushbike in the snow, skidding down Lodge Hill like a bloody comedian and nearly breaking my neck, getting a puncture outside the factory with no blighter offering me a lift home, and finding our Gary frozen to the blinking crossbar early one Saturday morning when I dropped him off at his gran's.

It's thanks to all the weekend working and double shifts in the week that I can manage the first instalment on the '56 Anglia. It might be getting on for twelve years old, but it's in fairly good nick, with no rust on the bodywork and a reconditioned engine, so it should last me a while. I'm paying for it in six instalments of twenty quid a month, but if I can scrape the money together before that then all well and good, because being in debt is something that goes right against the grain with me. I don't even like club books, but Eddress had her nose in one all the time.

As well as getting myself and Gary around, and Florrie to bingo now and again, it's going to be a great relief to be able to drive up and down to the school on Sundays. Taking the bus is no joke, what with having to change at the Centre, and all the waiting around at bus stops means our Susan's exeats don't last very long when we have to spend so much time getting back and forth across town.

Returning her to school after Christmas turned into an

144

ordeal and a half, and that's putting it mildly. It didn't start off too badly, though. Bless her heart, she sat me down the day before she was due to leave to try and persuade me that it was best for Gary if she stayed.

'He really needs me to be here, Dad,' she said, so solemnly that I could see she truly believed it – and why shouldn't she when I'm sure he'd like nothing better. 'As his older sister it's only right that I should be at home to take care of him.'

'But you two argue all the time,' I reminded her.

'Only when he doesn't do as he's told, and you're too soft on him, Dad. I'd be much stricter, which is what he needs.'

I can't dispute that, because I know I'm not a dab hand at discipline, far from it in fact. The trouble is, even when he's misbehaved and I'm cross, I find myself remembering how he's trying to get along without his mother and straight away I lose the heart to tell him off.

'He's a good boy, most of the time,' I told her, 'and I think we're just about managing.'

'But think of how much easier it would be if I was here to help.'

'It's not your job, my love, to look after us. It's your job to do well at school and . . .'

'I can do well at The Grange,' she cried, her temper rising. 'Why does it have to be bloody Red Maids? I hate it there and I'm not going back.'

'Oh Susan . . .'

'Don't say "Oh Susan" like that. You have to listen to me. You don't understand that you're ruining my life sending me to that horrible place. I don't belong there. This is where I belong, with you and Gary and if Mummy was still here she'd at least let me be a day girl.'

The sting of the truth was sharp and I wanted to say, 'If Mummy was still here you would be a day girl,' but I knew it wouldn't help. So all I said was, 'One day you'll understand . . .'

'Stop saying that, stop, stop, stop,' she seethed, banging

her fists into me. 'I don't care about one day. All I care about is now and staying here and never having to go to that horrible place again.'

Catching her hands I tried to pull her on to my lap, but she tore herself free and charged up the stairs to her room. I could hear her sobbing her heart out, and I was pretty close to doing the same. It made me think of Christmas Day, when I'd had to take myself off to our Doreen's front room before I disgraced myself in front of the kids. All this crying. I know it's not manly, but sometimes I just can't help myself. I miss Eddress so much and it never seems to stop.

When I tried to get into our Susan's room later she had a chair jammed up against the door stopping me from opening it. I knocked and pushed, but she just kept telling me to go away.

'I'm not going back to school and that's that!' she informed me.

'You'll do as you're told.'

'No I won't, and you can't make me.'

'We'll see about that, now open this door or there's going to be trouble.'

'No! I'm never coming out again.'

In the end, after half an hour or more of arguing, cajoling, ordering, even trying to bribe with an ice cream when Mr Whippy came round, I got the ladder out of the shed and climbed up to her bedroom window. She got such a fright when she saw my face that she screamed and I nearly fell off the blooming thing.

'What are you doing out there?' she shrieked.

'Open this damned window, or I'll break it,' I shouted, brandishing a hammer to show I meant business. I wouldn't have used it, but I couldn't think of anything else more persuasive.

To my surprise, she did as she was told. What I hadn't bargained for was how flipping difficult it was going to be getting off the ladder and in through the window. I ended up sliding in head first and landing in a kind of handstand with my feet still up on the sill and our Susan laughing so hard she could hardly catch her breath.

After I got myself sorted out and the laughter had died down, I sat on the bed with her and as she started to cry again I came within an inch of telling her that she didn't have to go back after all. To tell the truth, I'd give almost anything for her to be at home with me, because I miss her almost as much as I do her mother. The lights seem to come on again when she's in the house, not in the same way as when Eddress was here, but she has so much of her mother's spark that I just want to hold her to me and never let her go. It would be selfish though to think of myself, when what really matters is her future.

So back to school she went the following day with more tears and tantrums, and a promise never to write to me again.

'I don't belong here. You're turning me into a freak,' were her parting words. 'Everyone hates me, including you.'

I have to be honest, I don't think I gave enough thought to how difficult it might be for her to make the change from our way of life to the one she's in now. I suppose, if I considered it at all, I imagined mixing with a higher class of people was something she'd get used to in time, and actually, I think she has to a degree. I just didn't expect her friends in Greenways to turn their backs on her the way they seemed to over Christmas. I'm sure they'll come round in time, kids always do, but it upsets me to think of how lonely she looked at times. It's as though she's not too sure who she is any more, or where she fits in. I'm sure she must be missing her mother terribly, and knowing that makes my heart break for her, but nothing I say or do is ever going to bring Eddress back so I suppose we just have to continue hoping that things will get easier with time. Perhaps it would help if I could make our Susan feel proud of how well she's doing at school, but she never seems to care very much, even though her marks are consistently above average, even good. And in spite of how miserable she says she is, whenever I see her with the other girls she always looks to me as though she's a lot happier than she makes out.

Nevertheless, I'm worrying myself sick about her in case I have got it wrong. Is it really so important for her to be the first in our family to go to university, and to have a profession, which would be really saying something when you consider how many relatives there are on Eddress's side. It fairly makes my heart sing to think of my girl in a barrister's robes, or a surgeon's coat. It's what Eddress dearly wanted, to see her excel, and I have to hand it to Eddress, she saw long before the rest of us that all sorts of opportunities were about to start opening up for girls. What she probably didn't see coming was the shady underside to all these tempting new prospects, and I have to admit they make me very uneasy indeed. Miniskirts and flower power are bad enough, but birth-control pills, burning brassieres and communal living is going way too far, especially when girls our Susan's age, who are so impressionable, are lapping it all up. It scares me half to death to think of her being taken advantage of by men, or drugged out of her mind, and I'm afraid to say that's the way plenty of girls seem to be going today.

This is reminder enough for me that, like it or not, she's in the best place. Being as headstrong as she is, I shudder to think of the trouble she might get into if she was at the local comprehensive with no mother to rule the roost after school. She needs the kind of supervision she's getting at Red Maids. They know what's best for her, and despite all her protests and unhappiness, they're far better placed to turn her into a fine young lady with decent morals and a healthy social conscience than I'll ever be.

For some reason this second term of her being away is proving even harder for me and Gary than the last. We rattle around in the house like two lonely peas in a cold old pod, with nothing seeming quite right about the place. Of course, we have a bit of fun now and again, lots of wrestling matches and bedtime stories, but I can see how much he misses our Susan, and his mother, I'm sure, though he never mentions her. I sometimes wonder how much he remembers her, but I don't ask. It's best not to remind him when it'll probably only upset him, so we carry on learning to get on without her.

'Dad, these potatoes are crunchy,' Gary complains.

I look down at his plate, and though I force my best hearty laugh I feel like groaning at how useless I still am at cooking. 'It's the new trend,' I tell him. 'We're going to have crunchy beans for tea, crunchy porridge for breakfast in the morning, and Crunchie chocolate when we go over to Grampy's this afternoon.'

His eyes light up. 'Crunchies are my favourite,' he tells me with great earnestness. 'And Milky Bars, because I'm the Milky Bar Kid!' He draws his hands like guns to shoot me, so I shoot him back.

'You're dead first,' he shouts.

I feign dead by clasping my chest and slumping over my own dismal dinner. Then scooping up our plates I put the crunchy potatoes back on to boil, and the sprouts and roast beef in the oven to keep warm. I'll have to get our Nance to show me how to do roasters, or I'll never get him to eat a proper dinner that doesn't include beans.

'Dad?' Gary says later as we're driving along in our new Ford Anglia.

'Yes?'

'If I score three goals in my next six matches, please can I have tuppence a goal to make sixpence?'

Curious, and proud that he worked out the sums, I say, 'Yes, I expect so. What do you want sixpence for?'

'To buy a new diver to go and look for the one that drowned.'

I'm a little perplexed until I remember the diver he used to play with in the bath that I must have thrown out by mistake. (I told him it had sunk.) 'But drowned means he's not with us any more,' I explain.

'I know, but just in case he's trapped under a submarine, I think we should send another diver down, don't you?'

How can I argue with that? 'Well,' I say, giving it a try, 'if there was a submarine in the bath we'd probably see it, so why don't you save up to get the bow and arrow you saw in Smart's last week?'

At that, excitement bounces him round in his seat to face me. 'Yes, and then I'll be Robin Hood, and you can be the Sheriff of Nottingham who's wicked and a robber, and everyone will be on my side because I'm good,' and apparently happy with that he turns his dear little freckled face to the window, where, if you were on the outside, you'd only be able to see the top of his crew cut and his eyes peeking over the bottom of the frame.

He soon starts chattering on again about football and school and *Animal Magic* one of his favourite programmes, until we reach our dad's. He and Beat, my stepmother, used to live behind Woolworth's up Kingswood, but a few years ago they moved into a semi-detached council house on Coronation Road, just behind the Tennis Court pub. We come here on Saturdays now, instead of Sunday afternoons, apart from when our Susan's at home when we try to squeeze in a visit with her.

Beat's already at the door waiting for us when we get out of the car. 'I saw you pulling up,' she says, opening her arms to give me a hug. 'How are you, my old love?'

'Very well,' I tell her, giving her a hug back. She's the only person I know who hugs me before the kids, but I'm not going to condemn her for that when she doesn't have any children of her own, so it probably doesn't come naturally to her to put them first. I think she's fond of me because I'm the only member of our dad's family who comes to see him now that our Bob's gone. Nance and Doreen have never given her a chance – they didn't want anyone replacing our mam, and that was that. They didn't even go to our dad's wedding. Our Bob and I did, and our Susan was bridesmaid. Eddress would have come too if she hadn't been in hospital on the day. We've got a lovely photograph of the event, taken outside Kingswood registry office, that shows all us men with our hands inside the top front lapel of our suit jackets, in a kind of salute, and our Susan standing in front of us all in a white frilly dress and carrying a great big white handbag over her arm that could have belonged to the Queen.

I watch Beat ruffle Gary's hair and hand him a bag of liquorice allsorts as we go down the hall, which is the first thing she always does when kids turn up. I suppose it's to keep them occupied while she has a chat with the grown-ups, a treat she doesn't often enjoy because they have so few visitors.

'Where's our dad?' I ask as she puts on the kettle.

I think I already know the answer, and the way she suddenly seems flustered confirms I'm right. The old man's still in bed, probably out cold after too much booze up the Legion last night.

'How is he?' I ask.

'Oh, you know, the same,' she replies. Her soft, fleshy face is crumpled with wrinkles, and her kind blue eyes show a level of honest bewilderment that always warms me to her.

'How are you?' I say. 'Are you managing to get out much?'

'Oh yes, I can make it down to the shops on my own and one of the neighbours is very good. He brings the heavy stuff up the hill in his car. We've got a telly now,' she adds, 'but I haven't managed to get it working yet.'

Knowing she's hoping I'll have a look, but is too timid to ask, I say, 'Oh, I'm sure we can sort that out. Where is it? In the front room?' I don't have a clue how the darned things work, but knowing Beat and our dad they haven't even grasped yet that it has to be plugged in.

'Can we go and watch it?' Gary asks.

'When it's ready,' I tell him. 'And don't eat all those sweets now, or they'll rot your teeth.'

'One fell out the other day,' he tells Beat, 'and the fairies left a threepenny bit under my pillow.'

'Well there's nice,' she smiles. 'I expect we'll be able to find you another threepenny bit to go with it.'

Gary's eyes light up. 'I'll have sixpence then, Dad, so I'll be able to get a new diver.'

'I thought we'd decided on a bow and arrow,' I remind him.

'Oh yeah, I forgot about that.' He nods happily and goes back to fishing in the bag of allsorts.

'Do you want me to go and see if I can get our dad up?' I offer, turning back to Beat.

She looks unsure, and I know it's because she's afraid of the ugly Welsh temper on him that usually boils up when he's hung-over. I often feel sorry for her that she ever married him, because he can be a dreadful bully when he wants to be, and she's such a dear old soul who'd never say boo to a goose. This is her first marriage, and she must still be wondering what hit her, especially when she grew up in quite a big house from what I can gather, where money was plentiful enough for them to have fine clothes, the best food and even a cleaner. I suppose it's why she's so bad at housework herself, she's never had to do it, and one look around the kitchen is enough to tell me that she probably hasn't washed up for a week.

Reaching for a couple of mugs I turn on the geyser to give them a rinse in some nice hot water, then look round for a tea towel to dry them. Seeing a greasy-looking rag on the back of a chair, I decide to let them stand while we wait for the kettle to boil.

'Oh, that sounds like him now,' she says, as the floorboards overhead start to creak. 'He'll be glad to see you. He always is.'

I want to ask if he ever gets rough with her, but that would be prying and I know that even if he does she'll never admit it to me. There's a bruise on her forearm though, and I wonder if it's from where he might have grabbed hold of her. 'Did you go up the Legion with him last night?' I ask.

'Yes, but I got a lift home with Bill and Ivy Olds, so I was back about nine. It was gone midnight by the time your dad came in. I think he must have walked down the hill, because his clothes were soaked through when he came up to bed, and he was cold to the bone.'

And blind drunk, I didn't add.

Hearing him on the stairs I go along the hall to watch him come down, ready to catch him in case he falls.

'Eddie, my boy,' he says when he sees me, 'I didn't know you were here.'

He sounds crusty and tired, but not particularly out of sorts. He's a short man, probably not more than five feet tall, with a cheery round face, a mop of white hair and a yellowish-brown stain under his nose from all the snuff he takes.

'Hello Dad,' I say. 'Button up your flies, there's a good chap. We don't want to see next week's washing,' *or last week's*, I think unkindly, and I feel so bad for it that I quickly ask God's forgiveness.

'Susan and Gary with you, are they?' he asks, staggering into me as he reaches the bottom stair.

'Just Gary,' I say, drawing back at the whiff of stale booze. 'Susan's at school, remember?'

'Of course I bloody remember. Do you think I'm stupid, boyo? Where's my lad? Ah here he is. Look how he's grown. You're going to be taller than your old dad one of these days, and twice as bright.'

'I got a star this week for my sums,' Gary tells him.

'Good boy. Keep it up and you'll be rich. Beattie got the kettle on, has she?'

'It's boiled,' she calls out. 'I'll bring the tea in the front room. Eddie's going to have a look at the telly.'

'Bloody thing,' he grumbles. 'I don't know what we want to bother with it for. The wireless is good enough for me, but she has to go spending her money.'

'Try and be a bit kinder to her, Dad,' I say quietly. 'She's a good woman and you're lucky to have her to look after you.'

'It's me what does the looking after,' he retorts gruffly. 'Can't do a bloody thing about the house, stupid bitch, not like your old mam. Kept everything as shiny as a brass button, she did.'

'Beattie has other qualities,' I murmur, 'and our mam would be the first to say so. Now sit down there in your chair, and remember to say thank you when she brings in your tea.'

He makes some growling noises under his breath and collapses into his old armchair that's got a lot more sag than spring these days. Beattie keeps offering to buy him a new one, but he won't hear of it. 'It belonged to your grandmother,' he tells me. 'She let me have it when we moved up from Wales. It's the only thing I got left to remind me of the old place.'

It wasn't true, because half the furniture in the room had come with us when we'd shipped up to Bristol back in '37. To think that old chair is older than I am, and has had to put up with all his farting and scratching and heaven only knows what all these years, it's a wonder it hasn't chucked itself out and gone off to the rubbish dump on its own by now.

'Here we are,' Beattie says, coming in with a tray. She's found an old doily from somewhere, and a bowl for the sugar, but the milk's in a pint bottle and there's something encrusted on the teaspoon. She seems not to see, or hear, things drop to the floor as she clears a space on the table. 'One sugar, isn't it, Ed?'

'That'll be lovely,' I say, going over to the telly that's been shoved into a corner between a plant that probably died before Churchill, and a standard lamp that's lost half its fringe. Checking behind I see that they have thought to plug it in, but there's no sign of an aerial.

'Do we need one?' Beattie asks, bemused.

'Course we do,' our dad grunts.

'Let's give it a go with a wire coat hanger for the time being,' I say. 'I've heard that sometimes works.'

'I'll go and fetch one,' Beattie replies, passing our dad his tea.

I wait for the thank you and when it doesn't come I turn to glare at him.

'What's the bloody matter with you?' he demands belligerently.

'I'm wondering what's happened to your manners,' I remind him.

'Manners is for nancy boys,' he snorts, 'like poems and books.'

'Oh, I think it's lovely the way your Eddie reads so much, and writes,' Beattie coos.

'Who's asking you?' he says rudely. 'Get me a biscuit, and I expect our Gary'll want one too, won't you, my boy?'

'Yes, please,' Gary chirps. 'Grampy, will you say electricity?'

Our dad chuckles and puts a shaky hand on Gary's head. 'It's called elec-trickery,' he tells him.

Gary laughs with delight. 'Because it is like a trick, isn't it Dad?' he says. 'You can't see it, or hear it, but it makes things work.'

A few minutes later, with a coat hanger plugged into the telly, I turn the set on and Beattie cries excitedly, 'Oh look, you've got it going already.'

There's no picture, just a lot of hissing and white dots. As I turn the knob I can hear some distant voices, and a few images appear like ghosts in a fog, then vanish again. 'We'll definitely have to fix up a proper aerial,' I tell her.

'Have your tea,' she insists. 'There's some orange squash for Gary if you want some, my love.'

'Go and get it then,' our dad tells her, 'and don't forget the biscuits while you're out there.'

When she's gone I have to bite back what I really want to say because of Gary, but that doesn't stop me telling my own father that he's rude, selfish, ungrateful and a boor.

'I didn't ask you to come,' he growls at me. 'If you don't like the way I am go and see your bloody sisters.'

'Don't swear in front of your grandson,' I retort, 'or I won't come again.'

'Good bloody riddance,' he mutters, and takes a mouthful of tea.

'Here we are,' Beattie sighs, coming back with a packet of chocolate fingers and a glass of squash. 'Sit here at the table, my old love, and help yourself to as many as you want. I'll just take a few for Grampy.'

'No more than two,' I warn Gary, knowing how fast he's able to wolf down an entire packet of most things given half a chance.

'So how are Flo and the girls?' Beattie asks, after giving our dad his biscuits and settling herself on a settee that was probably her mother's, it's so elegant, in spite of the worn upholstery and scratched wooden arms.

'They seem to be doing all right,' I reply, sipping my tea.

'So they bloody well should be,' our dad snarls, 'living over there in my house.'

'It's not yours,' I remind him. 'It was our Bob's . . . '

'I was living in it first, with your mother.'

'That was a long time ago, and you know you wouldn't see your own grandchildren out on the street, so stop making a fuss.'

'Course I wouldn't see his girls out on the street. I'm just saying, that's all. They've got theirselves a nice house to live in, which is more than you've got, boyo, because yours belongs to the council.'

Deciding it's best to ignore him, I turn to Beattie and ask about her family, who she rarely sees now, and I have to think it's because of our dad.

'Tell us about Susan,' she says. 'How's she getting on? Oh, we had a letter from her the other day. It's here, somewhere. She's got lovely writing for a girl her age, that's what we said, wasn't it, Ted?'

'She's not very happy,' our dad grunts. 'She wants us to make you let her come home.'

'Oh dear, she's not still sending letters like that, is she?' I sigh. 'I was hoping they might have stopped by now.'

'It's not natural having her shut away up there with all those toffee-nose buggers what think they'm better than they are. She's a good working-class girl, that's what she is, and that's nothing to be ashamed of.'

'I'm not arguing with you about this, Dad,' I say. 'We've been over it enough times before . . .'

'Dad,' Gary chips in.

'Ssh, you know better than to interrupt when grown-ups are speaking. Wait your turn.' To our dad, I say, 'She's doing very well up there, and one of these days she'll be thanking me for sending her.'

'It's what Eddress wanted,' Beat reminds him.

'But Eddress ain't here, is she? And if you ask me, that girl's missing her mother more than she's letting on.'

'I can't help that,' I say, wishing I could block our Gary's ears.

'Bound to be,' he grunts. 'What girl wouldn't? And no teacher, nor edification's going to make up for it.'

'Let's change the subject, shall we?' I suggest. 'What did you want to say, Gary?'

'Um, I can't remember,' he replies.

'Then it couldn't have been very important.' I turn back to our dad to ask what news there is of our relatives down Wales, but there doesn't seem to be any, so after finishing my tea I have another fiddle with their coat-hanger aerial, and get ready to leave.

'I know you're doing your best, boyo,' our dad says, after Beattie's walked out to the car with Gary, 'but you don't want to be alienating your own daughter. She thinks the world of you, always has, but if she's feeling as shut out as she sounds in her letter, you mark my words, she'll end up turning her back on you, and that's not what you want, I know.'

As I'm driving home his words are still ringing in my ears, causing me to feel all the guilt and anxiety he probably intended. He's a tricky old bugger, and sometimes I wonder why I still bother going to see him. I suppose it's out of duty more than anything, and because our mam would want me to. And because I know that deep down he cares about us all, even Beat, though, like a lot of men, he's got a funny way of showing it. I'm sure it was being married to Eddress that made me the way I am now, disdainful of men who treat women as though they're not much better than slaves. Eddress would never have put up with it, and I wouldn't want our Susan to either. The rest of the world can call me as henpecked as they like, but I know how much Ed and I meant to each other, and I don't think we could have been as close as we were if there hadn't been a mutual respect in our marriage. So all this women's lib that's going on now, it's nothing new, it's just coming out into the open more than it ever used to. I'm not saying that's not good, I just think that involving sexual promiscuity and drugs is going about it the wrong way, so our dad can go on all he likes, Susan is better off where she is.

Susan

Ages ago I wrote to the Lord Mayor of Bristol asking him to talk to Dad about letting me go home. I felt sure that someone with that much authority would be able to make Dad see sense, but the stinky Lord Mayor, whatever his name is, hasn't even bothered to write back to me. None of my relations are on my side either, and I'm just about sick to death of it. It's all right for them, getting on with their lives in a normal way enjoying all the freedoms of a civilised society, they've got no idea what it's like being trapped in this godforsaken hole with disgusting food to eat, freezing dormitories to sleep in and satanic teachers hissing down our necks every minute of the day. I swear I'm not going to put up with it much longer. One way or another I'm getting out of here, and the amazing thing is, we've only gone and found an escape hole in the bushes on the far side of the hockey field.

Thanks to an enormous old oak tree it can't be seen from the school, the only problem is getting there without being spotted. However, if we keep close to the walled garden, then dash like mad along the edge of the pitch, we can just about make it, and then you dive through the bushes into a secret lane.

We stumbled upon it yesterday afternoon when we had nothing to do before tea, so some of us first form decided to go exploring. (None of us have dared to venture down the tunnel outside Dot's study yet, and until someone reminds us we're not going to mention it.) Since discovering the lane I've been making a plan of how to get home. The trouble is, Bristol's a massive place and I'm not sure which way to go once I reach the other side of the Downs. Plus, I'll probably have to set out at night, because my own clothes are locked away so all I have are my uniforms, and if anyone sees me out of school bounds during the day they might wonder what I'm doing and call Dot. Going at night is a bit dangerous though, especially since the loony man's been hanging around again lately. I haven't seen him myself, but apparently he was lurking about the sixth-form common room last Friday night, and when Jessica Corner spotted him he flashed open his mac and showed her his willy.

Everyone thought this was hilarious, but funnier still was the note Dotty sent round after. This is what it said: *I regret to say that once again a troubled individual has trespassed upon the school grounds and revealed his penis to a member of Lower Sixth.*

Penis! She actually used that word. We couldn't stop laughing. It was the funniest thing we'd ever read.

It went on to say: *The police have been informed and it is hoped that a recurrence of this nature will not happen again. Should any of you see anyone suspicious loitering around the premises, please report it immediately to a member of staff.*

I wrote at the end: *because she wants to see a penis too,* and it went all round the school making everyone laugh so much that we could hardly sleep that night.

The next day I had another idea that made them laugh even more. I went to Seaweed to report Mr Hinton, the music teacher, for loitering around the premises. Laura, Peg and loads of others were listening outside, making it really difficult for me to keep a straight face, especially when I heard them sniggering. It was Seaweed's fault that I ended up exploding in her face; she shouldn't have said that Mr Hinton could be arrested if my childishness reached the wrong ears, because I could just imagine him in handcuffs being marched away with all of us waving goodbye from the music room.

'You're irresponsible, immature and ignorant,' she told me angrily. 'You are in immediate detention and I'll be writing to your father to inform him as to why.'

I nearly poked out my tongue then, but I didn't quite have the guts, and anyway, I wasn't laughing as much any more, because I didn't want to miss another exeat. Bloody Seaweed.

'I was only joking, miss,' I said.

'There was absolutely nothing funny about it,' she retorted, 'and if I hear you've repeated it to anyone outside this office I warn you there will be even more dire consequences to pay.'

When I came out everyone was holding their breath, waiting to see what I would say.

'Do you think she means you'd be expelled?' Laura asked.

'If it does then we all have to say Hinton's a loony,' Peg told her. 'Then we can all be expelled.'

Everyone agreed with that, because everyone wants to get out of here, so that could be a good way of doing it.

We haven't mentioned it again since, but we don't need to now we've found an escape route. It was so fab climbing out into the secret lane. Freedom! We weren't inside the school grounds any more. It was like being let out of prison, or breaking out of a straitjacket and flying. We hardly knew what to do at first it felt so strange, but then we crept along to the end of the lane to see what was there. Lots of houses, and a street that seems like it leads down to a main road, which is probably the one that runs along the front of the school.

The whole first and second form are working out an escape plan now, plus this could be a fantastic way to meet boys in secret, which we're trying to sort out too.

I got struck on Sadie at the beginning of term and it's fab. The best thing of all was that she sent Laura to ask me if I'd like to be struck on her and I said yes straight away. Now she comes to tuck me up at night, and I share my tuck with her (when I have any, which isn't very often) and I've bought her a couple of singles with my pocket money, 'Say a Little Prayer' by Aretha Franklin, which is really fab, and 'Pictures of Matchstick Men' by Status Quo, which I don't like very much because they're more freaks than mods, but Sadie likes them and that's what counts.

When we came back after Christmas I told everyone that I'd kissed Robert for a whole minute for a second time, because I'm scared stiff of walking the plank. I'd rather go down into Dotty's cellar than plunge to my death from a fourth-floor fire escape. It turned out that everyone else had kissed someone too, but I think they might have the same dread of dying as I do. Peg had to go one better than the rest of us and claim that her boyfriend, Nigel, had felt her up, which I don't believe for a minute. I don't think he even exists, because she doesn't have a photo of him, and it gets right on my nerves the way she always tries to make herself look bigger and more daring than everyone else when she's not.

Laura's best friends with Isabelle Phillips now, who's in Discoverer. I don't mind, because I spend most of my time with Sadie when we're not in lessons, and with Paula when she invites us into her room. Cheryl usually comes too, and a few others, but Laura's not really interested in all the groovy things we like, such as make-up and boys.

Oh, the fabbest and best news of all is that Robert wrote to me like he said he would, and this is what he said:

Dear Susan, how are you? I hope you're behaving yourself up there at that posh school and studying hard to make us all proud. It was lovely seeing you at Christmas and seeing how grown up you are now. I'm sorry if I upset you before you left, I didn't mean to. You know you're my favourite cousin and always will be. I hope when you come home at Easter that you'll come for a ride on the bike. Lots of love, Robert xxx

I've only let the others see the last sentence, and they're all really jealous and dying to know what he's like. I've told them Billy Fury, and when he sends me a photo they'll see for themselves that it's true. Paula's mad on Billy Fury so she's always asking if I've had another letter yet, and if Robert might come to church one Sunday. I don't think he will, because he's too cool to go to church, but maybe one day he'll give me a lift back to school on his bike after an exeat.

Today we're looking for slugs to put in third form's tea. It was Peg's idea so I'm letting her pick them up, because they're so slimy and fat that I can't stand to touch them. I keep thinking of the time Mum caught Gary eating one when he was a baby. Ugh, it makes me feel sick.

As a matter of fact, I'm a bit fed up out here doing this, the ground's all mucky after so much rain and if we're not going into the back lane I'd rather be in my cubicle having a look at my Monkees annual, or reading Robert's letter. Good job I took it out of my satchel the other day, because Scatty, our English teacher, confiscated the satchel yesterday and if she'd stolen my letter I'd have done something drastic. She took the satchel because one of the day girls accused me of pinching her hair slide. Bloody cheek! In fact, it was another day girl, Isabelle Luckins, who nicked it, but I didn't split on her, even though I probably should have since it landed me up in another bloody detention. Still, the good news is that Isabelle lives really close to my Auntie Phil's newsagents shop in Longwell Green. So now, to make up for the punishment I took on her behalf she's going to smuggle in the chocolates, crisps and sweets

Auntie Phil is happy to send, even though we're not allowed them. She's also going to bring us copies of *Honey* which Paula really likes, and *Jackie* which Sadie and I love because of all the romance stories and pin-ups of pop stars.

It's really cool having an auntie with a shop. She's my mum's older sister and we used to see her all the time when Mum was alive, but we don't so much any more. I'd like to work behind the counter when I'm older, then I'll be able to have all the sweets and magazines and cigarettes I want. Paula smokes, so do quite a few of the other sixth-formers, so Isabelle smuggles fags in for them too, usually five Park Drive which come with five matches in the pack for about a shilling, I think, or ten Embassy if they can afford it, at around one and ten. Auntie Phil allows her to buy them because sixth form are, by law, old enough to smoke, even if they can't do it at school, and Auntie Phil's always been kind. (By the way the girls do smoke at school when no one's looking, but we never split and would make anyone who did walk the plank and probably push them off if they didn't fall.)

'I'm going in now,' I say as Peg turfs up another slug. 'This is immature.'

'You're just a spoilsport,' she tells me.

I don't care. I want to go and find out if I had any post this morning. I've given up waiting for Davy Jones to write back, so I've written to Tommy James who's the singer with the Shondells, because 'Mony Mony' is the best record I've ever heard in my life. I was going to write to George Harrison, but the Beatles have gone all freaky now, growing their hair and beards long and straggly and going on about *peace* and stuff, which really puts me off. Although I might ask for *Sergeant Pepper's Lonely Hearts Club Band* for my birthday in August, because everyone's got it except me, and I don't have any LPs yet, so I suppose it's time I did. Anyway, I like 'Lucy in the Sky with Diamonds' so it makes sense for me to have the whole album (that's what they call it now, an album, instead of LP, which means long player).

I'm thinking of writing to all my relations again, letting them know that Dad can't manage as well as he thinks without me. When I was at home over Christmas I noticed that the house wasn't as clean as it used to be, and I'm very good at polishing and hoovering so he definitely needs me there to do it. I can bake cakes now too, because I've learned how in our housekeeping classes (they don't rise much, but they taste all right once the icing's on), and I can darn socks and stockings in quite straight lines, and embroider the borders of a peg bag that I made myself with a sewing machine. I can even plant bulbs and weed a garden. I've learned millions of things since I've been here that will come in very handy when I go home to live, but I'm not going to give Dad the benefit of my skills until he agrees to take me out of here.

He will, one of these days, I've already made up my mind about that and if getting expelled is the only way, then I think getting expelled is what I'll do.

Eddie

Dear Susan, I am very disappointed in you, my girl. If it wasn't bad enough that you should have to miss an exeat because of what you said about your music teacher, I now hear that you're missing another because you STOLE someone's hair slide. Theft is a very grave sin, Susan, and I will not tolerate it any more than the school will, so I certainly will not be writing to Miss Dakin to try to persuade her to let you come home on Sunday. Your punishment is well deserved. I hope you will spend the afternoon asking Jesus to forgive and guide you and writing notes of apology to those you have offended.

Now, I don't want my whole letter to be taken up with admonishing you, so I will move on to other things. The ink you asked for is in the parcel with this letter, along with some

deodorant and a small packet of Persil. When you do your washing
don't forget to rinse all the soap out before you hang it in the linen
room to dry.

You have asked me to help with your geography. Well,
geography is the science of the earth's surface, form, physical
features, natural and political divisions, climate, and populations.
Please don't be afraid of these strange words. Science means what
we know and are sure about. Earth's surface means the outside
surface of the Earth or the part you can walk on . . .

'Dad?' Gary says, drawing it out in a way that tells me
he's starting to get fed up.

'Yes.' We're sitting either side of the dining table with
some pieces of Lego, a few chewed pencils and some
blotting paper between us.

'I don't know what to say in my letter,' he tells me.

'Let me see what you've written so far,' I reply, and
reaching over to turn his page round I read: *Dear Susun, I*
hope yw ar getting on all ryt and I hope yw ar getting lots more
frends.

'That's lovely,' I say, itching to correct the spelling. I still
haven't had time to go up the school to find out more about
this new-fangled method of teaching, or to write to the local
authorities about it, but seeing this reminds me that I have
to. 'All you have to do is sign your name now,' I tell him.

He pulls a face. 'Do I have to put love and stupid stuff like
that?'

'I think you should, don't you?'

He gives a shrug and picks up his pencil again. The page
slides around the tablecloth as he presses down hard to
write. '*Fondist luv, Gary xxx,*' he says aloud as he writes.

'Very good.'

'Can I do my Thunderbirds painting now?'

'Ten minutes before tea.'

'What have we got? I'm starving.'

'Corned beef, mashed potatoes and peas.'

'Can I have beans instead?'

'No, or you'll turn into one.'

He finds that funny and picking up a small chair that belongs to our Susan's dining set, he carries it out to the kitchen so he can reach the tap to fill his paint jar with water.

Once he's settled I return to my letter and the explanation of geography. When it comes to the part about longitude and latitude I add a couple of diagrams, and I hope I'm correct when I say that there are fifty million people in Britain, forty million in France and one hundred and twenty million in America. I'm soon running out of paper so I have to bring it to a close, and because I began the letter with a reprimand I decide to be gentler at the end so we don't finish on a bad note. *Well, Susan, I expect all this seems like another lesson, but I hope you find it helpful. I haven't managed to find your copy of* Naughty Amelia Jane *yet, and I've searched your room, but I'm sure it'll turn up somewhere. As soon as it does I'll send it as you asked. I'm popping a letter from Gary in the envelope with this one. Now I shall say goodnight, my sweetheart. God Bless, try to keep smiling and don't forget to wash the back of your neck clean. Best love from Dad. xxxxx*

Mrs Jewell, our home help, very kindly peeled some potatoes for me before she left this afternoon, so after sealing up a parcel and letters to Susan, I put the spuds on to boil then see about opening a tin of Daisy peas. Once they're in a saucepan I take out my notebook and pen to start making a list of everything I need to remember for the weekend. Now our Susan's not coming home (*lying and stealing!* I can hardly believe it. Well, let's see what she has to say for herself when I see her at church). Anyway, with her not being here for the afternoon I should have more time on my hands. The lawns need mowing, front and back, the beds badly need weeding and I can't remember the last time I swept the path. The council are supposed to be coming round after Easter to paint the gates and front doors – we're yellow our side of the street, opposite they're blue – so I make a note to give them a quick wash the week before. I ought to make a shopping list for when I go up Fine Fare on Saturday too.

That done, I note down all the things our Susan's asked for: embroidery threads, a new leotard, white gym socks, envelopes, some new playing jacks . . . I mustn't forget that Gary's got a pony-riding lesson at nine on Saturday morning, and I promised Beattie I'd take her up Kingswood on Saturday afternoon so she can buy a candlewick bedspread for her nephew's wedding present.

When I popped into our dad's the other night I had the surprise of my life. The front room was crowded with a dozen or more chickens. What a row, and what a stink! Feathers and fallout everywhere. It turns out he'd won them at cards and the bloke (who was probably dying to get rid of them) had delivered them himself that morning. I'd better make some time to go over and rig up some sort of coop in the back garden, because they can't go on sharing the house with a brood of flipping hens. He tried to make me take the cockerel off his hands, but I was having none of it.

'Think of all the free eggs,' he told me.

'Cockerels don't lay eggs,' I reminded him.

'They make a nice Sunday roast though, and Beat and I'll be glad to give you some of our eggs. Bloody good win that, if you ask me.'

There was no point arguing, so I left the new aerial I'd picked up from Rediffusion on my way home and hurried out again before he could shove a squawking bird under my arm.

Noticing the potatoes starting to boil, I lower the gas and go to pop my head round the dining-room door to check on Gary. There's paint all over his face, up his arms and in his hair, and a couple of finished paintings are drying on the guard in front of the fire.

'Blimey!' I exclaim, leaping forward just as one of them starts to ignite. 'You silly boy. You can't put paper by the fire like that, you could have burnt the house down.'

He looks at me, then at his paintings which I've screwed up in my hands like a pile of rubbish. 'Look what you've done!' he cries angrily. 'They were for Gran and Auntie Nance, and this one's for Auntie Kath.'

'Her name's Mrs Jewell,' I remind him. 'She's not related to us so she can't be an auntie.'

'She tells us to call her that, and I want to.'

'Clear up that mess,' I say. 'You've got paint everywhere. Look, it's even on the wallpaper.'

He turns round to have a look at the jagged swathes of blue that are randomly joining a clutch of yellow sunflowers together. 'I didn't do that,' he protests.

'Then who else did? You're the only one in here, now go and scrub your hands and face. Use some Vim if you have to, and think yourself lucky you're not getting a smack for making all this mess.'

'Don't pick on me,' he shouts, his eyes filling with tears as he takes himself off to the kitchen. 'I hate you. You're always mean and making me do things I don't want to.'

'Stop being cheeky, or you'll go up to bed.'

'I haven't had any tea yet, and I don't want stupid peas. I hate them.'

'You'll eat what you're given and say thank you to Jesus that you're not one of the starving children in Africa.'

'I wish I was. I expect their dads are a lot nicer to them than you are to me.'

I join him in the kitchen. Reaching for the scrubbing brush, I turn on the tap and plonk him on the chair so he can reach. 'I don't want to see a speck of paint left on those hands,' I tell him.

Taking the brush, he leans over to jam it into a bar of soap. The chair tips, he goes down and the thump of his head against the edge of the sink turns my blood cold.

'It's all right, it's all right,' I cry as he starts to scream.

Blood comes pumping out of a gash over his eye. Seeing it, he screams even louder. I feel like screaming myself, but grabbing a tea towel I shove it under the cold water and press it to the cut.

'Ow, ow, ow,' he yells, trying to push me away.

'I'm trying to stop the bleeding.' I hold the tea towel in place, praying this isn't worse than it looks, but when I take a peek I can see that it is.

'I think you're going to need stitches,' I tell him and scooping him up, I press a kiss to his cheek.

'Am I going to die?' he sobs as I carry him quickly down the hall.

'No, of course not.'

'It hurts, Dad.'

'I know, my love, but it'll be all right,' and grabbing our coats off the end of the banister I dash down the path to the car. After plonking him in the passenger seat I get in next to him and start the engine.

Two minutes after driving out of the street we're back, and I'm running into the house to turn the gas off under the potatoes.

Back to the car, and I'm just reversing up the road when I think about the fire and what did I do with his paintings?

Back to the house. The fire's dying down, but the paintings are still too close, so I scoop them up, chuck them on the table, knock over his water jar and his paintbox goes crashing to the floor.

By the time I get him up Cossham Hospital the bleeding's more or less stopped, but the doctor says we did the right thing to come, because he needs a couple of stitches. As they're applied I stand watching him being brave, with my conscience weighing me down like a lead barrel to think of how much I'm to blame.

To try and make it up to him I take him to the Clock Tower on the way home to get some fish and chips – or in his case a Clark's pie and chips. The thick white pad plastered over his eye immediately makes him the centre of attention, much to his delight, and by the time we leave, with an extra portion of chips in a funnel of greaseproof for him to eat in the car, and our cod and pie keeping warm in a thick wad of newspaper, he's as thrilled with his injury as I am bitterly ashamed.

To be honest, I'm starting to feel that as time goes on my ability to cope is diminishing instead of building, and the longing I have to see Eddress, framed in the kitchen window when I turn into the street at night, is growing instead of fading. I shall have to do better than this or there's no knowing where we'll end up. Our Susan stealing, telling lies about teachers . . . I'm beginning to wonder if it was a mistake expecting the authorities at Red Maids to take charge of her so I wouldn't have to worry as she starts to grow up. They discipline her when she misbehaves, all right, and as far as I can tell they're teaching her well, but I'm more worried about her now than I ever was before. I keep trying to think of someone to talk to about it, someone who'd be able to give me good advice. Our Nance and Doreen do their best, so does her gran, but they don't have much of an idea about places like Red Maids, and more often than not all they manage to say is, 'She's her mother through and through,' as if that in some way excuses her rebellious behaviour.

I don't think it's a compliment Eddress would like very much. In fact, I know it isn't, because the very reason Eddress wanted Susan to go to that school was to try and smooth out the rough edges of her roots.

Chapter Nine

Susan

I'm up the fair (actually we call it the shows) on Rodway Common. I'm with my cousin Doreen and her friend Stella who are both nineteen and you should see their skirts! They're nearly up to their bums. I'm dying to wear mine like that, but Dad's still refusing to buy me any minis, because, he says, they're not decent for girls my age, which is so bloody old-fashioned I could scream at him to get with it! You only have to look around to see that everyone's skirts are really short now, and mine is *only just above my knee*. I feel so soft I don't know where to look, so I'm keeping my head down in the hope that no one recognises me.

It's the Easter holidays so I'm at home for a couple of weeks, at last! It seems ages since I last managed to get out of that prison, thanks to the exeats I've had to miss, and I'm definitely not going back next term. I don't care what Dad says. He can't make me, so I won't.

'Cheer up, my old love,' Doreen says, as we go round the slot machines feeding in our pennies, 'it won't be long before you're old enough to go out to work and earn your own money, so you'll be able to buy what you want.'

I can hardly wait for that day. I've already decided that I'm going to leave school the minute I can. I couldn't care less about sixth form or college or stupid university. I'm going to live my own life where I'm the only one in charge.

'How about a ride on the ghost train?' Doreen suggests.

I lost all my money on the one-arm bandit about half an hour ago, so I can't afford any rides now.

'Oh blimey!' Stella suddenly squeals as a noisy avalanche of pennies starts pumping out of the machine in front of her.

Everyone stops to watch, and we're all laughing and shrieking as we gather up Stella's winnings. There are so many coins we can't fit them all into our hands.

'Here,' someone says, and he passes us a couple of plastic bags.

It turns out to be the chap who works on the chairoplanes, and the way he's ogling our Doreen I reckon he wants to eat her, or shag her. (Everyone's saying that now, so I do too, but only to myself, because I think it's quite rude.) I wish he wanted to shag me, because he's the best-looking bloke I've seen since we got here. He looks just like a gypsy, which I suppose is only to be expected, when he works up the shows. His hair's all long, curly and black, and his eyes are bright blue. I wonder which caravan is his, and if he's got saucy pictures hanging on the walls the way our Robert has.

He winks at me and says to our Doreen, 'Fancy a ride, darling?'

Our Doreen goes red to the roots of her hair. 'We've already been on the chairoplanes thanks,' she says, as Stella gives her a nudge.

'Who's talking about the chairoplanes?' he grins.

'Oh, listen to him,' our Doreen giggles behind her hand.

He gives me another wink and I wish I had the courage to accept his offer, because I wouldn't mind a ride with him.

'He fancies you,' Stella whispers to Doreen.

'Get lost, it's you he's after,' Doreen tells her. Then grabbing hold of me she says, 'Come on. We're not supposed to talk to strangers.'

'Who said anything about talking?' he calls after us.

Doreen and Stella laugh, and Stella shouts out, 'You're a cheeky monkey.'

'Come here and say that,' he challenges.

They don't turn back, but I glance over my shoulder in the hope he might give me another wink. He's already walking away.

We can't count the winnings where we are, so we carry them out on to the common and hide next to a tump, where we empty them into the lap of my revoltingly long skirt. At least it's good for something.

'Bloody hell, nineteen bob,' Stella murmurs when we've totalled our piles of pennies and added them together. 'I can nearly afford that coat in C&A now.'

'Aren't you going to share it around a bit?' Doreen objects.

'Yeah, course,' Stella agrees. 'Why don't I treat us all to a ride on something?'

I'm hoping they'll choose the chairoplanes, but it turns out they're more interested in a bloke on the bumpers, so off we trudge. Because only two can fit in a car, I stand on the side to watch as they whizz and crash around, and keep peering over my shoulder to see if the gypsy on the chairoplanes is watching me. He's flirting with someone else now, and when he locks her in the chair he runs a hand up her thigh and she doesn't do anything to stop him.

I wish he'd do that to me. I think I'd die if he did.

Loads of girls are walking about with boys' arms round their shoulders or waists, and it's making me really wish I had a boyfriend too. He'd be someone who makes me feel really special and that no one else in the world matters more than me. We could have horrible rows and threaten to break up, but in the end he'd only ever pretend to leave, and would always come back because he loves me so much.

I saw a girl wearing a paper skirt just now, and then I spotted Linda Watkins who lives at the top of our street with a dress so short that I couldn't understand how her suspenders didn't show. I kept looking and looking, but even when she leaned forward to try and toss a ping-pong ball into a goldfish bowl there was still no sign of them.

I've seen loads of people snogging, and running off into

173

the bushes behind the shows. Some women are giving them dirty looks, but they're old and boring and if they don't like what young people do they shouldn't come here, should they?

'Hello. Are you on your own?' someone asks me.

I turn round to find Mandy Hughes who lives in the next road to us standing on the steps of the dodgems next to me. She's about two years older than I am and isn't someone I'm supposed to talk to because her family's a bit rough, and one of her brothers is in prison. I think her dad's been inside too, but I'm not sure. Actually, I've always been quite fascinated by the Hughes, because they seem to have a lot of fun in their house with music blaring out of the windows half the time and motorbikes revving up outside. Gary plays football with one of the younger boys, up on the green, and Dad always talks to the one who's a mongol. He even invites him into our house if he spots him wandering about in the street on his own, and gives him a marshmallow or a glass of squash before taking him home again.

Mandy's really pretty, even though her hair's got a lot of split ends and some of her make-up's smudged. She reminds me a bit of Lulu. I'm not wearing any make-up tonight, because Dad wouldn't let me go out with it on, so it was either take it off or stay at home. We had a big row about it, and he won in the end, but only because Doreen and Stella were waiting to go.

'My cousin's on the bumpers,' I tell her. 'Who are you with?'

She shrugs. 'No one, really. I came with my brother, Tommy, but he went off with some girl about an hour ago and I don't know where he is now.'

I look at her closely, trying to work out if she's scared about being left on her own at this time of night (it's not eight o'clock yet, but it's quite a long walk home and will probably be dark by the time she gets there). She might be, I decide, and that's why she's talking to me, so she won't have to go across the common alone.

'Are you still going to that posh school up Westbury-on-Trym?' she asks.

'Worse luck,' I reply with a roll of my eyes. 'I'm on holiday now though. Where do you go to school?'

She throws an arm loosely behind her. 'Over there at Rodway Tech.' There's a school at the edge of the common which is where some quite clever children go. It never occurred to me before that Mandy Hughes might be clever.

'Do you feel like a ride on the waltzers?' she asks.

'I don't have any money.'

She takes out a two-bob bit. 'It's enough for us both to go on twice,' she offers. 'Or we can have one go on the waltzer and one on the big wheel.'

'I'll pay you back,' I tell her, excitedly. 'I'll get some money from my dad, and bring it round to your house tomorrow.'

'It's OK,' she says, as we start weaving through the crowd towards the golden chariots. I know the waltzers are just behind, but I realise I probably shouldn't have gone off without telling our Doreen, so I turn back quickly to see if she's spotted me leaving. She's right across the other side of the dodgems, being shunted and bashed about by a load of boys, and the bloke she fancies is riding on the back of her and Stella's car. I can hear them screaming from here, and there's no way they'll hear me if I shout, so I keep on going after Mandy, afraid I might lose her and miss out on a go on the waltzers.

Mandy's waiting at the bottom of the steps when I get there, watching all the cars whirl and whip up and down and around.

'Have you ever been on before?' she asks.

'Loads of times,' I lie. Dad warned Doreen before we left that the waltzers and the octopus were off limits for me. 'They'll only make her sick,' he said, 'so make sure she doesn't go on them.' I'm really glad he didn't come with us, he'd have spoiled everything.

I hope he's all right at home on his own, because Gary's

staying up Gran's tonight. I don't want him to be lonely, but knowing him, I expect he's got his head stuck in a book. He usually has.

Mandy waits next to the balustrades, where loads of other people are waiting too. This is where all the cool and with-it people hang out when they're at the shows, so we stand with them, clicking our fingers and dancing to 'I Love Jennifer Eccles' which is making me think of Sadie, because it's one of her favourites. She'd really love it here with so many lush boys around and everyone snogging whenever they feel like it, or sneaking round behind the caravans.

'Have you got a record player?' Mandy shouts over the music.

I nod. 'Have you?'

She nods. 'I've got loads of records.'

'Me too. We should do swaps.'

'All right.'

I feel a bit awkward then, because I'm pretty sure Dad won't let me go round with her, or even invite her into the house.

'Come on,' she shouts, as the ride starts to slow. 'Get ready to jump on or we'll miss the next go.'

As a crowd of people, dizzied and laughing, stagger off the ride, another crowd surges forward to take their places. Mandy and I squeeze into the corner of one of the cars, and five other girls we've never seen before jam themselves in with us. We're all screaming and laughing and telling each other our names. It's really fab. I'm having the time of my life. Then this really good-looking chap jumps on to the back of our car to take our money, and I think how fab it would be if he was my boyfriend.

Mandy hands over our fares and gives him a smile. It's really cool the way she does that, with her eyes kind of going down then up again, so I try it too, but he's not looking at me.

I'm going to practise in front of the mirror when I get home.

Slowly the cars start to rise and dip, while gliding into a spin. 'Lady Madonna' comes on the speakers and as the waltzers pick up speed the music gets louder and louder, and we go faster and faster. We're all screaming and yelling, and the really dishy bloke is whirling our car round as fast as he can. The whole world turns into a blur. I can't see a thing. Mandy's grabbing my arm and I'm grabbing hers. I feel sick and giddy, but totally fab. I wish Sadie and Cheryl were here, and Paula Gates.

The ride goes on and on. The music changes to 'Congratulations', making me think of Cheryl again, and I start to feel as though I might burst. Colours are whizzing past my eyes. I cling on more tightly than ever. I want it to stop now, but it doesn't. Round and round, up and down, so fast I can hardly breathe. Cliff is singing his head off. I want to get off, but I can't.

Eventually, just when I think I'm going to spin right off the edge of the world, we start slowing down. I feel Mandy's hands clenched on the bar next to mine. Our heads are down, our shoulders hunched. This is the worst and best thing I've ever done since I went on the cat and mouse with Mum at Weymouth and I thought we were going to shoot right off the top runway into the sea. I wonder if she can see me now on the waltzer. I hope not, because she'd probably be as cross as Dad would if he could.

At last our car makes its final spin, and as the bars go back we all stumble and lurch over to the balustrades to make room for the next lot to get on.

I'm still too dizzy to see much. Everything around me seems to be swaying and swooping and as Amen Corner start singing 'Bend Me, Shape Me', Mandy and I stagger, all wobbly-legged, down the steps on to the grass. We're laughing and gasping, and still hanging on to one another, as though trying to keep each other up.

'That was really cool,' I manage to say.

'Want to go again?'

'No, not yet.'

'What about the big wheel?'

I look up to the top chair and wonder if I've got the guts to go that high. I don't want to admit that I might not have, but nor do I want to start puking or panicking while I'm up there. 'I should find my cousin,' I say.

'OK. I'll come with you.'

We link arms and start off through the fair. I notice the way Mandy smiles at the boys who wolf-whistle, and gives snotty looks to girls who do the same to us.

'Scrubbers,' I hear someone jeer.

'Look who's talking,' Mandy jeers back.

'She's not here,' I say, when we get to the dodgems. The cars are all full and bumping around, but there's no sign of Doreen and Stella.

'They're bound to be around somewhere,' Mandy assures me, and tugging my arm she leads me over to the toffee-apple stall. 'Want one?' she offers.

I shake my head.

'What about a candyfloss? Or a hot dog?'

'I don't have any money,' I remind her.

'Choose what you want. I don't mind paying.'

In the end we decide on toffee apples and take them out on to the common to eat, where it's a bit quieter, but starting to get dark.

'Aren't you scared being out on your own?' I ask her, as we crunch into the fruity toffee. There are lots of other people scattered around eating chips or candyfloss, or drinking beer or pop as they puff away on their cigarettes.

'Not really,' she says. 'I know my way home, and anyway, I'm used to it. I go out quite a lot at night on my own. Why? Are you scared?'

'I don't know,' I say, fascinated by the thought of going out in the dark on my own. 'Where do you go?' I ask.

She shrugs. 'Lots of places. Downtown, up Kingswood, over the park.'

'Doesn't anyone ever go with you?'

'I've got a friend, Julie, who I go round with sometimes,

but she lives over Downend so I usually only see her at school.' She takes a bite of her apple and watches some boys go by as she eats it. 'Your mum died, didn't she?' she says after a while.

I stop chewing as I think of what Mum would say if she could see me now.

'What was wrong with her?'

'Cancer,' I mumble.

She nods, seeming to understand. 'So what's it like at your school?'

'Horrible. I hate it. Everyone's stuck-up and teacher's pets or goody-two-shoes. I mean, there are a few nice girls, but they wish they could get out too. What's your school like?'

'I don't know. I hardly ever go.'

I turn to look at her.

'I knock off,' she explains. 'It's better than going and sitting in a bloody classroom all day, listening to those wanker teachers going on and on about the most boring things in the world.'

I couldn't agree more. 'So what do you do?' I ask.

'I just go places, either on the bus, or I walk, depending how much money I've got.'

I'm not sure what to say now. As much as I hate school, I can't imagine not going. I never even realised there might be an alternative. In the end I say, 'Do you have any boys at your school?'

'Yes, but they're all freaks and weirdos, and anyway, I'm not interested in boys the same age as me. They're too immature.'

'I know what you mean,' I sigh. 'If I had a boyfriend he'd have to be at least four years older than me, like my cousin Robert. He's sixteen and rides a motorbike.'

'I know. I've seen him around. He's really dishy.'

Feeling proud, I say, 'Have you got a boyfriend?'

'Yeah. Actually, I've got lots of boys after me.'

I can believe it, because she's really pretty, and I'm

179

thinking, if I start going round with her, I might have lots of boyfriends too. I imagine what everyone will say at school when all the letters start turning up. I might even get some of the boys to come to see me after church on Sundays, just so's everyone will know that I'm telling the truth.

'Have you ever snogged anyone?' she asks.

It's on the tip of my tongue to say yes, but I can't quite make myself lie to her, because I've got a feeling she'll know. So I say, 'Only a bit. What about you?'

She nods. 'Loads of times. How old are you?'

'Nearly thirteen,' I say, before I can stop myself. But I could be, because lots of girls in my year will be come September or October, and it's not fair that I'm only going to be twelve in August when they're already nearly in their teens and they act so much younger than me. 'How old are you?'

'I was fourteen last month. Have you ever been shagged?'

I almost say yes, but then I realise if I pretend I have she won't tell me what it is. 'Have you?' I reply.

She shrugs. 'Loads of times.'

'*Susan!* Thank God, there you are. I've been looking all over the place for you.' Doreen comes puffing up to me, Stella close behind. They look very pale and cross. 'You frightened the living daylights out of me,' Doreen complains. 'If I hadn't been able to find you your dad would have had my hide, so would my mum. Where did you go? You were there one minute and gone the next.'

'I met my friend Mandy,' I tell her, thinking it best not to mention the waltzer. 'She lives near us.'

Doreen eyes Mandy up and down. 'I think you'd better come with us now,' she says, taking hold of my arm. 'It's time we were getting you home.'

'Mandy's going to walk with us,' I say. 'She lost her brother and now she's all on her own.'

'It's OK,' Mandy interrupts. 'I can find my way.'

I see Doreen look at Stella. They obviously feel guilty about leaving Mandy on her own, but they still don't seem to want her to come with us. In the end, I seize Mandy's arm and say, 'Why don't we go across the common instead of down round the road? We'll be safe if there's four of us.'

Eddie

It's Good Friday. I've been queuing for nearly half an hour outside the Clock Tower for our fish and chips and I'm still the wrong side of the door. It's pouring down with rain, and bless her, the woman behind offered to let me shelter under her umbrella. I thanked her politely and said that I didn't mind getting wet.

I have to admit, I'm not really enjoying all the drip and trickle running down my back, but there's so much sex going round these days that you never know what anyone means any more. Even the most innocent little remark can end up being taken the wrong way, and standing that close to a woman I've never met before could easily lead to all sorts of rumours that I definitely wouldn't want to be the butt of.

A shocking thing happened down the factory yesterday. George Daily, who operates the cutter-grinder machine next to mine, was arrested for assaulting his wife. The police turned up, unannounced, and marched him away, while the other blokes began jeering and calling him names I wouldn't want to repeat, as if they'd already decided he was guilty even though none of them had a clue what it was really all about. I did, because George had told me earlier in the day what had happened between him and his missus the evening before. Apparently, he'd caught her red-handed having a bit of how's-yer-father with the bloke who comes to collect the rent for the council. George lost his temper and swung a punch at them both, and now he's the one in clink. Heaven only knows where the other two are now – I can only hope it's in church praying for forgiveness after committing a cardinal sin.

I swear the world's going mad. Blokes don't know what's going on with their wives any more, because the women are running out of control. They seem to think it's all right to go round flirting and drinking and showing themselves off like trollops, but that's not how a lady should behave. It's not what marriage vows are about, either. Thou shalt not commit adultery. I can only feel glad I don't have to put up with all the shenanigans myself, but I honestly don't think Eddress would be like it if she was still here. Not that she was a saint, mind you. Far from it, in fact, and she definitely enjoyed a bit of the other before she was ill. We used to do it every Saturday night, after bingo, and again on Sunday mornings if we managed a lie-in. There was even a couple of occasions during the week if we were in the mood, but there's a time and a place for everything and when you've got children rampaging about the house and flinging themselves into your bed at all hours, that doesn't arise very often.

Ah, at last, I'm inside the shop, and the rain's not running down my neck any more. Just as well Nance and I took flowers to the graves yesterday, while the weather was good. Two bunches, one for our Bob, the other for our mam. While we were sorting it out, that rascal of a son of mine managed to sneak out under a bush into the park next door so he could have a go on the swings. Frightened me half out of my wits when I turned round to find him gone. Luckily he shouted out to let me know where he was, which turned out to be close to rolling round the top bar, he was going so high. I had to rush down through the graveyard, shove myself under the bush and into the park before he managed to launch himself off to the stars.

I'd have liked to take some flowers for Eddress, but I'm ashamed to say I haven't been able to bring myself to go back to the crematorium since we scattered her ashes.

It seems Eddress was on our Nance's mind while we were at the graves, because it was while we were putting daffs in our mam's urn that she said, 'Do Susan or Gary ever ask after their mam now?'

'No, not really,' I told her. I often wish they did, but that's me being selfish, because I want to talk about her and they're too young to be burdened with my needs and memories.

'That's good.' Nance stooped to rearrange one of the fresh daffs. 'It shows they're getting over it. Children always do and it generally don't take long.'

I expect she's right, but even so, I say, 'I sometimes wonder if I ought to ask them how they feel about things. I was reading the other day that it can be good to get things unbottled…'

'Oh, all that new-fangled rubbish. I've heard about it too, but we never had time to go round talking about things during the war, did we, and we managed to survive.'

'But we're not at war any more, and the world's changing.'

She gave a sigh. 'You know your trouble, Eddie, you read too much. You've got enough to be doing keeping your head above water and making sure our Gary's all right, so why do you want to go and make things even more difficult for yourself by dredging up the past when it's the future what counts?'

I didn't disagree, but I had to say, 'Our Susan is bound to remember her, so I…'

'Look, how often do we talk about our mam? Not hardly ever, and that's a good thing, because it lets her rest in peace while we get on with our lives.'

Still not able to let it go, I asked, 'Does Flo talk to the girls about Bob?'

'No, not as far as I know. They were so young when he went that they hardly remember him at all, so Flo's doing the best thing and getting on with the hand she's been dealt.'

Since our Nance doesn't have the best relationship with Flo, I couldn't help wondering how much she really knew about the way Flo's coping, but it wouldn't do to dig any deeper. A person's business is their own, and thankfully

Flo's got her family to give her any support she needs. Like mine do for me, and I suppose Nance is right, it doesn't do any good to dwell on things, because no one wants to hear you going on and on about someone who's dead. It's embarrassing for them, they never know what to say, and anyway, missing Eddress isn't something I should discuss with the kids.

Our Susan went up the shows with young Doreen and her friend last night and came back full of it. She wants to go again tonight, but I expect they'll be closed in this weather. You should have seen the long face on her this morning when she got up and saw the rain. Kicked the bed, she did, then she started on Gary. Anyone would have thought it was his fault the weather was bad. Before I knew it they were at each other's throats and if I hadn't grabbed the ashtray off her I swear she'd have clobbered him with it. She's a bundle of frustration these days, always picking on him, or me, unable to find anything nice to say to either of us, and nothing we ever do is right. Then, out of the blue, one of us manages to make her laugh, and when she does it's like the sun's come out, full force. I even find myself blinking. We don't half love it when she's home, most of the time, it's as though the house fills up with colour again, but I'm careful never to tell her how pleased we are to see her because I know she'll use it to try and make me let her stay.

What a battle of wills this education of hers is turning into.

She's down our Nancy's now, with Gary, waiting for me to bring their dinner. They'll probably have been up the Tizer shop by the time I get back. I hope she remembers she's supposed to share the money they get back on the bottles with Gary. She wants to go downtown shopping tomorrow, on her own, she says. I told her she can go up Kingswood for an hour and I'll wait in the library to walk her home again, but downtown is much too far for a girl her age. Needless to say there was hell to pay, but I shan't give in. She won't tell me what she wants to buy, so I've said she can't have any money until she does, because I know she's after a miniskirt and make-up and all sorts of things she's still far too young for.

I had no idea it could be this hard being a parent. I just hope she doesn't start speaking to her teachers the way she sometimes speaks to me, telling me I'm stupid and old-fashioned and should keep up with the times. If she does, there are going to be a lot more detentions to come, which'll mean no exeats, and I can't help worrying how much more they'll be prepared to put up with.

I wonder what I can do to keep her occupied this afternoon. All she seems interested in these days is playing her records and mooning over pictures of pop stars. It's a pity Robert's gone down Weymouth for the weekend, because she usually enjoys seeing him. It gives our Doreen and me a bit of a smile to see the crush she has on him, and I can't say I blame her because he's a good-looking lad, in spite of his long hair. Thank goodness he hasn't turned into a hippy, I don't think any of us would know what to do with one of those, but even so, our Doreen and Alf still don't approve of the leather jackets and tatty jeans he's taken to wearing. Still, he's going on seventeen now, so what can they do?

I was thinking about driving down to George Daily's house later to see if they've let the poor bloke out yet. Trouble is, it's not really any of my business and I don't want his missus slamming the door in my face the way she did once before. Apparently she thought I was a debt collector. She's a handful, that one, and I can't help feeling sorry for George who's a nice bloke in his way. A bit of a rough diamond, the way he swears all the time, and tries his best to get under everyone's skin, but he always remembers to ask after Susan and Gary, and he's one of the few down the factory who don't take the mickey out of me for all the writing I do. I can't see why it bothers everyone so much that I like to take out my notebook and pencil during breaks, after all, it's not hurting them. I could explain, but I won't, how I find it soothing to put words on a page – any words will do, famous quotations, my own thoughts, song lyrics, poems I remember, news stories from the day, anything at all. It's a lot more pleasing to me than leering over the girlie magazines they get themselves engrossed in. That sort of pastime wouldn't do a chap like me, with no wife to come home to, any good at all.

At last it's my turn. 'Three pieces of cod, one Clark's pie, one fishcake and four portions of chips,' I say to the woman behind the counter.

'Coming up,' she says, 'and how are you, Eddie? Haven't seen you in a long time.'

It takes me by surprise to realise it's Rosie Maguire, who used to work down the pottery with Eddress before we were married. I didn't recognise her in her overall with her hair hidden under a hat and no lipstick – she was always well known for her ruby lips. 'Oh, I'm not too bad, thanks, Rosie,' I tell her. 'What about you?'

She gives me a wink. 'Oh, you know, keeping busy,' she replies, wrapping up the fish. 'I heard your Susan's at a posh school now. How's she getting on?'

'Lovely, thanks. And how are yours?'

'Blighters, the pair of 'em, but I suppose that's only to be expected at their age.' She gives a brief look over her shoulder to where her boss is serving the woman behind me, then quickly shovels an extra portion of chips into my order. 'Here you are,' she says, putting a big fat parcel next to the till. 'That'll be five and six, please, Ed.'

I hand her a ten-bob note and wait as she starts sorting out the change. 'Are you going to the dance down Made for Ever tomorrow night?' she asks, passing me a half-crown and a two-bob bit. 'I don't have a partner, if you fancy coming with me. Herb left me back last year.'

I feel myself starting to go red. I don't want to embarrass her by turning her down in front of everyone, but I don't want people thinking I've been picked up in the chip shop either. 'I'm sorry to hear that,' I say, keeping my voice down.

'Good riddance, is what I say,' she scoffs.

I give a jolly little laugh. 'Well, it was lovely seeing you, Rosie,' I tell her, grabbing my parcel. 'Happy Easter,' and before she can say any more I skedaddle out of there.

I suppose it's flattering that she wanted me to take her to the dance, but I'm not going to start giving myself airs and graces over it, because I expect she couldn't find anyone else.

Susan

It's almost the end of the Easter holidays now. After Bank Holiday Monday Gary and I spent most of the time here, at Gran's, while Dad went to work. There's not much to do, except play the games Gary brings with him, or hang around with my cousins Geoffrey and Deborah who live next door. Luckily, there's a park across the road where we go to spin as fast as we can on the roundabout (which isn't anywhere near as good as the waltzers), or see if we can go over the top bar on the swings. The swimming baths are next door to the park, but Dad's banned us from going there without him in case Gary drowns.

Actually, there hasn't been as much playing in the park as usual, because it's hardly stopped raining since Good Friday. It was lucky I went up the shows when I did with our Doreen, or I might not have been able to go at all, and then I wouldn't have met Mandy Hughes. I've been thinking about her a lot since that night, but I haven't seen her again, in spite of walking around the block a couple of times in case she was out in her garden. There was no sign of anyone either time, so I decided they must have gone on holiday or maybe they were hiding inside away from the police.

I wish I could just go and call for her, because I think she's really cool the way she does things I'd love to have the guts to do myself, like going out alone at night. If I could do that

I'd be able to run away from school without anyone spotting me. I think I'll write her a letter when I go back to ask if she'd like to go for a walk or something when I'm next at home on an exeat. I'd invite her round to our house, but I know Dad wouldn't allow it, which just goes to show how narrow-minded he is. Just because the rest of her family gets into trouble doesn't mean that she does too.

Thank goodness it's stopped raining today. I don't know what we'd have done if it hadn't, because Robert's coming to take us for a ride on his motorbike. (Gary has to be included, but I know Robert's coming to see me really. He even asked me when we were over Auntie Doreen's the other night if I was looking forward to seeing him.)

Gary and I have spent most of the morning sitting on the front doorstep waiting for him to arrive, and now at last he's here. Gary leaps up in the air with a cheer and I feel relieved that Geoffrey and Deborah's older sisters are at work, because I know they like Robert and if they saw him they'd be bound to come over and flirt with him, thinking they have more rights than me, just because I'm still at school. Robert doesn't see me like that, though. He knows I'm much more grown up than everyone else seems to think I am, and treats me as though I'm more or less the same age as him.

I wonder if he's still going out with Jenny.

I won't bother to ask.

'Hello,' he laughs as Gary launches himself at him. With a quick wrestle Robert swings Gary up in the air, then buries him under one arm.

'Ow, help, let me out!' Gary shouts. 'Gran, he's got me.'

That's the sort of thing Dad shouts when Gary gets him in a headlock.

'And how's our little beauty queen?' Robert says to me.

I really, really love him, and peer at him from under my hair. (I'm trying to do the kind of smile I saw Mandy Hughes do up the fair, but I'm not sure if I'm getting it right.)

Suddenly he grabs me into a great big hug and blows a

giant raspberry on my neck. (I'd have preferred him to kiss me, but I know he can't in front of Gary, and anyway, Gran's coming out of the sitting room.)

'There you are,' Gran says, holding open her arms for Robert to come and give her a kiss, which I think is really nice considering she's not his real gran.

'Granny Price, you're looking younger every day,' he tells her. I know he doesn't mean it, because she's the oldest person we know, and is all crinkly and grey, but it makes her chuckle so I can tell she likes it. I wonder if he minds about her whiskers as he plants a smackeroo on her cheek. I never do, they're a part of Gran, like her bandaged legs and great big pinny.

Straight away she starts asking about Auntie Doreen and Uncle Alf, and wants to know how Robert's getting on in his new job. (He's been taken on as an apprentice in a factory near Wick, but when he's seventeen he's going to pass his test and drive the lorries like his dad.)

After they've been talking for a while, Robert says, 'So who's coming on the bike first?'

'Me, me, me,' Gary shouts, jumping up and down.

I roll my eyes to show that I understand how youngsters don't have it in them to wait.

'Are you sure Uncle Ed said it was all right?' Robert asks, as Gary leaps up for a piggyback.

'Just as long as they hold on tight and you don't go fast,' Gran tells him. 'And no further than round the block. I'll put the kettle on while you're gone and make a nice cup of tea. Or would you rather have coffee?'

'If it's Nescaff I'll have coffee,' he answers. 'I'm not all that struck on the Camp stuff.'

'Nor me,' I say. 'It's too sweet.'

Gran gives me a bit of a look, because she knows I love it really, but she doesn't split, she only slips an arm round my shoulders as we watch Robert jog Gary out to the motorbike. I imagine what he'll be like when we're married and have children of our own. He'll be a really good dad.

'I reckon they ought to be wearing helmets,' Gran mumbles as Robert plonks Gary on the back, then sits astride the saddle in front of him.

'Oh no, only spazzos and squares wear helmets,' I tell her.

She rolls her eyes, and we wait as Robert makes sure Gary is holding tight before starting slowly down the street. When they turn at the church we give them a wave, but they're not looking, and then they disappear from view.

'There, that's cheered you up, seeing your cousin,' Gran remarks, as she waddles ahead of me into the kitchen. 'He's a lovely chap. Now, where's the matches to light the gas? Go and fetch the teapot from the table, there's a good girl, and bring out the dirty cups.'

While we're making the tea – and coffee for Robert (Gary and I aren't allowed to have Nescaff, because Dad says it'll overexcite us. Honestly, I wish he'd stop treating me like a baby all the time) – Reggie comes in from the garden.

'What the bloody hell are you doing in here, you dirty old sod?' Gran shouts at him.

'I came to get a light for me fag,' he answers.

'Use your own matches.'

'Haven't got none till I goes up the shop.'

'Here,' she says, thrusting a box at him, 'and make sure you replace it when you've got your own.'

I watch Reggie go off with his stub of a roll-up, feeling quite sorry for him, but at the same time I'm glad he's gone, because his nose is running and his clothes are all muddy and stinky. I wouldn't want Robert seeing him and thinking one of my relations on Gran's side is a tramp.

Robert and Gary seem to be gone for ages. When they eventually come back Gary charges in through the door, his eyes all bright with excitement. 'It was brilliant, Gran,' he tells her. 'We went right up past the church, round past the college and then back down again.'

'I hope you didn't let go,' she smiles, ruffling his crew cut.

'No, I didn't, did I?' he says to Robert.

'He was a very good boy and an excellent passenger,' Robert assures us.

'I'm glad to hear it. Do you want your coffee now, or when you come back with our Susan?'

Robert looks at me and I feel really soft because I start to blush. 'Up to you,' he says, giving me a wink.

I don't want to wait any longer, but I try to sound cool as I reply, 'We might as well go now.'

So he leads the way down the path, and Gran and Gary come to watch me climb on to the back of the bike. It's higher than I expected, and when I put my legs either side of the saddle my dress rides right up my legs. Embarrassed, I try to pull it down again, but I can't, because he has to sit in between my knees.

When he's on, he turns round and says, 'Are you all right?'

'Yes,' I tell him, feeling excited and scared. I look at Gran and give her a smile.

'Hold on tight,' she calls out.

Even though I've seen the way older girls lean back behind their boyfriends and sometimes don't hold on at all, I do as she says or I know she'll only worry. Once we're out of sight, I can do it the proper way. So I circle my arms round Robert's waist and think it's a shame we can only go round the block, but it wouldn't be fair on Gary if we went any further, at least for today.

After revving up the engine Robert lifts his foot off the ground and we start to move forward. It's so thrilling and terrifying that I want to laugh out loud.

'All right?' he shouts.

'Yes,' I shout back.

I hope I'm not squeezing him too tight. My cheek is squashed against his back, and my eyes are shut. In a minute I'll be brave enough to open them. When I do I see the houses passing by, and then we tilt all the way over to the right as we start to turn the corner. I think we're going to fall, so I hold on more tightly than ever.

'Just lean with the bike,' he tells me.

We go past some girls who are walking towards the park. When they see me I feel so proud I could burst.

We go faster. The wind is blowing my hair, and rushing through my ears. One of Robert's hands closes around both of mine, as though making sure I keep hold of him.

I'm so happy I could fly. This is the best thing I've ever done in my whole life. It beats the waltzers any day, and the big wheel, and being on telly on Founder's Day when there were so many of us you couldn't make anyone out at all. It's just me and Robert speeding along, holding tight to each other, not thinking about anyone or anything like stupid school, or who wants to be my friend, or why Mummy had to die, or anything bad at all. I want to go on doing this for ever and ever. If anyone sees me they'll wonder who my really dishy boyfriend is and I won't even bother to tell them. I imagine us roaring in through the gates at Red Maids and all the girls flocking to the windows to find out who's coming. By then I'll be brave enough to sit back in the seat, and every one of them will wish they were me.

We go past the technical college, up around the corner into Lansdowne Road, and then down into Hilltop. I wish there were more people around, but there are some and I smile as we go by with my cheek still squashed up against Robert's back.

Eventually we turn out on to the main road where there's more traffic, and a bus is going by. We seem to be going faster than ever and I'm loving it. We're on our way to Gretna Green. We're going to get married and live in a lovely house and go for rides on the motorbike whenever we like. No one will be able to tell me what to do, except him, if I let him. I don't think I'll be an obedient wife, but it won't matter because he'll love me anyway the way Dad loved Mum, who never, ever did as she was told.

Just before the swimming baths we turn right, bringing us back into Church Road. We slow down a bit and by the time we pull up outside Gran's I've managed to let go with one arm. It feels really lush, and I wish we could just carry on, all the way through Soundwell and Kingswood, down Two Mile Hill and into town, but I know Gran won't allow it.

'There, how was that?' Robert asks as he holds the bike steady for me to slide off.

'Really fab,' I tell him, hardly able to catch my breath. I want to give him a kiss to say thank you, but I haven't got the guts.

He puts his fingers under my chin and laughs as he looks at me. With a laugh myself I throw my arms around him and say thank you with as much feeling as I can.

He comes in to drink his coffee and eat the Spam sandwiches Gran cut while we were gone, but he doesn't stay long, because he's on his dinner break so he has to get back to work. I walk with him down the path to his bike, loving the way he's holding my hand.

'Right,' he says, sitting on, 'time to be off. Are you going to give us a kiss before I go?'

I feel my face burn all the way into my hair, but instead of saying no, which I nearly do, I go up on tiptoe to kiss his cheek.

'Robert! You forgot your gloves,' comes a yell from the house.'

Robert looks up and my mouth touches his by accident. I draw back fast, feeling softer than I ever have in my life. He laughs and gives me one of his winks.

'Here you are,' Gary says, hurtling down the path.

'Good boy,' Robert tells him. 'I'd have been looking all over for them.' He turns on the engine and twists the handle to make it rev. 'Be seeing you,' he says, and with a giant roar he speeds off down the street, going ten times faster than he did with me and Gary on the back, but I expect the next time he takes me for a ride we'll go that fast then.

I can hardly wait.

Chapter Ten

Eddie

A terrible thing's just happened in America. Someone's only gone and shot Robert Kennedy. The news is still coming in, so I don't know many details yet, only that he was giving a speech in California when it happened. They've rushed him to hospital, apparently, and someone's been arrested. They're saying it's a dark-skinned chap who might be Mexican or Cuban, but no one's sure yet.

It makes you wonder what on earth's going on over there. First the President himself is assassinated, then barely a month ago that marvellous chap Martin Luther King was shot dead, and now this. It's like the Wild West, by the sound of it. All those guns! They should never be allowed. I'm just glad we're living in this country. Not that we don't have our problems, because we do, but when you weigh them up against the madness that seems to go on in America, and all the riots breaking out across the Channel in France, well, it makes you wonder what the world's coming to. The French students have gone and occupied their university now, and half the country's on strike so rubbish is piling up in the streets with rats running about all over the place, and normal people are terrified to go out. It's all in a good cause, I have to say, but is this really the right way to go about it?

The only good bit of news is that there's some serious talk at last about ending the Vietnam War. Twice Albert Pitman and I arranged to join a protest march about that, but I had to back out both times, first because I couldn't afford the coach fare to London, and then some extra overtime came up at work that I had to take.

I'm sitting here in my corner of the factory now, writing down what I've heard on the news today, and thinking what a relief it is to express myself this way. It cuts across my faults in speech and disguises my ignorance, without forcing me to withhold my opinions and remain silent. It would be hard to get into an exchange with the ruffians around me about the graveness of Robert Kennedy's shooting, because I know most of them couldn't give a tinker's cuss about what's going on in America. However, to be fair to them, they're not scoffing at my notebook today, in fact most of them aren't saying anything at all.

There's nothing being broadcast on the wireless about the shooting at the moment, but we're all waiting for the next announcement and hoping the news will be good and that he's survived.

I sometimes wonder how it's possible to be pleasant and gentle when there's so much bad in the world, but then I think of our Lord Jesus and it usually helps to unravel the knots.

I expect someone from management will be around any minute, ordering us back to work. I don't think anyone's going to bother though until they do.

Gary's too young to understand the gravity of the shooting, but I wonder how they're breaking it to our Susan and the other girls at Red Maids. It's a mightily serious situation, what with America becoming such a big power in the world, so I expect they'll sit the girls down to explain the impact it could have on us all. I don't suppose I've really worked that out myself yet, but I'll look forward to discussing it with Albert tomorrow night, and of course a lot will depend on whether the poor chap lives or dies.

It's Saturday June 8th now and very early in the morning. Robert Kennedy was pronounced dead about twenty-four hours ago.

I won't be going into work today, but it doesn't have anything to do with that. I've got some very serious news for our Susan now, which I'd be telling her if she was coming home tomorrow, but I had a letter yesterday informing me she's back in detention. This means she'll have to miss another exeat, and for the first time I won't be able to go up to the church to see her. So, I'm afraid the news will have to wait. I can't believe it's happened. I'm so shaken up I hardly know what I'm doing or saying or even thinking. I don't know how any of us are ever going to get over it.

Susan

Everyone's been talking about what happened to Robert Kennedy. Some of the girls cried, and lots were saying that there's an evil force taking over the world, so we must pray extra hard in church today in order to be saved. We were all very quiet at breakfast this morning – you could even hear the crunching of warm, crusty rolls as we devoured them in our usual hungry way. Then we had to go to our classrooms to memorise the collect for St Philip and St James's Day. We always have to do this in silence, but today it felt different, as though all kinds of holiness and devilry might be mingling about in the room with us.

Robert Kennedy's brother, John, was assassinated too, while he was President. That happened about four years ago, and I sort of remember it. His wife, Jacqueline, was in the car with him and she got covered in his blood. It was horrible. America sounds like a very dangerous place, and I feel extremely sorry for Robert Kennedy's family. I hate death, I wish God would stop making it happen. He never listens though, except when He wants to, and that's almost never where I'm concerned. I'm taking charge of my own life from now on, which means I won't be writing to anyone any more asking them to talk Dad into letting me out of here. I'll do it myself.

We've just come out of church and I'm looking around for Dad, but he's nowhere to be seen. I bet he's not coming because he's angry with me for being in detention again.

'Ah, Susan, there you are, dear.' It's Mrs Beach, Glenys's mum. 'I had a telephone call from your father this morning asking me to tell you that he can't make it today. He says he's very sorry, but he'll be here next week as usual.'

Straight away I think, *he doesn't want to see me any more, and now he's going to leave me here to rot.* I'd feel even more upset if a whole gang of us weren't in detention together, so at least I won't be on my own today, but Dad doesn't know that. I start to feel very angry with him for being so mean. I'm already being punished by having to stay here, so he doesn't have to make it worse. I don't think I'll write him any letters this week, and if he sends me any I'm not going to bother to read them.

The reason we're all in detention is because we got caught out of bounds the other night. We'd sneaked out to the back lane to meet some day girls who were supposed to be bringing some boys to see us. The next day they swore they had come, but as soon as they heard Cluttie shouting they scarpered before they got caught too.

We spent half the night facing the wall on the staff landing, which is where boarders get sent if they've done something seriously wrong when they're supposed to be in bed. It is the spookiest place in the entire school, and I was extremely glad not to be on my own. The staffroom is definitely haunted. We all jumped out of our skin when something banged against the door, and when we heard something being dragged around inside we fled upstairs to our dorms without permission.

Dot gave us a good talking-to the next morning about how dangerous it could be for girls our age to wander out of bounds without supervision.

'There are a lot of undesirable people out there,' she told us, 'and girls' schools are often a magnet to some of society's most unpleasant individuals. If you were to find yourselves in their hands the consequences could be very serious indeed. Do you understand me?'

'Yes, miss,' we mumbled. I know it probably was a bit dangerous, going out at night like that, and actually we were all dead scared, but what do they expect when they keep us locked up here like a bunch of criminals? Anyone in their right mind would try to escape.

'While you're here you are the school's responsibility,' she droned on, 'and I do not want to find myself in the position of having to contact your parents to inform them that something terrible has happened to you. Please try to think of how upsetting that would be for them, and what a dreadful impact it could have on the rest of the girls. You're grown up enough now to know the difference between right and wrong, and to behave in a responsible fashion, not only towards yourselves, but towards other people. You will all stay behind for detention this Sunday, and I'll be writing to your parents to inform them why you are unable to go home.'

I wanted to try and persuade her not to bother my dad, because he's got enough to worry about without her adding to it, but I knew she wouldn't listen, so I just left with the others and agreed with Sadie that Dot was a coward for not expelling us. At least then we'd be able to go home and never have to come back. And anyway, even if Dot's letter does make Dad upset and worried, it'll be his own fault for sending me here in the first place.

We thought, after Robert Kennedy was shot, that she might let us off, or even forget all about it, but no such luck. So here we are, walking back to school while everyone else disappears off to the zoo or Blaize Castle with their families if they don't live in Bristol, or home if they do.

Little does Dot know that we're supposed to be meeting Slash and his mates at four this afternoon, if we can manage to sneak out to the lane. I keep imagining how fab it would be if I met someone who really loved me, and you never know, I might.

We eat our lunch in the dining room. Cook serves us herself, because the rest of the kitchen staff have the day off. The food's quite decent for once, roast beef, mashed potatoes, carrots and gravy, with jam roly-poly for pudding, yuk! Celery (Miss Ellery) eats with us, but she doesn't speak to us because we're in disgrace, and we're not allowed to utter a word either. When we've finished we have to clear the table, sweep the floor, wash and wipe up, and hang the dish towels on a line to dry. Then we're sent off to bed to lie down quietly for two hours, no records, no talking, no anything, and at three we have to report to the nursery to find out what our punishment is.

It turns out to be folding endless piles of bed linen, which is as rough and stiff as cardboard it's so full of starch, but luckily it doesn't take long, and by a quarter to four we're free to do as we want for an hour.

Straight away we run up to Speedwell dorm where Sadie and I have hidden everyone's make-up, and we quickly start using it on one another ready to meet the boys. Cheryl does the mascara, Sadie the foundation, I put on the lipstick and Peg draws in the eyebrows for those of us who need it. Then we make our stockings as long and our suspenders as short as we can, before putting on our day kilts, because we can roll them over at the waist to turn them into minis. Worse luck there's nothing we can do about our black lace-up shoes, because they're all we have, but Peg has a fantastic idea.

'We can leave them next to the tennis courts and go barefoot,' she says. 'Like Sandie Shaw.'

So that's what we do.

It's quite a warm day, and there's no sign of anyone as we creep outside. Woe betide us if we're spotted with all our make-up and back-combed hair, but so far, so good. We tip-toe past the classrooms round to the walled garden, and when we're safely tucked out of view we kick off our shoes and run as fast as we can to the opening into the lane.

Sadie looks through first.

'Can you see anyone?' Cheryl asks in a whisper.

'No.'

'They definitely said four, did they?' Peg wonders.

'That's what Christine said,' Sadie replies. Christine's the second-form day girl who's bringing the boys. She lives in Westbury-on-Trym and apparently she's been out with Slash and says he's a really good kisser.

I wonder which one of us he's going to fancy.

I know it won't be me.

'Ssh, someone's coming,' Sadie whispers, and spinning round she bumps right into us as she tries to dive out of sight.

Giggling and squealing, we all tuck ourselves in behind the bushes to wait. Sure enough there are voices, and then someone, a boy, is saying, 'Is anyone there?'

Sadie nudges me to go out first.

I shrink back, shaking my head. 'No, you,' I whisper.

'You go,' she tells Peg.

Peg won't either.

'All right, I will,' Cheryl declares, and giving her hair a quick pat she steps up to the gap in the hedge. 'Hello,' we hear her say. 'I'm Cheryl. Who are you?'

'I'm Slash,' someone answers, 'and this is Jimmy, Mike, John and Christopher.' That means there are five of them, and six of us, so someone's going to be left out. 'Where are the others?' he asks. 'We were told . . . '

'They're here,' Cheryl tells him. 'We had to hide until we were sure it was you.'

Sadie's grinning all over her face. So are Peg, Sally and Melanie. They're all really excited. I am too, except I don't want to be the one who ends up being left out. I'm bound to be though, because the others are all much prettier than me, so I say, 'You go, and I'll keep a lookout in case anyone comes.'

'No, you have to come too,' Sadie insists. 'It's not fair if you don't.'

'I don't care,' I tell her.

She doesn't argue any more, and one by one they jump down into the lane leaving me on my own under the tree.

Actually, I really don't care. Why should I when I've got Robert? I've told everyone how we kissed after he took me for a ride on his motorbike, and I told them all about Mandy Hughes and what we did up the shows at Easter. I've done lots more things than they have, so it's only right that they have a turn with the boys first.

I wonder what Slash is like. Christine says he's really dishy. I bet he goes after Sadie, because she's the prettiest. Actually, I can imagine him thinking Cheryl is, or Peg. Sally and Melanie are really sexy too, so it could be any of them. I know he wouldn't like me very much, because I've got ginger hair and freckles and I'm starting to get spots now too. Cheryl's covered most of them up with Hide 'n Heal, but I can't help thinking my eyebrows look silly, all thick and black, although everyone insists they look really cool. Even if they do, Slash wouldn't like me, because no one does. I used to think Dad did, but I know he doesn't now. It was all a pretence, just like with Mum. She went off and left me too, but I don't care. They can all get lost as far as I'm concerned.

I can hear everyone chatting and laughing down in the lane, then suddenly I spot a car coming up the drive. Bloody hell! It's only Dot's.

'Everyone stay where you are,' I hiss, pressing myself into the undergrowth. 'Dot's going by. Don't make a move.'

'Who's that?' one of the boys asks.

'Ssh,' Sadie says sharply.

'It's Su Lu,' Cheryl whispers. 'She's our lookout.'

'What's she like?'

Everyone goes silent and I feel myself turning hot and cold. I can imagine them screwing up their noses and pretending to be sick. I expect Peg is mouthing *Really ugly* and I want to smash her face in. I could easily run over to Dot now and report them all. I don't of course, but if they're being horrible about me it would serve them right.

When we get back to the dorm they're all chattering non-stop about who said what in the lane, which one they fancy and when they're going to see them again, so I take out my pictures of Davy Jones and the letter I had from Robert. I don't mind that I can't join in, because they're talking about immature boys who are nobodies, and my photos and letter are from grown-ups who are famous and ride motorbikes.

I wonder what Dad and Gary are doing now.

I'm nearly crying, which makes me mad. It's Dad's fault I'm upset. He should have come today.

Eddie

Doubt. Despair. Demoralise. Depress. Dismay. Degenerate. Despise. Death. Destination. Difficult. Devastating.

I wrote all these words down because I've been feeling a bit depressed and demoralised lately with all that's been happening in the world, and in our family, but having worked hard on the washing today, and sat for a while watching the sun shine after some rain with the clothes drying nicely on the line, I started to feel more hopeful. Then my thoughts began to degenerate, and very soon I was filled with doubt and dismay again.

Death is hard. It leaves us full of despair. I despise it, even though I know, as a Christian, I should embrace it. Or at least I shouldn't fear it, or reject it as though I have a choice. Sometimes I long for it, but then I think of our Susan and Gary and I know with all my heart that I don't want to go anywhere until I've done my best to bring them up, and I can be sure they don't need me any more.

The road to that destination seems to stretch a long way ahead of me, and I'm certain it's going to traverse some very difficult terrain. It's already as bumpy as one might imagine the road to hell, full of sorrow, and the kind of confusion that tests my belief in God.

Back to doubt.

If it weren't for my religion I doubt I could have coped over these last two years since Eddress went. Her death sometimes seems to fill up the whole of my life. I miss her in ways I could never have imagined before it happened, and I'd never dreamt that time would just go on and on making it feel worse. I am incomplete as a person, inadequate as a man and incapable as a father. I try to stay cheerful, playing football out on the grass with Gary, writing jolly letters to Susan, taking Florrie to bingo and getting as involved as I can in the union. World affairs have always interested me, but the way things have been happening lately, I have to wonder what it's all about, or if it's even worth going on.

Earlier in the week Gary came first in the tunnel ball relay. He was as pleased as Punch, and so excited to tell me when I came home from work that he tripped as he ran to me and cut his mouth on the step. I thought we might be on our way back up the hospital, but it didn't turn out to be as bad as it looked.

What kind of God trips up a little boy in his happiness?

What kind of God leaves two young children without their mother?

What kind of God could do what He has to our family?

I could ask the question a thousand times over and no one will ever be able to give me the answer. I know it's wrong to question my faith, but after what happened at the beginning of June, how can I help it?

We're three weeks into July now and our Susan's home for the summer holidays. I know she's still upset with me for not going to see her at church on the day she missed an exeat, but the time hasn't been right yet for me to explain why I couldn't come.

If I live to be a hundred the time will never be right to break this news. I'm still trying to come to terms with it myself, but I don't think I ever will.

She's in bed now after a long day coming home from school and unpacking. I don't know if she's asleep. I turned her light out a while ago, so she might be. I'll have to wake her up if she is, because I can't let her find out what's happened from anyone else.

'Susan?' I whisper, going into her room.

She doesn't answer, so I go to sit on the edge of her bed.

'Are you awake, my love?' I ask.

I turn on her bedside light and her eyes flicker open. 'What do you want?' she complains. 'I was asleep.'

'I've got something to tell you,' I say. 'It's not very good news, I'm afraid.'

I sense her stiffen and wish there was something I could do to make this easier, but there isn't. 'Robert's been killed on his motorbike,' I tell her as gently as I can.

I see her eyes grow wide with shock and feel the cruel punch to her heart. It's brutal and devastating. I sense her shrinking away, as though trying to escape me, yet she hasn't actually moved. I know she's trying to fight off the truth, and who can blame her? I remember when I told her about her mother, and how after a few tears she decided to go back to school. She wanted to carry on as if nothing had changed, as though if she ignored it it wouldn't be real. It upset and confused me at the time, but I understand it now. It was too much for her to take in, and I feel this is, too.

'It happened over on Warmley Hill,' I tell her. 'A car was coming up as he came down . . . He was on his way home after seeing his girlfriend.'

Tears well in her eyes and spill on to her cheeks.

I smooth her hair. 'I'm sorry, my love,' I murmur, close to crying myself. How many tears have I already shed for that lovely young boy who was so full of life, who we all loved, but who didn't make it to his seventeenth birthday? How many for our Doreen and Alf whose lives have been shattered? For young Doreen whose world isn't making sense any more?

What kind of God rips out a family's heart? How many times will He do it to ours? First Bob, then Eddress, now Robert. They were all so young, but he was still a boy.

'Would you like to say a prayer?' I ask.

'No,' she answers. Her tone is unequivocal and savage.

How can I not understand her fury, or her rejection of the Lord? What can I do to soothe her pain? What can I possibly say to make her world whole again? The answer is, nothing, because there are no words that can right this wrong, nor any actions that can turn back time.

Chapter Eleven

Susan

I haven't done very much since we broke up from school. I was going to, but then I didn't feel like it any more, so I've mainly stayed in my bedroom playing records, or reading books, or writing in my diary. I hate God for taking Robert away. I really, really hate Him. He's broken Auntie Doreen's heart and mine too and everyone else's. Why do all the people I love have to die? It's not fair. I'm never going to love anyone again, because there's no point when God just takes them away. I want Mummy and Robert and Uncle Bob to be here with us, where they belong. Dad keeps saying what he always says, that we have to take one day at a time, but I think we should just snatch whatever we want when we want it, because for all we know the next day might not even come.

That's what I'm going to do from now on.

Sometimes I go downstairs to watch telly. Gary likes *Crackerjack* and Dad's favourite is *The Dick Emery Show*, so we usually watch those two programmes. It's quite funny the way he hits people with his handbag and says, 'Oh you are awful, but I like you.' (I mean Dick Emery, not Dad.) I have a bit of a smile at the idea of Dad with a handbag.

Some rich people are getting colour televisions now. It's just started, but only on BBC2 and we can't get that channel anyway, so it doesn't count for us. Mum always liked *Coronation Street* and *The Billy Cotton Band Show*. Sometimes she'd let me stay up late on a Saturday night to watch Billy Cotton. He's not on any more. It seems a really long time ago that we used to shout along with him, 'Wakey Wakey!'

I wonder if Robert's with her and they like it where they are.

Dad's on holiday from work next week so we might go down Bowleaze Cove for a few days. I expect Gran will come too, and one or two of my cousins, like Geoffrey and Deborah. Auntie Doreen and Uncle Alf rented a caravan down there, but they're not going now, so we might use it instead to save it going to waste.

I saw Auntie Doreen last week and gave her a great big hug. There were tears in her eyes, but she didn't cry. She told me how a young policeman came to the door in the middle of the night to tell them about Robert, and he got so upset that she sat him down in the front room and went to make him a cup of tea.

'He wasn't much older than our Robert,' she said. 'Must have been a terrible shock for him.'

That's typical of Auntie Doreen, to think about other people before she thinks about herself. She's lovely and gentle and kind and I don't understand why God had to do this to her.

Towards the end of last term I started to read the *Treasury of Devotion*, because in between getting into trouble I kept worrying that I might be making God cross, and if I was then He might never forgive me for whatever I did to make Him take Mummy away and send me to Red Maids. I've stopped reading it now, and I'm never going to read it again.

Ever since the weekend I've had a terrible stomach ache, and on Saturday night my head hurt so much that I wanted to bang it against the wall. Dad sat with me, trying to make me feel better, but it pounded and hurt so badly that in the end I started to be sick. The doctor was visiting one of the old-age pensioners in the bungalows at the bottom of the street so Dad asked him to pop in and see me. He said I had a migraine, and there was nothing he could give me except more aspirin. On Sunday I had a nosebleed that lasted so long I was afraid I might end up with no blood left.

It's quite early in the morning now and I'm still in bed.

Dad's gone to work, but Auntie Kath, our home help, is downstairs making our breakfasts. We're supposed to be going to her house today, instead of Gran's, which I was really looking forward to until I woke up to find out that I'm dying. I'm trying to comfort myself by thinking that Mum and Robert and Uncle Bob will be waiting for me when I get there, but what if they're not? I might go to a different place to them, like hell, because I've stopped saying my prayers and thought bad things about God.

I don't want to die. I want to stay here with Dad. It would be really mean of God to take me away from him, because he's already lost his wife and his brother – *and* his nephew, but maybe he wouldn't mind if he lost me. He wouldn't have to worry about me any more, or tell me off for getting into trouble, or put up with my cheek when he won't let me wear minis or make-up. I think I probably deserve to die, so that's why it's happening.

I have another look under the sheets and start to cry. There's blood everywhere. I haven't cut myself or anything, it's coming out from between my legs, lots and lots of it, all over my nightie and the sheets.

'Susan! Are you awake?' Auntie Kath knocks on my door, and when I don't answer she puts her head in. She's a little woman with wiry ginger hair, a long freckled face and quite big teeth. Gary and I like her a lot. She's very kind and down to earth and is a champion dart player at her local pub.

I look at her with only my eyes showing above the sheets, because I make an ugly face when I'm crying.

'Oh, my love, what is it?' she says, coming to sit on the bed. 'What's got you all choked up?'

I can't answer straight away because I'm sobbing too hard. In the end, I manage to say, 'I'm – I'm dying.'

She takes a drag of her cigarette and the smoke comes out of her nose and mouth in little white curls as she says, 'Well, that sounds like a load of old nonsense to me. Why do you say that?'

I'm still trying to catch my breath. 'Because – because I'm bleeding.'

She looks a bit puzzled at first, then resting her cigarette on the edge of my dressing table, she asks, 'How old are you again?'

'I'm twelve next week.'

She nods. 'And where are you bleeding?'

'Down – down there.'

I can hardly believe it when she starts to laugh. 'Oh, my love,' she says, smoothing my hair, 'didn't anyone tell you about that? No, obviously not. It's nothing to be afraid of. It happens to everyone . . . Well, girls, anyway. That blood is your periods starting.'

I don't know what she's talking about.

'It'll happen every month for about a week,' she goes on, 'well, maybe not as regular as that at first, but it'll settle down after a while. You might get some bad stomach aches when it's about to happen, or headaches, but they're nothing to worry about, it's perfectly normal.'

'But why does it happen?' I want to know, wishing it would go away.

She laughs again. 'It's all a part of growing into a woman and having babies,' she explains. 'When you bleed, it's your body washing away the egg that hasn't been used that month.'

'What egg?'

'The one you make so you can have children.'

I'm feeling quite confused, thinking she might have something wrong, but I'm not sure what. 'So was I pregnant?' I ask, feeling quite doubtful, but excited.

She laughs again. 'I should hope not,' she says, 'but now your periods have started you can get in the family way – that's a phrase they use for getting pregnant – or up the spout, or in the pudding club . . . But you're still a bit young for that, so we won't want it happening just yet, will we?'

I shake my head.

She peers at me closely. 'Do you know what goes on between a man and a woman to make a baby?'

I swallow and shake my head again.

'It's when a man puts his dicky-dye-doh, as Gary calls it, inside a woman's private parts. That's how babies are made.'

She's blushing, and so am I, so I'm glad when she gets up saying, 'Well, we'd better get you sorted out, hadn't we? I don't suppose you've got any Dr Whites, so stay where you are. I'll fetch some toilet paper to pad between your legs, then I'll go round the shop to get what you need. Poor love.' She strokes my hair again. 'When I come back I'll run you a nice warm bath so you can clean yourself up, then I'll sort out the sheets. OK?' She gives a happy little chuckle. 'There's a thing, Susan Lewis is a young lady already. It doesn't happen to everyone as young as you, my girl, so that makes you quite special, you know.'

I've always felt quite special, actually, so I'm not really very surprised when she says that.

Ever since my period started last week I've been feeling quite mature, and I'm sure people are noticing. I haven't told Dad, I just couldn't, but I think he knows, because I forgot to put my packet of Dr Whites away yesterday, so he probably saw them next to my bed when he came to tuck me in last night. He might not know what they're for though, unless Mum used to use them, but I've never seen any in our house before, so maybe she stopped having periods after she had Gary. I expect that's what happens when you decide you don't want to have any more children.

I've asked a couple of my friends in the street if they've started their periods yet, and no one has, which only goes to show how immature they are. I wonder if anyone my age at school has, but I don't think they can have, because I'm sure they'd have told me. I can hardly wait to get back to tell everyone. I don't want to be big-headed or anything, but I've always felt more grown up than them, especially Peg, and this just goes to prove that I am.

I must admit, I don't like the stomach ache much, and it feels strange trying to walk with a thick pad between my legs. I keep thinking people can see it under my shorts, but Auntie Kath swears they can't. I wonder what I'm going to do when I need some more pads, where I'll get the money from? I suppose I'll have to ask Dad. That'll be really *really* embarrassing, so maybe I should borrow the money from Auntie Kath.

I really want to tell Robert, even though I know I wouldn't if he was here. I just can't stop thinking about him, even when I'm doing something else, and I get so angry inside about what happened to him that I want to scream and hit out at someone. Dad says we'll never be able to make any sense of it, and that we shouldn't try because ours is not to reason why. Well I think it is, because I don't care what anyone says, it was wicked to make Robert die like that, and to take my mum and Uncle Bob. And the fact that God never shows Himself to us just goes to prove that He doesn't love any of us at all, especially not me, because He keeps punishing me for things I didn't do by taking away the people I love. I'm really scared He'll take Dad or Gary next. If He does I'll kill myself.

Oh yes! I found out something extremely interesting yesterday. The reason I can never see Linda Watkins' suspenders under her short dresses is because she's wearing *tights*. Not the thick woolly sort that children wear, but ones made of stockings. They go all the way up the legs and have knickers at the top, just like, well, tights. I have to get some and take them back to school to show everyone how with-it I am. They'll all want some, I know, but I'll be the first to have them, or I would be if I could afford them, but I don't have any money, and I can't see Dad giving me any for something like that. He'll say they're indecent, the way he does about everything, but I think they're much better than stupid stockings and suspenders. I'm going up Kingswood with Auntie Nance tomorrow, so I might ask if she'll get me some and I'll pay her back as soon as I can. I need some new brassieres too, because my old ones are much too small, but I don't want to ask her for them. She teased me about my bosoms when we went swimming last week, which I really hated.

'Oh, look at the big bosoms she's got,' she laughed, reaching in through the cubicle curtain like she was going to grab them. The next minute she was really angry, because I thumped her hand away and hurt her. I'm glad, because it was a stupid and childish thing to do, and she has no business even coming into my cubicle when I'm changing, let alone looking at my chest.

I hate everyone so much sometimes I could scream.

I saw Mandy Hughes yesterday walking across the top with her mum. She was wearing a really lush psychedelic minidress and white sling-back shoes with heels. She didn't see me, because I was in our garden playing rounders with Gary and she wasn't looking our way. I'm hoping I might bump into her up the shows again, because they're up Siston Common for the summer. As it's not too far Dad's promised to let me walk up there without him when we come back from our holiday in Bowleaze Cove.

We're supposed to be going tomorrow, but the car's playing up so Dad's taken it to someone he knows to see if they can mend it. Gary's gone fishing somewhere with his friends Geoffrey and Nigel, and I'm over by the brook with Diane and Carol, two girls who live right up the top of our street, and don't seem to mind about me being posh. They're the same age as me, and we always went to the same school until last year, so I've known them since I was five, just not all that well. My other friends in Greenways are all either on holiday, or have gone off without me as usual. I don't care, they're just stupid and childish anyway – and thick. (I wish they wouldn't leave me out really, because I'd rather have them as friends than anyone else.)

Diane and Carol haven't started their periods yet, they tell me. Diane's sister Jane has, but she's fourteen, so that's not very surprising. Carol's really jealous.

212

'I can't wait till I'm grown up and able to have babies,' she says. 'You're really lucky, Sue.'

I think I am too, apart from the stomach ache, and I hope I never get one of those migraines again.

It's very hot today, which is why we decided to come over to the brook so we can paddle in the water to cool down our feet. I thought Gary and his friends might be here with their fishing nets and jam jars trying to find sticklebacks, but they must have gone over Hanham. There are some other boys here though, who are about the same age as us and who live along Champion Road. We've seen them lots of times before, mainly in the park around the corner, and they're all right, I suppose. One of them's called Bruce and he's probably the best, apart from his great big ears; the other two are twins called Anthony and Alan. They're sitting a bit further along the bank, closer to the bridge, where they've left their bikes propped against the wall, and they keep shouting things out to us like 'Got any sweets?' or 'Want to come over here?'

None of us has answered yet. We just giggle and pretend to ignore them, even though we all want to go really.

'I dare you to go first,' Diane whispers to me.

'Why don't you?' I cry, giving her a push.

'You go,' she says to Carol.

'Get lost, you're the one who wants to.'

'I'm not going on my own.'

One of the boys shouts out, 'Anyone fancy a snog?'

We all gasp, then burst into giggles. The boys are grinning, and slapping each other on the back, obviously very pleased with themselves.

'I've never snogged anyone, have you?' Diane whispers.

Carol shakes her head.

They look at me.

I flick back one of my bunches and say, 'Quite a few times, actually.' I suddenly think of Robert and the fact that I'll never really kiss him now, and my heart gives such a horrible twist that I nearly start to cry.

'Who?' Carol demands.

'No one you know,' I answer shortly. I'm not going to tell them about Robert. It's none of their business anyway. 'He comes into the back lane at school sometimes,' I tell them. 'I meet him there.'

Their eyes grow wider still. 'What's his name?' Diane asks.

'His real name's Steven, but everyone calls him Slash.'

Diane and Carol look at one another, then at me. 'What's it like?' Carol wants to know.

I'm starting to wish they'd shut up, but I don't want to argue with them, so I say, 'Really lush.'

'Come on!' Bruce shouts. 'Or are you too scared?'

'They're just babies,' Alan jeers. 'Let's go and find someone else.'

'It's you who's a baby,' Diane tells him. 'I bet your mum still tucks you in at night.'

We all laugh. 'Diddums,' Carol says. 'Little baby Alan.'

I can see he's getting angry, but then Bruce says, 'If they were so grown up they wouldn't be afraid to come over here, so just ignore them, Al. They're only kids.'

'Look who's calling who a kid,' I sneer. 'I bet you're not even twelve yet.'

'That's just where you're wrong, because I'll be thirteen next month.'

'So what? It still doesn't make you a grown-up. I know boys who are much more mature than you.'

'Yeah, I bet, locked away in that posh school for stuck-up girls.'

'She meets boys in the back lane,' Diane informs him snootily, '*and* she's started her periods, which makes her much more mature than you.'

I pull myself upright, wishing I'd thought of that blinder myself.

The boys are looking puzzled.

'What is it?' we hear one of them whisper. They go into a huddle, and when they come out again Bruce's grin seems

king tights into the bag with my new dress. I
ed while I was doing it that I was shaking like
r ages after I kept expecting a policeman to
d arrest me. Luckily he didn't, and I didn't end
guilty for long. Why should I when I'm always
e to suffer for things I didn't do? Now I've
ne something bad, at least I'll deserve it if any-
wrong. Anyway, it's better than having to ask
ance for the money, because she'd only start on
bosoms getting big again and I'd end up wanting
again.

am I going to do if God punishes me by killing
elt so frightened when I thought that that I really
ave gone back to the shop if it hadn't been closing
ft.

I got home I went straight upstairs to my room to
my dress and new smalls. The brassieres are still a bit
ut at least they're better than my old ones. What I
want is to be like everyone else and go without a
re – or bra, as everyone calls them now – but I feel all
nscious when my bosoms bounce as I walk, and
than that, it makes me feel a bit sick to think of Dad
able to tell.

tights are massive, so I have to roll them over and
at the top and even then they still bag round my
es, so I'm having to wear a suspender belt to help keep
up anyway, which is very annoying.

till, my dress is fabsville, and miracle of all miracles,
hasn't tried to make me take down the hem.

I don't think it's right for a girl your age to show her
ees,' he told me, 'but as long as it's no higher than that,
u'll do.'

I chucked my arms round him and gave him a great big
iss, then realising my dress was riding up my legs I quickly
ot off his lap and pulled it down again.

I'm wearing it now as I bump about the dodgems with
Mandy, who I waited for down by the garages. When I saw

to be hooked on to each of his great big ears. 'We don't believe you,' he says.

'It's true!' I shout.

'Liar. You've got to be fourteen or fifteen before you have them.'

'No you haven't, and I can prove it.'

His grin gets even wider. 'Go on then,' he says.

They all fall about laughing and I want to hit them.

'See, you can't, because you're lying,' Anthony jeers.

'I am *not*.'

'Then show us.'

So I tug down the waistband of my shorts, hike up my sanitary belt and the top of the pad and let them see it.

They all hoot with laughter, then suddenly they're jumping on their bikes and pedalling away like the wind.

Diane and Carol are looking a bit stunned.

I wish I hadn't done it then, but it's too late to take it back, and I'm afraid they're going to tell everyone, and if Dad ever finds out . . . Why does everything always keep going wrong? I don't want to be here any more, I want to go home, so I climb the bank and step out onto the pavement.

'They're really stupid,' Diane says, coming after me. 'You shouldn't let them upset you.'

'I'm not.'

'It was a good job you shut them up,' Carol says, 'they were really getting on my nerves.'

'Ssh, quick, look who's coming,' Diane suddenly hisses, putting her head down and stamping her feet in excitement.

Carol and I both spin round. I'm half expecting it to be Dad on the warpath, but it's not. It's three really dishy-looking chaps, much older than us, all wearing jeans and denim jackets. They're on the other side of the road, but walking towards us with their thumbs hooked into their belt loops and swaggering like pop stars.

'Who are they?' I whisper, unable to take my eyes off the tallest one.

'The two on the outside are Lizzie Sawyer's brothers,'

Diane answers, 'and the other one lives up Pound Road. His brother's usually with them. They go round in a foursome. Oh, there he is behind, *with a girl.*'

My heart gives a jolt when I see who it is.

'Isn't that Mandy Hughes?' Carol says.

'She always gets all the boys,' Diane murmurs.

Someone wolf-whistles and I realise it was one of the chaps, and the tallest is laughing and looking straight at me. He gives me a wink, and I feel myself turn as hot as the sun.

'Hello, Sue,' Mandy calls out as she passes us with her boyfriend.

Glowing with pride, I say, 'Hello, Mand.' *Fancy calling her Mand, as if she's my best friend.*

'You don't know her, do you?' Diane whispers, sounding impressed, and shocked.

'Course,' I reply.

Diane and Carol look at one another, but I'm too busy watching the chap in front to notice what kind of faces they're pulling.

He winked at me. I want to jump up and down, or swoon, or spin round and round, because he's the best-looking chap I've ever seen in my life and *he noticed me.*

We didn't go to Bowleaze Cove in the end. Dad was too worried about the car letting us down, so we stayed at home. I'm in my bedroom now, writing Kev Sawyer's name in kisses all over my diary and drawing love hearts around our initials.

I found out his name from his sister, Lizzie, who I went to infants school with ages ago. I saw her outside Tanners, the shop where we go if we need anything on Sundays. Dad had sent me round to get the Bisto he'd forgotten up Fine Fare yesterday, and when I saw Lizzie was there with her mum who was gossiping with Mrs Tanner, I was able to ask how she was, and what her brothers' names were.

'Why do you want to know?' she snapped nastily.

I leaned in to whisper. 'Don't tell anyone,' I said, 'but one

of my friends is really m
the oldest, anyway. He'
find out what he's called.

'Well, if you must know,
other one's called Rich, bu
they won't be interested in y

I blushed really hard. 'It
reminded her. 'I couldn't care
what their names are. I'm just t

'What's her name?'

'I'm not telling, or you'll tell y

Lizzie shrugged, and change
like up that school you go to?'

'Vile. I hate it, but I'm probably
soon. I'll be going to the same scho

I was thinking about making he
now I've decided not to. She's no
actually, she doesn't smell all that ni

I'm twelve now. It was my birth
Auntie Nance baked a cake and af
Kingswood so I could spend some of m
found this really sexy dress in Harris's,
old-fashioned shop full of hats for wedd
to my surprise the woman behind the cou
just the thing for you.'

It's black and white with a round neck
and, best of all, it's about two inches above
sure Auntie Nance was going to tell the lady
again, but she didn't, so I tried it on, and bec
so fab Auntie Nance said I could have it.
pounds fifteen and six, which didn't leave me
from my fiver, but I had to have it, so I didn'
much it cost. The trouble was, I needed to get
brassieres and a pair of stocking tights, but if I bo
I wouldn't have enough left to go up the shows.

So, I waited until Auntie Nance and I were in Jo
when she wasn't looking I slipped two brassieres

her coming I asked if she was going up the shows and she said yes, so we came here together. We're both showing loads of leg, and giggling like mad at the boys who keep wolf-whistling and staring. I hope we don't bump into anyone I know or they might tell Dad who I'm with, then there'll be hell to pay and I won't be allowed to come again.

All the boys who hang around the Anchor and Made for Ever club are up the shows tonight, strutting about like they own the place, but not one of them is anywhere near as dishy as Kev. I've told Mandy that I like him, so she's going to try and help me get off with him. I feel really sick and excited when I think about that, and a bit worried in case Robert minds.

'Do you think he'll be bothered about my age?' I asked while we were walking here.

'He won't know unless we tell him,' she replied.

'Let's say I'm fourteen, shall we?'

'Definitely. It's how old you look, so he's bound to believe it.'

I have a feeling she's going to be the best friend I've ever had.

Apparently she's been going out with Kev's brother, Rich, for about a month, on and off. She's been out with Larry and Clive Frost as well, Kev and Rich's friends, but that was ages ago. She's never been out with Kev, she told me, and as far as she knows he doesn't have a steady girlfriend at the moment, so his sister was lying.

I thought as much at the time, and now I feel so excited that I could whirl round and round the big wheel and fly off like a firework, fizzing and sparkling and going off with a bang.

'Do you think they'll come?' I say as we join the queue for the octopus.

'When I saw Rich earlier he said they would,' she answers. 'If they don't it'll be because they've gone to the other shows over at Rodway.'

This flattens me. 'Do you think we should go over there to have a look?' I suggest.

'Don't be mad. It's miles to walk, and it's starting to get dark.'

'I thought you weren't scared of being out in the dark.'

'I'm not, but even if they're over there, they'll have gone by the time we turn up, so it's not worth it. If we don't see them tonight, there's always tomorrow.'

Twirling and swooping about on the octopus cheers me up a bit, and winning a goldfish on the firing range makes me shriek with triumph and shock. I've never hit a target before. Dad's always the one who wins up the shows.

I'm beaming as the bloke on the stall hands me the goldfish, which is swimming about in a little plastic bag with strings so I can carry him home.

'Don't look now, but guess who's just turned up,' Mandy mutters in my ear.

My heart does a giant somersault and I don't dare to turn round. 'Is it him?' I gasp, feeling as though the ground has turned into one of the fairground rides. What if he sees me and thinks, *that's the girl I winked at the other day. I've been wondering who she is. She looks really fab in that dress.*

'It's all of them,' Mandy tells me. 'They've gone to stand next to the waltzer, so do you want to get on?'

I dare to look round, and my heart does another giant leap as I spot him, going to lean against the rails of the waltzer, where all the cool boys stand to watch the girls on the ride. His hair's long and really dark, and he's got one hand stuffed in his jeans pocket, while he holds a cigarette in the other.

I glance down at my goldfish and wonder what to do with it. I can't give it back because I want to show Dad and Gary that I won it, but I can't take it on the waltzer either.

Realising my dilemma, Mandy takes the goldfish and hands it back to the bloke on the stall. 'Can you look after it til we come back?' she asks. 'We won't be long.'

He rolls his eyes, but takes it anyway, and we set off towards the waltzer. 'Are you going to speak to them?' I ask, feeling all fluttery and nervous as we reach the steps.

'Depends,' she replies. 'Look, it's slowing down. If we're quick we can get straight on.'

I'm certain Kev's watching me as I wait for a car to empty, and when I slide into one corner I cross my fingers, hoping he might get on with me. That's what happens sometimes: if a boy fancies a girl, he gets into the car with her, but our car ends up full of girls, worse luck.

The first couple of swoops round I can see Kev standing with his mates, still smoking, and listening to Gary Puckett and the Union Gap singing 'Young Girl', but I can't tell if he's watching me or not. I feel the words of the song rushing through me as we start to gather speed, and I can imagine Kev thinking them about me. He'll be thinking that his love is wrong, so I ought to go, because I'm too young for him, but really he wants me to stay. It makes me feel exhilarated and sexy and on top of the world.

He must be watching me. I know he is. My head's back and I'm laughing and screaming along with the others. My legs are showing. I'm really glad I took my socks off before we got here. I've hidden them behind a stone to pick up on the way home.

It seems ages before the waltzer starts to slow. By then the music's changed to the Equals singing 'Baby Come Back'. I love this song, too. Doreen gave it to me for my birthday, so I know all the words. I can't sing though, I'm too dizzy. I can hardly see.

I stagger into Mandy as we step off the platform and we shriek with laughter. I steal a quick look over my shoulder and my heart sinks right through the floor. Kev's gone.

I look at Mandy in panic. 'Where are they?' I ask.

'I don't know. Probably by the dodgems, or somewhere?'

We hurry over to check, but they aren't there. They're not by the octopus either, or the chairoplanes, or the big wheel.

Eventually we spot them buying hot dogs from one of the vans, which is what everyone does when they're about to walk home.

'They're leaving,' I choke.

'They might go and sit on the grass,' Mandy says. 'Pretend we haven't seen them, OK? We'll go and get a hot dog too, and follow them out.'

I don't have any money left, but I'm not hungry anyway. My stomach's too tied up in knots. 'I have to get my goldfish,' I remind her, and while she joins the queue at the hot dog stall I whizz back to the rifle range. Thankfully the bloke remembers me and within seconds I'm back at Mandy's side.

'Did you see where they went?' I ask, looking around.

'Between the caravans over there,' she replies, 'which means they're probably going to sit on the grass.'

'So shall we do the same?'

She nods. 'But not too close or they'll think we're after them.'

After she's bought herself a bag of chips we wander out of the throng of the fair into the quiet of the summer's night where the common is turning pink in the sunset, and, in the distance below, street lights are starting to come on.

'There they are,' Mandy whispers.

I follow where she's looking and spot them slouching on the grass about fifty yards away. At first I think some girls are with them, but then I realise the girls are part of another group a little way past. Something's going on between the two groups though, because we can hear them all shouting and laughing. I'm terrified Kev might get off with one of them, and feel I should get over there as quickly as I can to stop it happening.

'Let's sit here,' Mandy says, as we reach a clump of bushes where the grass starts to dip.

I wonder why we can't just go and join them, as she knows them, but I can tell she doesn't want to, so I sink down next to her with my goldfish and hold him up to watch him swimming round the bag.

'I think I'll call him Kev,' I say.

She chokes on a chip as she laughs. 'You're really mad about him, aren't you?'

I nod glumly and happily.

'You know he's eighteen, don't you?'

I didn't, but I remind her that we're going to say I'm fourteen, which should make the age gap all right.

'I'll tell you what, when I've finished my chips, I'll go over and ask if he wants to get off with you, shall I?'

My mouth turns dry. 'What if he says no?'

'Don't worry about it. He won't.'

I don't know how she can be sure, but I don't question her, because she should know.

We sit quietly for a while, staring down at the lights of New Cheltenham while she finishes her chips. I try to spot where our house is, and wonder what Dad would say if he could see me now. Relieved that he can't, I put him out of my mind and try to stop myself looking over at Kev. Does he know I'm here? Is he wondering if we're going to go over? Perhaps he's thinking about coming over here.

He probably can't remember who I am. I expect he winks at all the girls, and everyone falls for him on sight, so I'm nothing special. I'm just a stupid fat twelve-year-old with spots and ginger hair. No one's ever going to like me, especially not someone like him.

Mandy screws up her chip bag and tosses it into a bush. Then, taking out a packet of No. 6, she lights one up. 'Do you smoke?' she asks, offering me one.

I look at it, but before I can answer she says, 'If this is your first don't have it now, because you don't want to cough your guts up in front of them.'

Agreeing, I watch her put the packet away and get to her feet. 'Wait here,' she tells me. 'I won't be long.'

'What are you going to say?' I ask, looking up at her. I feel so sick with nerves now that I don't want her to go.

'Just leave it to me,' and with a wink she starts off across the grass.

I stay where I am, stiff with fear. I look at my goldfish and hold it a little higher so they can see I've won it. I'm not sure if that'll help, and suddenly afraid it might make me look stupid, I put it down again.

A long time seems to pass. I daren't look over, I'm too embarrassed. I try to imagine what they're saying, but I can't think of a thing. He won't be interested, anyway. He's bound to have all the girls after him, so why would he want me? I wonder if I should have told Mandy to let him know I've started my periods. That would make me seem more grown up. It's not fair that I'm still only twelve when I feel – and look – so much older. My bosoms are bigger than anyone else's I know, and I'm growing hair under my arms now, and in other places. I reach a hand behind my head to show my armpit, in case he's looking my way. There aren't many hairs and they're fair, but if he can see them at least it'll prove I'm not a kid.

Eventually, when it's almost dark, Mandy comes back. 'Come on,' she says. 'Let's go home.'

Misery engulfs me. I struggle to my feet, still holding on to the fish. 'What did he say?' I ask.

'He wants you to come back when you're older,' she replies, and hooking an arm through mine she starts to walk us down over the common.

'So he didn't say an outright no?'

'Not exactly. He's never heard of you, he can't even remember seeing you before, but he asked if you know how to snog. I said yes, you've done it loads of times.'

I swallow hard. 'Are you going to see Rich?' I ask.

'He said I should be by the Anchor tomorrow, and we'll probably come up the common together.'

'You mean to the shows?'

She gives me a look that I don't quite understand.

Chapter Twelve

Eddie

I've been having a dreadful struggle with my faith, though the talks I've had with Canon Radford lately have gone a way towards helping. Losing our Robert came as such a terrible blow to us all. I just couldn't make any sense of it, and I'm still not sure I can now. Or that I ever will. I know our Doreen and Alf won't be able to, and I can't help wondering how I'd be if I was in their shoes and Gary was taken in his prime. It hardly bears thinking about, which is why I try to project my mind out to the wider world, and the problems that should make my own seem very minor by comparison.

I often ask myself how we would all feel, here in England, if we were starving to death like the poor souls in Africa and South America. Or if we had riots on our doorsteps like they're having in Los Angeles; or earthquakes like the one that's just devastated thousands of homes and families in Iran. That's not to say we don't have problems here, because of course we do, just not on that sort of scale. What's making headlines in our papers today is the number of Tories joining the National Front, and that maniac Enoch Powell who's stirring up hatred for the blacks. As if they don't suffer enough of it already, poor blighters. And then there's the trouble brewing up in Ireland . . . How do any of them manage to sleep peacefully in their beds at night, I'd like to know, and I strongly suspect they don't.

It's no wonder I sit down and write as often as I can, when

the very act of it calms and nourishes me like nothing else. As the words stream from my mind they settle on the page like the gentle notes of a musical score and I feel myself floating along in the melody, leaving all the angst and strife of my insignificant little life behind.

I'm in a tea shop at the moment, on a Saturday afternoon, with a cup of Nescaff next to my notepad and a chocolate biscuit in a saucer. A well-dressed lady is smoking at the next table to me. I see what people mean by having plenty of money; if you do you can eat anywhere, or drink and mix with just whoever you fancy. Our Susan could be like that one day.

I make a quick note to myself: *Must work on my conscience as there are so many conscientious people about.*

I'm hoping it might be easier to get our Susan back to school at the start of her second year, but sadly I can't say I'm seeing any signs of it yet. If anything, being home for the summer seems to have settled her back in with us in a way that I fear means trouble when it's time for her to go. Already I only have to mention that she should think about sewing name tags into her new smalls, and she says she'd rather kill herself than do anything about going back there.

What do I do with her? I only wish I knew. She seems to have it stuck in her head that she's at Red Maids as some kind of punishment, or to push her out of our family, and I can't make her see it any other way. What's worse, and tugs at my heartstrings mercilessly, is how we don't seem as close lately as we used to be. I suppose that's only to be expected now she's growing up, but the occasions when we have a bit of a laugh and a great big hug are becoming fewer and fewer. She doesn't want bedtime stories any more (though I know she's listening when I read to Gary), and she's started refusing to walk on the same side of the street as me.

'You're embarrassing,' she tells me. 'I don't want people seeing me with you.'

I know a lot of parents have to go through this, but

amusing as it can be, I'm afraid that this newfound self-consciousness has more to do with the crush she's developed on one of the Sawyer boys who live up around the corner than with her age. It's when we walk past their house that she doesn't want to be seen with me. I haven't spoken to her about it yet, but whichever one of them she's keen on hardly matters, because they're both far too old for her, and I can only hope that they know it, because it turns my blood cold merely to think of their sort leading her astray.

Twelve she might be, but there are times, when I look at her, that I see her mother at eighteen. The transition's happening so fast I can hardly keep up with it. I tell myself that her body's stealing a march on her and she doesn't have any idea yet of how grown-up she looks, but I'm not always so sure of it, because half the time her attitude, and even her behaviour, belongs to a girl twice her age. But then there are other times, when she doesn't know I'm watching, that I see the child she still is, vulnerable and innocent, and still very much in need of her old dad. She seems lonely too, which catches at my heart, though I'm not sure why I think that when she's out so much of the time. She's obviously got some friends somewhere, I just wish I knew who they were.

I've thought about following her to find out where she goes, but if she were to spot me, I dread to think how she'd react. Luckily she'll soon be out of harm's way, so rather than cause any more friction now, I've decided to let things be and hope that being back amongst the Red Maids will help return her to the straight and narrow.

The trouble is, I'm not sure how straight and narrow things are going up there with all the detentions she keeps getting. Dear oh dear, what a worry she is. I've heard people say that girls are the hardest and I'm not having a problem believing it. She needs Eddress more now than ever, but there's not a lot of point in thinking that way when that's all it'll ever be, a thought, a wish that can never come true.

'How have they been today?' I ask Florrie when I go to pick them up after work one night.

'To tell the truth, I haven't seen much of them,' she answers. 'Gary's been in and out, the way he usually is, but Susan's been over that park all day again, hanging about with all and sundry, not even coming back for her dinner.'

'She hasn't eaten all day?'

'Oh, she has now. Wolfed down two Marmite sandwiches and a bag of potato puffs the minute she came in the door, about half an hour ago. Smelling like a bloody tart's boudoir she was too, so she must have been next door raiding our Kay and Wendy's bedrooms again. They'll be after her when they find out. And have you seen what she's done to her arm? She's only gone and scratched some boy's name on it. *Kev*, it says.'

I feel myself starting to tense. 'It's the name of one of the Sawyer boys,' I tell her.

'You mean the family that lives up around the corner from you? They're no good, Ed. You ought to keep her away from them.'

'Believe me, I'm trying, but she seems smitten with him at the moment, his name's all over every book she owns, and now you say she's scratched it into her arm. What am I going to do with her?'

Florrie gives a troubled sigh. 'She's as headstrong as her mother, I know that much, and woe betide us all if we don't let her have her own way.'

'Woe betide us if we do,' I correct.

Florrie doesn't argue with that, only sits with the worry of it all, wondering, like me, what's best to be done.

'Where is she now?' I ask.

'She went next door with our Gary about ten minutes ago. Are you going to stay for a bit of tea? I've got some nice pork chops our Arthur brought in earlier. We can have them with some mash and runner beans.'

Arthur's one of her sons who works part-time at a butcher's shop in Staple Hill. 'Those chops are for you,' I tell her. 'I expect he'll be wanting one too. How's he getting on with his young lady?'

Florrie rolls her eyes. 'She's a queer little thing, if you ask me,' she tuts. 'What she sees in an old goat like him God only knows, when he's old enough to be her blooming father. And if she thinks he's got any loot stashed away, she needs to think again, because he's poorer than a church mouse, and twice as dim.'

'Oh, he's not that bad,' I say loyally, though I have to admit it's not far off the truth, because Arthur's never been the brightest of Eddress's brothers, and it's a bit of a mystery to me too, why someone as young as Cherie Amos is going after him. 'They say she was down Barrow Gurney for a while,' Florrie tells me (she means the mental hospital the other side of Bristol), 'and I can believe it, because she behaves like someone out of the loony bin, with all her dancing in the middle of the garden and lighting candles round the toilet at night. What on earth do she want to go and do something like that for? She's touched up here, that's what she is.' She taps her head, sighing.

Actually, I think Cherie's more of a hippy than a halfwit, but if she's taking drugs, which is what it sounds like, I suppose that could be one and the same thing. She's someone else I was afraid would have a bad influence on our Susan when she first turned up, but luckily that doesn't seem to be happening. In fact, I wouldn't mind too much if she were to take our Susan shopping with her, because I'd much rather see my girl in long dresses and flowery headbands than all these flipping miniskirts that seem to be getting shorter by the day, and the new-fashion hipster trousers that are coming in now. I hardly know where to look when I'm walking along the street these days with all that bare flesh on show – it makes me feel like a peeping Tom when all I'm trying to do is mind my own business.

Anyway, I suppose I'd better go and turf them out of next door, then decide whether or not to tackle my girl about where she's been all day. If I do, it'll be bound to lead to a row, followed by tears and more tantrums, storming up the stairs, doors slamming, and more yelling from inside her room. We could all do without it, especially our Gary who hates it when she flies off the handle and starts lashing out at us. What a temper she's developing, and Florrie's right about how headstrong she's becoming. A lot worse than her mother, I know that much. If I didn't have more sense I'd think a flipping devil was trying to take her over.

It's five o'clock on Sunday morning, and here we are, the three of us, rolling around my bed laughing our heads off like we don't have a care in the world. Gary's so beside himself I'm afraid he might choke, and Susan's holding her sides in pain she's laughing so hard.

'Ssh, ssh,' I warn, 'he's about to do it again.'

And right on cue the cockerel our dad dumped on us yesterday teatime, now shut up in the rabbit hutch under my window, goes, 'Cock-a-doodle-errrrr!' and off they go in fresh gales of uncontrollable mirth.

I told them just now that we knew the cock was Bristolian because of the errr, and I'm not sure whether it's the fact I said 'cock' that's making them laugh so much, or whether it's the bird's regional burr. Probably both, and I don't mind if they're laughing for the wrong reason, because after all the ups and downs we've been through lately it's lovely to be having these precious moments together, especially as it won't be long now before Susan has to leave.

Heaven only knows what the neighbours are thinking about the darned cockerel. Being woken up at this time on a Sunday morning won't be making them happy, of that I'm sure. I'll have some apologising to do later, and then I'll have to work out what to do with the blinking thing, because we won't be able to keep him. I wouldn't be a bit surprised if it's the reason our dad brought him here, because his own neighbours have been complaining, and who can blame them? Graham, Eddress's eldest brother who lives next door to Florrie and keeps chickens himself, would no doubt offer to come and wring its neck so we can have it for Sunday dinner, but I don't think even I could stomach that. And I definitely wouldn't want to be the one to tell the kids it was what they were eating.

After a while all the hilarity dies down, and we lie quietly together, getting our breath back and eventually starting to doze off again. I can't help thinking what a shame it is that I have to take Susan back tomorrow, but of course I'd never be foolish enough to tell her that. I'd never get her out of here if I did. The truth is though, we feel more like a proper family when she's around, in spite of all the tantrums and frustrations she throws in our faces. Still, Gary and I will soon get used to being without her again, even though we might not like it much, and God willing, she'll take a lot less time to settle into her second year at Red Maids than she did her first.

Susan

Dear Governors of Red Maids School,

I am a pupil in the second form and I am writing to tell you that my dad has made a terrible mistake in sending me here, and so I am asking if you will talk to him to make him see sense. He needs me to be at home taking care of him and my brother. I can go to the local comprehensive, called The Grange, or to Rodway Technical College, which is a very good school, just like Red Maids, but I wouldn't have to board.

I think it would be in everyone's best interests if I do go home to live, so I am depending on you to help me to put my family first.

Yours faithfully,

Susan Lewis, RM 74

I then add our address in Greenways so they'll know how to contact my dad, and after I've finished writing, I read the letter through, before showing it to Sadie.

'It's really good,' she tells me, 'especially the bit about putting your family first.'

I'm actually particularly proud of that, so I take the letter back and placing it into an envelope I write on the front, *Governors of Red Maids School, Bristol,* because we don't know their names or addresses. I'm hoping someone at the post office will, and after licking the shiny strip I seal the envelope up.

'There,' I say, once the stamp is on, 'my dad's going to have a real shock when one of them orders him to let me go home, and he won't be able to argue because they're much too important.'

Sadie's looking a bit worried. 'What are you going to do if they write back to you first?' she asks.

I frown as I think. 'I suppose it depends what they say, and actually, I hope they do, because then I'll be able to tell them exactly how vile it is here, and I think someone should, don't you?'

'Absolutely,' she agrees forcefully. 'And if they ask me, I'll say the same thing.'

'Good, so let's go and put it in the post basket ready to go tonight.'

As we walk down the back stairs together Laura suddenly comes rushing up the other way, followed by a couple of her friends. 'Ah, there you are,' she gasps, all out of breath. 'We've been looking everywhere for you. Apparently some coffee's gone missing from the kitchens and everyone's saying you took it. Seaweed's on the warpath. So's cook.'

Furious, I turn to Sadie. 'Bloody cheek assuming it's me,' I rage. 'What do I want with their fucking coffee?' I'm swearing all the time now, and I can tell the others are impressed by the way they keep copying me.

'Go and tell Seaweed,' Sadie says to Laura, 'that she can bloody search Su Lu's bloody cubicle and mine too, if she wants, so she can find out for herself that we fucking don't have her coffee.' Sadie's not all that good at swearing yet, but she's getting better all the time.

'Where are you going?' Laura asks, turning to follow us down the stairs.

'We're posting a letter,' I inform her, 'and then we're going to listen to some records before prep. You can come too, if you like.'

'Susan Lewis! Is that you I can hear?' Cluttie bellows down the stairs.

I look up through the stairwell. 'What do you want?' I say rudely.

'Report to Miss Sayward immediately,' she commands. 'She's waiting in her office.'

'Then she can carry on fucking waiting,' I mutter, and as the others giggle we continue down to the main hall.

The post basket is still there, so I drop my letter on top of everyone else's, then Sadie and I link arms and wander on through to the rec area to play jacks and dance to the music we bought during the summer hols.

I can hardly believe that only a week has gone by since Dad forced me to come back here. It feels like a year already, and I hate it so much I can hardly keep my temper any longer. It was bad enough before, but now I've met Kev, and Mandy has become my best friend (apart from Sadie who's my best friend here), I really, really, really can't stand it. What's making it even worse is that Paula Gates isn't here now. Of course, I knew she wouldn't be, because she left at the end of last term, but I didn't want to think about it when it was happening, so I pretended it wasn't. I thought if I did that, then something might happen over the summer to make her come back again. I can see that doesn't really make any sense, and anyway, I should have known better, because no one ever comes back.

It's a pity she's not here though, because I know she'd want to hear all about Kev, and how every time he sees me he always looks over, and sometimes gives me a wink. I'm so in love with him that I can't think about anything else. She'd be able to give me advice about how to get off with him because she's really experienced with men. Still, at least there's Sadie to talk to, who's a very good listener, and she understands how miserable I am about not being able to see

233

Kev. I've told her, and the others, that I'm actually going out with him, because I don't want them thinking that it's not serious, when it is. Or it will be just as soon as I manage to meet him properly – and that's not going to be possible *while I'm here*, is it?

After the night up the shows, when Mandy tried to get me off with him, she's tried lots of times since, but he keeps on saying I'm too young which is driving me mad.

'It's not that he doesn't fancy you,' Mandy insists, 'it's just your age that's a problem, because his sister's obviously told him how old you really are.'

That cow Lizzie, she should mind her own fucking business. Still, at least she's said I'm thirteen, instead of twelve, which goes to show how much she knows.

Almost every day during the holidays while Gary and I were up Gran's and Dad was at work, Mandy came to meet me in the park and we either went up Staple Hill or Kingswood to do some shoplifting; or down to Brains, the factory where Kevin and his mates work, to wait outside for them to come out. Sometimes Rich walked along with Mandy, and I'd have to follow behind, which made me feel a bit stupid, but I didn't want to be a gooseberry and walk with them, and nor did I have the guts to go and walk with Kev and his mates.

Sometimes I only just made it back to Gran's before Dad came home from work, and once he found all my knocked-off stuff hidden in one of Gran's bandage drawers. Luckily, I was quick enough to say that it belonged to Uncle Arthur's weirdo girlfriend, Cherie the loon, so he left it where it was, and I was able to smuggle it out to Mandy the next day so she could take it home to her house for me. There was loads of it, mascara, eyeshadows, pansticks, rouge, tights, a hairbrush, shampoo, soap, and a really fabsville miniskirt that I wore out of the shop under my own longer skirt.

It's fantastic when you get away with it. We run off screaming down the street and hide somewhere as soon as we can. Doing it is the most terrifying thing in the world though, in case we get caught. We haven't yet, but we did see someone who was. Lucky for them the manager of Woolworths didn't call the police, but he told the girls never to set foot in the shop again. We didn't go there ourselves for ages after, just in case, because I definitely don't want to swap one prison for another.

I know it's wrong to steal, and I do feel bad about it sometimes, but it's a really good way of getting the private things I need, like bras and tights and knickers without asking Dad. I know I take make-up too, but that's because it's easy to drop in my pockets, and anyway, I have to have some for when I go out. It's the smalls that are the most important though, because I can't stand Dad even to see my knicks and stuff when I hang them on the line to dry, never mind to think about me getting new ones. (Usually I peg them right down the bottom of the garden, out of view of the house, but then I end up forgetting them and the next thing I know he's brought them in and I want to curl up and die of embarrassment.)

Lucky Mandy, she's got a mum to do her washing and buy her Dr Whites, and so has Julie Archer who goes to Mandy's school and comes around with us sometimes. Julie's all right, but she can be quite bossy and if she doesn't get her way she usually goes off in a sulk, which is really childish, especially for someone who's nearly fifteen. She's got a great big crush on Larry Frost, one of the brothers who goes round with Kev and Rich, but he packed her up a few months ago and keeps saying he doesn't want to go out with her again. I feel sorry for her when she gets upset, because I know how I'd feel if Kev ever packed me up, but at least Larry sees her sometimes and takes her for walks up the common, which is more than Kev ever does with me.

I've heard other girls who hang around the Anchor and Made for Ever club calling Mandy horrible names, which I think is really mean when they don't actually know her. She's the kindest and friendliest person I've ever met, and if I was older, and tougher, I'd tell them all to shut their faces, because she's not a scrubber or a groupie. They're just jealous because Rich Sawyer likes her better than them, and I don't blame him, because she's much prettier and more intelligent than all those fat tarts put together. Actually, I suppose some of the older ones are OK, like Judith Prince and Christine Flowers who work up the corset factory in Kingswood, and Ruby Gosling whose dad owns the pub. (Mandy says that Kev's been out with Judith Prince and shagged her quite a lot of times, but he packed her up last June and now she's going out with Pete Newman who's got a scooter that he takes her up the common on.)

Because everyone's so horrid to Mandy she doesn't go down Made for Ever club very much, and I can't anyway, because you have to be fourteen to get in on Thursday nights, which is when everyone goes. Instead, we go to the bus shelter along Anchor Road, where we sit talking for hours and hours, hoping that Kev and the others might go past on their way up the Horseshoe. If they do, sometimes they stop to see if Mandy wants to go for a walk with Rich, and then they all go along too, leaving me behind to wait on my own for them to come back. Mandy's sure they'll ask me to go too one of these days, but it can't be until bloody half-term now, because the exeats are no good when I have to be back at fucking school by six.

I've written in my diary that I've been having lots of shags in case anyone reads it, because there are lots of snoops around the school. The real truth is I haven't even snogged anyone yet, but I'm dying to. I wish I'd snogged Robert, but it makes me feel really upset when I think that, so I have to stop myself and think about something else. That's how I got over Mum, by thinking of something else, though I still have times when I get very angry and frustrated inside about not being able to talk to her any more. It just doesn't seem fair, but nothing is, at least not for me, so why should I care?

Anyway, if I could, I'd practise snogging on Slash, or one of the other boys who come to the lane, so I'd be good at it by the time I snog Kev, but I don't want them telling Peg and the others that I'm rubbish at it, or they'll guess that I'm making things up about Kev.

Bloody hell, here comes Seaweed, foaming at the mouth and looking like she's just been chucked up on the shore by Neptune's dog.

'Susan Lewis, were you not told to report to my office?' she squawks.

'Yes, miss,' I answer, sounding bored.

'So what are you doing here?'

'Playing jacks with Sadie, miss.'

'Very clever. Cook wants to know what's happened to the large tin of coffee that's vanished from the kitchen, and I feel sure you can enlighten her.'

I glance up and treat her to one of my dirtiest looks. 'Why does it have to be me who's taken it?' I enquire. 'Did anyone see me? No, because I haven't even been in the kitchen.'

'Miss Clutterbuck is searching your cubicle as we speak,' Seaweed informs me, 'and if anything is found you'll be reporting to Miss Dakin, do you hear me?'

'Yes, miss, but I'm not worried, because nothing will be found, unless someone's planted it on me, and if they have, they'll be sorry.'

I'm aware of all the first-formers listening, who are already dead scared of me, and now they'll be scareder still.

'Miss Sayward,' someone calls, coming through the dining room into the back of the hall, 'Cook's looking for you. She's found the coffee. It got put into the wrong cupboard after the delivery.'

Seaweed's face goes purple and starts to twitch. 'I see,' she says, her mouth as tight as a duck's arse, as Granny would say. 'I'll come right away.'

As she follows Carol Beadle from fifth form back through the dining room, I say, 'Don't bother to apologise. I don't mind being called a thief, thank you very much.'

She either doesn't hear, or pretends not to, because she keeps on going, and I don't much care, because someone's just put 'Young Girl' on the record player, and I get so full up with longing for Kev that I can't think about anything else. I'm going to write him another letter later that Mandy's promised to pass on, just in case his mother, or that smelly little sister of his, stole the first one I sent.

After the record's over I feel restless and stroppy. I want to get out of here so much that I could scream and scream. Maybe I should, they might let me out if they think I'm going mad. I start sifting through the records, trying to sort out which ones are mine. Someone's put 'Mony Mony' on now, which reminds me of the shows, and I feel as though I'm going to burst with frustration. I start to dance with Sadie, but I'm too angry to keep going, so I storm off to the bogs to be on my own. I can't stop thinking about Kev and feeling terrified that he might be getting off with another girl. I wish I could run across the grounds, out of the gates and all the way home to Kingswood. I need to do something, anything, or I'll go off my head.

Returning to the rec area I say to Sadie, 'Come on, let's go and blow up bloody first form. I caught one of them looking at me just now, and it's not allowed.'

Sometimes I feel sorry for the first years and how mean I am to them, but then I think about how horrible it was for me when I first started, and if I had to go through it, why shouldn't they?

Eddie

Another exeat comes and goes with our Susan remaining at school in detention. As usual I go to see her for an hour after church, but to tell the truth, she doesn't seem very interested in seeing me. She's always keen to walk back with Sadie who's generally in detention with her, linking her arm and whispering the whole way to make sure I can't hear what they're saying. Under any other circumstances I'd be heartened to know that she's made such a good friend of a Red Maid, but considering how often they're in trouble I can only carry on worrying about where it's all going to end. With Sadie being a year older I feel inclined to say she's leading our Susan astray, but I very much fear it's the other way round.

Headstrong's no longer the word to describe my daughter, because from what I've been hearing from Miss Sayward, she's downright defiant, disruptive and offensive. She doesn't seem to care about anything any more, neither her lessons, nor her behaviour, not even me or Gary. She's even stopped begging me to let her come home to live with us, which, not so long ago, would have allowed me to hope that she was finally starting to settle down. Now, it's making me more anxious than ever, but for reasons that I haven't yet been able to put into words.

Miss Sayward wants me to talk to Susan, so I tried last Sunday, but to no avail. She was too distracted to listen, and for the few minutes she did she looked at me as though she was tired of the sight of me.

'Do you have to go on and on and on?' she sighed. 'I only see you for an hour on a Sunday, and here you are, picking on me already, accusing me of being hostile and uncommunicative, when it's you who put me here, so if you don't like the way I'm turning out, you've only got yourself to blame.'

She's got an answer for everything, and an attitude that's as unpleasant as it's annoying. Sometimes I find myself wanting to slap her, and I will if she keeps it up. She might be twelve, but that doesn't make her too old for a damned good hiding, and our Nance, and her gran, think it'd do her the world of good. I'm inclined to agree, but showing her up in front of her friends at school won't get us anywhere, and as she's never at home these days, it'll have to wait till she is.

With all my heart I want everything to be right for her, which is why I'm writing to her now, in the hope that reading what I have to say might have more of an impact on her than hearing it, and indeed than a good hiding.

To give myself guidance I start by writing down a list of words as they come to my mind so that I can sew them in as I go. Goodness. Obedience. Kindness. Respect. Understanding. Tolerance.

My dear Susan, I'm sorry we had a bit of a falling-out when I was at the church last Sunday. You're right, I shouldn't pick on you when the time we have together is so short, so I will try not to do it again. I would like to explain though, how important it is for you to understand the value of obedience and kindness, not only towards me, but to all your elders, whether they be staff at the school, old people like Gran, our neighbours here in Greenways, or strangers you come across in the street. These are qualities that will stand you in very good stead for the future, my love, and will help you a great deal now.

I know you don't think so, but your teachers at Red Maids are full of goodness. They have a tolerance that is most admirable when dealing with so many girls at once. It would make me very happy if you would respect them, Susan, because they have your best interests at heart and can do more to help you achieve your goals in life than I will ever be able to.

Perhaps, when you come home at half-term, we can have a longer chat about all this, and I'll be happy to help you with your schoolwork, the way I did last year.

I won't mention how her marks have gone down since the beginning of this term, she knows, so I don't need to rub it in. Nor will I mention Miss Sayward's suggestion, which has come from Miss Dakin, that Susan might benefit from some sessions with a psychiatrist. I'm too afraid of how she might take that, so it would be better to leave it until she's at home.

No one's asked me if I think it's a good idea. Florrie reckons it'll end up disrupting her even more, having some stranger probing about in her head, asking all sorts of questions she won't want to answer, and she might have a point. If our Susan resents it, the way she is now she'll only take it out on everyone around her, and I certainly don't want her picking on Gary any more than she already has.

However, something has to be done to get her back on the rails, and if our betters at the school think she needs to see a psychiatrist I mustn't allow myself to dismiss it without at least giving it some consideration.

A psychiatrist, for heaven's sake. What on earth would Eddress say? I know what I say – she'd be a different girl now if her mother was here. I'm a failure as a father, useless, no good to her at all.

Chapter Thirteen

Susan

It's the night before half-term and I'm so excited, and nervous, that I don't know what to do with myself. Kev's only agreed to see me next week! Or that's what Mandy said when she came up to school last Friday, and I don't see why she'd be lying.

She met Sadie and me in the back lane during the hour before tea and prep. That's the really fabsville thing about her life, she can knock off school whenever she likes, while it's impossible for us to, stuck here round the clock. Slash and the other boys were there too, but Mandy, Sadie and I didn't take any notice of them. They're too juvenile, especially compared to Kev and his mates. Let Peg and her friends have the *boys*; Mandy, Sadie and I are much more interested in chaps who wear jeans and denim jackets and shave every morning while having a smoke, instead of those with spots, braces and bumfluff chins.

Oh, that reminds me. I smoke now. I decided to take it up when the school governors never bothered to write to me or Dad. It made me realise that I have no choice but to take matters into my own hands – if I want to get out of here then the only way of doing it is to *get expelled*. I'm serious about it now, no more messing about and saying wouldn't it be great to get chucked out, because it really would be. So, I'm going to make it happen and that's that.

Taking up smoking is part of my plan, though I have to admit I didn't like it all that much at first. Nor did Sadie, but we're getting used to it now and don't choke quite so much. We still haven't inhaled properly yet, we keep heaving and spluttering every time we try, but Janet Crawley-Phipps and Lisa Dunlop, the older girls who are teaching us behind the stable block before prep, keep insisting it gets easier in time.

Isabelle, the day girl, still brings the cigarettes from my Auntie Phil, and Auntie Phil still thinks they're for the older girls, but not all of them are any more, because some are for us. We've only bought one packet of No. 6 so far, because that's all we've been able to afford, but we should have more pocket money by the time we come back after the break, so we might even splash out on some Embassy which is what Mum used to smoke. (Dad would go completely berserk if he knew because he hates smoking, but I'm sorry, if he won't do as I ask and get me out of here, then he'll have to find out that this is what happens.)

It's *Top of the Pops* tonight, so, as usual, we're allowed to stay up until the programme's finished. We all give a groan at the end when it turns out that Mary Hopkin is at number one with 'Those Were the Days', because it's really soppy and square and useless to dance to. It'll be all the mums and grannies who are buying it, who should have their own chart instead of messing up ours.

By the time we're ready for bed I'm getting so worked up about going home tomorrow that I don't want to sleep, so I suggest to Sadie that we play Johnny on the first form. Babies that they are, they get terrified every time we glide down the dorm under a sheet, clumping a broom handle on the floor to make the sound of Johnny's wooden leg, and putting on spindly, Seaweed-type voices to tell them they're all going to die.

Sadie's all for it, but we decide to blow them up first, so we turf them out of bed and start marching them up and down the dorm singing grace. It's hilarious when we make them dance a jig, you should see them hopping about like idiots, and after forcing them down on their hands and knees to crawl back to bed we dash out to the corridor to laugh our heads off. Serves them right. I had to do it, so why shouldn't they?

Next comes Johnny, but instead of using a sheet tonight, I climb on Sadie's shoulders and we wrap two capes around us, making us look like a giant. It's so funny that we end up collapsing on to Natasha Furloe's bed, which frightens her so much that she actually wets it.

What a weed!

After that I still can't sleep, so Sadie and I have the brilliant idea of spending the night in the loo. We take our counterpanes, blankets and pillows and wrap ourselves up either side of the toilet. Next thing we know bloody Cluttie's banging on the door, and we're sent down on the landing.

'What for?' I cry as she marches us off in a southerly direction.

'You know very well what for,' she replies.

'We're loo mates, so we have to sleep in the loo,' Sadie tells her.

'Try to grow up,' Cluttie snaps.

This really annoys me, so I say, 'Why don't you, you old bag?'

Cluttie stops in her tracks and turns me round to face her. 'What did you just call me?' she demands.

I tilt up my chin, and I'm about to repeat it when I wonder if they can keep me in detention for the entire half-term. Not wanting to risk it, I say, 'Nothing, miss. Sorry, miss.'

She eyes me nastily, then shoves me on down the stairs.

We have to hang around in the draughty, cobwebby dark for over half an hour, jumping out of our skin when the stupid grandfather clock chimes for no reason, and practically belting back up the stairs when we hear footsteps dragging across the staffroom. That place is definitely haunted, and I'm not surprised, given all the old witches that go in there every day.

I wish Sadie was coming home with me tomorrow, I'd love her to meet Kev, except I'm afraid he might fancy her more than me. Anyway, she has to go to Dover to stay with her parents, which is miles away, so we won't even be able to meet halfway. Still, they have a phone at her house, so I'll be able to ring her from the phone box at the bottom of Holly Hill if there's anything to tell her, which I've already promised to do.

At last Cluttie comes to send us back to the dorm, where we wait about half an hour before returning to the loo. We end up spending the whole night there without being disturbed again. So now we really and truly are loo mates, and will be for ever!

'You are not going out of this house wearing that!' Dad is shouting.

'Oh yes, I am,' I inform him.

'Get back up those stairs and put on some decent clothes now.'

'There's nothing wrong with these,' I scream. 'It's the fashion, in case you hadn't noticed.'

'I don't care what it is. It's disgusting. You're showing your legs right up to your backside, and I'm not having it. Where did you get that skirt?'

'It's none of your business.'

'Don't you dare take that attitude with me, young lady, or you'll be back in your room and you won't be coming out again tonight. Now, I want to know where it came from.'

I'm fuming mad. 'Sadie let me borrow it, OK? Her parents aren't square, like you. They understand about things like being mod, now let me go.'

'I've already told you, you aren't going anywhere in that. Now upstairs and change, and while you're at it you can take that muck off your face.'

'It's not muck!' I rage. 'And I'm wearing this whether you

245

like it or not, so get out of the way or I'm going to be late.'

'Stop shouting you two, I can't hear the telly.'

'Bog off,' I yell at Gary.

'Drop dead,' he yells back.

'I've had enough of this,' Dad growls. 'Up to your bedroom now and don't come out again until you're dressed decently and you're ready to apologise.'

'I am going out *now*,' I seethe.

He grabs hold of me and turns me to the stairs. 'Do as you're told this minute, or you'll get what for,' and he starts shoving me up the stairs, holding me so tight that I can't break free, even when I try to throw myself down.

'If you don't let me go out, you'll be sorry,' I warn. I'm sobbing with outrage and fury by now. My make-up's running and my tights are falling down. I'm supposed to be meeting Kev, so I have to go, but typical of my dad, he's spoiling everything. 'If you don't let me go, I'll burn the house down,' I scream at him.

'Get in there,' he roars, and shoving me into my bedroom he slams the door so hard it nearly breaks.

When I try to open it he's hanging on to the handle outside, so I start kicking and punching it and telling him how much I hate him. 'I'm going to be late now,' I sob, 'everyone'll go without me and it'll be all your fault.'

He doesn't answer.

I try the door again, but he's still there.

'Dad, please,' I beg. 'I'm sorry I shouted at you. I'll come home by nine, I promise.'

'You're not going anywhere,' he tells me.

I raise my fists and slam them into the door again. 'I hate you,' I scream. 'You spoil everything, you even killed my goldfish and now you're trying to kill me.' He did, he killed my goldfish. OK, maybe not intentionally, but when I got home yesterday Kev wasn't in his bowl any more, and Gary admitted they forgot to feed him. So he died and then they flushed him down the loo. So that's what my dad thinks of me and the prizes I win!

'Don't be ridiculous,' he snaps. 'Now get ready for bed, and once you've calmed down we're going to have a talk.'

I'm about to start shouting again when I realise I'm never going to get out of here in time if I wait for him to open the door. The only other way out is the window, so dashing across the room I push it open and climb up on to the window sill. It's nearly dark out by now, but I can see the grass below, and bloody fucking Gary is only out there picking up his toys. I thought he was watching telly!

'Psst!' I hiss down to him.

He looks round.

'Up here, stupid.'

He looks up and his mouth drops open. 'What are you doing?' he asks.

'What does it look like? I'm going to jump.' I'm not sure yet if I've got the guts to, but it would serve them both right if I do, after what they did to my fish. Anyway, Kev's waiting round by the Anchor, so I have to jump.

'You can't,' he says.

'Yes, I can, now stand there ready to catch me.'

'Get lost! You'll flatten me.'

'Don't be stupid. All you have to do is hold out your arms and I'll jump straight into them.'

'Dad!' he yells.

'*Shut up!*' I seethe.

'Dad!' he yells again. 'Our Susan's jumping out the window.'

My bedroom door bangs open, and Dad comes in so furiously that I nearly go over the edge.

'Oh dear God,' he cries, seeming not to know what to do. 'Get in here now!'

I inch carefully on to the outer sill. 'No! If you don't let me go out, I'm going to jump.'

He takes a step towards me, then backs off again. 'All right, all right,' he says. 'You do as you want, just come down from there.'

I'm about to answer when I suddenly realise that I'm in a

stronger position than I ever was downstairs. It doesn't take me long to work out what to say next. 'I'm not coming in until you promise to let me go out,' I tell him.

'I just said, you can do as you want.'

'Wearing this skirt?'

'If you have to.'

I look at him warily. He's giving in too easily. Then I get it. The minute I come down he'll tie me up, or lock me in a cupboard, or call the police or something equally drastic. 'You have to go outside,' I tell him. 'You and Gary have to go into the shed and stay there until I've gone.'

'Susan . . .'

'I'm not coming in until you do as I say.'

'You're being very childish.'

'All right then, I'll jump.'

For one horrible minute I think he's going to tell me to, but then he turns around and I hear him going downstairs.

I stay where I am, shivering in the cold and feeling cramp creeping up my legs, until finally he shouts out, 'Gary and I are in the shed.'

Quickly I spring back into my bedroom, snatch up my handbag and charge down the stairs so fast that I'm at the gate long before he can get to the front door. Then I'm dashing up the street, along the lane at the top and out into Holly Hill. I'm praying I won't bump into Kev and the others on their way to the Anchor, or they'll wonder why I'm running like a loony with make-up streaking down my face and my tights bagging like socks round my ankles.

Eddie

I had to let her go. If I hadn't she might have jumped and I just couldn't risk it. It could have killed her from that height, or she'd have broken her neck and ended up crippled for life.

I haven't got any idea where she is now, or when she'll be

back. I'd have tried to follow, but I probably wouldn't have caught up with her, and besides, it's too late to leave Gary on his own. There'll be merry hell to pay when she does finally show her face, I hope she realises that.

What a trollop she looked in that skirt and make-up.

I don't want to believe that was my girl.

What would her mother say?

Susan

I'm round the Anchor now, sitting on my own on the wall outside the car park. I'm not thinking about Dad and how angry he must be, or what he's going to say when I get in. I mean, I don't like upsetting him, because I love him really, but he shouldn't upset me, saying I look like a tart and trying to stop me from going out. I don't expect he loves me any more now. So what, he didn't anyway.

Everyone else is up by the pub, drinking pints and joking with each other. A couple of chaps pulled up on scooters just now, and Stella Phelps got on the back of one. I used to go to junior school with her sister, Linda, but I don't ever see Linda now. I'd love to have an older sister, especially one who went round on scooters.

It's horrible being the only girl. No one understands me.

Mandy's gone down Made for Ever club to see if Kev and his friends are there, while I wait here in case they turn up. They told her to be outside the Anchor at seven and she was, but it's nearly half past now, so it doesn't look as though they're coming. Unless they forgot and went down the club, in which case Mandy will probably come back with them.

I'm feeling really soft sitting here on my own. A couple of girls keep staring, and one of them gave me a filthy look just now, so I'm making sure I keep turned away. I don't want them coming over to beat me up, because they do that sometimes. They just pick on someone out of the blue, and start scrapping with them. I saw them do it to a girl from Cadbury Heath during the summer. She was walking along with her mates, then suddenly one of the girls from the Anchor, I think it might have been Stella, or Kathleen, started shouting out at her. She shouted back and next thing she was being kicked around the ground while her mates ran away.

I wish Mandy would hurry up. It's getting cold sitting here, and I'm right on the roundabout so everyone can see me as they go past in their cars. The headlights are flaring over me like torches as they go by. Someone slowed up just now, looked at me, then drove off again. I don't know what he wanted, but in case he had any funny ideas I slammed my eyes and turned my head away.

I hope it wasn't someone who knows Dad.

The number fourteen bus is across the road parked next to the stop. The driver and conductor are sitting on the wall having a chat and a fag. It makes me think of Uncle Bob, who used to drive the buses. I wonder if he's in heaven. He was so kind it's where he should be.

No it isn't.

He should be at home with Auntie Flo, Julie and Karen.

I can see Mandy coming up Fisher Road now. She's on her own and I feel so upset that I almost start to cry. Why isn't Kev with her? He must be around somewhere, so we have to find him.

'Where is he?' I ask as Mandy reaches me.

'Apparently, they've gone down Torquay for the week,' she replies.

I can't believe it. I want to scream at her that he can't have, or that she's a liar, but what I say is, 'I thought they were supposed to be meeting us tonight.'

'That's what they said, but Tony Skitting reckons they went down Torquay yesterday, and won't be back till Saturday.'

I really, really, *really* don't want it to be true. 'What are they doing down there?' I snap.

'They're on holiday, I suppose.'

'But it's winter.'

'Not yet, and sometimes people go on holiday after the summer. The caravans are cheaper and there aren't so many people jamming into the pubs.'

I'm imagining him down Torquay with loads of girls after him, and it's so horrible that I press my fists to my sides and clench my teeth to stop myself from crying. I took ages getting ready to come out, then I had that awful row with Dad, and now it's all gone wrong.

'Oi, Hughesie, what are you doing round here?' someone shouts from up by the pub. 'Why don't you get lost?'

'Come on,' Mandy says, 'let's go,' and linking arms we make ourselves scarce before anyone has a chance to come and smash our faces in.

We decide to walk up to the Horseshoe, where we bump into Julie who's been with Greg Bowen, she tells us. I don't know who he is, but apparently he's in the pub now with his mates. Julie can't go in because she's not old enough, so she's waiting outside for him to bring her a shandy and bag of crisps.

'He probably can't get to the bar,' she says. 'It's really crowded in there.'

'Let's go in the offy and get some limeade,' Mandy suggests. 'Have you got any money?'

I shake my head.

'Nor me. We'll just have to beg as people go in and out.'

There's no sign of anyone at the moment, so we sit with Julie on one of the benches, our hands stuffed in our pockets and our shoulders hunched against the cold. Mandy starts telling Julie about how we were supposed to meet Kev and Rich, but Julie doesn't seem very interested, so they talk about people from their school who I've never even heard of, never mind met. In the end I decide to go home.

'Don't worry,' Julie says as I get up. 'He'll be back next week.'

I don't bother to reply.

'You're not sulking are you?' she teases.

'No, I'm just bored. And it's all right for you, you're here all the time. I have to go back to that stupid school next week, so how am I going to see him then?'

'You should run away,' Julie tells me. 'I know I would.'

'You wouldn't catch me dead in a boarding school,' Mandy chimes in. 'It's bad enough going to the one we do.'

'When we bother to go,' Julie says and they burst out laughing.

I start to walk off, then suddenly turn back. 'Is it true Kev wanted to see me tonight?' I say to Mandy. 'Or were you making it up?'

'Cross my heart and hope to die,' she insists.

'You ought to go out with other chaps to make him jealous,' Julie advises. 'It always works.'

I don't want to go out with anyone else, but I can't help wondering if she's right. The trouble is, there isn't anyone else.

'If he thought you'd already had a shag I bet anything he'd be interested,' she adds.

I look away, not sure what to say.

'Will I see you tomorrow?' Mandy asks.

'I don't know. My dad's got a couple of days off work, so I might not be able to go out.'

She's never asked why Dad won't let me go round with her, she just seems to accept it, which makes me feel sorry for her in a way, because apart from Julie, no one's ever very nice to her, and it's not her fault that her front garden's always a tip and her family keeps getting into trouble with the law. Not that Dad's ever come right out and said that I mustn't have anything to do with her, it's Mum who used to say that, but I know Dad'll think the same, which is why I've never told him.

He's waiting when I get home, looking all angry and upset. I feel really guilty now, but before I can say sorry he starts on me.

'I'm disgusted with the way you behaved earlier,' he

shouts, 'you're a disgrace to yourself and a very bad example to your brother. Now where have you been?'

'Out!'

'I know that. Who were you with?'

'A friend.'

'Which friend?'

'No one you know.'

His eyes go all boggled. 'How can you be out with someone *I* don't know?'

'Because you don't know everyone.'

'I'll have less of that lip, thank you very much. Now I want to know who you were with and where you were.'

I drop my weight on to one leg and heave a sigh. 'I went for a walk with Diane Grant, OK? If you don't believe me, go and ask her.'

He doesn't believe me, I can tell, but all he says is, 'Then why did you say it was someone I don't know?'

I give a shrug.

'I want an answer.'

'Because I don't have to tell you everything all the time,' I shout.

He shakes his head. 'I don't know what to do with you,' he says. 'Look at the time. It's gone nine o'clock . . . '

'That's early! And I'm not at school, so why can't I stay out late?'

'Because you're twelve years old, it's dark out and you're dressed like a common tart. Now get off to bed this minute, and I don't want another peep out of you till morning. And don't forget to brush your teeth.'

'I'm not a child!' I seethe as I push past him. 'And I'm not going to bed yet. *The Champions* is on tonight and you said I could watch it.'

'That was before you ran out of here like a wild animal. You'll do as you're told now, and that's an end to it.'

I stomp up the stairs, not caring if I wake up Gary, but he's not asleep because I catch him peeping over the banister. He doesn't say anything as I slam into my room, but after a while I can hear him talking to Dad, so I put 'Silence is Golden' on my record player, to give them a hint to shut up.

After the record's finished Dad knocks on the door and asks if he can come in.

'No!' I shout.

He waits, then knocks again and cracks open the door.

I don't say anything, so he comes in and when he sees I'm in bed he comes to sit on the padded stool that matches my dressing table. 'I don't want us to fall out,' he says, 'but you know what you did tonight was wrong, don't you?'

I turn my head away.

'I was worried sick about where you were. If anything happened to you . . . '

'It won't! I'm old enough to take care of myself.'

He starts to smooth my hair, and I want to push his hand away, but I don't.

'Mrs Jewell is coming to get your breakfast in the morning,' he tells me.

I feel my mouth go tight. 'Why? I thought you were on holiday.'

'I am, but I've got to be up the doctor's by half past eight and I thought you'd rather have a lie-in than come with me.'

I'm feeling all stiff and angry now. 'What are you going up the doctor's for?' I demand. See, he's going to die, just like everyone else. I knew it. I want to die too. *Please let me die.*

'I've got a verruca on my big toe.'

That doesn't sound very serious, so I stop feeling stiff.

'Gary wants to go up Blaize Castle tomorrow afternoon. Do you want to come with us, or shall I drop you at your gran's?'

I think about meeting Mandy, but she's always got Julie, so I say, 'I'll come with you, but only if you let me wear my turquoise dress, and can we go downtown after so I can buy some boots?'

'I'll think about it, provided you promise not to run out of here again.'

'I promise,' I say, even though I'm not very sure I can keep to it, because if he won't let me see Kev I don't know what I might do.

Eddie

I don't know if I really managed to get through to her, but at least we didn't end up shouting and bawling at each other. That never does either of us any good, and going over how badly she behaved earlier will have to wait, because I don't want a situation developing where we become like enemies. We'll never be able to talk about anything then.

I know in her heart she's a good girl really, I just can't always get through to her heart and I don't know why. We used to be so close, she was my little angel, and now I'm frightened out of my mind that I'm losing her.

Susan

'There you are, my old loves,' Auntie Kath says, putting our bowls of cereal on the table. 'Do you want a cup of tea, or some orange squash?'

'Tea please,' I reply, 'with two sugars.'

'Squash please,' Gary says, his mouth already stuffed full of cornflakes. 'We're going up Blaize Castle today.'

'Yes, I saw your dad before he left, and he told me. That'll be lovely.'

'When are we coming down your house again?' he asks. 'I like it down there.'

I do too, so I'm interested to know the answer.

'Well,' she says, going out to the kitchen to get our drinks, 'there's something I have to tell you.'

I don't know why, but I suddenly get a feeling that I don't want to hear what she has to say.

'What is it?' Gary asks cheerfully when she comes back in the room.

She puts a glass in front of him, and starts to spoon some sugar into my tea.

'Have you still got a kite that we can go on the green and fly?' he wants to know.

She laughs. 'That old thing got caught round someone's aerial and we never got it back,' she tells him.

'Oh.' He looks a bit put out, but then shovels another spoonful of cornflakes into his bottomless gob.

'What have you got to tell us?' I remind her, in spite of not really wanting to know.

She takes out her fags, lights one and blows out a great big cloud of smoke. I'm tempted to ask for one, but don't dare because I know she'll give me what for if I do. 'Well,' she says, taking another drag, 'do you remember I told you Uncle Les might be taking over a baker's shop on Two Mile Hill?' Uncle Les is her husband.

I look at Gary as he says, 'Yes.'

'Well, he's decided he's going to, so we'll be moving in a couple of weeks. I'm afraid that means, my old loves, that I won't be coming here any more, but you haven't got to worry because the council will find someone else to take my place. As a matter of fact, I think they already have.'

I don't say anything. I don't even move.

Gary's bottom lip is starting to quiver. 'I don't want anyone else,' he says. 'I only want you.'

She sticks her fag in her mouth and goes to give him a hug. 'I know, my love, but you'll still be able to come and see us, and I expect the new lady's . . . Where are you going?' she asks me, as I get up from the table. 'You haven't finished your breakfast.'

'I'm not hungry,' I tell her.

'You have to eat something. What about a piece of toast?'

When I get upstairs I close my bedroom door and go to sit on the edge of the bed. My old ted's on the floor where he fell during the night, so I pick him up and sit him on my lap.

I don't really care that Auntie Kath's leaving. It makes no difference to me, because I know everyone leaves, but I think it's really mean on Gary. He's got used to her now, and it's not right that she should just go off like he doesn't matter. Also, I'm not very happy about someone else coming into the house to take her place. I'm the one who should be doing the housework and getting Gary off to school, not a person we've never met before.

I start wondering what it might be like to live in a baker's shop, then I think about Dad's verruca, and whether it's hurting him. He'd better not be lying about it, pretending that's all it is, when really he's got cancer or something, or I'll be really mad. My fists are going all tight and I can feel my eyes filling up with tears, but I'm not going to cry. I'm not going up Blaize Castle this afternoon, either. Dad and Gary can go on their own and I'll stay here, because I don't want to do anything any more, except wait for Kev and his mates to come back from Torquay. He's the only one who really cares about me, that's why he's running away, because it's just like in the song, 'Young Girl'. He's scared of what people will say, but it'll be all right as soon as I'm older.

'Can I come in?' Auntie Kath says, putting her head round the door.

'If you like.'

She comes to sit next to me and puts an arm round my shoulders. 'Are you all right?' she asks. 'Feeling a bit upset?'

'No. Why should I be?'

'Oh, I don't know, maybe you're not very happy about me leaving.'

'It's up to you,' I tell her. 'It doesn't make any difference to me.'

She gives me a hug. 'That's all right then, isn't it?' she says.

It's not, but what does she care? I get to my feet. 'I have to clean my teeth,' I tell her, and leaving her sitting on the bed I go and shut myself in the bathroom.

*

It's Saturday afternoon now and after four days of feeling really down in the dumps and like I want to run away, I just don't know where to, the best thing in the entire world has happened. It turns out that Kev and his mates are back from Torquay, and they only want to see me and Mand. Rich called round for her last night, so she went out with him, and told him off for standing us up the other night. He said they were really sorry, but they want to make up for it today.

Lucky Dad's taken Gary down the Rovers ground, so I've been able to put on my make-up and miniskirt without having to worry about how to get past him. He wouldn't be able to complain about my black patent kinky boots though, because he bought them himself to cheer me up after we went to Blaize Castle.

Mandy and I are sitting on one of the benches outside the Horseshoe now, shivering like mad, because it's freezing cold out today. I'm not wearing a coat, because I've only got my stupid anorak, or school gaberdine, and I wouldn't be seen dead in either of them. Mandy's got a lush reefer jacket that she says she nicked from a shop downtown, and she's going to get one for me the next time she's there, if she can. She's wearing boots too (the heels on hers are higher than mine), and her hair's more back-combed, but I don't mind because secretly I think hers is too high.

There's no one else around, because the pub's not open yet, and not many people live up this way, so hardly any cars are going by. There's a huge patch of green across the road, and at the bottom is the brook where I was the very first time I ever saw Kev. When I think back to that day it makes me feel all happy inside. I really love him, and I'm so glad I've met him.

When the time ticks on past five I start getting worried that they won't come again. I even wonder if Mandy was making it up, just to get me to come out. I've already told her that I have to be home by six, because that's when we watch *The Munsters* so Dad will be expecting me, and I don't want to have another row with him in case he tries to stop me going out again. Of course, if Kev does turn up and we get off together, I won't worry about what time I get home then.

'Here they are,' Mandy suddenly whispers. 'And it's only Rich and Kev.'

I stop breathing and duck my head. I can't look. My heart's banging like anything. After a bit I peep out from under my fringe, and it *really is them*. They're coming across the green towards us looking really mod, and like they know they're it.

'Quick, light up,' Mandy says, getting out her fags, 'it'll make you look older.'

The wind blows out her first two matches, and I start to panic that we won't be able to get them going in time.

'Remember what I said,' she whispers, as I suck in the smoke, 'I told them that you've already gone all the way, so they don't have to worry about you being a virgin or anything, OK?'

I start choking.

'Don't do that. It makes you look stupid.'

I'm trying not to, but my throat and nose are on fire. I want to ask what a virgin is, but I still can't speak. The only one I know about is Jesus's mother, and I can't work out what she has to do with it, so it's probably best that I don't show myself up and just keep quiet.

'All right,' Rich grunts as they come up to us.

'All right,' Mandy grunts back.

I keep my head down, feeling too soft to look up.

'Coming?' Rich says.

Mandy gets to her feet and I start to panic again as she links his arm and walks off round the corner of the pub. I want to ask where they're going, and how long they're going to be, but then I look at Kev who's hunched in his denim jacket as he smokes, and kicking his feet to keep warm. Wanting him to see that I smoke too, I take another puff of my fag, and this time I manage to take back without choking.

After a while he comes and sits next to me. I go all shy and wonder what I should do. He stretches his legs out in front of him and I notice his winklepickers, but I don't say anything, like they're really mod, or cool, or fabsville, because I'm afraid of how my voice might sound. I can smell the denim of his jacket, and the smoke in his hair, and for a minute I want to run home, but I never would. I just stay where I am, smoking and staring down at his feet.

He doesn't say anything for ages, so in the end I have a quick look at his face. He's so good-looking that I know I'll do anything for him, because I'm deeply in love. I wish I could think of something to say. I wonder what other girls talk about when they're with their chaps. I'll have to ask Mandy, she'll know.

'So you're Sue,' he says, flicking his ash on to the ground between us.

'Yes,' I answer. My voice comes out all hoarse and I wonder if he heard.

'The one who writes me the letters?'

I swallow hard and colour right up. I wish I hadn't written them now, because I've never felt so soft in my life. He probably thinks I'm a loony.

'What's it like up at that school?' he asks.

I try to find my voice, by clearing my throat. 'Horrible,' I reply. 'They keep us locked up all the time, as though we were babies, but we always manage to sneak out.'

He gives me a quick look. 'Where do you go?'

'Just in the back lane to meet b . . . friends.'

'Boyfriends?' he says, like a tease.

I laugh and blush again. It'll probably make me seem quite mature if I say yes, but I'm not sure I want him to think I already have a boyfriend, so instead of answering I say, 'What's it like working down Brains?'

He shrugs. 'Like anywhere else, I s'pose.'

'I love faggots,' I tell him. That's what they make down Brains.

He takes a long drag of his fag, then looks at me with one

eye closed as he blows out the smoke. 'So you're fourteen,' he says. 'That's still a bit young.'

'I'm nearly fifteen.' The lie seemed to pop out all on its own.

'Mm,' he says, like he's not sure whether to believe me. 'Have you ever snogged anyone?' he asks.

My heart turns over and I feel myself going beetroot red. 'Oh yeah, loads of times,' I say, tucking my hair behind one ear. 'What about you?'

He laughs at that, and so do I. It was a dumb thing to say, but quite funny too, and it's nice that I made him laugh.

'So do you fancy a snog now?' he asks.

I don't know what to say, because I do, but at the same time I don't.

He carries on looking at me.

I swallow, and try to nod, but I think I just look like I twitched.

He moves a bit closer and slides an arm round my shoulders. 'You're cold,' he says, pulling me against him. 'Where's your coat?'

'I didn't want to wear one.' My heart's pounding so hard I can hardly hear myself. I wonder what he's going to do. I'm scared stiff, and excited, and shaking, and wishing I had loads of experience so I'd know what to do next.

Ages go by with us just sitting there. It starts to feel quite nice, the way he's trying to keep me warm. I imagine being in the back row of the pictures with him, or sitting on a settee in front of a fire.

'What's your favourite record?' I ask.

He throws down his fag and grinds the end under a heel. 'I s'pose it would be, "Jumping Jack Flash" or "Hey Jude".'

'Oh yeah, they're great,' I agree, though I'm a bit disappointed that he didn't say 'Young Girl'.

'"I Get by with a Little Help from My Friends",' is cool too,' he adds.

'Really cool,' I agree. 'Do you watch *Top of the Pops?*'

'Sometimes, if I'm home. I used to prefer *Ready Steady Go* when it was on. Did you ever watch that?'

261

'Yes, all the time with my . . . ' I was about to say with my mum, but stopped myself just in time. I don't really won't to bring her into this. 'It was brilliant. Did you ever go up to London to see it?'

'No, I wasn't *that* keen.'

'Me neither.'

After that I can't think of anything else to say, and he doesn't bother, so I dig into my bag for another fag. 'Want one?' I offer.

'I just put one out.'

I have too, but I feel too stupid to put them away again, so I ask him for a light.

He flicks open his lighter and cups his hands round the flame as I start to suck. I pretend not to hear my hair singe as the wind blows it into the flame. I'm sucking like mad and at last some smoke starts coming through. I cough a bit, and my eyes start watering.

'How long have you smoked?' he asks.

'Oh, ages,' I reply, 'ever since I was a kid.'

He tucks me back in under his arm, and doesn't say anything else until we hear someone unlocking the pub door. 'Want a drink?' he offers.

'OK. Thanks.'

'What'll you have?'

I can't say lemonade and lime, or Tizer, which is what I usually have, or he'll think I'm a right baby, but I don't know any other drinks, apart from whisky and beer. Then I remember shandy, so I say that.

When he comes back he has a pint for himself, a shandy for me and two bags of salt and vinegar crisps.

'You're turning blue,' he tells me, and taking off his jacket he puts it round my shoulders.

He's acting like my husband already, and I love it so much that I want to tell him I'm ready for a snog, but I still don't know how to do it. If only I'd had some practice with someone else, because I know you're supposed to open your mouth, and sometimes people use their tongues, but I

262

don't know how it's really meant to go, and I don't want him to end up thinking I'm an idiot or a weirdo or something.

We eat our crisps and drink our drinks. The beer in the shandy makes me feel lightheaded, but it's nice so I take another sip. A couple of old blokes go into the pub, but I don't know either of them, so I don't have to hide my face. If it was anyone who knew Dad it would be a different story, but luckily I can just sit here pretending I'm out on a date with my chap, and actually it's not pretending, because I am!

After he's thrown our empty crisp bags away and put the glasses on the windowsill, he tilts up my chin and tucks my hair behind one ear. I'm shuddering and shaking, with cold as much as anything, and being too embarrassed to look back at him I keep my eyes down.

In the end, all he does is tweak my nose then look up as Rich and Mandy come back round the corner of the pub.

'What are you doing still here?' Rich says, sounding surprised to see us.

'What the bloody hell do you think?' Kev retorts. 'And where the fuck have you been? I thought you were never coming back.'

'All right, keep your shirt on. I'll go and get some drinks.'

'Fuck that,' Kev says, and taking his jacket off me, he gets hold of Mandy and walks her back round the corner of the pub.

My head starts to spin as I turn ice cold. He's gone off with Mandy right in front of me, leaving me alone with Rich. I don't understand. I thought he was with me, and she's supposed to be my friend, so why did she go with him?

I look at Rich. He's not nearly as tall as his brother, nor anywhere near as dishy – in fact he's got a bit of a snidey look, I always think, but I don't care. When he says, 'Fancy going?' even though I don't really know what he means, I reply, 'Yes, all right,' because I'm going to teach that Mandy a lesson. If she can have Kev, then I can have Rich, and we'll see how she likes it when she comes back.

Chapter Fourteen

Eddie

Our Susan's back at school now, and I have to say, knowing where she is from morning to night has been such a weight off my mind that I might be feeling ten years younger, if Betty Williams hadn't told me she thought she saw her last Sunday up Siston Common with Mandy Hughes and a gang of boys. I didn't even know she knew Mandy Hughes, and as far as I was concerned she was in detention that day, so she either lied, and I'm very much afraid I think she did, or Betty had got it wrong.

When I saw Susan the following Sunday she swore black and blue it couldn't have been her. 'You can ask Sadie, or Cheryl, or even Seaweed, if you like,' she cried. 'I was here, in stupid, bloody detention for chalking a zebra crossing between the gym and the art room. Can't anyone take a joke around here?'

She directed the last words so loudly towards Miss Sayward that I put a hand on her shoulder to calm her down, and led her over to the car. I waited until we were on our way back to school before broaching the next serious issue, which was the school's repeated insistence that she, and I, go to see a child psychiatrist.

She looked at me as though I was off my head. 'Get lost!' she sneered, in a way that's becoming typical of her lately, and makes me wonder what's happened to my daughter. 'I'm not seeing any psychiatrist. I'm not a *child*.'

'In the eyes of the school, and the law, you are, and the way you're constantly misbehaving is causing everyone a great deal of concern.'

'Well, why doesn't everyone just mind their own business?'

'Because you are their business while you're in their care, and they're trying to help us get to the bottom of why you're being so disruptive.'

'I don't need a psychiatrist to work that out,' she shouted. 'I've been telling you till I'm blue in the face that I want to come home to live, but you won't let me, so I've decided to get myself expelled.'

This wasn't the first time she'd thrown that at me, but it worried me a lot more hearing it then, because it was starting to acquire a ring of serious intent rather than something clever she'd thought up to impress her friends.

'You realise, if you're expelled, there are no guarantees they'll let you come home to live,' I told her.

Her face turned sour. 'They can't tell you what to do,' she retorted. 'If you say I can, then that's that. It's up to you.'

'No, it isn't. Someone came to see me from the Education Authority last week and they're afraid that I'm not a strong enough influence on you. You need a firmer hand, they said, and if I can't manage one now, while you're at Red Maids most of the time, they don't see how I can manage you on my own at home.'

Just as I expected, her temper exploded. 'Of course you can,' she shouted. 'And who the hell do they think they are, poking their noses in our business? You should tell them to get lost, or slam the door in their faces. That's what you should do.'

'Susan, it's precisely this sort of attitude that's causing the problems.'

'But I'll be good once I'm home,' she insisted. 'It's being here that gets me all riled up.'

'Yet you've made some lovely friends . . . '

'Don't keep going on about that. I know I have, but it doesn't make a difference. I want to come home.'

I'm sitting at the dining table now, holding a letter from Gloucestershire County Education Office that's giving me the date and time of our first appointment at the Child Guidance Clinic. It's set for a week tomorrow. On the back are some notes I made earlier, and because I don't want to read the letter again, I read them instead.

I won't apologise for wanting to educate myself in subjects I've barely even heard of. Oology, die-cast aviation, orthography? 'A load of old bunkum,' is what they'd probably say down work. 'Give me the Rovers and a pint of bitter any day.'

And who could blame them? Simplicity is a kind of purity, a bed to lie down on, a place to be free, whereas stuffing your head with all sorts of information you might never need . . . It can keep you awake at night working yourself up into a sweat over things you can probably never change, even if you wanted to, and it's not as if I don't have enough to keep me awake as it is.

I give a sigh, and turn the page over again. In spite of trying my best since Eddress went, this letter's telling me loud and clear that my best just isn't good enough.

Now, if I can, I have to find the energy to go outside and kick a football around with Gary and his friends, because I promised I would. It won't be easy, when I haven't felt this drained since I realised Eddress was going to die. I don't like thinking about those days, but they're coming back to me a lot lately, reminding me of how helpless I was to change things then. It's no different today, and now it's my children I'm letting down, because it's not only our Susan who's worrying me, it's this ridiculous new system of learning our Gary's still being put through at Falconride. ITA they call it, Initial Teaching Alphabet, and while I can see what they're on about, if anything's a load of old bunkum, that is. You can't teach a child a made up form of spelling when they're six and seven and expect them to learn a different one when they're eight and nine. Or not to my mind you can't.

'But the initial results have been positive,' Mr Lewis, his headmaster, insisted when I finally managed to get a morning off work to go up there. 'And Gary's doing very well with his reading.'

'He can't spell,' I told him, 'or not in the traditional way, and apart from the books you give him here, he can't read, so I don't see how you can say he's doing well. He doesn't even put a capital letter on his own name.'

'The transitional learning period is underway,' I was informed. 'I don't want you to worry. This revolutionary new method is being very closely monitored by the education authorities, and I can assure you they know what they're doing.'

Frankly, I don't think they know what they're doing at all. The trouble is, I can't fight them on my own, and I don't know of anyone else who's worried. I was considering asking Miss Dakin her opinion when I was up at the church last Sunday, but she's got enough on her hands with one of my children, so I'm sure she won't want to hear about my concerns for the other.

The truth is, I don't know who to turn to about anything any more, so I suppose I ought to try and look on the appointment with this psychiatrist as a bit of a blessing in disguise, instead of proof of my failings as a father.

Susan

Apart from Sadie, Cheryl, Laura, Peg and a few others, I haven't told anyone about Kev and how we snogged and shagged and did everything else while I was at home during half-term. It's my secret and I know they'll keep it, but it doesn't really matter if they don't. They all want to know what 'everything else' means, but I keep telling them they'll find out when they're going steady themselves.

Actually, it's not really true about the shag. That night at the Horseshoe was the only time I saw Kev, and when I went round the back of the pub with Rich, well, it was revolting. At first I thought he was yawning, but then I realised he was snogging, but his mouth was so wide I thought he was going to swallow me up!

All the time we were there I kept wondering where Mandy and Kev were, but I didn't find out till the next day, when I crept out to meet her before coming back to school. She told me that they'd climbed the stile together, crossed over a field full of cows, *in the dark*, and then gone into the old railway hut just over the bank.

'But I thought I was supposed to be going out with him,' I reminded her angrily.

'You are,' she said. 'He kept talking about you, saying how cool he thinks you are, and funny and pretty, but you've got to grow up. Everyone's having sex with everyone these days, so you have to do it too.'

I would if he'd let me, and now I'm determined to show him that I'm mature enough to have sex with lots of boys, and I will, the minute I can get out of this dump.

I've had one bloody exeat since I got back after half-term, but I didn't tell Dad about it, so he went home without me after church, then Sadie, Cheryl and I caught the bus to the Centre, then another to Warmley. From there we walked along Tennis Court Road to meet Mandy outside the Anchor, before going up Siston Common to meet Kev and his mates. I was so excited and nervous I kept thinking I was going to wet myself. We all felt like that and the way we couldn't stop laughing was making it worse.

When we got there Kev seemed really pleased to see me, but I think he was a bit more interested in Sadie really, but she's my best friend so she wouldn't do anything to take him away from me. In the end she and Cheryl started to get bored, which got on my nerves a bit, so I walked off without them and Kev only followed me over to Lover's Dip! (Lover's Dip is full of bushes and trees and all sorts of secret places where you can go to be private.) All we did was snog, because there wasn't time for anything else before we had to get the bus back to school, but it was so fabsville and fantastic that I haven't been able to stop thinking about it since.

The way he kisses is completely different to his brother. He doesn't open his mouth as wide as it'll go, instead it's open just a little way, and he doesn't press really hard like Rich, who nearly crushed my teeth. He didn't use his tongue either, which I was quite glad about, because I was afraid it might make me gag.

Anyway, we're back at school now and it's so boring it makes us all want to do something insane, like blowing up the science lab, or throwing Cluttie out of a window. I can just see her plunging down and going splat on the ground. Yesterday we decided to raid the wine cellar under Dot's study, but when we got to the bush where the entrance is hidden, we ended up chickening out.

'What if she comes and rolls a boulder over the entrance,' someone said. 'We'll be buried alive.'

Since none of us fancied that we came back inside and played jacks, or read magazines until prep. That's where we are now, stuffed in the classroom having to do more work, even though we've been studying all day. I'm writing about *The Planets* by Holst. What I should really be doing is working out how to get expelled.

'I know,' I suddenly say. 'Why don't we go and break a window?'

Everyone looks at each other, and then Peg says, 'Great idea,' and abandoning our desks we traipse off outside, leaving the goody-two-shoes and teacher's pets behind.

'Which one?' I say once we're out there.

'What about the next classroom to ours?' someone suggests. 'No one's in it.'

So we pick up some stones and start to throw them at the bottom panes of glass. After a while a crack appears, and we give a cheer. Then deciding to get it over with, I take off a shoe and hurl it with all my might. The window smashes, glass flies into the classroom and we leap up and down in the air.

By the time we get back inside Seaweed's already in the classroom, holding my shoe aloft and inspecting our feet like the demon opposite of Prince Charming.

Off I go to stand outside Dot's study. I might have to sign the black book for this, which is great, because it'll be one step closer to getting me out of here and back home to Kev, where I belong.

He promised to write to me, but I haven't received anything yet. I reckon that's because Cluttie or Seaweed are censoring our letters. They do that sometimes, which might be a criminal offence, because no one's supposed to interfere with the Royal Mail. I've written to him lots of times, telling him how boring it is here and how much I'm looking forward to seeing him at Christmas. I don't suppose I'll be able to spend it with him, Dad would go mad if he found out I was seeing someone so much older than me, and anyway, I expect Kev'll have to spend it with his family too.

Mandy caught the bus up here the day before yesterday and met me in the back lane. She's really fed up, because she hasn't seen very much of Rich. It's so cold out now that she doesn't like waiting around in the open for him, and she can't go down the club because the other girls keep threatening to beat her up.

Oh blimey, here comes Dot, her witch's cape billowing out behind her, and her lace-up shoes squeaking like a couple of squashed mice. I suppose I'm in for it now.

'Susan? What are you doing there?' she asks, sweeping by me and opening her door.

'Miss Sayward sent me,' I tell her.

'Well, I didn't imagine you came for the view. Why did Miss Sayward send you?'

'Because I threw my shoe through a window, miss.'

'I see. You'd better come in.'

Her study's all brown and dreary and full of ancient books that look all crumbly and crusty, a bit like her. 'Why did you throw your shoe through a window?' she asks, putting her stuff down on her desk and going to sit behind it.

'I just felt like it,' I say.

She looks at me long and hard. 'Did it strike you that such

270

foolhardy behaviour might be considered an act of vandalism, for which I could report you to the police?' she asks.

I turn cold. Being in trouble with her is one thing, with the police is another altogether.

'Well?' she prompts.

'No, miss,' I reply.

'I thought not. You understand I will have to inform your father about this, and the cost of repair will be deducted from the funds you have deposited with Miss Sayward.'

'But miss, I won't be able to buy any yoghurts or records on a Saturday if you do that.'

'What a pity. You'll be in detention for the next exeat, when you will report to me here to enter the details of your offence into the punishment book.'

I surprise even myself as I suddenly start to cry.

'I have no sympathy for you,' she informs me harshly. 'Your behaviour since the start of this term has been appalling. I can only hope that your sessions with the psychiatrist will help bring you to your senses. You can go now, but straight up to bed without supper. I'll see to it that Miss Clutterbuck is aware of why you are in disgrace *again*.'

Sadie and the others are waiting at the bottom of the back stairs as I round the corner. 'What did she say?' Sadie whispers, putting an arm around me.

'Are you in detention?' Cheryl wants to know.

'Did you sign the black book?' Peg asks.

We're all moving up the stairs in a huddle as I say, 'Yes, I'm in detention, and yes I have to sign the book. Silly cow. She's only going to charge me for the bloody window and tell my dad.' I don't mention anything about the psychiatrist, because if she thinks I'm going to see one of them, then she's got another bloody think coming.

I'm only here in this stupid clinic because it means I'm able to get out of school for the day. The others were all dead jealous when I told them my dad was coming to pick me up so I could go to my grampy's funeral. It doesn't matter that someone's dead, any excuse to get out is good enough for us. I don't really like telling that sort of lie, but it's better than having them think I'm a loony. Anyway, it's true that Grampy's dead. Dad rang the school the same night as I broke the window to tell Dot, who called me back to her office to break it to me.

See, this is God punishing me again. Every time I do anything wrong He takes away someone I love. I couldn't stop crying that night, and everyone was making a fuss of me, but I just wanted them to go away. They don't know what it's like to have everyone die.

Dad was very quiet in the car on the way here, and I was expecting him to have a real go at me about breaking the window. So far he hasn't even mentioned it, which is how I know he doesn't really have his mind on what's going on. He's upset about his dad dying. I try for a minute to imagine how I'd feel if anything happened to him, and it's so horrible it makes me start panicking and want to throw myself out of the car. I don't let it show though, and to stop it, I force myself to think of something else.

Actually, if Grampy hadn't died, I'd have refused to come today, but when I saw how unhappy Dad looked I decided not to upset him any more by kicking up a fuss. He said he might take me to see Auntie Beat when we've finished talking to the psychiatrist. I hope she doesn't cry, because if she does I'll start crying too. I know Grampy was a bit daft sometimes, and always getting drunk, but I really loved him, and I think it's horrible that he's not going to be here any more.

The trouble is, God never listens to me.

We're the only ones in the waiting room, even though there are lots of chairs. Dad's sitting with his cap in his hands, staring at nothing, so I watch the rain on the windows, telling myself if the drop I'm following reaches the bottom without blending with any others I'll get married to Kev.

I wish I could light up a fag. I wonder what would happen if I did. I won't be able to find out, because I haven't got any, and even if I had, I don't want to make Dad any more upset than he already is.

I wonder if I should say something about Grampy.

A door opens and a tall, stooped man with saggy skin and little round glasses comes into the waiting room. 'Mr Lewis? Susan?' he says. 'I'm Dr Leigh, it's nice to meet you.'

Dad stands up and shakes the man's hand, so I do too. Behind his glasses his eyes are quite friendly, and when he smiles his face doesn't seem to sag quite so much.

'Come in,' he tells us, and standing back he waits for us to go past into his office. It's quite big, with lots of children's drawings on the walls, toys in one corner, a telly in another, and hundreds of books on the shelves.

He invites us to sit down, and once he's behind his desk he looks at me and kind of twinkles as he says, 'I expect it's rather good to be having a day off school, isn't it?'

I nod, and wonder if Dad's happy to be having a day off work. I expect it's hard for him to be happy about anything now Grampy's dead.

I wish Grampy wasn't dead.

Dr Leigh opens a file in front of him and has a slow read through.

I start wondering what Kev's doing now, and what he'd say if he knew where I was. I'm not even going to tell Mandy about this, because I don't want everyone thinking I belong down Barrow Gurney. What if they do send me away to a place like that, where no one can find me any more? Dad might not come to visit, and Gary will grow up without me. Mandy and Sadie will make other best friends, and Kev will marry someone else.

I feel like I'm starting to panic.

'Mm, yes,' Dr Leigh says. He looks at Dad. 'I think it might be helpful if I interview the two of you separately to begin with, what do you say?'

Dad twists his cap between his hands. 'Whatever you think best,' he replies.

Dr Leigh gets up and goes to open the door. 'I'll have a chat with Susan first,' he tells Dad. 'Do help yourself to a coffee or tea from the machine, Mr Lewis.'

After Dad's gone the doctor sits down again and fixes me with his friendly eyes. 'So, you're not very happy at school?' he says with a sigh.

I shake my head.

'Why is that?'

'Because I hate sleeping there and not having any freedom. I want to be like other girls who go to school in the day and come home at night.'

He nods, seeming to understand that, which makes me think I might be able to get him on my side. 'Do you have many friends at Red Maids?' he asks.

'Loads.' I don't want him thinking I'm one of the smelly people who no one ever talks to.

'And you're fond of them?'

'Of course. They're really great.'

He steeples his fingers. 'Would it be true to say that you have more friends there these days, than you do where you grew up?'

'I might, but that's only because I don't see the others very much any more. If I was with them all the time, they'd still be my friends.'

He looks down at his file again. 'You don't seem to be doing as well in your lessons as you did during your first year,' he comments. 'Are you finding the work more difficult?'

The truth is, I'm not, but coming bottom of the class all the time is part of my plan to get expelled. I can't tell him that though, and I don't want him to think I'm stupid either, so I say, 'Sometimes.'

'Do you ever ask a teacher for help?'

'No,' I reply. *He must be joking.*

He picks up a pen and makes a couple of notes. 'Tell me some things you like about the school,' he says.

I have to think for quite a long time before I can come up with anything. 'Chocolate-spread sandwiches for tea. Warm crusty rolls for breakfast on Sundays. Listening to records and dancing in the rec room.'

'What about lessons? Which are your favourites?'

That's easy. 'French and history. Oh, and English I suppose, if we're reading an interesting book.'

'What kind of books do you find interesting?'

'Um, Shakespeare's my favourite.'

He looks surprised and I think he might know I'm lying. 'Any others?'

I think of the rude stories I've got tucked away in my cubicle that one of the day girls smuggled in. I wonder what he'd say if I told him about them. '*Little Women*,' I say, 'and *Alice through the Looking Glass*.'

He writes the titles down, then says, 'Do you enjoy being in detention at school?'

'No!' *Is he mad*?

He looks a bit puzzled. 'You seem to have acquired quite a number this term, so if you don't enjoy them, I have to wonder why you behave in a way to earn them?'

'I get them because the teachers all pick on me,' I tell him.

'Really? In what way?'

'They give me detentions and make me stand on the landing.'

'For no reason?'

'Sometimes, yes.'

His eyebrows go up, and I think he knows I'm lying again.

I'm starting to get fed up now. These questions are boring and aren't getting us anywhere, so why doesn't he just let me go? I'm sure he's got some real loonies he has to take care of.

It seems he's read my mind, because he gets up and goes to the door. 'I'll speak to your dad now,' he says, 'if you'd like to take a seat in the waiting room.'

Eddie

So much has happened over the last week that I hardly know whether I'm coming or going. The session with the psychiatrist is a bit of a blur now, with it being the day before our dad's funeral. I don't know how helpful I was with my answers, or how well our Susan did either. By the time I took her back to school she looked all in. It couldn't have been easy for her, getting dragged across town to be interrogated, then over to our dad's to see Beat, before having to go all the way back again. I'd have kept her home for the night if it was allowed, but I hadn't asked permission, and with the funeral happening the next morning, it was best she wasn't around. Funerals are no place for children.

Dear old Beat, she looks a proper lost soul now our dad's not there shouting at her and giving her something to do. Someone had obviously been round to clean the house before we went back for the wake, because everything was looking crisper and shinier than I've seen it in a while. I wonder why it's called a-wake, when the sleep is endless, eternal?

Not many came, just a couple of his mates from up the Legion, me and Beat and some neighbours. No one made it up from Wales, and our Nance and Doreen didn't put in an appearance either. Made me feel really sorry for the old soul, who's only crime was to get married again after our mam died. I wonder if Susan and Gary would turn on me if I ever decided to marry again. I don't think Gary would, but I'm not so sure about our Susan. It won't happen anyway, so no point bothering myself about it.

I'm afraid Susan's turning into a bigger worry to me as each day unfolds. I've started dreading the post in case it brings yet another letter telling me she's in detention, or some equally upsetting news like they're stopping a shilling a week out of her pocket money until she's repaid what it cost them to repair the window. She's signed something called the punishment book now, which she calls the black book, and heaven help us, she seems proud of it instead of ashamed.

We have to go back for another session with the psychiatrist in the new year. Perhaps he'll tell me then what he made of his first meeting with her. It's going to need several visits to get to the bottom of things, he's already warned me about that, and I'm inclined to let him make the decisions about how often we should go. What else can I do? I'm at the end of my tether, and if Dr Leigh can't help us I'm not sure that anyone can. Just thank goodness no one outside the family knows, because it's a terrible thing having to go and see a psychiatrist.

I'm having a sit-down now, next to the fire. Gary's at the table with one of his friends playing blow football, so I'll leave him be for another half-hour while I carry on writing things down. I don't want to dwell on our Susan, or our dad, so I'm going to write some thoughts I think about myself.

I'm wondering if I'm the landlord of my body, or the tenant of a greater landlord. If I am the tenant then I have a lot of duties which I would not have if I belonged to myself. No need to bother if you are only to live ten years, but if for ever, I'd better bother. My bad temper, jealousy, greed, cowardice, conceit . . . Does God know? Did He take Eddress as a punishment for my wrongdoings and failings? Have my communist tendencies angered Him? I sometimes wonder if it's why the doctors let Eddress die. Someone high up in government told them to withdraw treatment in order to teach us commies a lesson. So is it my fault our Susan and Gary don't have a mother?

'Dad?'

'Yes, my love?'

'Can I have a brown-sauce sandwich?'

I look round and see to my surprise that Gary's friend has gone. 'You've just had your tea,' I remind him.

'I know, but I'm still hungry. And then can we write a note for Father Christmas?'

Only yesterday he was saying that there was no such thing, but today he seems to be hedging his bets. Do I deserve the gift of such a wonderful son? Will he be taken away, the way our Robert was?

I go and make him his sandwich, then sit down at the table with him to write his list. A *Beano* annual; some battling tops; a box of Lego with animals in; an Action Man; a new football; a Bristol Rovers scarf; a puzzle and some crayons with a crayoning book.

'Is that all?' I ask, making him laugh.

'I expect I can think of some more.'

'I'm sure you can. So shall we send it up the chimney now?'

He folds the list into a neat little square and is just handing it over when he says, 'Do you think we should send one for our Susan too?'

Loving him for thinking of her, I say, 'Have you got any idea what she might want?'

He looks defeated. Then suddenly brightens. 'What about some record tokens? She'll like that. And we could ask for a Sindy doll, she likes them.'

'It's been a while since she played with her dolls,' I remind him, wishing we were back at a time when she did.

'All right then, we could ask for some smelly things, like bubble bath and scent, and I know she likes red liquorice so we could put that on the list too.' He frowns. 'Except I was going to buy her that, and I won't be able to if Father Christmas brings it.'

'We'll leave it off then, and put some new gloves on instead. How does that sound?'

'Yes, the furry ones that don't have any fingers. They keep you the warmest.'

'Are you going to write it down, or shall I?'

'You can do it. I want to go to the toilet.'

He runs to the door, then hopping from one foot to the other, turns back and says, 'Don't forget to put a Monkees album on her list, she'll definitely want one of those. Oh yes, and . . .'

'Up the stairs now, before it's too late,' I interrupt.

'Get her some book tokens,' he shouts as he thunders up the stairs.

As I sit writing out our Susan's list I'm trying to stop my thoughts from anchoring in troubled waters. I must think of buoying subjects that will allow me to chart calmer seas and improve my mind. *A sound taste in literature is a guarantee against boredom, the key to a fuller mental life. The man or woman who can talk intelligently about books bears the hallmark of a cultured mind, and therefore, apart from any consideration of personal enjoyment, a knowledge of literature is a great social asset.*

By the time Gary comes down again I'm ready for our dispatch to the North Pole, so making him stand well back, I remove the fireguard and send the notes on their way. I then quickly replace the guard before he can stick his head up the chimney to make sure they've gone, and going back to the table I sit listening as he tells me, between mouthfuls of sandwich, about our new home help, Sarah – or Mrs Moon, as I'd prefer to call her. She's much younger than Mrs Jewell, mid-twenties I'd say, and Gary's obviously taken quite a shine to her. That's a relief, because I know he missed Mrs Jewell when she went. He's talking now about getting Mrs Moon a sachet of bubble bath for Christmas, and he thinks it would be a good idea to buy them for Gran, Auntie Nance, Auntie Doreen and young Doreen too.

'Oh yes, and Auntie Beat, we mustn't forget her,' he says.

'No, we certainly mustn't,' I agree.

It's going to be a funny old Christmas this year without our dad, and our Robert. Two more big holes in our family, left for time to fill, except it never will. Still, won't do any good getting maudlin about it, it's not going to bring them back, and whatever else I do, I have to keep a stiff upper lip, if only for the children's sake.

Susan

Christmas was all right, I suppose. We had quite a nice time up Auntie Nance's and then Gran's, and I had some fab presents (and some grotty ones too), but it wasn't the same, not being at Auntie Doreen's. We saw her on Boxing Day, because she came over for Dad's birthday (Gary and I gave him some Brylcreem and a bar of Bournville), but she didn't stay long. No one talked about Robert, but I know we were all thinking about him. I wonder if he could see us, or hear our thoughts. He'll know how much we all miss him if he can.

I still really love him and I always will.

After Auntie Doreen left we went to see Auntie Beat. She cried about Grampy, so I cried too. Then Gary did, and Dad ended up making us all laugh by mimicking the cockerel Grampy gave us. (The cockerel's gone to live on Critchley's farm now, because the neighbours complained. Still, it's better than having him served up as a Sunday roast, which Uncle Graham was threatening to do. I've seen him wring a chicken's neck, and it's not very nice when they carry on running round the yard even though they're supposed to be dead!)

Auntie Beat's still got her chickens, but Dad's arranging for someone else to have them now, because she can hardly take care of herself, let alone a coop full of hens. I explained to Dad, after we left, how good it would be if I was going to The Grange, because Auntie Beat's is on the way home, so I'd be able to cook and clean for her too.

'I could even make her breakfast in the morning, if I left early enough,' I said, which I think was very nice of me, but as usual he didn't seem to be listening.

He's always somewhere inside his head, thinking about politics and religion and all kinds of stuff that make him say really weird things sometimes. Like last night, when he started going on about English.

'Our language is a growth from Anglo-Saxon, which is

German,' he said, even though no one had asked, 'and Old Norse, which is from the Vikings. Then in 1150 there was a transition to Middle English. Early modern English started around 1520, which is about the same time as the printing presses were first used.'

Sometimes I think he reads too much and it's not good for him, but if I say that we only end up rowing, so I just let him drone on and then, as soon as I can, I escape.

It's three days after Christmas now, so it's taken me quite a long time to be able to sneak out and meet Mandy. We're in the bus shelter over on Anchor Road, tucked into a corner each, while it pelts down with rain outside. It's bloody freezing, so, grotty as they are, I'm glad to have my new furry gloves to keep my hands warm. If Kev comes along I'll stuff them straight in my pockets before he can see them.

Mandy had three lush new minidresses, some hipsters and a white polo-neck jumper for Christmas, plus loads of other stuff like records, and Estée Lauder talc, and some Fry's Turkish Delight, which she loves and I hate.

She looks really cool tonight in the new Afghan coat she bought when her mum took her downtown to spend her Christmas money. I thought Afghans were supposed to be hippyish, but if Mandy's wearing one I must have that wrong, because we're definitely mods.

We're not sure if Kev and his mates are going to come tonight. We don't have an actual arrangement and with all this rain, they probably won't. Still, it's nice to be here chatting with Mandy about everything while we wait, just in case they do turn up.

She hasn't seen them at all over Christmas, or even very much before, mainly because of not being able to go into Made for Ever club, or the pub, which is where they usually are when the weather's bad. Still, we've decided to walk up and down past their house tomorrow in the hope they might see us and come out, and if they don't we'll wait outside Brains about five o'clock in case they're already back at work.

I've definitely decided to go all the way now. I'm not scared. I understand a bit more about what will happen, and it's quite funny how I managed to find out. There's this first-former in our dorm called Ros, who's really pretty and lively and is struck on me. Anyway, she sleeps in the next bed to Sadie and one night when I was tucking her in she only asked me, 'Su, do you know what a virgin is?'

Honest, I don't have a clue why she asked, but she did, and then I had to give her an answer, didn't I? Lucky for me, Sadie was listening, so I said to Ros, 'Are you saying you don't know what a virgin is? You are so juvenile. Sadie, tell her, will you?'

So Sadie did. 'A virgin is a girl who's never had sex,' she said. (I don't know how Sadie knows, but it sounded right to me.) 'Do you know what sex is?' she asked Ros.

'Oh yes,' Ros replied, 'it's when a man puts his thing inside a woman's thing and moves it up and down to make babies.'

Of course, I knew it was that, but I wouldn't have put it that way exactly, and I had to wonder how she knows so much when she's younger than me! It's probably because her mum's a doctor. It must be handy that, having a mum as a doctor.

I'm trying to think what I'd like my mum to be if she was still here. I decide I wouldn't mind just as long as she was here.

'Someone's coming,' Mandy whispers.

I go very still and listen. The rain's muffling the sound of voices and footsteps, but I can definitely hear them coming our way. We wait, hardly breathing, hopeful and excited, until a man and woman hurry past under an umbrella. I'm just biting down on my frustration when someone comes into the shelter and to my horror it's Dad.

'What are you doing here?' I cry.

'I might ask you the same thing, young lady,' he says in a deep, angry voice. 'Now get yourself home.'

'No!'

'I'm not arguing with you, you'll go home now or I'll drag you there.'

'You wouldn't dare.'

'Oh yes, I would.'

I can tell he would too. I think about trying to dart past him and running away, but he's blocking the exit and even if I managed it he'd chase me and probably catch up.

I look at Mandy, who's still hunched in her corner. 'Are you coming?' I say.

She glances nervously at Dad.

'It's up to you,' he tells her, and grabs hold of my arm.

I snatch it away. 'I can walk on my own,' I snap.

He stands back for me to go by, then says to Mandy, 'She's too young to be out with you . . . '

'Shut up!' I seethe. 'I'm not a child, so stop treating me like one.'

'Home,' he barks, and taking my arm again he begins marching me along the road.

If Kev and his mates come round the corner now I'll die.

Luckily they don't, and there's no sign of anyone outside the Anchor either, so no one to witness the awful humiliation of being dragged home by my dad.

By the time we get there we're both soaked through, so he tells me to go upstairs and get ready for bed, then to come back down again. I know I'm in for it, so once I've got my nightie on I snuggle up in bed, instead of going downstairs to get shouted at. I'm really worried, because I know he's going to try and stop me going round with Mandy, and if I don't see her I'll never see Kev.

In the end, when he comes into my room, he stands next to the bed looking down at me so angrily that I suddenly want to shout at him.

'I don't want you going out with that girl again,' he tells me. 'She's too old for you . . . '

'It's up to me who I go round with.'

'If you chose girls your own age . . . '

'They're just childish and stupid.'

'And so are you, saying things like that. How many more times do I have to remind you that you're twelve years old . . .'

'I'm nearly thirteen . . .'

'Not until next August.'

' . . . and anyway, everyone says I'm really mature for my age.'

'Then act it and stop behaving . . . That's *enough*,' he shouts as I start to speak again. 'I'm turning out your light now, and I don't want to hear another peep out of you till morning.'

After he's gone I lie in the darkness trying not to cry, but I can't stop myself. Everything's always going wrong for me, and I don't know what to do to make it go right.

Eddie

It was Mrs Drake who lives along the lane that came to tell me she'd seen our Susan walking along Anchor Road with Mandy Hughes.

'We were driving back from our mam's,' she said, 'and when I realised who it was I said to Colin, I bet her father doesn't know she's out with that girl, and in this weather. So I thought I better come and tell you.'

I thanked her for taking the trouble, and after checking our Gary was asleep, I put on my coat and went off in search of Susan.

I've told her now that she's not allowed to see Mandy Hughes again, and if she does then she won't be going out at all. I know she'll play merry hell, but it's the only way to stop her getting into trouble, and seeing that Sawyer boy's name still covering all her books tells me that's exactly where she's heading. It'll be Mandy Hughes who's encouraging it, and from what I've heard about her . . . Well, I can't even bring myself to think about our Susan going the same way.

Chapter Fifteen

Susan

Made it!

I'm out of breath after running all the way here, but I'm at the Horseshoe now, sitting on a bench outside with Mandy, waiting for Kev and Rich. She saw them yesterday, on their way home from work, and apparently Kev asked where I was.

He definitely wants to see you, Mandy wrote in the note she gave her brother to give to Gary to pass on to me. (Gary won't split because he's old enough now to understand that everyone hates splitters.) *Meet me outside the Anchor at quarter past nine and we'll walk up the Horseshoe together,* she wrote.

This is the latest I've ever been out on my own, but it was quite easy sneaking out, because Dad was in the front room with Mr Pitman talking about Russian stuff and once they get going on that they're lost in another world. I left by the back door so he wouldn't hear me open and close it, and now I just have to hope Gary doesn't decide he wants to come in and sleep with me, like he does sometimes, hoping for a story, because if he finds I'm not there he'll be bound to think I'm downstairs and go down to find me.

I'm not worrying about that now though, because Kev and Rich are coming across the green, their collars up to keep out the cold, but at least it's not raining. My heart's thundering like a big bass drum. I know I've already necked with him (that's what we call snogging now), but that was ages ago, and I'm afraid I might have put him off by not being any good.

'He wouldn't be coming if you weren't,' Mandy assures me.

That seems to make sense, so I say, 'Where are we going? Did they tell you?'

'No, they just said to be here.'

I take a quick puff of my fag and start to cough.

'Oh for God's sake. Can't you do it right yet?'

'Of course I can. It just got caught in my throat.'

'Well don't choke in front of them, and whatever you do, don't start acting babyish if they want to go all the way. It's time you did, or he definitely won't want to see you any more.'

I swallow dryly. I'm not sure I want to do this really.

'Don't worry about what to do, he'll show you, OK?'

'OK,' I whisper, and I cross my fingers tightly inside my pocket. *Please God don't let me show myself up and give me the courage to do it.*

'All right?' Rich grunts to Mandy.

'All right?' she grunts back.

'All right?' Kev says to me.

'All right?' I say back.

'Fancy coming down Larry and Clive's house?' Rich asks. 'Their old dear and her bloke have gone up London for New Year, so they've got the place to themselves.'

Straight away Mandy says, 'Yeah, we'll come.'

Even though I feel nervous, I'm excited too, and when Mandy tucks her arm through Rich's to start back across the green, I look awkwardly at Kev.

'Are you going to walk with me?' he offers.

I fill up with pride to find myself walking arm in arm with him, just like a proper boyfriend and girlfriend. I wish the whole world could see me, but I suppose it's better they don't or someone, like that old busybody Mrs Drake, would be sure to go rushing back to tell Dad. So I keep my head down every time a car goes past, until we're walking up the lane to where Larry and Clive Frost's house is all lit up with twinkling Christmas lights.

Clive answers the door and once we're inside he takes us into the front room which is quite posh in a way, with all kinds of brass ornaments on the brick fireplace and a three-bar gas fire that's making it lovely and warm. Larry's sprawled out on a black leatherette settee watching something on the telly, but when we come in he gets up to turn it off and starts to grin.

'All right?' he says to Mandy and me.

'All right?' she says back.

'Fancy a drink?' Clive offers.

'What have you got?' she asks.

He looks at his brother and shrugs. 'Cider?'

'Or sherry,' Larry adds.

I've only ever had sips of sherry, usually over Auntie Doreen's at Christmas, but tonight I get a full glass all to myself. It's really lush.

Larry puts on some music, so we start twisting and dancing, and it's funny, but no matter how much sherry I drink my glass always seems to be full. When Joe Cocker comes on I remember how Kev said that 'I Get by with a Little Help from My Friends' was one of his favourites, so I try to do my best dancing to that, but it's not easy because the record's quite slow and I'm starting to feel quite dizzy. It turns out all right though, because Kev comes and smooches with me and it's so fantastic feeling him up against me that I could die. I saw this film the other night on telly where a woman was kissing a man on his stomach and I'm thinking how much I'd like to do that to Kev.

'Fancy going upstairs?' he whispers in my ear.

My stomach turns over, along with my heart. I want to say yes, but at the same time I don't. I notice then that Mandy's no longer in the room, nor is Clive. Larry and Rich are sitting on the settee smoking and drinking beer and talking about something that might be football.

I let Kev lead me up the stairs by the hand. It's lovely how masterful he is.

When we get to the bedroom he leaves the light turned off, and closes the door. I can't see a thing, and I'm dizzy again, but then he puts his arms around me and we start to neck. I love the way his mouth tastes of beer and fags.

We lie down on the bed together and he starts to unzip his jeans. I'm trying not to feel scared, so I lie very still, remembering that Mandy told me he'd show me what to do. I hope I get it right.

Somewhere deep, deep down inside me a voice is screaming 'Mummy' but I won't let myself listen.

Mandy and I are on our way home now. I'm not sure what time it is, and I'm more worried about being able to get in without waking up Dad than anything else. It's freezing cold, and I feel a bit sick and strange.

'So are you still a virgin?' Mandy asks.

'I think so,' I answer miserably. I know I am, because we didn't go all the way.

'Oh God,' she groans. 'Was he mad?'

'No, not really. I don't think so.'

'How about the others? What did you do with them?'

'Not much,' I mumble, feeling really horrible now about the way Kev told me to stay where I was when he'd got fed up with me because Larry wanted to come up and get on the bed with me. I didn't say no in case Kev packed me up, but I wish I had, even though all I did with Larry was some necking and a bit of touching up.

'Come on, cheer up,' Mandy says. 'At least you got to go with him, even if it wasn't all the way.'

'I'm all right,' I insist feebly.

'No, you're not, I can tell. Did any of them put it in your mouth?'

I want to gag. 'No,' I answered. I feel so immature and ashamed. What must Kev be thinking now? I've got to make myself be able to do things properly, or he'll never want to go out with me.

Linking my arm, Mandy says, 'Don't worry, you wait, once you get used to it you'll love it.'

I'm finding that quite hard to believe, but I don't bother to argue.

Hearing someone whistling out behind us, we turn to see Kev and Rich walking fast to catch up with us.

'All right?' Kev says to me, putting an arm round my shoulders.

Amazed, I find myself breaking into a smile. I definitely am now, and I snuggle into him, wishing we were married and that we could go home together and sleep in the same bed.

'Are you OK?' he whispers, kissing me on the lips when we reach the garages, where we have to go different ways.

My heart soars. That must mean he wants to see me again, which would be fantastic if I didn't have to go back to bloody school on Monday.

I'm not going.

'Get on your knees,' he says, pressing down on my shoulders.

I hear a noise next to us, and looking round I see that Mandy's already on her knees in front of Rich.

I feel really angry with myself. I have to do this, or I'm going to look like a great big baby.

The way his fingers are digging into my shoulders really hurts. I try to think about something else, like dancing in the rec room, or what days I'll be down for a bath next term. I imagine everyone grouped round me fascinated to hear everything I did with Kev during the holidays. I'll say we've gone all the way – I have to, because I've already told them that anyway.

I hear footsteps coming along the lane and we all go very still. Mandy sniggers and quickly clamps a hand over her mouth.

Please God, don't let it be Dad. Please, please, please.

Whoever it is walks on past and doesn't even seem to notice us.

'See you then,' Kev says, and taking a packet of fags from his pocket he lights up as he and Richie walk away.

'I ought to go home now,' I say to Mandy, 'before my dad finds out I'm not there.'

Luckily, I manage to sneak into the house without waking anyone up. I get undressed in the dark, being as quiet as I can, then snuggle up in bed with my old ted to keep warm. I think I'm happier than I've ever been, because I've spent all evening with Kev, so I don't understand why I'm starting to cry. I'm not sad, I know I'm not, but I can't seem to stop crying. I cling on to Ted even tighter, and inside my head I start screaming. I wish Mum was here. She'd make everything better, the way she always used to. Not that anything's wrong, because it isn't. I just wish she'd come back. I don't want to be without her any more. It's been long enough now. I don't want it to go on any longer.

Please, please, please God don't let her be dead so she can come back.

Eddie

It's half-past six in the morning, pitch black outside and cold enough to freeze the whatsits off a brass monkey. I don't blame our Susan for not wanting to get up, I found it hard enough myself, but if we don't get a move on we're going to be late.

There's no answer when I knock on her door, but she was in the bathroom just now and I can hear her moving around, so I know she's up.

'Have you got your toiletry bag?' I call out, trying to keep it to a whisper so I don't wake Gary.

She doesn't answer, so I knock again, and say, 'What are you doing in there?'

'Nothing,' she answers sulkily.

With a sigh, I leave her be for now and go downstairs to pack up my flask and sandwiches to take to work. The house is as cold as a fridge. I went to fetch some coal in just now and nearly ended up on my backside thanks to all the ice on the path. I'll have to be careful driving this morning or we'll be skidding off the road into a ditch.

I've set the fire ready for when Mrs Moon, the home help, comes to get Gary out of bed. She should be here about seven. This'll be her first day back after Christmas, and it's a pity she's not going to meet Susan, but then again, given the mood our Susan seems to be in this morning, it's probably just as well.

Putting on my cap and scarf, I go back upstairs to see what she's doing. 'Are you dressed?' I ask from outside her door.

'Get lost.'

'Come on now,' I say. 'I told Mrs Beach we'd be at her house by a quarter past seven, and we don't want to make her late.'

'I'm not going.'

Bracing myself for battle, I crack open her door. 'Can I come in?'

'No!'

In I go anyway to find her sitting on the edge of her bed, dressed in the denim jeans and jacket she bought with her Christmas money. Since they're allowed to wear their own clothes back to school, I'm not surprised by that, or by the mutinous look on her face.

'Have you finished packing?' I'm able to see my breath, it's so cold in her room.

'What does it look like?' she growls.

The old suitcase Eddress and I took on honeymoon is sitting on the floor next to her with the lid down. 'Then put your coat on and get a move on,' I tell her.

'I'm not going.'

'Susan, we haven't got time for this.'

'I don't care. I'm not going.'

She starts to cry, but we've been through this enough times for me to know better than to start being soft with her.

'I can't go,' she says.

'Do as you're told now.'

'I'm not very well.'

Something else I've heard before. 'Then you can go and see matron when you get there.'

'I don't *want* to see her! I want to stay here, and you can't make me go.'

Maybe it's the cold, maybe it's guilt, or maybe I've just had enough, because I suddenly snap. 'You'll get down those stairs right now, my girl, or you'll be sorry.'

It's rare I lose my temper, so she looks startled for a second, then she's in for the battle. 'I'm not going,' she seethes.

I'm just not having this, so grabbing the suitcase I seize her arm and drag her across the room, out to the top of the stairs.

'Get off me, you're hurting,' she shouts.

'Keep your voice down, Gary's still asleep.'

'I don't care.'

I go ahead down the stairs, pulling her after me. She's still resisting, but I don't let go, and when she tries to make herself fall I tighten my grip and keep her upright.

'Now put your bloody boots and coat on,' I tell her when we reach the bottom.

'Don't swear at me.'

'And don't cheek me back. I've had about all I can take of you, young lady. I'm just thankful your mother didn't live to see what you're turning into.'

'Don't say that!' she screams, launching herself at me. 'That's a horrible, wicked thing to say.'

'And you're a horrible, wicked girl. Now get out of that door.'

'Don't push me!'

'I said go.'

By the time we're on our way down the path, ducking

under frosty branches, and trying not to skid on the ice, she's sobbing so hard I hardly know whether to say sorry or slap her. 'I hate you for making me go,' she chokes. 'I don't want to be me any more. I wish I was dead. You'll be sorry then.'

I left the car up the top last night, so when she goes the wrong way at the gate I grab her hard and force her up the hill.

'Don't!' she shouts, tears streaming down her face as she tries to shake me off.

I shove her along. 'Do as you're told or you'll get a damned good hiding.'

'Why are you being so mean?' She skids and starts to fall, but I haul her up again. Then I slip and drop the suitcase and the bloody thing bursts open, spilling her stuff out on to the street.

'Look what you've done now!' she shouts.

'It's your own damned fault,' I shout back. 'Now get in the car while I pick it up.'

There's no time to fold anything. I just shove it back in the case, handfuls of slush and all, snap shut the one clasp that's working and throw it on to the back seat.

'I hate you,' she wails as I get in the driver's side next to her.

'Shut up,' I bark. 'I've had all I can take from you this morning, now I don't want to hear another word.'

She turns her head away, but I can still hear her crying.

'Stop that damned snivelling,' I snap, annoyed by the sluggish turn of the engine.

'I can't help it!' she cries. 'You're being horrible to me, and you threw all my clothes in the street, so why don't you do the same to me?'

'Don't tempt me,' and sending a silent thank you to God as the engine catches, I start driving gingerly along the road.

Getting out of Greenways and Dawn Rise is a risky business, but at least we don't bang into any of the parked cars, and when we get to Tennis Court Road the gritters have already been round so it starts to get easier.

We might just make it to Mrs Beach's in time, if not I'll end up having to take her the whole way myself, and I can't afford to be late for work this morning, not with how much we've spent over Christmas. I need to put in all the hours I can now.

By the time we get to Fishponds Mrs Beach and Glenys are already in their car, so I quickly apologise for being late, and after dumping our Susan's case in the boot I turn round to give her a kiss. It's only now I'm having to let her go that I start to feel terrible about the way I shoved her out of the house and dropped all her clothes in the street.

'I'm sorry, my darling,' I say, giving her a hug. 'I shouldn't have shouted at you. Are you going to be all right?'

'No,' she sniffs.

I tilt up her face. 'I'll be up to collect you on Thursday afternoon, all right? We've got another appointment with Dr Leigh.'

'I'm not going,' she mutters.

Now isn't the time to argue. 'Off you go,' I say, 'or you'll make Glenys late.'

Mercifully, she does as she's told and I stand watching her, wishing with all my heart that I could start this morning all over again.

Chapter Sixteen

Susan

'Sssh,' Sadie giggles as we hug ourselves tightly to the art-room Terrapin, trying to keep out of sight of the main school. (A Terrapin is a big hut with steps up to it and lots of windows – a bit like a portable classroom, I suppose.)

'I'll go and see if anyone's inside,' Cheryl gamely offers, and tiptoeing on ahead, she climbs the steps and peers in through the porthole window of the door.

'All clear,' she calls back.

The rest of us, me, Sadie, Peg, Sally and Ros, scuttle as quickly as we can to the steps and disappear like we're being swallowed up into the art room.

'OK, everybody grab one,' I say, 'the biggest you can find.'

'What colour?' Ros asks.

'It doesn't matter. Any will do.'

Moving like a tornado we rush round the art room scooping up giant cans of powder paint, and when everyone has one tucked under their arm, we tiptoe out again, even though there's no one around to hear us.

Getting back to the main building is chancy, because for some of the way we're in full view of the sixth-form common room *and* Dot's private flat. If anyone sees us we've got a story ready, the trouble is I've forgotten what it is, so I'm really hoping that either someone else remembers, or, better still, that we don't get caught. (This might get me expelled, but we have to commit the whole crime before anyone finds out, or it won't be serious enough.)

By the time we get round to the stable block, no one's come out to ask what we're up to so it seems we're in the clear.

'I can't open the fucking door,' Peg swears, shoving herself against a small one that leads into the boiler rooms.

'It was open just now,' Sadie hisses. 'Someone must have locked it.'

We look round cautiously. If someone's split on us, and we find out who, they'll be paying for the rest of their lives. There's no one about, and all the windows that overlook the stable yard are empty. No one seems to be watching, but we're very exposed standing where we are like this, so we have to get out of sight soon.

'Give it another push,' I say. 'All of us together.'

Sadie gets hold of the handle, we all surge forward and go flying in through the door, landing in a tangled, hysterical heap on the cobwebby floor.

'Didn't you think to turn the handle?' Sadie accuses Peg.

'It doesn't matter,' Cheryl says as we pick ourselves up. 'We're in now, so let's get on with it.'

The room is dark, hot and smelly, and probably full of rats and spiders, but we try to ignore all that as we set about doing what we came here to do.

It was my idea to empty powder paint into the water tanks to change the colour of the water. I overheard a couple of fifth-form girls talking about it at supper last Friday. They were saying how someone had attempted it once, expecting to turn the water red, but it hadn't worked, which was a pity because it was a brilliant idea.

I thought so too, which is why I decided we should give it a go, and we shouldn't limit ourselves to just red, because maybe whoever tried it before us hadn't put in enough tins of powder.

I think it's fantastic the way everyone is helping me to get expelled. They understand how important it is for me to go home and be with Kev, especially since we got engaged over Christmas. (That's what I've told them, and they seem to believe me, even though I don't have a ring yet, but I've said he's still saving up to get me one, which, for all I know, he might be.)

'When's he coming up to see you?' Peg wanted to know.

'He can't, you idiot! Remember how old he is. If he gets caught he'd really be in trouble.'

'I don't think he exists,' she scoffed.

I wanted to whack her, but instead I turned to Sadie. 'Does he, or doesn't he exist?' I demanded.

'I've met him,' Sadie told Peg, which really shut her up.

'So have I,' Cheryl added, which shut her up even more. Stupid cow.

She's all right though really, especially when she's willing to get into trouble herself in order to help me get out of here.

'What shall we do with the cans?' Ros asks when they're all empty.

Since she's only a first-former, and is struck on me, she's allowed to ask stupid questions.

'We take them back to the art room,' Sally answers sarcastically.

'No, we don't,' I tell Ros. 'We leave them here. Now let's go before someone comes.'

By the time we get to the rec area we're all in hysterics again, but we refuse to tell anyone why, which gets them all worked up, and snooty, making us laugh even more. I'm glad I'm not one of them, it's much more fun being us.

'How long do you think it'll take for the water to change colour?' Sadie whispers to me when we're on our way up to bed.

'How do I know? Let's hope it's soon and it's black.'

Eddie

'Thank you for coming again, Mr Lewis,' Dr Leigh says.

I quickly tuck my cap under my arm in order to shake his hand.

'Please sit down.'

Our Susan's outside in the waiting room. I'm still feeling wretched about the morning she went back to school, even though I wrote her a letter that same day to apologise. I said sorry again while we were on our way here. She told me she'd already forgotten it, but given how shirty she was with me, I don't think she has.

I've no idea what Dr Leigh said to her during their session, or what she said to him. She still hasn't told me much about the last time we came, except she thinks it was boring and a waste of time.

'Did you have a good Christmas?' Dr Leigh asks.

I wonder if he's making pleasant chat, or if this is relevant to our session. 'It was lovely, thank you,' I say, and I immediately wonder if he asked our Susan the same question and got a different reply.

He smiles. 'That's good. And did Susan enjoy it?'

Is he trying to trick me? I'm not sure, but I don't want to be rude, so I say, 'She had a nice lot of presents, and I think she was glad to be home for a while.'

'What did she do during the break?'

I shift about in my chair as I recall the night I frogmarched her back from the bus stop, and the other times she disappeared without telling me where she was going. I'm sure she won't have told him about that, and though I'd dearly love to ask his advice on how to handle her, I'm too afraid that if he thinks I can't cope he'll end up recommending that she doesn't come home for holidays any more. That'd break both our hearts. So all I say is, 'We went to see her aunties, and her grandmother.'

He nods. 'Does she have many friends around where you live?'

I swallow hard. 'Yes. She's grown up with most of them.'

'And what about a boyfriend?'

Though it feels like a blow, I have a go at laughing it off. 'She's too young for that,' I remind him. Then, afraid she might have told him about the Sawyer boy, I add, 'Of course, she has a few crushes, mostly on pop stars, and friends' older brothers, you know the sort of thing. Girls her age, their heads are full of romantic nonsense.'

He smiles again and seems to agree, which is a relief.

'Do you talk much, the two of you?' he asks.

I wish I knew the best way to answer that, but without knowing where it's leading all I can say is, 'Quite a bit.'

'What about, mainly?'

'Oh, you know, all sorts of things. I try to help with her lessons, and get her interested in what's going on in the world.'

'And does she readily engage?'

I swallow again. 'Usually.'

He nods and looks down at his notes. 'Tell me, Mr Lewis,' he says, 'does Susan ever talk about her mother?'

The question throws me so much that I feel myself starting to sweat. 'Not really,' I reply.

'Do you ever mention your wife to your children?'

I wouldn't mind leaving now, but then I decide there's probably no harm in telling the truth, so I say, 'Not very often. I don't see the point in upsetting them, and I think it would if I started talking about her when I've already explained to them that she's gone to heaven.'

He writes something down on his notepad, then asks, 'Do you think Susan's behaviour at school might be in some way connected to losing her mother?'

I have to admit I do think that, but we can't bring Eddress back, can we – and if he thinks she is still missing her mother he might wonder if it's because I'm not doing a good enough job with her. I'm not, I know that, but I'm so afraid they'll stop me from seeing her that all I say is, 'Obviously it hasn't been easy for her, a mother is a big influence in a child's life, but I think what's happening now is that she's trying to grow up too quickly. She's a headstrong girl who, if she doesn't get her own way, makes us all suffer. Even her grandmother says that.'

He makes some more notes, and I feel like getting out my

own notebook to show him that two can play at that game. 'Is Susan's grandmother on her maternal side, or paternal?' he wants to know.

'Maternal.'

'And does she have a close relationship with her?'

'I think so, yes.'

'If you don't mind me asking, how old is her grandmother?'

'Eighty-two.'

'And is she in good health?'

'She's got diabetes, and she has a job walking, so she doesn't get out much, but other than that, she's not too bad considering her age.'

'How many other grandchildren does she have?'

'She says it's forty-five, but I'm sure that includes great-grandchildren too. Probably even some great-great-grandchildren by now.'

Off goes his pen again, and I can feel mine starting to twitch, a bit like a sword sharpening up for a fight.

'Tell me, do you think it would be in Susan's best interests for her to return home to live?' he asks.

He's really gone and floored me now. If I say yes, it might let her out of Red Maids, which would deprive her of the lovely future her mother had planned, and if I say no they might think I don't want her and take her out anyway and send her even further away. 'I was hoping,' I hear myself say, 'that you might be able to give me some advice about that.'

Susan

'It has come to my attention,' Dot's saying in her deepest manly voice, 'that the water in this school has turned purple.'

We're all doing our best to keep a straight face, but it's really hard. Laura nudges me, even though she wasn't a part of it, but she knows it was me, and her shoulders are shaking with laughter. I sneak a look behind me to where Sadie and Cheryl are standing in the third-form rows. They're doing their best to look all innocent too, but I can see they're nearly splitting their sides.

We're in morning assembly, with Dot up on the stage and several of the teachers standing along the side of the hall like ravens about to go in for the kill. I feel a bit like a tasty snack as they eye me up, so I deliberately turn away from them.

It's taken four days for the water to change colour, but it finally has, and we were all laughing so much this morning, when we went into the bathrooms and turned on the taps, that we nearly missed the breakfast bell.

'I won't ask who's responsible for this childish act of sabotage,' Dot goes on. 'Susan Lewis, I'll see you in my study straight after morning prayers.'

'What?' I cry. 'Why me? *Ouch!*' Bloody Scatty's only given me a clout on the back of the head. She's going to suffer for that in our next English lesson, just let her wait and see.

'Everyone kneel,' Dot orders.

Down we go, catching our stockings on the rough wooden floor and splintering our knees as we put our hands together and close our eyes. I feel a nudge in my back and turn round. It's come down the line from Sadie, who gives me the thumbs up. I grin, then quickly put my head down before Scatty can biff me again.

'Almighty and most merciful Father, we have erred and strayed from Thy ways like lost sheep . . . '

As Dot drones on I think about the reason Sadie gave me the thumbs up. I know it's because this might get me expelled, or at least one step closer. It would be fantastic if it happened today, because I've been back for two weeks now and Kev hasn't answered even one of my letters. Everyone says that's typical of men, so I shouldn't be worried, but I know they're all thinking it's really strange when we're supposed to be engaged. Privately I've wondered if he can actually write, but I wouldn't say that to anyone because I don't want them to think he's thick, and really, I'm sure he can.

Yesterday, Dad and I went to see Dr Leigh again. It was horrible and boring and I wish we could stop going, because he keeps on asking questions I don't want to answer.

'Do you feel angry inside?' he asked.

'No,' I answered, even though I sometimes do, quite a lot.

'What would you say to your mother if you could see her again?'

My insides turned over when he asked that because I thought she might be about to walk in the room. I even looked at the door in case it opened. It didn't, though, and for a minute I wanted to hit him for making me think she was there. 'I wouldn't say anything,' I told him.

He didn't look as though he believed me. 'Do you feel she's let you down?'

Yes, I do, but I wasn't going to tell him that, when it wasn't her fault she died. So I said, 'No.'

'Do you think you should be taking her place at home, looking after your father and brother?'

'Yes,' I answered, hoping he would agree.

'How would you feel if your father got married again?'

I felt my face turning red when he asked that, and I almost got up and ran away. 'He's not going to,' I told him fiercely. 'He doesn't want to.'

He wrote something down, then said, 'Do you believe your mother loved you?'

'Of course she did,' I snapped. I keep worrying that she might not have, but I'm not going to tell him that.

'And what about your father? Do you believe that he loves you too?'

I know he does, but I found it hard to answer because I was nearly crying. So I nodded.

'Do you think, when you get into trouble, that you could

be testing him, to find out if he'll love you no matter what?'

I didn't know what to say to that, because me getting into trouble has nothing to do with Dad, apart from wanting to be at home with him.

He went on waiting for an answer.

'No, I don't think I'm testing him,' I said, still trying not to cry, because I hate the thought of upsetting Dad, even though I have to sometimes or I'll never get to go home.

'What would you like to do when you leave school?' the doctor asked. 'What kind of career would you like to pursue?'

That one was easy. 'I want to get married and have children.'

He looked surprised. 'Any desire to go to college or university?'

'No.'

'Any ambition to become a lawyer, a social worker, a manager of some kind?'

'No.'

'Do you think you're helping yourself by always saying no?'

'No.'

He raised an eyebrow, then I realised he'd caught me out.

'Tell me about your friends,' he said. 'Are they mostly older or younger than you?'

'Older.'

'Very much older?'

I thought about Kev and said, 'Some of them, yes, but I'm not like other girls my age. I've had to grow up more quickly.'

'Why do you say that?'

'Because I haven't got a mother.'

He wrote something down again, then luckily the buzzer sounded on his desk and it was Dad's turn to come in, and mine to wait outside, so off I went. I kept my head down as Dad went past so he wouldn't see I was still on the verge of crying.

Actually, being left on my own in the waiting room gave me a good opportunity to run away, because I know how to get from the clinic to Kev's factory, but I was in my uniform and I'd rather die than let him see me in that.

Later, when we were driving back to school, Dad said, 'How did you get on with Dr Leigh?'

'All right,' I replied. I thought again about the way he asked if I was testing Dad. Why did he have to say that? Of course I wasn't testing him.

'What sort of things did he ask you?'

'Just dumb things. What did he ask you?'

He took his time answering, and in the end he said, 'Just dumb things too,' and then we didn't talk about it any more.

I'm in Dot's study now, standing in front of her desk while she talks to someone on the phone. It sounds like it's about the work they're having to do to clean out the hot-water tanks.

When she's finished she replaces the receiver and looks at me with her witchy eyes. 'Are you going to own up to this crime, or do we have to go through a time-wasting process of denial?' she asks.

What I really want to say is, up to you, but actually I'm quite scared of Dot so instead I say, 'All right, it was me.'

She nods, and I think she's quite pleased that I've decided to be honest. 'Now I'd like the names of the other culprits please.'

She's got to be joking! 'I did it on my own,' I tell her.

She seems to sink with disappointment. 'Are you trying to tell me you stole six large cans of powder paint from the art room single-handedly?' she asks.

I can see why she's finding it hard to believe, but she's not going to get me to split on anyone, so all I say is, 'No, miss.'

'Then what are you trying to tell me?'

'Nothing, miss.'

She sighs. 'The theft alone is putting you straight into detention,' she informs me. 'The mindless act of tipping all that powder paint into the water tanks is earning you another, plus a bill for the plumber's work that is now being carried out. Your refusal to co-operate with the names of your accomplices means that you will have to serve their detentions for them. It would seem logical to assume that there were at *least* four of you, so you will now serve six detentions, one after the other, which, by my calculations, means you will not be going home again this side of half-term. Now, please get out of my sight.'

I don't think that was a very nice way of telling me to leave, but I'm more than ready to go, and absolutely gutted about the detentions. She was supposed to expel me, the stupid cow, not keep me locked up even more than I already am.

Everything's going wrong, and now I haven't got a clue when I'll be able to see Kev again. I'll have to get Mandy to persuade him to come up to the back lane. If he does, then I'll pack everything I can into my satchel and run away with him. We can live somewhere in secret together until I'm old enough to get married and be his wife.

Eddie

I'm sitting in Fishponds library again, my usual place on a dinnertime, especially when the weather's bad. I love it in here, where everyone's quiet, as though respecting the solemnity and grandeur of so much knowledge. Sometimes, when I browse around, I feel as though I'm visiting old friends, or making new ones. Other times, I think of the bewildering variations of subject and content, the men and women who created these works, and the thousands, millions of people who've read them. I imagine that each volume that sits along the shelves contains a single piece of an enormous puzzle that would, if I could track all the pieces down, create a full and glorious understanding of life itself.

Today, in order to exercise my pen and free my mind

from the awful captivity of worry, I have been writing out Shakespeare's Sonnet 18.

Shall I compare thee to a summer's day?
Thou art more lovely and more temperate:
Rough winds do shake the darling buds of May,
And summer's lease hath all too short a date:
Sometime too hot the eye of heaven shines,
And often is his gold complexion dimm'd;
And every fair from fair sometime declines,
By chance, or nature's changing course untrimm'd;
But thy eternal summer shall not fade,
Nor lose possession of that fair thou ow'st;
Nor shall Death brag thou wander'st in his shade,
When in eternal lines to time thou growest;
So long as men can breathe, or eyes can see,
So long lives this, and this gives life to thee.

Since I first started to read the sonnets, back when I was a boy and our priest gave me an old copy that belonged to someone who'd died, I've loved every one of them. Their music sings through my soul as I read them, whether silently to myself, or aloud, as I used to for Eddress. She didn't read them herself, she never had time, she'd say, but whenever I started to recite one she'd pause in what she was doing and let the beauty of the words fall around her like summer blooms. That was how I liked to see her, radiant and refreshed by the master's verse. She always claimed not to understand it, it was my voice she liked to listen to, she said, but there were times when she'd recite some of Sonnet 18 along with me, and whether she understood the words or not, they always brought a light to her eyes.

I said that to her once and she called me a daft old sod. That was Eddress, always ready to quash romance, while thriving on it really.

I'd love to think there was a sonnet that could reach our

Susan. I fear it's going to take a lot more than that, though, to alter the course that's about to unfold.

I went to see Dr Leigh on my own yesterday morning, and he was very polite and regretful when he told me that Miss Dakin would like me to remove Susan from Red Maids School at half-term.

She's too disruptive and is leading other girls astray. It wouldn't be fair for their education to suffer any more than it already has, so the bad apple that is spoiling the barrel must be cast out.

Those weren't his words, of course. It's what I'm writing down now, with my sandwiches next to me, uneaten, unwrapped, and my flask of tea, also untouched. I don't know yet where they're intending to send her, Dr Leigh was talking about somewhere in the Midlands, but I told him I didn't want that. If she's not going to be at Red Maids, then I want her at home with me.

I'll have to see about borrowing a car when I go to pick her up for half-term next week, because the Anglia's packed up on us, and I expect she'll have quite a lot to bring home. He said I can break the news to her myself after church this Sunday. It'll be a good opportunity to pray for guidance before I see her.

I think I'll borrow Kant's *Metaphysics of Morals* today. He always gets my mind going, and a busy mind is a far healthier mind than one that is steeped in misgivings and dread.

Oh Eddress, my love, what am I to do with our girl?

Chapter Seventeen

Susan

That's it! We've definitely got to run away now. I've just managed to push Seaweed down the stairs – by mistake – and I think she's broken her neck. Or her leg, or her nose – definitely her record for getting on people's nerves.

'It was her own fault,' Sadie gasps, as we race into the dorm. 'She shouldn't have pushed you first. And all you did was turn around. You didn't actually shove her.'

It's true, I didn't, but I know she's going to say I did, so before everyone can start blaming me for something I didn't do, Sadie and I are going to make ourselves scarce. We've been plotting our escape all day anyway, drawing maps and working out how to get to Temple Meads station from here, so we're already quite well prepared.

Word that we're going spreads round the dorms like wildfire, and by the time we've dressed in all five of our uniforms to keep warm, and collected up as much tuck as we can get into the inside pockets of our cloaks, we find that everyone's been donating as much cash as they can spare to help us on our way.

Cheryl hands us the money. 'Ten pounds thirteen and eight,' she says. Her eyes are brimming with tears. She doesn't want us to go, and we don't want to leave her, but we don't have a choice now Seaweed's gone and injured herself.

'I'll go and make sure the coast is clear,' Cheryl tells us, and as she zooms off to check, we start saying our goodbyes to everyone else. It takes ages, because all the first, second and third years from the other dorms have managed to sneak up to Speedwell to wish us good luck.

'Don't forget to write,' Peg says, giving us a hug. 'And don't worry about paying me back.'

I don't think either Sadie or I have even considered it, but it is nice of her to be that generous, so we thank her, then creep out of the dorm to see what Cheryl's up to.

'Everything's really quiet,' she whispers, when we reach her at the top of the stairs. 'They must be in Seaweed's office.'

'We should go before the ambulance gets here,' I say to Sadie.

'Or the police,' Cheryl adds.

I turn cold and can't wait to get out of there.

It's Saturday night and the older girls are either in the sixth-form common room, or watching telly in the main hall. That's where Sadie and I were when Seaweed found us. We'd crept down after lights out to watch the entries for *The Eurovision Song Contest*. Honestly, the fuss she made when she discovered us. You'd have thought we'd committed a major crime, and if she hadn't kept poking me in the back all the way up the stairs, before shoving me really hard on to the nursery landing, I wouldn't have got angry and turned round so fast. I think I frightened her, because my hand was up, but only to stop her hitting me again. She probably thought I was going to whack her, so she took a step back and the next thing we knew she was bouncing down the stairs – in so far as someone that thin can bounce!

I hope she's still alive, even if she isn't in one piece, but only because I don't want the blame for her death, otherwise I wish she'd bugger off to the pearly gates as soon as she likes and leave us all alone.

I could be in really big trouble for this, and I'm actually scared stiff, but it's best not to let it show.

I wish there was a way of letting Mandy know what we're doing, because she could get word to Kev and he might come to find us. We'd be a lot safer going out at night with him around, and he'd probably know exactly how to get from here to the station. When half-term comes next Thursday I'll go home as normal, but until then Sadie and I are going to her parents' house in Dover, because they're in the Caribbean at the moment so there's no one there. It would be great if Kev could come with us, and Slash, because Sadie's got a big crush on Slash now. We could spend five days, just the four of us, cooking and smoking, and lazing about in front of the telly. It would be like we were all married.

I suppose I'll have to get a note to Dad somehow to let him know I'm all right, or he'll only worry – or end up calling the police

It's pitch black outside and *freezing* cold. There's no moon, only a howling wind and things scuttling about the undergrowth as we scurry down the drive, making us shudder and jump.

Once we're out on the main road we can see a lot better, thanks to street lamps and headlights. We walk top speed towards the Downs, certain we know how to get across them to Clifton. From there we're going to follow the same route we take on Founder's Day, down to the cathedral, and after that we're not sure where Temple Meads is, but I expect we'll find it.

The Downs are really spooky at night. Trees are looming up all over the place like monsters ready to pounce, and I'm sure loads of bogeymen and loonies are hidden inside the bushes waiting to jump out and flash us. I'm starting to feel quite afraid, and I think Sadie is too. We hold tight to one another's arms and walk so fast we're almost at a run.

A car slows up on the other side of the road.

'Don't look,' Sadie hisses. 'Keep going.'

We walk and walk and the Downs never seem to end. There's nothing but a sea of black grass all around us, and I'm starting to wonder if we've taken a wrong turn.

After a while another car slows up alongside us. I take a quick peek and my heart nearly jumps out of my chest. 'It's the police.' They're going to arrest me for hurting Seaweed, I know they are. We have to run.

'Madams! Madams!' one of the policemen calls out. They're driving alongside us, keeping up with our pace.

'Don't listen,' I tell Sadie.

'Madams, could you stop a minute please?'

We don't. We just keep going, holding tight to each other and trying to pretend they aren't there. But then they drive past us and stop the car.

'They're getting out,' Sadie gulps.

We stay where we are, frozen to the spot, watching them coming towards us.

'Are you from Red Maids School?' one of them asks.

I try to swallow. I'm going to be arrested now, I know it. I'll go to prison and I'll never see Dad or Gary or Kev again.

'You are, aren't you?' he says. He sounds quite nice, but you can never tell, it might be a trick to get us to trust him. 'So what are you doing out here on the Downs at this time of night?' he asks.

It's either still a trick, or he doesn't know about Seaweed. 'We're . . . We're going home for half-term,' I tell him.

'I see. And do your parents know you're coming?'

I feel Sadie's arm tighten on mine. Neither of us replies.

'Do you know what?' he says. 'I have a feeling you might be running away. Am I right?'

We only look at him, not saying a word.

'I think I am,' he decides, 'and it's too dangerous around here for young ladies to be wandering about on their own, so you'd best get in the car. We'll take you back to school.'

I don't want to do as he says, and I don't think Sadie does either, but neither of us has the guts to argue with the police. Also, if we are lost, we could be out here all night, and if we aren't murdered we'd probably end up freezing to death anyway.

As they turn the car around I start to panic about

Seaweed again, because if the police don't know yet, someone will be bound to tell them when we get there, and there's no knowing what they might do, especially if she's dead.

The policeman in the passenger seat says, 'It's not that bad at your school, is it, that you have to run away?'

Sadie doesn't hold back. 'It's horrid,' she tells him. 'We hate it there, don't we, Su? The teachers are really mean to us. They treat us like slaves, or as though we're in prison. I don't think it should be allowed.'

'No, it shouldn't,' I say. 'We have to go to bed at seven o'clock, and when we get up in the mornings we have to do offices, like servants, and we're never allowed to go out of the grounds, except for church on Sundays.'

'And if we do even the slightest thing wrong,' Sadie continues, 'they put us in detention to stop us going home on our exeats.'

'That's right,' I confirm. 'I haven't been home now since Christmas, which is ages ago. They're wicked, our teachers, so we're glad to have the chance to report them.' If I can let them know how foul and mean everyone is before we get there, they might be a bit more understanding about what I did when they find out.

Neither of the policemen says any more after that, but I think they might be wondering if it's a good idea to return us to such a terrible place.

They do though, because a few minutes later we're going up the drive, and when we reach the front door Dot and Cluttie are only standing there waiting!

'Go inside,' Dot orders us in a voice that's as deep as the Devil's. 'Miss Clutterbuck will see to you.'

As we pass her she says to the police, 'Thank you, officers. You've been most helpful.'

'Happy to oblige, ma'am,' one of them replies, and then we're on our way up the front stairs – *front stairs*, we're never allowed to use them normally – to Dot's private flat. I wonder if I should ask about Seaweed, but I don't dare to say a word as Clut makes us stand outside the flat, facing the wall, until Dot comes up.

When she does she says, 'Susan, you'll sleep in the lower nursery tonight. Sadie, you will sleep in the upper. Miss Clutterbuck has already collected your night clothes and toiletries from your cubicles, so there will be no need for you to return to the dormitories. I'm sorry that it's going to be necessary to lock you in, but your actions this evening have left us with no choice. Now off you go, I'll speak to you again before church in the morning.'

Not a word about Seaweed. Does that mean she's all right? I really hope so, because I swear I didn't mean to hurt her, even though I hate her guts and wish she'd get carried off by aliens.

I'm on my own in the lower nursery, because no one's sick. I wonder if Sadie's on her own too, over the other side of the landing, at the end of a spooky corridor. I'm glad I didn't have to go there, I'd never have been able to get to sleep if I had. As it is, I might not be able to anyway.

'Can I keep the light on?' I ask Clut when she comes to check on me.

'It's "may I", and the answer is no, you may not.'

Typical. She's such an old bag. I'd never be like her if I was in her position.

'It's lucky for you, young lady,' she goes on, 'that Miss Sayward only twisted her ankle when she fell. There might have been some serious consequences to pay if it had been any worse.'

Well, that's a relief anyway, at least I won't be going to prison, except I'm in one already.

As soon as I hear Cluttie turn the key, I wait for her footsteps to clomp and creak off along the landing, then I turn on the light. No way am I going to stay here on my own in the dark.

I wonder if the other girls know we've been brought back yet. They'll all be talking about it if they do. If they don't they'll find out in the morning, when I expect they'll want their tuck and money back.

Remembering the tuck in my cloak pocket, I go and dig out an Aero and take it back to bed. I wish I had a book to read, but there's nothing in here at all, apart from five empty beds, a curtained cubicle at one end where the doctor does his examinations, piles of clean linen on the shelves next to it, and all sorts of medical stuff. We finished the best book I've ever read in English Lit the other day. It's called *Pride and Prejudice*. I love Darcy so much that I've already started reading it again. He reminds me of Kev, moody and handsome, and pretending not to be interested in Elizabeth, when really he's madly in love with her. Well, actually, he looked down his nose a bit at her at first, but then it all ends happily, which is what really counts.

Yesterday, because I was bored, I decided to pay attention during Latin, just for something to do. To my surprise I didn't find it very difficult, which made me wonder why everyone gets such bad marks. I probably got it all wrong though, and what do I care? It's a dumb language anyway. No one speaks it, except doctors and Catholics, and so I don't see why we have to study it unless we want to be nuns or nurses.

I think about that for a while, mulling over the idea of being in a convent or working down Frenchay Hospital. I'd much rather be an air hostess, or a model, or a fashion designer. I'd have people working for me who could do all the sewing, like the girls who work up the corset factory. I'd be the boss and tell them which machines they have to work on, and when they can take their breaks.

Yes, I think I'd like to be in charge.

It's morning now and I'm standing outside Dot's flat waiting for her to open the door. Cluttie says Dot knows I'm here, so I don't have to knock, I just have to face the wall and keep my lips together. As she walks away I open my mouth as wide as it'll go, then poke out my tongue.

There's no one else on the landing, but I can hear plenty of footsteps charging down the back stairs as everyone gathers outside ready to crocodile off to church. I hope they're going to let me go too, otherwise I won't see Dad.

I had the most terrible thought earlier, when Cluttie brought my breakfast into the nursery. What if they're going to keep me in detention for the whole half-term holiday? I'll go mad if they do. I won't let them get away with it, because I've gone long enough without seeing Kev, I can't go any longer.

Dot's door opens. 'All right, Susan, come in,' she says.

I've never been in her private quarters before, so I'm feeling quite important as well as a bit nervous as I step inside. Her sitting room turns out to be not very different to her study, dark and old-fashioned and full of books that smell. She's got some nice armchairs either side of her gas fire, and some paintings of the countryside hanging on the walls. There's a grand piano in one corner close to the window. I didn't know she could play. I wonder if Celery sings when they have their private evenings together in here. Everyone says they're lezzies and I expect it's true.

'Sit down,' Dot says, pointing to one of the armchairs.

She's never let me sit down before, so it makes me feel a bit suspicious to be invited to now.

She sits down opposite me, and rests her elbows on the arms of the chair. 'I don't think you're aware yet,' she says, 'that you are due to leave this school on Thursday, when the half-term holiday begins.'

My heart gives a jump. No, I didn't know that. *Please don't let her be about to tell me she's changed her mind now, and is going to punish me for last night by keeping me here.*

'In the light of your escapade yesterday evening,' she continues, 'I am going to ask your father to remove you today.'

It takes me a second to realise what she's said, then a weird thing happens: my head starts to spin.

'Miss Clutterbuck has brought your suitcase and personal clothing out of storage, and once we've all left for church, I'd like you to go upstairs to pack your belongings.'

I don't know what to say. This is exactly what I wanted, except now it's happening I'm not really sure . . . It's all a bit fast. I mean . . . I can't make myself think . . .

'I'm truly sorry it's come to this, Susan,' she goes on, sounding quite friendly for her, 'but I'm afraid I can't allow you to continue disrupting the education of the other girls. Last night was the final straw. If Miss Ellery and I hadn't spotted you and Sadie on the Downs as we were driving by, I dread to think what could have happened to you. So, it's for your own safety, as well as the safety of your friends, not to mention the reputation of the school, that I'm being forced to let you go.'

I feel my eyes starting to sting with tears, but I don't want her to see, so I put my head down. What's Dad going to say? He's going to be really angry and upset . . . What am I going to do if he says he doesn't want me at home? I don't think he does, that's why he's always made me stay here. *Dad! Dad!* I want to shout. I wish he was here. I want him to say that everything's going to be all right.

'I'd like to wish you the very best for the future,' Dotty says, standing up and holding out a hand to shake. 'I hope you'll find greater happiness in your next school.'

I still don't know what to say, but my throat's too tight to let out any words anyway.

She walks to the door with me, and puts a hand on my head before I go through. 'God bless you, my dear,' she murmurs, which is the only nice thing I've ever heard her say. It makes me even more upset, but I'm not going to let it show. I wish she'd been nice to me before, I think I could get to like her if she wasn't always telling me off.

Cluttie is waiting for me in the nursery. My suitcase is standing in the middle of the floor, and my denim jacket and jeans are hanging on the door. I'm so pleased to see them that I forget, for a minute, how scared I am. 'Take your things up to the dorm,' Cluttie says. 'I'll be along to help you once I've spoken to Miss Dakin again.'

She drapes my clothes over my arm, and hands me my empty suitcase. The broken clasp is sticking out at an angle, reminding me of the morning it sprang open and everything fell out.

I'm going along the corridor to the dorm when Sadie comes out.

'What are you doing here?' I whisper. 'I thought everyone had gone to church.'

'Dot's taking me in her car,' she replies. 'Why have you got your suitcase?' Her eyes suddenly go very wide. 'Are you being expelled?' she gasps.

I nod and try to look pleased.

She claps a hand over her mouth, and then we throw our arms round one another. I'm trying not to cry and I think she is too. I make myself laugh and have a go at jumping up and down with glee, but nothing seems to be coming out quite right.

Eddie

I'm standing close to the back of the church with Gary. The Red Maids are all in now, filling up the front rows in their smart gaberdines and jaunty black hats. I didn't see our Susan go by, but that's not unusual, because sometimes we manage to miss her, and we arrived a bit late today. Not too late to see Sadie come in last with Miss Dakin, and after she took a place in one of the pews the whispering started up, buzzing along the lines like a current of electricity. Instinct alone tells me it's about our Susan, and the fact that her best friend was escorted here by the headmistress can only mean they've been in trouble again. Normally, I'd be working myself into a state of anxiety by now, but since the worst has already happened, I'm only feeling embarrassed and apologetic that she's caused so much fuss.

For once I find it difficult to pay attention to the service, though Gary and I sing along with the hymns, and go down on our knees to pray. I'm aware of the other parents around us and I can't help wishing my life was as easy as theirs. Of course, I don't know anything about their lives really, but one thing I do know is that their daughters aren't on the verge of being expelled.

I feel as though the future is collapsing in front of us. All the wonderful opportunities are turning to dust, the hope has already slipped away.

> . . . the world, which seems
> To lie before us like a land of dreams,
> So various, so beautiful, so new,
> Hath really neither joy, nor love, nor light,
> Nor certitude, nor peace, nor help for pain;
> And we are here as on a darkling plain
> Swept with confused alarms of struggle and flight . . .

When the service is over the girls start filing out, and, as usual, most of them call out a cheery hello to Gary. He's become a bit of a favourite with them, so he'll miss coming here, I'm sure.

'Good morning, Mr Lewis,' Miss Dakin says when I walk outside. 'Susan didn't come to church today. She's still at school.'

'Is she all right?' I ask.

'She's in good health. Do you have your car with you?'

'No, we came on the bus.'

'Then perhaps I can offer you a lift back in mine.'

This honour doesn't bode well, but I expect she wants to talk to me about what's happening on Thursday, so I open the back door of her Humber for Gary to climb in, then slide into the passenger seat myself, feeling everyone's eyes watching us. I wonder if anyone knows yet that Susan's being expelled on Thursday. The shame of it is crippling me, but I manage to keep my head up and behave with as much dignity as I can muster. Maybe it's what the whispering was about in church, someone let the cat out of the bag, and now it's all round the school. I suppose some of them will be thinking she wasn't good enough to be here anyway, so good riddance. It hasn't been easy for her, mixing with her betters, I wonder if any of them have considered that. Did they make allowances for her? If they did, they're not going to any more, and I suppose I can't blame them.

'I'm afraid,' Miss Dakin says, as we drive along, 'that it's been necessary to ask Susan to leave school today. She should be packed by the time we return.'

This new blow comes right out of the blue, so it's a moment or two before I can say, 'I see.' My throat's turned so dry that my voice sounds scratched and unsteady.

'Last night, she and Sadie Hicks left the school premises without permission,' she continues. 'They were picked up on the Downs by the police. I believe it was their intention to run away. As to their intended destination, I have no idea. Fortunately, they were discovered before any harm befell them.'

'I see,' I manage to say again.

I'm not sure what else I want to say, until remembering my manners, I apologise for the inconvenience and concern she must have caused. Then I feel a flash of blinding anger, though I'm not sure whether it's towards our Susan, the school or life itself.

When we get back to school Susan's waiting with her suitcase at the front door. She's wearing her denim jacket and jeans and looks very pale in the face and red around the eyes.

Angry as I am, I can't help thinking of how hard things have been for her, trying to fit in, wanting to be at home, missing her mother, being all confused about growing up. And she looks so lonely and afraid standing there. 'It's all right my love,' I say, going to give her a hug. They might not want her any more, but I always will, and that's never going to change. And what's the point in telling her off, much as I'd like to? It's too late for that now. The damage has been done, and over time she'll see for herself what a mistake she's made throwing away this chance of a marvellous future. By the look of her though, I think it's already starting to dawn.

Miss Dakin wishes us well, and disappears inside the school. She probably can't wait for us to be gone.

'Have you got everything?' I ask Susan.

She nods, so I pick up her suitcase in one hand and take Gary's hand in the other to start walking down the drive.

We're about halfway along when a stampede of Red Maids suddenly rushes towards us. It seems half the boarders of the school have raced back from church to try and get here before she leaves.

Gary and I stand to one side watching as she hugs all her friends, most of whom seem to be crying. Susan is too, but I can see she's trying very hard not to.

'Congratulations,' some of them are saying.

'Well done, you did it!'

'We're really going to miss you.'

'Don't forget to write.'

'We love you Su Lu.'

'Come and see us on a Sunday.'

Sadie and Cheryl are sobbing as they cling to her. She's clinging to them too. I know in her heart she doesn't want to leave them, and it's breaking mine to see it. This is a very bitter lesson she's learning in being careful of what you wish for. How much am I to blame for this? What could I have done differently to make sure she fitted in and was happy?

In the end, I hear the bell ringing, summoning the girls for lunch, so I tell Susan it's time to go.

A large crowd walks to the gates with us, gathering round like they aren't going to let her go. I don't think she's ever felt so popular in her life. At the boundary they stand watching us walk away, waving and calling out 'Good luck' and 'We love you' until we're out of sight.

As we turn the corner I feel our Susan's hand slip into mine. I know she's still afraid of what I'm going to say, and trying her hardest not to cry, so I don't say anything as we carry on along the main road towards the bus stop. There'll be plenty of time for talking – and no doubt ranting and raving – when we get home; the important thing now is to get there.

Can you see us, Eddress? Are you watching us from wherever you are? What would you do with her now? Give me an answer please, because we've lost our way and I hardly know what to do any more.

I look down at Gary to find his little face turned anxiously up to me, and it's all I can do not to sweep him up in my arms and squeeze him to within an inch of his life. Instead, I force a smile and say, 'Well, here we are, three little pigs, wee, wee, wee, all the way home.'

Chapter Eighteen

Susan

This is the letter Gloucestershire County Education Office sent to my dad, which he let me see:

> *Dear Mr Lewis,*
>
> *I have now received the report of the Consultant Psychiatrist at the Downend Child Guidance Clinic and note that you are willing for Susan to return home. Arrangements have been made for her transfer to The Grange School for Girls, Kingswood, after half-term, i.e. 26th February, and I shall be glad if you will kindly telephone the school to make an appointment to see the Headmistress, Miss D.I.S. Fisher, as soon as possible. The telephone number is Bristol 674149.*
>
> *Yours sincerely*
> *C.P. Milroy, M.A.*
> *Chief Education Officer*

It was a huge relief to find out that I wasn't being sent hundreds of miles away to a place where I'd never see Dad or Gary or Kev – or put into care. Dad said they'd threatened to do that, but he'd told them he wouldn't allow it, and that I had to come home.

He made me stay in my room for two whole days when we got back from Red Maids, because he was so disappointed and angry he couldn't bring himself to look at me, or talk to me. 'If I do,' he said, before he closed my bedroom door, 'I can't promise not to give you the hiding of your life, and you damned well deserve it, my girl, I hope you know that.'

I lay on my bed crying and crying and hardly eating any of the meals that Gary brought up for me on a tray. I was really scared that Dad was thinking up a way to get rid of me again, or considering contacting the authorities to tell them to take me. I kept calling out to him, but he either didn't answer or he'd come to my door and say, 'I haven't forgiven you yet, and I'm not even sure that I can, so learn to be quiet instead of making things worse for yourself.'

I got so terrified that I started pushing the sheets down my throat to try and stop myself screaming. I kept wanting Mummy, but then I'd think of how disgusted she'd be with me too, and I hated myself so much that I wanted to kill myself – I would have if I'd only known how. I tried to get Gary to smuggle a note to Mandy letting her know I was being kept a prisoner, but he refused to. He even punched me for upsetting Dad. I didn't hit him back, because I know I deserved it, but I definitely would have if he'd done it again.

In the end, when Dad finally managed to bring himself to look at me, he came to sit on my bed and because I was sobbing so hard he pulled me on to his lap and told me to stop being silly. 'Of course I still love you,' he said, 'but what you've done, Susan, the way you've behaved . . . Well, I hope you realise by now how serious it was, and how hard it's been for me to forgive you.'

'But you have now?' I sobbed.

'Only because Jesus tells us to be forgiving and we can't go forward unless I do, but I want your promise that you'll try hard at your new school, and that you'll carry on going to see Dr Leigh.'

'All right, I promise,' I said, really meaning it, 'but you have to promise never to send me away again.'

'All right, I promise,' he said, and then he gave me one of his giant bear hugs which made me feel quite a bit better, because he seemed more like his old self.

After that he let me go back downstairs. I wanted to go out and see Mandy, but I didn't have the courage to ask, so we all sat and watched telly together until it was time for bed. He came in and kissed me goodnight and even read *The Taming of the Shrew* which is one of my favourite Lambs' Tales from Shakespeare. That Kate was really difficult and horrible to everyone, but in the end she became meek and obedient and her husband really loved her.

I wonder if Kev will love me if I'm meek and obedient?

I've been home for over a week now and I haven't seen Mandy at all. I found out yesterday that she's down at her gran's house, on the Isle of Wight, and won't be back until the end of the half-term break. In a way I'm quite relieved, because though I'm dying to see her and Kev, I'm a bit nervous about it too. Dad'll go completely mad if he finds out, and if I make him angry again he might break his promise and put me into care. So I've been spending most of my time writing letters to all my friends at Red Maids, and crying because I won't see them again. I mean, I'll go up the church on Sundays, but it won't be the same as sharing a dorm with them every night, getting into trouble together and complaining about our lessons and prep. I never, ever dreamt that I'd feel homesick for that vile place, but I have to admit that I do. I keep thinking about my bed with no one in it, and my chair in the classroom pushed up against the desk. It was horrid when *Top of the Pops* came on this week, because now I don't have them or Mummy to dance with any more.

I know it's my own fault, and I definitely don't want to go back there, but it's horrible losing people you love. I feel all miserable and fed up whenever I think about them. If only I could see Kev I'd probably feel all right again.

Actually, something that's good is that we've got a groovy new home help called Sarah Moon. I didn't get on very well with her at first, mainly because she was all full of herself and thought she could boss me around, but it didn't take me long to put her in her place. I was sorry after for upsetting her so much, but she shouldn't have walked into my bedroom without knocking. It wouldn't have been so bad if I was dressed, but I was only wearing my bags, and I *hate* anyone seeing me without any clothes. The way I screamed at her sent her running down the stairs, then she grabbed her coat and dashed out of the house. I stayed where I was, with a chair jammed up against my door so no one else could get in, and I was still there when Dad came home for his dinner.

We made up in the end, after Dad went round her house to explain that she has to knock on my door before walking in, and now we're almost like sisters we're so close. She looks quite a bit like Cathy McGowan, but with shorter, curlier hair. Her husband, John, works for the Pru, and they have an eight-month-old baby, Josephine, who's so sweet and cute you want to eat her all up. Sarah's mum takes care of Josie when Sarah comes to our house, which is every weekday morning to make breakfast, and again in the afternoon so she's there for when Gary gets home from school. I don't need anyone there for me at my age, but quite often when Sarah goes at five I leave a note for Dad to let him know that I've gone to her house with her, and that Gary's either with us, or in the Williamses' or the Lears'.

Sarah lives in one of the smart private houses over on Willis Road. I can just imagine me and Kev living somewhere like that when we get married.

I've been at The Grange School for about two months now, and I suppose it's not too bad. At least it's a brand-new building, so not fusty and creepy like Red Maids. There are loads more girls here than there were at Red Maids, and they all talk Bristolian, like me, and live around Kingswood and Warmley, like me. The ones I go round with think I'm really it for getting expelled and keep wanting to hear all about it. They think it's hilarious when I put on my posh voice. (I never let on that I don't always mean to, it just keeps coming out, or they'll think I'm a snob.) The lessons are quite easy, because I've already done a lot of them, and most of the teachers are loads younger than the ones I had before and even a bit trendier.

Actually, the best part of going to The Grange is having some freedom after we finish at quarter to four, when I can do more or less what I want until Dad comes home at twenty past five. If I don't go to Sarah's, I usually meet Mandy over at the bus stop where we wait for Kev and his friends to go past on their way home from work. Sometimes Mandy's friend Julie is there too, and if we walk over to the railway hut on the common with the chaps she usually goes with Larry or Clive, while Mandy goes with Rich, and I go with Kev. If Kev's not there I have to go with one of the others or Mandy and Julie say they won't let me go round with them any more, and if I don't go round with them I'll never see Kev, so I don't have a choice.

Most of the time when I'm out at night Dad thinks I'm in bed, or over Sarah's, but he caught me sneaking out last weekend, so I haven't dared to try it again since. Mandy's managed to creep into my bedroom a couple of times though, and we sit in the dark whispering about Kev and Rich until the coast is clear and she can creep out again.

I'd never tell Dad this, but actually going to The Grange isn't turning out to be anywhere near as fabsville as I thought it would be. I mean I like it some of the time, but I really miss Sadie and Cheryl and Laura, and even Peg and her gang. We write to one another every day, and I've even been up to visit them after church some Sundays. It feels really strange when the bell rings and they have to go in. I stand at the end of the drive watching them, waving until I can't see them any more, then I walk off to the bus stop wondering what they're having for dinner, and thinking about all the laughs we used to have. It's horrible having to go home on my own, and even remembering that I don't have to lie on my bed for two hours doing nothing doesn't seem to cheer me up very much.

They say they really miss me too, and that life's become

very dull now they're all behaving themselves. I can imagine that's true, because if we weren't getting into trouble, we were always bored stiff. Even the teachers ask about me, apparently, and Mrs Lear, the Latin teacher, only gave me a Commended for the last Latin homework I handed in.

We don't do Latin at The Grange, and because I'm already on top of most of the lessons, I've started spending a lot of my time in class making catapults to fire at the teachers, or thinking up all sorts of practical jokes to play on them, or on other girls. I've made a special friend called Lainey Burrows who's in my year and is the leader of a gang in Cennick house, which I'm in too. She lives quite close to us, on Grace Drive, so we walk to school together most mornings, or ride two on a bike until someone catches us and makes one of us get off. Yesterday, during English, we jumped out on Miss Doors and made her scream, and the other day in rural science we locked Mr Lee in the cupboard and left him there while we went off for break. It was so funny hearing him shouting out for help that we're thinking about doing it again the next time we have a lesson with him.

One of the teachers told us that we might like to think we're as clever as the kids on *Please Sir!*, but we aren't.

Lainey said, 'You're right, miss, because we're cleverer,' and the whole class screamed with laughter.

Actually, we get some of our best tricks from that programme, but worse luck our teachers aren't anywhere near as dishy or understanding as Mr Hedges, who all the girls fancy, in his class, and in ours.

Lainey's definitely the prettiest girl in the school. She's a real laugh too, and so are most of the others in our gang – Tina, Carol, Marilyn and Jess. We're always getting told off for not wearing our uniforms; sometimes we're even sent home to fetch our ties which we all hate wearing. It's not as if we're boys, so why should we have to dress like them?

I've told Lainey all about Kev and she's really under-standing. She's mad about an older boy too, Greg Phillips, who goes down the club sometimes with Kev and his mates. She's already shagged Greg, loads of times, she says, but she's made me swear not to tell anyone else. It seems as though everyone's done it, so I'm really glad I have too, because I wouldn't want to be the odd one out – or one of the squares who always pays attention in class, and never has any boyfriends at all. Or if they do, it's usually one of the ugly bugs in the school next door, who make me and Lainey want to gag, because they're all spotty and smelly and really immature.

Our form mistress is Miss Vaughan. She teaches domestic science and invites all her friends into the cookery room at break times – Miss Batt, Miss Hawkins, Miss Perry and sometimes Mrs Webber, who's twice as old as the others. If we've got nothing else to do we creep up to spy on them through the windows, watching them eat the food Miss Vaughan makes for their dinners, then after they smoke cigarettes with their feet up on chairs showing all their legs. Miss Vaughan is definitely the prettiest, and really young for a teacher, but she's always going on at me to tie back my hair, which really gets on my nerves. Nag, nag, nag, nag. She's just said it again now and I'm getting really fed up with it.

'No!' I say. 'I don't want to tie it back.'

'You'll do as I tell you,' she snaps, going all red in the face.

'No, I won't.'

She starts winding through the stoves and mini-kitchens towards me, looking as though she's going to slap me. 'I'm sick to death of you cheeking me,' she rages, grabbing my arm. 'You think you're so grown up, but you aren't. You're just a nasty disobedient little child.'

'Don't you dare speak to me like that, you old cow!' I shout back, feeling my fists starting to clench.

Lainey and the others are sniggering, and Miss Vaughan's

looking like she's going to fry me up with the eggs. She lashes out. I dart back, but she's suddenly on me, and is grabbing my hair in both hands.

'OW, ow! That hurts! Let me go!' I scream.

'You're coming with me,' she shouts, and keeping hold of my hair she hauls me out of the classroom, across the playground and up to the headmistress's study, never letting me go once, even when I trip and nearly fall to my knees. I would have, if she hadn't yanked me up by my hair.

'I'm going to smash your face in,' I warn her, as she drags me into the office.

'What on earth's going on?' Miss Fisher demands, coming out of her door.

'I can't take any more of this girl,' Miss Vaughan shouts. 'She cheeks me all the time, calls me names, refuses to do as she's told . . . '

'Let go of me!' I yell. My scalp's on fire. I really want to kill her.

'You'll do as you're told!' Miss Vaughan seethes, shaking me by the hair and making me scream again.

'Miss Vaughan, you have to let her go,' Miss Fisher tells her.

It's only when I part the nest Vaughny's turned my hair into that I see what a state she's in too. Mascara's streaming down her face and her hair's not looking all that much better than mine.

'Now, what's all this about?' Miss Fisher asks.

Miss Vaughan's sobbing. 'She won't tie back her hair,' she gulps, trying to flatten her own.

Miss Fisher turns her beady eyes on me. 'Why won't you tie back your hair?' she demands. 'You know it's school rules.'

'I don't want to,' I say. I'm still watching Miss Vaughan, who can't stop sobbing. It's like someone's put a shilling in the meter and she won't let up till it runs out.

'You aren't given a choice in the matter,' Miss Fisher tells me.

I look at her, then back at Miss Vaughan, who's in such a state now that she can hardly catch her breath. 'I'm – I'm sorry,' she stammers, 'but I – I can't take any – more of her.'

'There, there, dear,' Miss Fisher says, patting her arm. 'Fetch her a drink of water,' she instructs the secretary.

I'm still staring at Miss Vaughan, hardly able to believe my eyes. I mean, I'm the one who got dragged here, and whose hair has been torn out by the roots, so if anyone should be sobbing their heads off surely it should be me.

'Are you proud of upsetting your form mistress so much?' Miss Fisher asks me.

I glance at her, then back to Miss Vaughan, who I'm actually starting to feel a bit sorry for, and glad for her sake that the others can't see her like this, because they'd take the mickey out of her forever if they could. 'No,' I say.

'Then perhaps you'd like to apologise.'

I baulk at that, because I don't like saying sorry to anyone. On the other hand, poor Miss Vaughan's so upset that I'm starting to wonder what else I could have done to get her so worked up, and if she's not splitting, then maybe I should say I'm sorry before she does. 'I didn't mean it,' I mumble. 'I'll tie it back now, if you like.'

Miss Vaughan looks at me. Her eyes are all red and black and her head's jerking about like a puppet's, she's sobbing so hard. 'Yes, you do that,' she says, taking a tissue from the box Miss Fisher's offering her.

The trouble is, I haven't got anything to tie it back with, but Miss Fisher soon solves that by digging an elastic band out of the secretary's drawer.

I ought to brush my hair first, but I don't like to ask for one, and anyway, it would probably be agony with all the knots I've been left with. Plus, my head's still smarting like I've been stung by a thousand bees. Come to think of it, I reckon Miss Vaughan ought to be saying sorry to me, but I don't have the guts to suggest that either, so I twist the elastic band into my hair, dreading how much it's going to hurt when I try to get it out again.

'So, are we friends now?' Miss Fisher asks, looking from one of us to the other.

Miss Vaughan tries to nod, but suddenly she's off again, sobbing as though someone's just whacked her, or something, and I didn't do a thing.

'Miss Vaughan, is something else bothering you?' Miss Fisher asks.

My stomach goes over in case Miss Vaughan's about to go on about something else I've done.

She shakes her head. 'No, I'm all right now,' she sniffs, even though she clearly isn't. (I bet it's the time of the month – and she's taking it out on *me*. Blooming cheek.)

'Good, then perhaps you'd like to take Susan to the toilets so you can both clean yourselves up. Can I trust you to do that without a fight breaking out again?'

I can't believe she's talking to Miss Vaughan as though she's a child, and what's more, Miss Vaughan doesn't seem to mind. I'd go mental if I was Miss Vaughan's age and someone spoke to me like that. Still, when it's Miss Fisher talking no one answers back, apparently not even a teacher.

After Miss Vaughan's drunk her water and blown her nose a couple of times, Miss Fisher gives us a hairbrush and off we go to the nearest bogs to sort ourselves out. Because the school is brand new the toilets are nice and clean, but they stink of smoke, so someone's obviously just been in for a crafty fag.

I glance at Miss Vaughan's reflection as she starts brushing her hair, wondering if she's going to mention the smell. For ages she doesn't say anything, just tidies herself up, and after passing the brush to me she pats some cold water on her face. Then she gets some bog roll to try and clean off the mascara under her eyes.

I'm wincing like mad as I struggle to get the brush through all my knots and tangles. It's not that I'm trying to make her feel bad, or anything, because it really does hurt, but she's watching my face in the mirror and then she only goes and says she's sorry.

'I shouldn't have pulled your hair,' she says.

'That's all right,' I manage to reply, even though it isn't. 'I suppose I deserved it.'

She gives a little smile, then taking the brush she starts to tidy me up, going very gently to make sure she doesn't hurt me any more.

I don't much like the ponytail I end up with, but she's being so nice that it would be mean to complain, and anyway, I don't want her going mental on me again. 'Thank you,' I say.

She slips an arm round my shoulders and we look at one another's reflections for a while. She's taller than me, blonde, and a bit like Petula Clark. I remember the day we saw her and the other teachers dancing in the cookery rooms on a dinner time. They'd kicked off their shoes and they were twisting and jiving to something we couldn't hear, and I remember thinking how cool she was for a teacher.

'I wonder what the rest of the class is up to by now,' she says.

I keep my eyes on her, waiting for what she's going to say next. I'm sure she's going to blame me if we get back to find there's a riot going on. Then I blink as I realise that she's trying not to laugh.

Suddenly I start to laugh too, and the next minute we're both in hysterics and weakly holding each other up. I'm not sure what's so funny, except being in the bogs with a teacher laughing our heads off is pretty hilarious. If anyone came in they wouldn't believe it.

'Friends?' she says when we get our breath back.

'Friends,' I reply, meaning it, because actually, I really like her now.

'If you want,' she says, as we walk back to the cookery room, 'you can come and have some dinner with us today. I'm making mushroom omelettes.'

I can't believe it. I give her a quick look, expecting to find it's a joke.

'I mean it,' she says. 'You could tell us about your old school, Red Maids, if you like. I expect it was an interesting place, and we'd love to hear about it, if you don't mind, that is.'

All of a sudden I feel really important, and I can hardly wait to hear what Lainey and the others have to say when I tell them where I'll be going instead of the canteen today.

Eddie

My thoughts are taking me deep down inside myself. Down and down, passing doors that must remain closed, all the way to the bottom, where there's what . . .? Emptiness? Death? The asylum where I fear I belong?

I come up again, bursting into daylight, dazzled and breathless and glad to be alive, because I can hear Gary laughing. Susan is too. There's no greater pleasure in life than seeing my children happy. Knowing I can make them laugh so easily always lightens the darkness inside me.

Gary climbs on to my lap and Susan watches us hug. I know she wants to come too, but holds herself aloof, considering herself too grown up for these childish things now. I hold out an arm anyway, and let her decide. It takes a while, but in the end, with an exasperated roll of her eyes, she says, 'Oh, all right, if it'll make you happy,' and in she comes, doing me the biggest favour she possibly can.

We're in the dining room after breakfast on Easter Sunday. It's a gloriously sunny day, providing an understanding of why the season is called spring. It makes you want to leap and bounce with the joy of birdsong and blossom. I'm going to church soon, taking Gary with me. I wish Susan would come too, but she's going to stay here to do her homework.

Do I believe her?

Alas no, but I don't want to spoil the day with more rows. She's both demon and angel. She makes me think thoughts that belong only in darkness, never to be spoken, or even written by my hand. They remain inside me, falling through my conscience as silently as leaves fall from a tree. When she smiles, showing us glimpses of the tenderness deep in her soul, the tenderness she tries hard to hide, I am reminded of why I am so happy to have her at home.

I try not to think of what the neighbours are saying.

'A girl Susan's age shouldn't be living in a house with two men. It's not right. She needs a mother.'

'Eddie won't get married again.'

'She's going off the rails, anyone can see that. They threw her out of her last school, and the way she's going on now, it's not hard to see why.'

I'm sure they don't know I can hear their gossip, because they aren't normally malicious. They've watched my children grow up with their own, but they're coming to a point now where they don't want Susan mixing with their girls. Susan doesn't want to anyway. She says they're all square and childish. Her friends are much more trendy and grown up, she tells me, which is all that seems to matter to her.

There's so much sex on TV these days. It's everywhere, and now, added to the legality of abortion there's a new pill they're saying will stop a girl getting pregnant. One little pill and she can have as many sleeping partners as she likes. Bad enough for girls of a legal age, but what's happening to the youngsters, is anyone asking themselves that? Is anyone watching?

I thought the crush on the Sawyer boy would have burned itself out by now, but I can see no sign of it happening yet. I'm sure she's still friendly with Mandy Hughes, even though she swears she isn't. I know she lies to me about many things. The demon sends out words of duplicity and deceit, and I wonder where the angel is hiding. So few glimpses, but each one as precious as the child she still is. Where is that child? How can I get her back?

Is it weak to admit I need help?

We still go to see Dr Leigh every second Thursday in the afternoons, but I haven't noticed any improvement in her manner, and I don't think he has either. If anything, she seems to be more unruly and insolent than ever. I'm not sure what she's like with him, he never lets on, and she never wants to talk about it after. I've considered telling him about this boy and her friendship with Mandy Hughes, but I haven't forgotten that he was the one who recommended she be taken out of Red Maids. It's left me afraid that telling him too much might lead us down an avenue we can't get back from, so I end up keeping a lot of things to myself.

I know there's more trouble going on at the school than she's telling me about. I rang Miss Fisher a couple of weeks ago and she admitted she's worried, but that they aren't giving up on her yet. Apparently she's become quite attached to her form teacher, Miss Vaughan, who's a very pleasant young woman, judging by the couple of times I've met her. So something good is happening for her there, but the rest of the time she's disrupting lessons, making the other teachers' lives a misery and leading her friends into trouble. It was when I rang that I found out about all her detentions. Miss Fisher assures me she's sent a letter each time to inform me, but Susan must be getting to them first and throwing them away.

'I don't know what you're talking about,' she shouted when I challenged her on it. 'I haven't seen any letters.'

I knew she was lying, it was written all over her, but I could see too that I was never going to get her to admit it.

The sigh inside me curls around the words that need to be spoken, but I have no one to listen to them. Every time I try talking to her she just accuses me of nagging and not understanding and being an old fuddy-duddy dad who knows nothing about girls.

She had another migraine a few weeks ago. I presumed it was connected to her time of the month, but Mrs Moon, our home help, told me that wasn't the case. (It was a very embarrassing conversation to be having with a woman who's not even a member of our family, but it was the only way I could find out without asking Susan, who hates talking about those things with me.) It seems the migraine came out of nowhere and Miss Fisher herself ended up driving her home. The first I knew of it was when I came back from work to find her in bed and in so much pain that she started to throw up. It had more or less worn off by the morning, but she stayed home from school that day, on her own after Mrs Moon had gone, and I popped back at dinnertime to make sure she was all right. I'd half expected not to find her there, but she was fast asleep under the blankets with her worn old copy of *Alice in Wonderland* next to the bed, always her favourite when she's not very well – and old Ted, who's never far away.

I sometimes wonder if it's the effort she puts into not thinking about her mother that makes her head hurt, but maybe I'm attributing the cause of my own headaches to her.

It's a bit of a weight off my mind to know that she's getting along with Mrs Moon now, after the difficult start they had. I think our Susan's erased it all from her mind now, and maybe it's best that way. Mrs Moon's a lovely young woman who was very generous to forgive as readily as she did. She's as good as gold with Gary and does an excellent job about the house.

It was only a couple of nights ago at a parent's evening that I found out what had happened between our Susan and her form teacher. It was a great relief to learn that this was another unpleasant episode that had turned out well in the end – certainly Miss Vaughan can do no wrong in our Susan's eyes now, unlike every other teacher who she accuses of picking on her and blaming her for things she didn't do. However, it was very worrying indeed to think of her causing the same sort of distress to Miss Vaughan that she had to Mrs Moon, before establishing a more friendly relationship with them.

I mentioned both incidents to Dr Leigh when we saw him last week, and he was clearly quite interested to hear more, so this time I didn't hold back so much and I told him what I knew. When I'd finished he gave it some thought, then started to talk about Susan taking out her frustrations on an older woman who then forgave her, which wouldn't be unusual for a girl in her position. He intimated that she's punishing them for her mother dying, as if they were her mother, then she forms strong attachments to them, again as if they were her mother.

Susan doesn't want to go and see him any more. She hates the way he keeps talking about her mother, she says, and I have to admit, the visits are starting to get me down too. If I'd noticed an improvement in her schoolwork over the time we've been seeing him, or some sign of her settling down at home, I'd be more convinced he was helping. As it is, her last school report made me want to weep, it was so bad, and the lies she tells to get out of the house to get up to heaven only knows what come close to breaking my heart. Dear God in heaven, what's she up to with those boys? My worst fears are so awful that I cannot bring myself to describe them with words. All I can do is pray to the Lord for guidance and hope, *believe*, that He will deliver us safely from the depths of my despair.

Chapter Nineteen

Susan

Dad's gone all strict and even more religious lately. He's hardly let me out for a month, and sits over me while I'm doing my homework, which is really, really annoying. I haven't even been able to sneak out, because he lies in wait, ready to catch me when I try. We keep having terrible rows, but he won't give in. He says I'm turning into a lazy, good-for-nothing madam, who's selfish, opinionated, ungodly and much too big for my boots.

Very nice, I must say!

'Imagine your father saying that to you,' I wrote to Sadie in one of my regular letters. 'I thought he wanted me to come home to live, but now I'm not so sure. I wish I could run away with Kev.'

Someone's been chalking *Sue loves Kev* on the pavement outside his house, which is really childish and probably why he doesn't want to have anything to do with me lately. If I ever find out who's been doing it, I've made it known that I'll smash their faces in. (Although I've never actually hit anyone, and don't really want to in case they hit me back and manage to beat me up badly, I find that threatening to often has very good results.)

On the nights I do manage to give Dad the slip I go to meet Mandy in the bus shelter, where we've started doing this really cool thing, provided Julie's not there. Either Mandy pretends to be Kev, or I pretend to be Rich, and we make up these chats as though we're married to them. We imagine what it would be like on our wedding days, or honeymoons, or telling them we're pregnant. We even have rows sometimes, but we always make up, and Kev is so nice to me then that it leaves me feeling quite sad that none of it's real.

The nights are getting lighter now, so we're hoping they'll start coming to find us again soon. Someone said that Kev's going out with a girl called Katherine who lives over Downend. I'll want to kill myself if it's true, but I don't think it is, because I've never seen him with anyone. The trouble is, I hardly see him at all. Mandy says he doesn't go round the Anchor much, or down the club, so maybe he is going to see this girl in Downend. *Please God don't let him be. It's not fair that no one ever loves me.*

Dad keeps going on about how aggressive I sound when I speak, but he goes on about everything these days. He still makes me laugh sometimes though, like when he told me about the day he hid under the stairs from Flirty Gertie, and ended up getting caught. When he's in a good mood he comes outside and cheats at rounders, which always makes everyone fall about laughing, he's such a clown. We keep telling him he ought to be in the circus, he might make us all rich.

Usually though, he's having a go at me about something, saying I'm driving him to the end of his tether and he doesn't know what to do with me. I keep telling him he doesn't have to do anything, except keep his hair on and stop treating me like a child. He won't listen though, and last week, after he found out I'd been knocking off school with Lainey, Julie and Mandy, he only got some nuns to come and have a chat with me. *Nuns!* We're not even Catholic, so why he had to go and talk to them I'll never know. I wasn't having anything to do with them, anyway. The minute I saw them standing at the door like three giant crows ready to peck me to bits, I tore upstairs to my room and refused to come out till they'd gone.

Honestly! Everyone knocks off, and no one else's parents

call in the nuns. I think Dad might be going off his rocker, which is very worrying, because I really love him, when he's being normal that is, and I don't want him ending up down Glenside or Barrow Gurney with all the nutters.

The last couple of weeks he's been making me go up the library with him at weekends and though there are a thousand other things I'd rather be doing, I've found some great books by Jean Plaidy and Georgette Heyer. I love reading them more than anything (apart from going out with my friends, or Kev), and can't put them down. I can easily see Kev as the hero in all of them, and it's fantastic imagining us being a lord and lady with tons of money and living happily ever after. (That's Georgette Heyer, who's my favourite. Jean Plaidy writes about people who actually lived, so her books are more tragic, but still really good.)

To try and keep Dad happy I've been cooking his tea ready for when he comes home at night. Miss Vaughan's taught us some easy recipes for baked potatoes and lamb chops, or toad in the hole, which I'm useless at, but I keep giving it a go. It seems to work out all right when I'm in her lesson, but by the time I put it on a plate for Dad it looks like a pile of sick with a lost sausage poking out the top. He always eats it though, and says it's delicious, but he would because he's like that. I think he prefers the fairy cakes I let Gary help make, with icing on the top and currants in the middle.

I've been doing some housework too, polishing all our ornaments in the front room and hoovering the carpets the way Mum used to. I don't like washing sinks and the toilet much, so I try to get Gary to do them, but he just tells me to get lost and goes off outside with his friends.

There are two reasons I'm doing so much round the house: first, so that I can get some practice in for when I'm married to Kev; and second, because Sarah's going to be leaving at the end of June. She's having another baby, so her husband doesn't want her to work any more. They're moving house too, but I can't remember where they're going. I only know that it's close to Chippenham, which is miles away. She keeps saying she's going to miss us, and hopes we'll get the bus to visit her sometimes, but I don't expect we'll bother. I don't tell her that, because it would be rude, but I've already stopped going round her house, and I'm not telling her any of my secrets now. It's up to her if she wants to move away, I'm not going to stop her.

I don't care, anyway.

'Dad,' I say, after he's finished his tea. 'Can we have a dog?'

He sits back in his chair and covers his mouth as he burps. 'No, my love,' he replies.

'Why not?'

'Because there's no one here all day to take care of it, and besides we don't know anything about dogs.'

'I think we should get one,' Gary pipes up.

'We can always learn about them,' I say.

'You can get a book,' Gary suggests.

'Yeah, like you did on sewing,' I remind Dad, 'when I started to make my own clothes. We learned how to do it from one of your books.'

'And Mrs Taylor had to finish it off for us, because we weren't any good,' he reminds me. 'No, we're not having a dog and that's that.'

'I think you're really mean,' I tell him, 'because you and Gary have got one another, and I don't have anyone.'

'Don't be silly, you've got us, and you don't need a dog. You won't look after it, and I don't have the time. Now, let's change the subject please. Who's got homework tonight?'

'Me,' Gary groans. 'I have to learn twenty spellings.'

'Well, at least they're proper spellings,' I retort snootily, 'instead of all that rubbish they were teaching you before.'

'It wasn't rubbish, was it Dad?'

Dad gives a sigh. 'It's better that you learn the correct way to spell,' he replies, 'and I have to admit I'm glad that experiment is over. Now, do you want me to test you?'

'In a minute. I haven't learned them all yet.'

341

'What about you, Susan? What homework do you have?'

'None,' I lie. I'm not bothering to do it, because I won't be there to hand it in tomorrow. Julie, Mandy and I are going shoplifting over Staple Hill, and after that we're going to see if we can find Philip Bird down the garden centre so Mandy and I can ask him if he'll go out with Julie. Then we're going to wait outside Kev's work so that Julie and Mandy can ask him if he'll go out with me again.

Eddie

I keep wondering what use I am, if I have any real purpose here. I seem to have lost my foothold and am now falling endlessly, aimlessly through life. My only purchase is in the pages of a book, my anchor is when my pen touches paper. I register the factory noise around me and cringe from it. The thump, grind, hiss and squeal of machinery. The stench of burning metal and sweat. The coarse, loud voices of men. I shrink from the crudeness of their humour, and feel saddened, sickened by the way they discuss, debase the women in their lives. Sometimes I seek to change their views, but why? They only mock me, so let another missionary convert them. I turn away from the explicit nudity of the pictures they hang on the walls, embarrassed, but not unstirred. I feel concern and shame for the girls who are photographed that way, and terrified that our Susan should ever find herself there.

For the past few months, since she left Red Maids to start afresh at home, we have been through the valley of the shadow of death. Sometimes I feel as though I'm losing her completely, but then she returns to my side, settling back into the child she still is and struggles so hard not to be. I watched her despair when Mrs Moon left us, and felt helpless to soothe it. I tried, but she pushed me away, saying she didn't care, we could manage on our own. Her focus now is her teacher, Miss Vaughan, who can do no wrong, and who, as far as I can tell, is working hard with Miss Fisher to keep Susan at the school. There are others who would prefer her to go. She continues to be disruptive, arrogant and rude, they say, and when I search for words to defend her I can find so few that I feel treacherous and of no use to her at all.

We no longer go to see Dr Leigh. I don't think he was surprised when I told him after our last visit that we wouldn't be coming again. He asked if I understood that Susan's behaviour is a reaction to losing her mother, a cry for help, I think he said. 'She needs to talk about it,' he went on, 'and come to terms with why it happened – and the fact that neither she, nor anyone else, is to blame.'

I didn't argue with him, he knows more about these things than I do, but if he can't get our Susan to talk about her mother, I'm sure I don't know how I'm going to when I don't have any of his expertise. And would it *really* do any good to dredge it all up again? Eddress has been gone for almost four years now and our Susan's unstable enough as it is, without trying to make her go through the process of grief, as he called it.

What's happened to my little girl, I keep asking myself. Where is she? Why is she turning into this stranger who is so hard to control, even to like? I worry about her day and night. My only refuge continues to be in books, but I dare not spend as much time as I used to reading, or writing, for fear of what she might do while my eyes are averted. I feel sick to my soul when I leave for work in the mornings, wondering whether she will go to school, or roam the streets with friends who are anything but. In desperation a while ago, I went to see Father Michael at the Catholic church. It was the first time I'd set foot in one for two decades or more, but I'd started to wonder if God was using our Susan to punish me for leaving the faith, so I had to find out. It would be cruel of Him to make her, a blameless child, suffer for my sins, and though she says she's never been happier, and I should stop worrying all the time, I know that deep in her heart she must be suffering indeed.

Father Michael spoke to the nuns at Our Lady of Lourdes, and three of them came to the house on an 'errand of mercy'. Susan wouldn't see them, and I had to apologise for wasting their time. Sister Benedict was very kind, and told me to call on them at any time. 'You are still one of us,' she assured me, and for a while I took some comfort in thinking I was. I wanted to belong to something, or someone, who might give me enough strength to get through each day.

Florrie keeps telling me I should get married again.

'Our Susan needs a woman to lean on,' she says. 'Someone with a strong arm and who can teach her how to behave. I'm doing my best, but I'm old now, and I don't see her often enough. And God bless you, Eddie, you're too gentle a soul to know how to handle that girl when she's got her mother's wilfulness about her.'

Is it her mother's wilfulness that's driving her? Of course, I see and hear Eddress in her all the time, but there's a distance between us that I never had with her mother, nor with her, until I sent her away to school. Is that what created the rift that I am finding so hard to close? Am I to blame for the way she is? As her father I must be.

As for getting married again, it's not what I want, and I don't think our Susan would like it either. Besides, what woman would want to take on a girl who behaves the way she does, cheeking back all the time, and dressing like a trollop twice her age? A picture of Anne who works in the charity shop over Staple Hill comes to my mind, and I shudder to think of how troubled her tender sensibilities would be by my unruly daughter. She's a refined and educated woman who's never been married, or had much experience with children, but she is kind enough to ask about Susan and Gary sometimes when I go in. Perhaps she's only being polite, but I always appreciate the friendliness, and am polite in return when I tell her that they're well, thank you very much. It's a pleasure to see her smile. She has pale blue eyes, and fair hair that I think she must have washed and set every week at the hairdresser's. She often keeps books aside for me when they come in, and seems very pleased when I buy one or two of her recommendations. She'll even ask me about them the next time I drop in.

I was thinking of going over there tomorrow afternoon and taking Gary with me, but I've just got home from work to find a dog in the house, and without having to be told, I know already that it's ours.

'Dad! Dad! This is Lucky,' Gary shouts as he skids into the kitchen behind the little beast. 'We got her down the pet shop this afternoon.'

The puppy is bouncing all over my feet, rotating her tail like a windmill and leaking pee with excitement.

'You were supposed to be at Gran's,' I tell him. It's the summer holidays now, so they're not at school. 'Where's our Susan?'

'I'm here,' she says, coming out of the dining room with a bag of biscuits. 'Isn't she cute, Dad? She only cost a shilling and they gave us a week's worth of food for free.'

'We can't have a dog, my love. They need training and walking . . . '

'We're going to do it, aren't we?' she says to Gary.

'Yeah. We've already taken her over the field and she can run even faster than me.'

'I'm sorry,' I say, going to fetch some newspaper to wipe up the mess, 'it's not fair on the dog when we're not here all day.'

'But we are now,' Susan protests. 'And by the time we go back to school she'll be trained so she can come with me and wait outside till I finish.'

I give a sigh and shake my head. 'You can't tie a dog up all day, especially not at school. She'll have to go back.'

'No!' they shout together.

'She's mine now,' Susan cries. 'She's my best friend in the whole world and if you make her go away I'll go too.'

'Susan, Susan,' I sigh wearily.

'Come on Lucky,' she says, scooping up the puppy, 'let's go somewhere we're wanted.'

'And me.' Gary jogs off down the hall after her. 'Where are we going?'

'Nowhere you can come,' she tells him unkindly.

'But I want to,' he protests.

'Neither of you are going anywhere,' I inform them. 'It's teatime and I want . . . '

'I'm not eating anything unless you let Lucky stay,' Susan shouts.

'Nor me,' Gary chimes in.

I close my eyes and shake my head.

'Please, Dad, please,' Susan begs. 'She's really cute and lovely and it'll be good for us to have a dog.'

I don't ask why, because I already know the answer. It'll be good for us because it's what Susan wants, and I have to admit, now I'm having a closer look, it is a happy-looking little thing and anything that's happy is welcome in our house. 'You'll feed and walk her, and clear up after her,' I say sternly.

Both their faces light up, and next thing I'm being bombarded by all three of them, with Lucky peeing on my feet again.

'What kind of breed is she?' I ask.

'She's a black Labrador,' Susan replies.

Well, she's certainly black, but as for being a Lab . . . 'Which pet shop did you find her in?'

'It was downtown, just off Old Market,' Susan says.

I blink hard. 'You went to Old Market to get her?' I repeat. 'And you took Gary with you?'

'We got the number fourteen straight there and back again. You're allowed to take dogs upstairs, and the man in the pet shop gave us an old collar and lead because we didn't have enough money to get that as well.'

I'm still stunned by the news that they were wandering about such an unsavoury area on their own. 'I don't want you doing anything like that again,' I warn them firmly. 'It's dangerous around there, what with all the drunks and . . .' I was about to say prostitutes, but quickly change it to 'hooligans'.

'We didn't see anyone like that,' Gary assures me. 'There was a nice lady who stuck her hand out to stop the bus for us, and the conductor helped us upstairs with Lucky, didn't he?'

'Yes,' Susan confirms, holding the dog up and letting it lick her all over her face.

'That's not hygienic,' I tell her.

'She's kissing me, because she's happy.'

'She does it to me too,' Gary says. 'Can I hold her now?'

'Only for two minutes, because remember, she's mine.'

'Where did you get the money?' I ask.

Susan doesn't meet my eyes. 'I had some,' she replies. 'I saved up.'

I can't think where she might have stolen it from, so I don't accuse her, I simply say, 'If you've borrowed any, I want you to pay it back.'

'I just told you, I saved up,' and turning on her heel she drags Gary and the dog back into the dining room.

I can already see all the work this new member of the family is going to create, but there's no point arguing when they both want her so much. I'll have to ask Anne to keep an eye out for a book on dogs so we can learn how to train the wretched thing, and I expect we'll enjoy the walks when we get time.

I find myself starting to chuckle. I suppose it's because I always wanted a dog when I was a boy, or maybe it's because I'm hoping that having something of her own to love will help our Susan to settle down at home and at school.

Chapter Twenty

Susan

We're having a fab time singing advertising songs from the telly as we walk along the street. The first one's about Double Diamond working wonders, then there's Opal Fruits making your mouth water and then we finish so loudly with the Heinz beans ad that people turn round and laugh.

'I know, I know,' I cry, 'what about the lady who loves Milk Tray?'

'That's not a song,' Mandy protests.

'Yeah, but it's really lush. Imagine if Rich climbed into your bedroom like that with a box of chocolates. I bet you'd wet yourself.'

Julie and I scream with laughter, while Mandy hits us, and Lucky barks and jumps up to try and protect me.

'We've got to find a song for Lucky,' Julie decides, and cupping Lucky round the face she says, 'What shall we sing for you, you naughty little thing?'

'I know,' Mandy exclaims. 'How much is that doggie in the window?'

We sing it at the tops of our voices and all laugh and cheer and Lucky leaps about on the end of her lead, just like she knows we're singing to her.

We're crossing the green in front of the Horseshoe on our way to see Kev and the others. He hasn't met Lucky yet, but I know he's going to love her, because everyone does, and she's so sweet that she always loves them back. I'm really glad I got her, and I think Dad is too, now he's had some time to get used to her.

I'm fourteen now. (Well, actually thirteen, but everyone else in my class is fourteen, or they will be by Christmas, so I think that makes me fourteen too.) I bought Lucky as a present to myself for my birthday, with two sixpences I pinched from the top drawer of Dad's dressing table. I'll pay it back as soon as I go out to work, which I can hardly wait for, because apart from Miss Vaughan I really hate school. It's a great big waste of time.

Kev and his mates are slouched on one of the benches outside the pub, drinking pints and chatting to some girls who I recognise from the Paige School. They're really common and mouthy and everyone knows they'll go with anyone. I don't know what they're doing around here, and I'm furious to see the way one of them is trying to get off with Kev.

'It's Sandra Hodge and her gang,' Mandy whispers.

'Why don't they fuck off?' Julie mutters.

'If one of them says anything to me, I'm going to smack her right in the mouth,' Mandy declares.

'Me too,' I say. Then suddenly I'm lurching across the road towards the pub, being dragged by Lucky who's spotted another dog just behind Kev.

As I whizz by, struggling to keep Lucky under control, I hear Kev and his mates starting to bark and howl, and I feel so embarrassed that I want to smack Lucky with all my might. I would, if I could get her to stop, but she's dragging me on past the pub, going after this little Jack Russell that's out on his own.

In the end the Jack Russell disappears into someone's garden, and Lucky finally calms down. I drop to my knees and grab her face between my hands, seething with fury for the way she's just shown me up. All she does is pant and wag her tail and give me a great big lick. She even looks like she's grinning, and because I love her so much I forgive her, but not before warning her never to do anything like that again.

I turn round to find Sandra Hodge and her gang still sniggering and gawping like the juvenile delinquents they are, but at least Mandy's talking to Rich and Julie's shouting out to ask me what I want to drink.

I tell her a lemonade and Sandra Hodge and her friends start mimicking me, saying 'lemonade', then pretending to be jerked along by a dog.

'Very funny,' I mutter.

'Why don't you grow up?' Julie sneers at them.

'Come here and say that?' Sandra dares her.

Julie goes to poke her face right into Sandra's. 'Grow up,' she says. 'Now what are you going to do about it?'

'Scrap! Scrap!' one of Kev's mates shouts. 'Go on girls, show us what you're made of.'

Suddenly Sandra's got hold of Julie by the hair and is spinning her round. Julie thumps her in the stomach and stamps on her foot, then they fall on the ground, screaming and kicking and clawing each other to bits. The boys are on their feet cheering them on. Mandy goes over and whacks one of Sandra's friends, then they're rolling about too, ripping at one another's clothes and hair.

'Come on, Sue, get one of them,' Mandy shouts.

I don't want to look chicken so I start running forward, holding on tight to Lucky, and the next thing I know Sandra and her gang are all scarpering across the green. It turns out they're scared of Lucky, and I shout after them that they should be, because if I tell her to she'll tear them to bits.

Right on cue Lucky growls, which I think is extremely clever, until I realise she's looking at Kev.

'Get that beast away from me,' he says, backing off.

'She won't hurt you as long as you're nice to me,' I assure him.

'Yeah, right. Just keep it where it is, OK? I don't want it coming near me.'

Lucky growls again and I feel so mortified I want to hit her. 'Stop it,' I snap at her. 'He's a friend.'

Lucky looks up at me and licks her lips.

'You're a bad girl,' I tell her, torn between hugging her and ignoring her.

'Where are you going?' I hear Kev shout.

I turn round.

'Where do you think?' Rich answers.

Mandy's holding his arm and they're heading towards the stile.

'You coming?' Kev says to Julie.

Julie goes beetroot and looks at me.

'I'm not going anywhere with that dog,' he informs me.

Lucky growls again and I slap her.

'I'll hold Lucky if you like,' Julie offers.

I look at Kev, not sure what to do.

His mates are muttering something I can't hear and they burst out laughing. So does he.

'Go on,' Julie says, coming to take Lucky's lead.

I let it go, but when I make to join Kev Lucky tugs Julie along after me.

'You have to stay there,' I tell her.

She just keeps coming.

'Stay!'

'I can't hold her,' Julie cries, trying to drag her back.

Suddenly Lucky's got hold of the bottom of Kev's flares and is growling like a wolf as she tries to tug them off him.

'Get that fucking thing off me!' he cries.

His mates are in fits, laughing. So's Julie, who only drops the lead.

I quickly snatch it up and grabbing Lucky's mouth I make her let go of Kev.

'That's it,' he says, looking all flustered and not very cool. 'No way am I going anywhere with you while you've got that dog. Come on, Julie,' and grabbing her hand he drags her up over the stile.

Aware of everyone staring, I look the other way as I go to wait on the grass opposite the pub. I want to scream and rage that Kev's gone off with someone else, especially Julie, who I could kill. I know she goes with him anyway, but only when I'm not there, and now she's gone and done it right in front of my face. All right, he told her to, but she should have said no – or held on to Lucky a bit harder.

Anyway, I don't want to go with him, so I don't care that he hasn't bothered much about me since I got expelled. I hate doing all the stuff he likes and I hate him, but I love him too and I expect, when he's finished with Julie, he'll come to find me and want me to forgive him. I'm not sure if I will, at least not straight away.

I'm keeping my back turned to the pub so no one will see that I'm trying not to cry, or know that deep down inside I feel like I'm the only person in the world. I'm so glad I've got Lucky. She's trying to bounce around after butterflies. I daren't let go of her lead in case she runs off, but a part of me is so angry with her that I wish she would. Immediately I feel guilty and give her a hug. She evidently likes that because she settles down very close to me then, and seeming to realise I'm upset she starts nudging me with her silly face. I love her too much to stay cross with her for long, but I warn her she can't come again when I'm meeting Kev.

'You keep frightening people,' I tell her, 'and you're not supposed to do that to people I like, only those who want to hurt me.'

Her funny little head tilts from side to side, as though she's trying to understand me. Then she gives me a great big lick and sticks a paw into my hand.

We've had her for over three weeks now, and she still isn't very good at doing as she's told, which is driving Dad mad, and getting me told off all the time. Gary loves her as much as I do, and is always taking her for walks, but we have to go together, because she's so strong she'd pull him over if he was on his own. Gran says she loves her too, which is very generous of her given the way Lucky ran into her house, leapt up on Gran's lap and knocked out her false teeth. Next thing Lucky ran off with them, and we couldn't stop laughing because it looked as though the teeth were hers. She's a real handful, but when she's behaving herself she's the best dog in the world.

Ages and ages go by, and still no one comes back. I know people are staring at me, wondering what I'm doing, but I'm just ignoring them. There's no law against sitting on the grass with your dog. I lean down to Lucky and whisper to her to be nice to Kev when he comes back. 'Please don't show me up again,' I murmur, and she makes me laugh as she gives me a lick.

'Talking to yourself is the first sign of madness,' someone says.

I look up. It's Bruce and his mates from Champion Road. They're the ones I showed my sanitary belt to when I first started my periods, and they've never let me forget it.

'Get lost,' I tell them.

'What are you doing here?' Bruce wants to know.

'Mind your own business.'

'Fancy a shag?' one of them asks.

'Grow up and drop dead,' I sneer.

'Come on. Everyone knows you're a . . .'

'Get lost, or I'll set my dog on you,' I shout.

Lucky's already on her feet, growling and straining at the lead, and they quickly start backing off.

'All right, all right,' Bruce says, holding up his hands.

As they walk away they're shouting over their shoulders, calling me foul names so that everyone over by the pub can hear. I feel so angry and ashamed that I want to run away, but I'm too embarrassed to move. I turn my back, and then I see Kev and Mandy and the others, miles away at the other side of the common, taking the other road back towards the Anchor. They've obviously gone that way to try and avoid me, and I feel so upset that I swear to myself I'm never going to speak to that Mandy again.

'Susan? What are you doing?'

I nearly jump out of my skin. Bloody hell, it's Dad!

Lucky starts jumping all over him, really pleased to see him.

Dad grabs the lead and holds her still. I can tell he's cross, but I haven't done anything wrong, so I don't know why. 'You were supposed to be home by seven o'clock to go over Auntie Doreen's,' he reminds me. 'Uncle Alf came to pick us up, but there was no sign of you.'

'I forgot,' I tell him.

'Well that's not good enough. We were waiting for you, and now you've spoiled the whole evening.'

'It's not my fault I didn't remember.'

'Then whose fault is it?'

I can feel everyone over by the pub staring at us, and I want to die. Fancy being told off by your dad in front of the whole world. 'Go away,' I tell him. 'You're showing me up.'

He looks amazed. 'In front of who?' he demands. 'No one's taking any notice of you.'

'That's what you think, now just shut up and go away.'

'Don't talk to me like that. I want you home, *now*.'

'I'm not walking along with you,' I cry. 'Everyone'll see me.'

'Oh, for heaven's sake. Walk on your own, if you have to, but you're coming home whether you like it or not. And take this dog. I'm not having her dragging me all the way.'

I can't have a row with him in front of the pub, so grabbing Lucky's lead, I start running down the green towards the brook. 'I'm going up round the top way,' I shout back at him. That'll save me having to go past the Anchor where Kev and everyone might see me.

Why are they trying to avoid me? It must be because of Lucky.

I'm almost at the end of Champion Road when I spot Mandy and Julie coming towards me. Thank goodness Dad's nowhere in sight. I suppose he's gone the bottom way, which is the quickest, so luckily he won't come across me talking to them.

'Where are you going?' Mandy asks. 'We've been looking for you.'

I know she's lying, but all I say is, 'I got fed up waiting. Where's Kev?'

'He's gone down club with the others.'

'So where are you going?'

'Up the Kleen-eze playing fields. Do you want to come?'

'There's this bloke, Mickey Lester,' Julie says. 'He works down GB Britain's during the week, but he's the park keeper on Saturdays and Sundays. He's gert lush, you wait till you see him. He's about twenty-four and looks exactly like Davy Jones.'

I know I'm supposed to be going home, but who cares? I'd much rather go up the Kleen-eze, especially if there's a bloke who looks like Davy Jones. If I can get off with him, that'll really show Kev.

I just hope Lucky doesn't growl at him, or she'll really be in trouble.

'Where have you been?' Dad's face is white with rage.

'Out with my friends.'

'I trusted you to come straight home, and now look at the time! It's after nine o'clock and I've been worried out of my mind.'

'What for? I'm old enough to take care of myself.'

'Don't backchat me, young lady. Now, I want to know where you've been.'

'I went up the Kleen-eze, all right?'

'No, it is *not* all right. I told you Uncle Alf had come to pick us up . . . '

'Stop shouting at me all the time.'

'Who did you go with?'

'My friends.'

'Which friends?'

'Lainey and the others.'

'You're lying. It's written all over your face.'

'Oh no, you two aren't rowing again, are you?' Gary complains, coming in the door.

'I thought you were sleeping in the Williamses' tonight,' Dad says.

'I am. I've come back to get my pyjamas. Hello, Lucky. Want to come with me?'

'She's mine, not yours,' I remind him, 'so she's staying with me.'

'You always get to keep her. Why can't I have a turn?'

'You can't take her next door,' Dad tells him. 'Now hurry up and fetch what you came for, and you, young lady, can get upstairs to bed.'

'Don't worry, I'm going. Come on, Lucky, we know where we're not wanted, don't we?'

'Have you eaten anything today?' Dad calls after me.

'I'm not hungry.' Actually, I'm starving, but I'm not going to give him the chance to get on at me about something else. I'm fed up with him. I wish he'd just leave me alone. I wish everyone would, especially Mandy and Julie who only made me wait over the other side of the park while they went to talk to Mickey Lester, in case Lucky attacked him. Anyone would think she's vicious, and she's not.

Anyway, he's not interested in either of them, because he's got a girlfriend who was there, and from what I could see she's lovely-looking, so it's no wonder he told Julie to grow up and get lost.

'I know your sort,' his girlfriend called after her, 'and we don't want you round here, so stay round your own way.'

Julie's threatening to go and bash her up now, but if you ask me she's all talk.

Lucky's lying on the bed gazing up at me, so I go to give her a cuddle before Dad comes in to get her. He won't allow her to sleep upstairs, even though she howls and scratches at the kitchen door for most of the night.

'She has to learn she can't always have her own way,' he says sharply, 'and so do you.'

He's so mean. I really hate him sometimes. In fact, I hate everyone, except Lucky and Miss Vaughan, because they're the only ones who are always on my side.

Miss Vaughan's going to be Mrs Philpott by the time we

start back in September. She only invited me to her wedding, which I thought was really nice of her, and I felt really honoured, but worse luck, we're going to be on holiday down Bowleaze Cove the week she gets married.

I'm thinking about running away and taking Lucky with me. It'll serve everyone right if I do.

Eddie

'Hello Mr Lewis.'

'Hello Anne.' I keep meaning to tell her she can call me Eddie, but I'm afraid it might seem too forward, so I never quite get round to it. 'How are you today?'

'Oh, I'm fine. A bit hot, but it's lovely weather we're having, isn't it?'

'Lovely,' I agree.

I have a look around the shop, wondering where to start first.

'How are you?' she asks. 'If you don't mind me saying, you're looking a little peaky. Are you getting enough vitamins?'

'Oh, I'm all right,' I tell her, even though I'm in a bit of pain. Our Nance keeps on that I'm developing an ulcer, and sometimes I think she might be right.

'It's worrying about our Susan that's doing it,' she says. 'She'll be the death of you, that girl, the way she carries on.'

I wish she wouldn't say things like that in front of Gary, but I suppose not having any kids of her own, she doesn't realise how much they pick up. Of course he went straight home and told our Susan I was going to die because of her, and the next thing I knew they were at one another's throats. I managed to break them up before any blood was spilled, but our Susan ended up crying so hard that she started to retch.

She's gone over our Doreen's today, with Gary. I put them on the bus first thing this morning, and Alf's bringing them back tonight in time for *Top of the Pops*. Woe betide us all if we make our Susan miss that. The latest is that she's going to run away and be a groupie for the Monkees. I can only hope she doesn't know what that actually means.

The dog's at home, shut up in the kitchen in disgrace after she chased one of the neighbours up her own stairs yesterday, and kept her trapped under the bed, barking and growling at her, until her husband came home and managed to get Lucky out of the house. I don't know what we're going to do about all the havoc she's causing, but I'll have to think of something, because I'll never get our Susan to part with her now.

'I've kept something back for you,' Anne says, and going behind the counter she pulls out a brown envelope and hands it over. 'It's some photographs of the Concorde. I thought you might like them, because you used to work down Rolls-Royce at one time, didn't you?'

'It was the BAC,' I tell her, which is on the same site and part of the same company, so all of us who've worked there, even if we've left now, feel a sense of pride about Concorde.

'Did you go down to watch it taking off, back in April?' she asks, as I sift through some of the best photographs I've ever seen of the plane. They're all in black and white, and my goodness, they're impressive.

'I couldn't get the time off,' I reply, 'but I'd have loved to be there. Who on earth brought these in? They must be collectors' items. I can't believe their owner doesn't want them.'

Her cheeks go slightly pink as she says, 'I found them in with some books I was sorting out this morning, so I suppose Helen, who does Thursdays and Fridays, must have taken them in.'

'Well, it's very kind of you to keep them for me, but someone must have brought them in by mistake.'

'Oh no, I'm sure they didn't,' she insists.

I have a look through them again, marvelling at how clear and well taken they are. 'These are really something to treasure,' I comment, 'pictures of her maiden voyage out of Filton, is what it looks like. They say she'll be flying across the Atlantic by '73, you know.' I give a chuckle. 'I don't suppose the likes of us will be able to afford the tickets though. Come to think of it, I'm not even sure I can afford these photos. How much do you want for them?'

She waves a hand. 'Oh, don't worry about that. You spend enough in here already, so take it as a gift, but mind you don't tell anyone, or you'll get me into trouble.'

It's not until I'm back home later, and flicking through them again, that it occurs to me Anne's brother, or was it her father, used to work at the BAC. I don't know the family well, because they're quite well-to-do, but as far as I remember, her dad used to be quite high up in Rolls-Royce. He's dead now, but I think her brother still works there, and I'm guessing that these photos are his, and she's had some copies made, just for me.

I have to sit with the shock of that for a minute or two, not sure why she'd do something like that, and actually hoping she didn't, because it would make me very uncomfortable to think of her spending all that money on me. It wouldn't be right, when we hardly even know each other, but at the same time I can't help feeling touched by her kindness. Of course I can't ask her if that's what she did, because it would embarrass her terribly, and anyway, I'm sure she'd only deny it.

I expect I've got it wrong though, because the more I think about it, the more unlikely it seems that she'd go to all that trouble. That's typical of you, Eddie, I say to myself, thinking you're a bit special, when very likely all that's happened is that some poor bloke really has handed them photos in by mistake. I'll tell her next time I'm up there, that I'll be very happy to give them back, should anyone come looking for them.

Now it's time to start packing for our holidays. Florrie's not coming this year, because we're having to get the coach, and her legs aren't up to all that walking and getting on and off the bus. So it's going to be just the three of us, and Lucky, who's sitting here looking very sorry for herself, having just been told off. You should have seen the state of the kitchen when I got back. She'd torn half the wallpaper off the wall, scratched all the paintwork, and she must have jumped up on the draining board to try and get out of the window, because the venetian blinds were all buckled, and the dishes I left drying were all over the place.

'For two pins I'd take you down the flipping dogs' home right now,' I tell her. And I would too, if it weren't for how our Susan would react. I suppose I could always tell her the dog got run over, or wandered off and hasn't come back. It wouldn't be right to lie to her though, and much as she doesn't deserve to have anything of her own the way she carries on half the time, I don't have the heart to take away her dog.

I've got a couple of things I need to ask her about though, one in particular that's been playing on my mind for a long time now. It's hard getting round to it when I know how much it'll embarrass her, me too, and try as I might I can't seem to think of the right words. I've written them down I don't know how many times, and in a dozen different ways, but nothing ever seems right. I'll have to ask her though, because if there is something wrong with her, the quicker we get her up the doctor's the more chance we'll have of putting it right.

Just thinking about the doctor brings the soreness back in my stomach that makes me want to groan out loud. I suppose I'll have to get something for it, or the next thing I know I won't be fit to go back to work after my holidays, and apart from needing the money, it scares the kids to death when I'm not well.

I lie back and close my eyes, waiting for the burn to pass. When it finally does I become aware of the dog's head under my hand, and looking down at her I can't help but smile. She's gazing up at me with her doleful brown eyes, as though saying, 'It's all right, Ed, I'm here for you.'

A bit of fanciful nonsense, but it makes me feel better, and then I look at the photos on the arm of the chair, and realise that bit of fanciful nonsense – thinking Anne had copied them specially for me – made me feel better too.

Susan

I didn't realise Auntie Nance was going to be here as well today, and I wouldn't have minded, if I hadn't heard her and Auntie Doreen talking about me. They were in the kitchen and I was in the front room having a look through young Doreen's records, which she keeps in their sleeves, all pristine and shiny, with no scratches at all.

This is what Auntie Nance said: 'That girl's running wild and something has to be done.'

'Oh come on now, Nance,' Auntie Doreen said, 'she's not that bad.'

'Don't you believe it. She's making her father's life a misery, and our poor Ed doesn't deserve it. He works hard bringing up those kids on his own, and if she goes on the way she is . . .'

'Ssh, or she'll hear you. Where is she?'

'She was outside just now, with our Gary. What I'm saying is, our Ed's not well, and if it turns out to be something serious that young madam will be to blame. She goes and gets herself expelled from school, now she's running riot down the Grange and the things I've been hearing . . .'

'Now, now, Nance, girls will be girls, and you've got to remember, she's lost her mother, poor love, so you have to make allowances.'

'That was a long time ago,' Auntie Nance barked, 'and I'll tell you this, her mam wouldn't put up with the way she's behaving, not for a minute.'

'I daresay you're right, because Eddress was always strict with 'em, but our Ed's a good dad and he loves those kids.'

'I'm not saying he doesn't, but he's too soft on her, Doreen. She needs a firm hand, or before we know it she'll be right off the rails and in a borstal, or blooming well pregnant.'

'Oh, you're exaggerating, Nance. She's too young for all that. She's only just thirteen.'

'And look at her. She's more like a girl of sixteen the way her bosoms are growing and how tall she's getting. You mark my words, she's on the road to ruin, and that's where she's going to end up if someone doesn't talk to her soon.'

'Does she know about the birds and the bees? Has anyone told her?'

'Well I haven't, and I don't know that her gran has. I think you should sit her down and . . .'

'Why me?'

'Because you've got young Doreen, so you know more about girls our Susan's age. What did you tell our Doreen?'

'Let me see. You know, I don't think I told her anything specific like.'

'Auntie Doreen,' Gary shouts, bursting in through the door, 'some boys down the bottom said I could go and play with them, is that all right?'

'Go on then, my lovely, but make sure you stay on the green where I can see you. Where's our Susan?'

'Dunno.'

After he's scuttled off I hear Auntie Nance say, 'I hope she hasn't gone and run off. It would be typical of her though if she has, because she never thinks about anyone but herself.'

Eddie

It's early evening now, and Susan's in her bedroom sorting out what she's going to take down to Bowleaze Cove tomorrow. She had a face as long as a fiddle when she came back from our Doreen's earlier, apart from when she saw

Lucky, but now she won't even let the dog into her room.

I try knocking on her door again. 'What's the matter, my old love?' I call out.

'Nothing,' she snaps back.

'Then why won't you let us in?'

'Because I want you all to go away,' she shouts.

I glance down at Lucky, who glances up at me. 'Well that's not very nice, is it?' I say.

'I don't care. Just leave me alone. And I don't want to go on holiday tomorrow. I'm staying here.'

'We don't want you to come anyway, do we Dad?' Gary shouts from his room.

'Yes we do,' I tell him, 'now, if you've finished your packing you can go outside and play football for a while. I want to have a chat with our Susan.'

'I'm not talking to you,' she informs me. 'Nothing you say is of any interest to me.'

I don't know what the dickens happened over our Doreen's to put her in such a bad mood, but something's obviously rubbed her up the wrong way, and I don't know whether to leave her be, or try to make her tell me what it is.

In the end, because my stomach's starting to play up again, I take myself off downstairs to put the kettle on. Someone said bicarb in hot water is good for stomach ache, so I'm giving it a try.

When it's ready I go and sit down in the dining room, where the windows are wide open and the smell of freshly cut grass is wafting in on a breeze. The lovely pictures Anne gave me are on the table – I expect Gary will enjoy looking at them, but I'll have to make sure his hands are clean, because I don't want him mucking them up. Even he feels proud that parts of Concorde are being built in Bristol, the whole city does.

I'm taking Faulkner's *The Mansion* away with me on holiday. He says it's a writer's job to put things clearly so that others can read and form their own conclusions. I think he makes a very good job of putting forward his points about class and race, and I'm looking forward to reading more. Certainly it'll keep my mind off the acid in my gut, and beef up my meagre knowledge of our wonderfully, frighteningly complex world.

I shall also make a study of Swinburne's 'Ballad of Burdens' if I have time. I imagine I will, because the children will be off with new friends, splashing about in the sea, exploring the local attractions. I find myself wondering what Anne does for her holidays, where she goes, how she occupies her time? Perhaps I should return the photographs, but how can I without causing offence?

I can hear music coming from our Susan's room now – 'Something in The Air' – so I'm hoping this means that her black mood has lifted. I must say, I'm partial to this song myself, so I think I'll write the lyrics down for her. She often asks for them, so I'm sure it'll please her to have these.

I reckon we're leading up to some kind of revolution, with all that's going on in the world. We were told the Vietnam War was coming to an end, but there's no sign of it yet. All that waste of life, never mind the abuse of it. At the same time the Americans go and put a man on the moon, and what good's that going to do anyone, I ask myself. It was impressive though, and we all stopped work to watch when it happened. At the crucial minute the picture went, but the sound carried on so we heard the already immortal words '. . . one small step for man, one giant leap for mankind'. I wonder who wrote that. I'm sure Neil Armstrong didn't make it up on the spur of the moment. I expect they had some great minds working on that for years.

Oh, to have a great mind, to be a respected thinker, a philosopher of lasting merit.

My stomach seems to have settled down a bit now, so when the record stops I decide to go up and check on our Susan.

Instead of asking if I can go into her room I stand at the top of the stairs and call out to her. 'Are you all right?' I say.

'Yes thank you,' she replies.

I stay where I am for a minute or two, looking out of the landing window to where Gary's kicking a ball round our grass, and a couple of girls from across the street are playing touch. They're the same age as our Susan, but I have to admit, they look a lot younger. They behave it too, with their skipping and hopscotch and decent clothes. I doubt they go wandering off at night so their mothers don't know where they are, or what they're up to.

'Susan?' I shout.

'What?'

I brace myself, because I know already she's not going to like this question, but I have to ask it, so here goes. 'Are your bosoms all right?'

I can almost hear her cringing with embarrassment, and I have to say I'm glad she can't see my face, because I know I've gone pretty red myself.

'Of course they are,' she snaps.

I've obviously upset her, but I can't leave it at that, so I say, 'Are you sure?'

'Why don't you go away? There's nothing wrong with me, so go and ask someone else your stupid questions.'

'It's just that your mother . . . ' There's no point continuing because she's put on another record, obviously to drown out my voice.

If we'd realised sooner that the lump in Eddress's left bosom was going to turn out to be the cancer that ended up killing her, there's a good chance we wouldn't be where we are today. Can I say all that to our Susan? Maybe I should try, but it's about such an intimate part of her body that I can't bring myself to put her through the shame of it.

Chapter Twenty-One

Susan

I've been trying on Mum's clothes. There are loads of them hanging in her wardrobe, her black and white check skirt, her blue polka-dot dress, her best suit with satin lapels, her trousers with loops under the feet . . . They're all miles too big for me, so are her shoes, but I put them on anyway to see how much more I have to grow until I'm as big as her. When I was little I used to play dress-up in her clothes. It always made her laugh.

I had a look in her dressing-table drawers after, where she kept her jumpers and brassieres. They're all much too big for me too. I went on sorting through, trying on her earrings and necklaces and then her perfume, which made it seem like she was in the room. That spooked me a bit, in case she was a ghost about to tell me off for poking around in places I had no business to be.

There were some letters from people I don't know, but they all asked about Dad so that was all right. No more photographs of a bloke called Michael, like the one I once found in her cookery book. I don't want to find anything like that again. I used to think he might be the bloke she'd run off with, but that was when I was trying to pretend she wasn't dead. I don't do that any more.

I went on looking through her stuff, trying on her brooches and sprinkling her talc on my arms. There were lots of nylons, but they're all too long for me, and anyway, I don't wear them any more. I wonder what she'd think of tights.

Then I found her engagement ring all snug inside a little velvet box. When I tried it on my wedding finger it fell straight off again, so I slipped it on my middle finger instead and held up my hand to have a look. It's gold with three little sapphires. I can remember her wearing it. She never used to take it off, or her wedding ring.

For ages I sat inside her wardrobe with the door closed. I don't like remembering her because that's when the screaming starts, but sometimes I can't help it. We used to lie on my bed together singing the nursery rhymes on my wallpaper. I've got different wallpaper now, I made Dad change it after I left Red Maids. Sometimes I think I can hear her laughing, or shouting at me, or saying something to Dad. I know it's not real, but it feels like it is. I wonder where she is and if she can see me. I don't expect she can, because like Auntie Nance said to Auntie Doreen, she'd never let me get away with the way I behave. Except being dead, she can't do anything about it.

When I got out of the wardrobe I made a promise to myself that I would never think about her again if I could help it. I don't think Dad does, or Gary, because they never mention her, so I won't either. It'll serve her right for not being here to take care of us. If she was I might not have all that screaming inside, or feel that I want to hit people and smash things up.

I liked her engagement ring so much that I thought I'd keep it, so I'm wearing it now, holding my fingers tightly together to stop it slipping off. It's on my third finger and I'm hoping, if Kev sees it, that he'll think I've met someone else and be jealous.

We've been in the bus shelter for ages now, and he still hasn't come. I don't think he will, but Mandy wants to wait a bit longer, just in case. I wish I'd brought Lucky. She looked really sad when I left without her, but I was afraid Kev might be mean to her if she growled at him again.

I wonder what Dad would say if he knew I had this ring. He'd probably go mental, but I think I should have it, or it won't ever get worn again, and that would just be a waste. I wonder where her wedding ring is. I think I ought to have that too.

We're back at school now, which is such a waste of time that I don't know why we bother. I hate leaving Lucky at home – Dad and I had a terrible row about it, but I can see his point, I suppose, that she'd be unhappy tied up outside the gates all day and besides, someone might come along and steal her.

Lainey and I were going to knock off all this week so we could stay at home with her, but I came in today because there's a trip up to Gloucester that I quite fancied going on. It's where I am now, sitting on the grass outside the cathedral that we've just had a look around. It was quite interesting, if you like that sort of thing, and actually I do, because history's one of my favourite subjects. Miss Hawkins, who takes us for the lesson, gave a fascinating talk all about Edward II whose tomb is here, and about the sculptures and stained-glass windows. Then we went down to the crypt, which was lovely and spooky and made me think of the one where John Whitson's buried in Bristol Cathedral.

I haven't heard from Sadie and the others for ages, and I haven't been up to see them either. I got a bit fed up with it to tell the truth, because they were always going on about things that were happening at school, and laughing their heads off at stupid stuff that I didn't really get. It's not that I want to lose touch with them, but they're not the only ones who are too busy to write.

Miss Hawkins is in a café at the moment with Mrs Webber, the Cennick housemistress. They're next to the window, keeping an eye on us all as they eat their dinners, while we tuck into our sandwiches out here in the cold. Still, at least it's not raining and it's a lot better than being at school. I just wish I had a packed lunch, because I'm starving. I told Dad last week about the trip, but he must have forgotten, because there was nothing waiting for me when I came down this morning, and there was no time for our new home help, Mrs Bees, to make anything for me.

It would be nice if someone offered me a crisp or a finger of their Kit Kat, but, selfish pigs, they're just sitting there stuffing their faces and watching me starve. If my real friends were here that wouldn't happen, but this is A group History, and Lainey and the others are all in B and C. I keep meaning not to work so I can go down a group too, but the trouble is, I can't help listening because Miss Hawkins (she's one of Miss Vaughan's – oops, Mrs Philpott's – dinnertime friends) has a way of telling us about what happened in olden times that nearly always makes us laugh. She does crafty things, too, like asking us which year Guy Fawkes blew up the Houses of Parliament. Everyone stuck up their hands and said 1605, but she kept shaking her head and they couldn't understand why, when she had the date chalked up on the board. In the end, she said, 'Susan, you haven't put your hand up yet. Can you tell me the answer?'

'I think it's a trick question, miss,' I replied, 'because he was caught before he blew them up.'

She laughed, and so did everyone else, and I felt quite proud of myself for having guessed the joke.

She's always nice to me, but we did have a bit of a row once, when I turned up late for her lesson. We ended up friends though, and later she said that with my red hair and fiery temper I was probably Queen Elizabeth I in an earlier life.

I think she could be right.

She's coming across the grass towards me now looking very concerned.

'Susan, don't you have anything to eat?' she asks.

'No, miss,' I reply. 'My dad forgot all about me, and I don't have any money, so I have to sit here and starve.'

I swear she nearly laughs, which actually I meant her to. 'Well, we can't have you going hungry, can we?' she says. 'You'd better come inside with us.'

And now here I am, sitting in the café eating shepherd's pie, which is so tasty I might ask for seconds. I know everyone's watching me, green with envy, but I don't even bother to look out at them. Let them eat cake, as Marie Antoinette would say – or in their case, worms!

When we've finished our meals Mrs Webber gets out her cigarettes and offers one to Miss Hawkins. Then she only goes and offers one to me. I can't believe it. She's obviously gone off her rocker.

'I know you smoke,' she tells me, 'so don't pretend you don't.'

I look at Miss Hawkins, who's clearly as shocked as I am.

'Well, do you want one or not?' Mrs Webber is shoving the packet towards me.

I grin at her. 'You're going to put me in detention if I take one, aren't you?' I challenge.

She sighs and starts to put the packet away.

'All right, I'll have one,' I say, and to my amazement she not only lets me take one, but she strikes a match herself to give me a light.

This is the most hilarious thing I've ever done, sitting in a café with two teachers, smoking a fag while the rest of the class look on, hardly able to believe their eyes.

I know Mrs Webber is waiting to see if I take back, so I do, and I think she's quite impressed by how expert I am.

She shakes her head. 'What are we going to do with you, young lady?' she asks.

'I don't know, miss,' I reply.

She takes a puff of her fag. 'You're like a Stradivarius that could play beautiful music if we only knew how to tune you,' she says.

I don't know what a Stradivarius is, but I think she's given me a compliment, so I blow out my smoke and say thank you.

'Do you know what Miss Fisher said about you the other day?' she goes on. 'She said, "Imagine what a joy it would be if we always saw Susan at her best."'

That sounds quite a nice thing to say, so I thank her again.

'What do you want to do when you leave school?' Miss Hawkins asks.

I shrug. 'I haven't really made up my mind yet,' I tell her, 'but I definitely don't want to work up Fantasy.'

'Fantasy?'

'It's the corset factory up Kingswood,' I explain. 'I'll probably join the commercial group next year, to learn office practice, so I can get a job as a typist or secretary, or something like that.'

'Why don't you join the general group, and go on to take your O levels?' Miss Hawkins suggests. 'I'm sure you'd pass them.'

I'm quite flattered that she thinks that.

'And then you could go on to sixth-form college to take A levels,' Mrs Webber adds. 'Which subjects would you choose for that, I wonder? There have to be three.'

It doesn't take me long to decide that. 'English, history and French,' I announce.

'Mm, yes, I hear you're doing very well in French,' Mrs Webber says. 'And we know you're good at English and history, so I think there's a fair chance you'd achieve some excellent grades. You might even be able to go on to university. Would you like that?'

I screw up my nose. 'No, thanks. All that studying would do my head in. I'd rather get married and have kids.'

Miss Hawkins says, 'Wouldn't you like to travel the world and get lots of experience under your belt before you settle down?'

I give it some thought, and soon find that the idea of visiting different countries is quite appealing. Not if I have to go on my own though, and I can't see Lainey wanting to come with me, because she wants to work up Fantasy. Mandy might, but it would mean leaving Kev and Rich behind and we definitely don't want to do that. And what if I got lost and ran out of money, or was abducted for the white-slave trade? I might end up in a harem and never see

England again. 'I think I just want to get married and have kids,' I say again.

'Do you have a special boyfriend?' Mrs Webber asks.

I think that's rather nosy, but they're paying for my dinner and letting me smoke, so in return I decide to tell them a bit about Kev. I make it sound as though we're going steady and that he's really mad about me, or they probably won't be very impressed.

'And he's already at work?' Miss Hawkins says. 'What does he do?'

'He makes faggots down Brains,' I tell her. 'I don't know if you've ever had them, but they're delicious.'

'I'm sure,' she murmurs. 'And how old is he?'

I decide I'd better not say nineteen, so instead I say, 'Sixteen.'

'Has your dad met him?'

'Um, not yet, but I expect I'll take him home soon.'

A waiter comes up to collect our plates, and empty the ashtray. When he puts it back down again I flick my ash, and because they're being chatty with me, I decide I can be the same with them. 'Did you go to Mrs Philpott's wedding?' I ask.

'Oh yes, we both did,' Miss Hawkins replies. 'It was such a shame you couldn't come. She looked lovely.'

I can imagine it, because Mrs Philpott's very pretty. 'She said she'll probably have the photos back soon, so she'll bring them in to show me,' I tell them. I can't wait to see them, as much to find out what her husband's like as to have a look at her dress. 'Are you in them?' I ask.

'Probably,' Mrs Webber chuckles, and leans forward to stub out her fag. 'I expect you're going to miss her when she leaves at the end of term,' she adds.

I feel my face drop.

Miss Hawkins starts to look worried. 'Oh dear, she hasn't told you yet that she's leaving?' she says.

I shake my head. I wish I could go outside now.

Miss Hawkins glances at Mrs Webber.

'It doesn't matter,' I tell them. 'I don't mind if she leaves.'

Mrs Webber watches me put my fag out.

Miss Hawkins says, 'She'll miss you when she goes, we know that, because she's become very fond of you.'

I just shrug. So what? 'Are there any toilets in here?' I ask.

'Uh, yes, they're over there, behind the till,' Mrs Webber replies.

I stand up. 'Thank you for my dinner,' I say politely. 'I'll see you outside.'

When I get there the other girls start flocking around me, wanting to know how I got the teachers to let me smoke, and what we talked about. Since none of them are my friends, I don't want to tell them anything, so I push my way past and start walking away.

'Look at her,' Anita Cooper sneers, 'she thinks she's it, just because she went in that café, when really she's just a common little tart.'

I spin round so fast that she catches her breath. I am so close to whacking her that my hand's already in the air, but then I see the priest from the cathedral watching me like he's God waiting for me to commit a sin. 'You're going to be really sorry you ever said that,' I hiss at her.

As I turn away I hear someone whisper, 'Anita, she'll smash your head in as soon as we get back to school.'

'Her and whose army?' Anita sneers.

'You'll find out,' I tell her, 'and when we get hold of you, you'll wish you were never born.'

Actually, that's how I feel, that it would be better if I'd never been born. There's no point being here, it's horrible, I hate it. All the way back on the coach I sit staring out of the window, wishing I was dead and trying to think of a way to do it. I wonder where Mrs Philpott's going, and if she might be able to take me with her. She won't want to though, and who can blame her? Why would she want me when I'm ginger and ugly and nothing more than a common little tart?

Eddie

I keep wondering if I should take a present into the shop for Anne to say thank you for the pictures of Concorde. The trouble is, if they weren't a gift and someone really did hand them in by mistake, I could end up making a proper chump of myself. Of course, it would be good manners to acknowledge her kindness in holding them back for me, I think she'd appreciate that, but the question is, what to get her? I know she likes the Brontës, because we've talked about them once or twice when I've been in, but she's probably got a full set that's far nicer than anything I could ever afford. It can't be scent because that's much too personal and anyway I don't know what she likes, and the same goes for nylons, or headscarves or handkerchiefs, that would be going several steps too far. I can't ask our Nance or Doreen, because they'll wonder who it's for, and I don't want them getting the wrong idea, which I know they will. The blokes down work aren't any good either, because none of them knows anyone as refined as Anne, so they wouldn't have any more of a clue what to get than I do.

I haven't been back to the shop since she gave me the photographs, because I don't want her thinking I'm reading things into her gesture that she didn't intend. I only ever used to go in once a month or so anyway, generally on a Saturday, so it wouldn't look right if I started going in more often now. She might think I was after more gifts, or some other kind of special treatment, and that wouldn't do at all. She could be wondering what's happened to me by now though, because it's been closer to two months since I was last there. I hope she doesn't think I've taken her generosity for granted, because that certainly isn't the case. Maybe I should go in this weekend. There's probably a nice new stock of books by now, and that's what I go over there for really.

I decide to make up my mind what do on to Saturday morning, because I've got other things to worry about tonight. I should have left half an hour ago to go up the union, but there's no sign of our Susan, and Gary says he hasn't seen her since she came home from school.

'Are you sure she didn't say where she was going when she went out?' I ask him.

'I already told you, no,' he replies. 'All she said was she couldn't take Lucky because she scares people, and then she went.'

'What was she wearing?'

'I don't know.'

'Was she still in her uniform?'

'*I don't know.*'

I'd be worried anyway, but ever since she found out her favourite teacher's leaving at Christmas she's been in a terrible mood. Mostly she takes it out on me, shouting and screaming and saying she wishes she was dead, or she shuts herself up in her room refusing to come out. I suppose I'd rather that than think she was getting into trouble at school, or was out wandering the streets with the likes of Mandy Hughes, but the trouble is, she's doing that too. Three nights running last week she managed to sneak out after we'd all gone to bed, and once she didn't come back till gone midnight.

I was waiting at the bottom of the stairs when she came in but she wouldn't tell me where she'd been, and when I got hold of her to give her a damn good shake she threw herself down on the floor to escape me.

'What the heck have you been doing until this hour?' I asked her.

'It's none of your business,' she shouted, picking herself up. 'Now let me go past.'

'You'll stay right where you are until I get some answers.'

She folded her arms and glowered at me as though she might put an evil spell on me.

Taking a different tack, I said, 'Susan, my love, you're ...'

'Don't speak to me like that,' she raged. 'I'm not your love. I hate you, now get out of the way.'

'Who were you with? Was it boys?'

'I don't have to tell you anything . . . '

'If you've been with boys, young lady, there's going to be some . . . '

'I expect you think I'm a prostitute,' she spat. 'Well, for your information I am.'

I felt as though she'd punched me, even though I knew it couldn't be true. I wasn't even aware she knew what a prostitute was, and to be honest, I don't think she does, but I've been worrying all along about how far she might be going with these boys, and now I'm scared half to death that my worst nightmares have already come true.

Is that where she is now? Letting them do things to her that a child her age shouldn't know anything about? Dear God in heaven, please give me guidance, because I just don't know what to do.

'I don't think Lucky's very well,' Gary says.

I look down at the dog and think he's probably right, because she's not her usual lively self. 'She's probably eaten something that disagrees with her.'

'Yeah, like one of my football boots,' he grumbles.

I had to buy him a new pair a couple of weeks ago, because she'd torn his others to shreds.

'Shall I stay here and look after her while you go up the union?' he asks.

'No, you go in to Mrs Williams's,' I tell him. 'She'll be all right once it's gone through her.'

I won't worry myself now about the mess I'll have to clean up when I get back, I'll just deal with it then. That's if I go. I can't think about going anywhere when I don't know where our Susan is. I should go out to try and find her. That's what I should do.

I've been walking around for an hour now, up and down Anchor Road, over to the Horseshoe, the brook, the bus shelter, along Fisher Road and down Made for Ever club. There's no sign of her, and no one I've asked has seen her.

I return home, hoping to find her there, but the house is

empty, apart from the dog. Just as I expected, she's been sick all over the kitchen, so I set about clearing it up before going upstairs to make sure our Susan's belongings are where they're supposed to be. To my relief they are, so it doesn't seem that she's run away.

So where is she?

If something's happened to her I'll never forgive myself. I'm scared half out my mind that the police are going to come knocking on the door any minute, the way they did our Doreen's after Robert was killed. Anyone could have got hold of her, God only knows what they might be doing to her. I've got a panic flaring up in my gut that's worse than any ulcer, if that's what it is burning my insides. It's all my fault. Everything I've done has been wrong, from the minute her mother died. I've made one bad decision after another, after another, and I've never been nearly strict enough with her. Is it too late to get things back to the way they should be? I'm not even sure I know what that is any more, apart from wanting her to do well at school, and behave in a respectable manner. How am I to get her to do that? What's wrong with me that I can't get through to her?

I fetch my notepad from the pocket of my coat and go to sit at the table in the dining room. Though my hands are shaking and my mind is spinning, writing is all I can think of to help blunt the edges of my fear. Maybe moving the pencil over the page, recreating words by Keats and Shelley, Shakespeare and Burns, will soothe my troubled mind and bring some relief into my heart.

Fill for me a brimming bowl
And in it let me drown my soul;
But put therein some drug designed
To banish women from my mind.

Keats's lament at least brings the ghost of a smile to my lips. Funny that I should have chosen that one first, or perhaps not funny at all.

Lucky pads across the room and puts her head on my knee.

'Hello, girl,' I say, giving her a stroke. 'Are you feeling better now? I expect you want to go for a walk.'

Her tail starts to wag, showing her understanding of 'walk', so I put my pencil down and go to find her lead. I'm hoping that by the time I come back our Susan will be here. If she isn't, then all I can do is sit and wait, because Gary's going to be home any minute, and I can't leave him on his own while I go roaming the streets looking for her again.

Susan

I can hear Dad going to take Lucky for a walk. He's telling her to stop pulling him the wrong way, because he doesn't realise that she knows where I am and is trying to get to me. In the end he wins, and tugs her on out to the street.

I heard him going out earlier too. I think he probably went up the union, he usually does on Wednesdays. Gary's next door with Geoffrey and Nigel, and I'm here, under our old tent in the shed. It smells all fusty, and I think there might be spiders around, but I'm not particularly scared of them. I should have been going out with Mandy and Julie tonight, but when we got round the Anchor Kev was there with his new girlfriend who lives over Longwell Green. Her name's Debbie, apparently, and she works over Brains, which I suppose is how he met her.

He didn't even bother to speak to me. He just looked the other way and pretended I wasn't there. Then he walked past us with her holding his arm, and from the direction they went in he must have been taking her down the club, where he's never taken me. I know I'm too young to go in, but he's never even let me hold his arm in front of everyone else, and to flaunt her in front of me like that was just mean.

Before Mandy went off with Rich, and Julie went with Larry, they told me to wait for them round the bus shelter, but I didn't bother to go. I just came back here and got into my special place where no one can find me, or get on my nerves any more.

I think I'll stop going round with Mandy and Julie from now on, and just go round with Lainey. We had a bit of a row in school today because I was nasty to Mrs Philpott, but we made up again on the way home. I feel a bit bad for telling Mrs Philpott that I didn't want to see her wedding photos, because I suppose it was quite rude. What's the point, though? I won't know anyone in the pictures except a few teachers, and I see them every day already so I don't need to see them again. And who cares what her new husband looks like anyway?

I think Dad's got a girlfriend called Anne. I don't normally read his tiny little writing, but for some reason I did the other day, and this is what it said:

Anne dresses so attractively and modestly that it makes me feel devastated. A vision of gentle beauty, colours and contours, carefully chosen to suit her. Her taste is reflected in her clothes. Her heavy shoes show resourcefulness, stamina, strength and health. It sets me wondering about her religion, politics, education and ambition. Her hair is blonde. She is strong-limbed, determined, but has an easy carriage, and elegant poise. What does she see when she looks at me? The misshapen dwarf gazed upon by the beautiful princess. Her fairness makes my Nordic type ache for I don't know what.

I ripped the page out of his book and kept it. I wonder if he's noticed yet. I don't expect so, because there are thousands of pages he's written, and I don't think he ever reads any of them back. He's funny like that, but there again, I suppose I don't read my diaries after I've written them either, so I wonder why I bother. Why does he?

She sounds nice, this Anne, but I don't expect she'd like me. Anyway, we don't want another mother.

'We're all right as we are, aren't we?' I said to Gary after I read it.

'Yes, I suppose so,' he replied.

I could tell he didn't know what I was on about, so I said, 'We don't want Dad to get married again, do we? She'd only be telling us off all the time, and you know what she'd be, don't you?'

'What?' he asked.

'A wicked stepmother.'

He turned a bit pale at that. 'We definitely don't want one of those,' he agreed.

I keep wondering what I'd do if Dad did get married again, especially if it was to someone who didn't like me. I don't want him to love anyone except Mum and us. We don't need anyone else. We're all right as we are.

I can hear Dad coming back now, and Lucky's trying to get to the shed again. He still doesn't take any notice, just pulls her inside and closes the door.

I don't know how long I'll stay here, maybe until I die.

Chapter Twenty-Two

Eddie

'Oh, Mr Lewis, you shouldn't have done that.'

Anne's smile is lovely. Her cheeks have turned pink, showing how pleased she is.

'I just wanted to show my appreciation for the way you hung on to those photographs for me,' I tell her.

It's a box of Maltesers, which I thought was a good choice, not too personal, but something she was sure to like. I nearly got Milk Tray, until I remembered the advert. It makes my toes curl up to think of myself trying to swoop into her bedroom at night, dressed all in black with a mask over my face, so heaven knows what it would do to her. Frighten the living daylights out of her, I'll bet, and who could blame her? Eddie Bond 003 and a half!

'Oh, I'm glad you like them,' she says. 'And these are my favourites, not too fattening, but a little bit of naughty all the same.'

She blushes fiercely at the innuendo, and I think I do too.

Trying to cover her embarrassment, she puts the chocolates down and starts searching for something under the counter. 'Someone brought a book on dogs in last week,' she tells me. 'It should be here somewhere. Ah, here we are. I remember you saying you wanted one to try and help train yours.'

I give a chuckle as I take the manual and leaf through it. 'You don't know how much we need this,' I say. 'The blinking thing's close to running wild.'

She smiles in a fond sort of way. 'I expect the children love it though, don't they?'

'Oh, there's no doubt about that, and she's not a bad little thing in her way, very affectionate, but not a clue about discipline.' I cock a playful eyebrow. 'I'm sure there are some who'd say that about my children too, so if you find any books on how to control them . . . '

She laughs heartily at my joke, which isn't a joke at all where our Susan's concerned, but fortunately she doesn't know that.

'How old are they?' she asks.

'My daughter's thirteen, and my son's nine. Susan and Gary,' I tell her, sounding as proud as Punch, when inside I'm crippled with shame for the way our Susan's staying out at night and getting up to heaven only knows what with God only knows who. It was nearly midnight again on Thursday, and when she came in, chilled to the bone and stinking of cigarettes, I couldn't get a word out of her about where she'd been.

'Wherever it is, you've been smoking,' I shouted at her, 'and you know I won't have it.'

'No one's asking you to.'

'Don't cheek me or you'll get the back of my hand.'

'You wouldn't dare.'

'Test me once more and you'll wonder what's hit you. Now I want to know where you're getting cigarettes. You're not old enough to buy them, so who's giving them to you?'

'Mind your own business.'

I grabbed her and started to shake. 'Cigarettes can kill you, don't you realise that?' I shouted. 'It's because of them we're in the position we're in now.'

'What are you talking about?'

'They kill people . . . '

'I don't care. I want to be dead.'

'Don't talk stupid.'

'I'm not. I'd rather be dead than go on living here.'

I pushed her to the bottom of the stairs. 'I've had enough

of you,' I growled, as she fell, 'now get up those stairs and you'd better start asking God's forgiveness for the way you're behaving, or you're going to end up in a very sorry place.'

'Good!'

'You're going to hell,' Gary told her, over the banister.

'Get lost,' she snarled at him, and slamming her bedroom door behind her she screamed, 'I hate you all. Do you hear me? I hate you, so go away and leave me alone.'

Our Gary was upset, naturally, so I sat with him until he went back to sleep and stayed on sitting with him long after, too exhausted, too defeated to move. Thank God he's not showing any signs of going the same way as our Susan, but the way she's carrying on is definitely starting to affect him. I'm terrified I'll end up calling in the authorities to help control her, because I have to keep things stable at home for our Gary's sake. He doesn't deserve any of this, and if we go on this way I could end up having them both taken away.

My dear little souls. Eddress's babies, Susan and Gary. They look to me to protect them, but no matter what I do it never seems to be right.

'They're very nice names,' Anne says kindly.

'Thank you,' I say, managing to summon a smile.

'I expect they're good company, aren't they?'

Thinking only of Gary, I reply, 'Oh, they have their moments. A bit of a handful at times though.'

'Like most children, but it's important for them to have character, is what I always say.'

I think of our Susan and nearly smile at the wonderful euphemism of 'character'. The moment of cheer soon fades as I wonder what kind of character she's turning into. 'They're definitely not lacking in that,' I say lightly.

She looks round as an old lady comes into the shop, and when she greets her by name and starts to chat, I go on leafing through the manual, thinking I'd probably be wagging my tail if I had one, I'm so delighted with how gracious she was about accepting the chocolates. And for remembering that I was on the lookout for a dog book. My optimism hits a brick wall when I entertain the prospect of her meeting our Susan, but as it's not likely to happen I cheer myself up by thinking about how well she'd probably get on with Gary.

Realising I'm being very presumptuous indeed with my thoughts, I tuck the book under my arm, and carry on looking around to see what else has come in during the past couple of months.

By the time the old lady's gone I've found a very handy book on gardening, another on the discovery of Australia, and a Penguin edition of *The Cloister and the Hearth*, which sounds very interesting indeed.

'Will that be all for you today, Mr Lewis?' she asks, when I take them to the till to pay.

I want to tell her to call me Eddie, but what I say is, 'Four's my limit, thank you,' which is true, though I'm not sure why.

'You've got a very eclectic taste,' she comments, looking through them.

I'm so thrilled by her use of such a scholarly word that I give her a little bow of thanks.

She laughs and blushes, and then starts busying herself with putting my books in a bag, keeping her eyes down as she says, 'Have you seen that film *Paint Your Wagon* that everyone's talking about?'

'No, I haven't,' I admit. 'Have you?'

'Not yet, but they're saying it's very good.'

'That's what I hear too. Do you go to the pictures much?'

'Whenever I can. What about you?'

'I used to, but these days it's usually only to take the children. Gary likes all the Westerns.'

'I'm sure. And what about Susan?'

'Oh, I suppose anything that's romantic would be up her street, especially historical. That's all she seems to read these days, Georgette Heyer, Anya Seton, Jean Plaidy, Jane Austen.'

'Really? Then I'll keep an eye out in case we get any of them in. Now, let me see, that'll be one and ten please.'

After counting out the coins, and giving her the exact amount, I pop the parcel under my arm and say, 'Well, it's been very nice talking to you, and thank you very much indeed for the dog book. I'll make a start on the little scallywag as soon as I get home.'

She laughs. 'Good luck with it, and if you do see the film, don't forget to let me know what you think of it.'

It's not until I'm as far along as Page Park and about to cross over the road that it occurs to me she might have been dropping a hint about the film, hoping I'd offer to take her. The thought of it leaves me feeling a bit flustered, so instead of carrying on over to Florrie's, I go into the park and have a sit-down on a bench.

I'm trying to decide whether I'm getting above myself thinking she'd want to go to the pictures with me, because she can't be short of someone to go with, or whether I should return to the shop and ask her. I have to admit, the thought of starting to court someone is causing me a lot of consternation. It's not something I feel inclined to do, but on the other hand she's a very nice woman and I'm sure it would be most enjoyable to have her as a friend. I don't expect she wants any more than that either, especially not with someone like me. *The misshapen dwarf gazed upon by the beautiful princess.* I wrote that once. I wonder if that's how she sees me. She'd be far too polite to say so if she did.

I don't think I'll go back, because if I've misunderstood it'll embarrass the heck out of us both. I probably won't even be able to face going in there again, and that would be a shame. Besides, what would I do if she says yes? I don't know which picture houses are showing the film, or what nights it's on. Of course, I could always get a paper to find out. I won't be able to pick her up though, because I don't have a car these days, so I'd have to meet her outside, and I'm sure that won't be good enough for someone like her. She'll be used to being treated like a lady, and though I'd do my best, I'm sure I'll be woefully lacking compared to the kind of gentrified people she probably knows. And then there's the children. Where would I tell them I was going? I wouldn't want to lie, though with Gary it would probably go in one ear and out the other. I don't really want to think about how it might go down with our Susan, though.

When all's said and done, I'm sure I'm giving myself airs and graces, so picking up my books I leave the park and carry on over to Florrie's. It's best to keep myself to myself, no misunderstandings or embarrassment that way, and no explanations needed either – or sadness to cope with, when I get home after spending time with a woman who isn't Eddress.

Susan

Kev's only finished with Debbie Cooper and wants to see me!

I'm rushing to get ready now, putting on loads of Hide 'n Heal to cover my spots, and drenching my neck in gallons of Aqua Manda, which is so lush I want to pour it all over me.

In her note Mandy said I have to be outside the Horseshoe by seven o'clock, or they'll go without me. I won't be late though, because it's still only twenty to, and it should only take ten minutes to run over there. I'm wearing my navy blue mini kilt, which I think makes me look dead sexy, a white V-neck cardigan with navy buttons, and my black PVC boots. I'm also wearing a new purple and white check bra that I bought up Mitzi's with some of my birthday money. It's really fab.

I'm just about to dash downstairs to grab my coat when Dad storms out of his bedroom and seizes hold of me on the landing.

'What are you doing?' I shout, trying to shrug him off.

'Not so fast, young lady,' he growls. He's obviously in a

rage, but about what I don't know, because I haven't even seen him since we had tea, and he was all right then. 'You're not going anywhere until you tell me what's happened to your mother's engagement ring,' he barks.

My heart gives a horrible lurch, because I've lost it, but I can't tell him that, so I say, 'How would I know? I haven't even seen it.'

'Don't lie,' he seethes. 'It was in a box in her dressing-table drawer, and now it's gone. So where is it?'

'Why are you blaming me?' I yell at him. 'You don't have any proof that I stole it . . .'

'It can't walk on its own, and who else would take it?'

'I don't know. Now let me go, or I'll be late.'

'Get back in that room,' he shouts.

'No!'

'Do as you're told.'

'You can't make me,' and with all my might I give him a shove and bolt down the stairs.

He's after me like lightning, and pushing me into the front room. 'I've just told you, you're not going anywhere . . .'

'Oh yes I am.'

'I want to know what's happened to that ring.'

'I told you, *I don't know*!'

'You're lying.'

'Don't you dare say that to me. I hate you, now get out of the way.'

He blocks the door and spreads out his arms. 'You're not taking a step further until you tell me where you're going.'

'Out!' I yell.

His face is all red and trembly with fury. 'I've had all I can take of you,' he shouts. 'I never know where you're going or what you're up to. I want to know if you're still a virgin.'

I shrink back, blocking my ears. 'Don't say things like that,' I scream. 'I hate you . . .'

'I want to know . . .'

'Shut up!'

'I want the truth out of you.'

I stick out my face, saying, 'You can't make me tell you anything . . . '

'Where's your mother's ring?' he roars.

'*I don't know.*'

His fist comes up and suddenly he's punching himself in the face.

I can't believe what I'm seeing. He's ramming his fists into his own face. 'Dad! *Stop!*' I cry. 'What are you doing?'

He punches himself again, and again. *Punch, punch, punch.* He won't stop. His nose and lips are bleeding. Tears are streaming down his cheeks. He's gone mental.

'Dad! Stop!' I scream again.

'I have to hit myself, or I'll hit you,' he shouts, and he goes on punching.

I can't stand any more. I don't know what to do. He's really scaring me, so I duck past him, tear open the door and the next moment I'm out in the street, running for my life.

Eddie

I'm at the kitchen sink dabbing my face with cold water, and still trembling, when Gary comes in the back door.

'All right Dad?' he says chirpily.

'Yes thanks, my love,' I croak.

'Can I have something to eat? I'm starving.'

'There are some cheese and onion crisps in the pantry.'

He swings open the pantry door, takes a packet from the bread bin and is about to stuff a handful of crisps in his mouth when he stops. 'What are you doing?' he asks.

'Just having a wash.'

'But what's all that blood?'

I look at the towel I should have hidden as soon as he came in. 'I cut myself shaving,' I tell him.

He looks a bit suspicious for a moment, then apparently deciding it's all right he goes on into the dining room to turn on the telly.

I give a sigh of relief and pick up a clean towel to start drying my face. I don't know what came over me. I only know that I wanted to hit her so much that I was afraid if I did I might kill her. Better to hit myself, punch my face and the walls, break my knuckles and split my mouth, than to subject her to all the pent-up rage inside me. If I had they'd have ended up taking her away for certain, and now I'm thinking that maybe that wouldn't be such a bad thing. She's running wild. She has no respect for herself or anyone else, and I've lost all hope of being able to reach her. She's a stranger to me, not my daughter at all. I know it was her who took the ring, because no one else goes in that drawer, except me. I don't know what she's done with it, but I don't suppose I'm going to see it again, and it's breaking my heart.

I wonder who you're supposed to call when you can't cope any more. The council? No, I suppose it would be the education authority. I hate even thinking it, but maybe it'll be for the best if they put her in a home for juvenile delinquents. They might be able to stop her stealing, playing truant, and going with boys.

It would be for the best.

Eddress must be turning in her grave.

I put my head in my hands and start to sob, but I have to stop in case Gary hears me. Poor chap, I know all the rowing and swearing is getting him down because he's been coming to get in with me at night, needing a cuddle and to know that I'm all right. He's usually been to check on our Susan first. All this chaos and anger, it's too much for a boy his age. I know he loves her, and he'll miss her when they come to get her, but we can't go on like this.

I wonder where she is now, what she's doing. I know I frightened her and I'm sorry about it, but it was better that than laying into her the way I wanted to. Shall I go and look for her? She'll be off somewhere with her friends, and will probably have forgotten all about what I did by now, because she's selfish, dishonest and determined to have her own way over everything. She doesn't spare a thought for anyone else and the effect she might be having on them. How do you love a child like that? I don't know, you just do. Because she's mine, I suppose, and I want to believe, I *have* to believe that there's still some goodness in her somewhere.

I go upstairs to check myself in the bathroom mirror. My top lip is cut and there's still some blood on my nose. My left eye is starting to swell, it'll probably be black by morning. I can imagine what the blokes down work will say.

'Whose wife have you been trying to get off with then, Eddie?'

Or, 'Turned you down, did she?'

I don't care what they say. All that matters is trying to sort out what's to be done with our Susan. It's tearing me apart to think of giving up on her, but what else can I do? Any day now she's going to come home and tell me she's pregnant, or the police will be at the door to arrest her, or to tell me she's been raped, or even murdered. Dear God in heaven, please guide me. I can't bear to think of anyone hurting her, but if she goes on the way she is, it can only be a matter of time.

Susan

After I left the house I ran and ran and didn't stop until I reached the Horseshoe, even though Lucky was nearly tripping me up as she bounded along with me. When Kev and the others saw her they started shouting at me to get her away, but I pretended not to hear and kept on going. Lucky was excited to see Mandy, but as she jumped up someone kicked her and she flew out into the road, yelping in pain.

'Get that fucking animal away from me,' Kev shouted.

'Take her home,' Mandy snapped. 'What did you bring her for?'

I held Lucky tight, with my face buried in her fur.

'Why does she always have to bring the bloody dog?' Rich grumbled.

'It's savage,' Kev snarled.

'She hasn't even got it on a lead,' Mandy added. 'You know she doesn't behave,' she shouted at me.

I thought Mandy was supposed to be my friend, but she was ganging up against me too, so without saying anything to any of them, I kept hold of Lucky's collar and took her away.

We're down by the brook now, under the bridge where no one can see us. I'm trying hard not to remember what Dad did, but I can't get it out of my mind. It was like he'd gone mad, punching and crying and making himself bleed. I've never known anyone do anything like that before, and now I'm scared to go back. I wish he'd come to find me, but what if he starts hitting himself again? I didn't mean to make him do that. I wish it hadn't happened. I'm going to stop thinking about it and pretend that it didn't.

I don't know where Kev and the others are, but I don't care. He kicked my dog, at least I think it was him, and that's a horrible thing to do. I know she can be boisterous and a bit frightening at times, but she'd never really hurt someone the way he tried to hurt her. If a car had been coming she could have been killed.

She's just had a long drink from the brook and now she's sitting next to me, panting and giving my face a lick every now and again, as though to remind me she's there.

I consider going up Gran's, but if I do she'll only ask why I'm out so late and send me home. I won't be able to tell her about Dad, because I don't want anyone to know what he did. They'll only blame me, and I know it's my fault, but there's nothing I can do about it.

I wonder what he's doing now. What if he's killed himself? Suddenly I feel sick and the next thing I know I'm retching. Nothing comes up, but I can't seem to stop. I want my dad. I don't want him to be dead. I really, really, really, really love him, but I'm scared of him now.

He shouldn't have hit himself like that. It was a daft thing to do. No one else hits themselves.

If he is dead then I want to die too, but then Gary would be all on his own.

I don't know what to do.

I have to stop crying, or I won't be able to leave here.

I hope Kev and the others don't come looking for me, because I never, ever want to see them again. He shouldn't have kicked my dog.

I want to kick him.

Suddenly I grab Lucky's collar and start dragging her up to the road.

When we get home Dad's in the dining room and the telly's on, so I try to sneak past, but he hears me.

'I'm going to bed,' I tell him when he opens the door.

'Are you all right?' he asks. His face is all swollen and there's a cut on his mouth. It really happened. He really did beat himself up.

I nod and wonder if I should ask how he is, but I'm afraid of what he might say.

'Do you want something to eat?'

I shake my head.

I walk on along the passage to the bottom of the stairs. Lucky's behind me, and I'm waiting for him to tell her to come back. Instead he says, 'Do you know what happened to your mother's ring?'

I hang my head.

'When did you last see it?'

'I can't remember,' I mumble.

'Did you take it out of the house?'

It takes me quite a long time to pluck up the courage to nod. 'I didn't mean to lose it,' I cry.

'You shouldn't have taken it.'

'I know, but I don't know what you're making all the fuss about because she's never going to wear it again, is she?' and before he can answer I dash up the stairs to shut myself up in my bedroom.

'And how long's it been since this happened?' Florrie asks.

'A few days,' I reply. 'I've been trying to make up my mind what to do . . . '

'How's she been since?'

'Quiet, especially for her. She seems afraid to come near me now.'

'Oh, dear Ed,' she sighs. 'You're such a good man, and she's such a lucky girl to have you as her dad.'

'I don't know about that. I'm not doing a very good job, am I?'

'You're doing the best you can, and that's what counts.'

'But it's not good enough. All the truancy and bad reports from school . . . I've had a letter from the headmistress telling me that some of the teachers want her expelled.'

'Oh no, not again,' Florrie murmurs.

'Apparently Miss Fisher's not ready to give up on her yet, and she's got the backing of a couple of other teachers, but if Susan doesn't start changing her ways . . . I never thought I'd say this about my own daughter, but she's not turning into a very nice person, Flor.'

'But she's not a person, Ed, she's a child, and the sooner she remembers that the better.'

'I don't know,' I sigh, shaking my head. 'I'm at the end of my tether with her. I only want what's best for her, I always have, but now I'm thinking that being with me isn't doing her any good.'

Florrie's starting to look bemused and upset. It's not that she hasn't had to deal with an unruly grandchild before, heaven knows she has enough of them, but I think with Eddress no longer being around she feels more of a responsibility towards my two. I feel bad about burdening her with this, but she's the only one I can talk to who loves our Susan as much as I do, and who I can trust to want the best for her.

'Do you think I should have her put away somewhere?' I ask. 'It's not what I want, but the way she keeps getting into trouble . . . She's going to end up on drugs, or with her throat cut.'

'Do you want me to have a talk with her? I don't know if I can do any good, but having her put away, Ed . . . Well, I don't know what our Eddress would say about that, but I don't think it's what she would want.'

'I know, but she could always handle her much better than I can.'

Florrie gives a faraway sort of sigh. 'Yeah, she could handle just about anyone, could our Eddress,' she murmurs, and her eyes well up with tears.

'There you are,' I say, picking up a hanky from the arm of her chair and handing it to her. It's funny how after all these years – five next May – we can all still have a good cry about her. You'd think we'd be over it by now and sometimes I think I am, but then suddenly there I am again, right back as if the last time I saw her was yesterday.

'Let me have a chat with her,' Florrie says. 'I don't know how much good I can do. I feel so helpless with these legs . . . If it weren't for them, you know I'd do more . . . '

'Now, now, I don't want you blaming yourself. You've got enough grandchildren on your plate as it is, and like it or not, you're not getting any younger.'

She gives a chuckle. 'Eighty-five next birthday. I must be wicked to have lasted this long, if only the good die young.'

I smile and squeeze her hand. 'You're one of the best, Florrie. Don't ever let anyone tell you different.'

Her rheumy old eyes twinkle, but then she seems sad again. 'We'll get this sorted out between us,' she promises, 'we have to or we'll end up losing her, and one thing's for certain, our Eddress would never forgive us if we did that.'

Chapter Twenty-Three

Susan

I'm only in Miss Fisher's office sitting on a chair in front of her desk, while she stares at me through her flick-up glasses. Her hands are folded together, and the sun's streaming in through the window like magical rays – I'm hoping they'll make her disappear, or turn her into a frog, or better still a handsome prince to whisk me away to a palace. Everyone's scared of her, including me.

'Do you happen to know if your father received the letter I sent him a couple of weeks ago?' she asks.

'No, miss,' I reply. 'He hasn't said anything.'

'Can we be sure that you didn't intercept it? In case you don't know what that word means . . . '

'I know what it means and no, I didn't intercept it.' Bloody cheek! I mean, I know I do try to get to the detention letters before he does, but she doesn't know that, so she's got no right accusing me.

'So you're not aware that there are certain members of staff who would rather you were no longer at this school?' she goes on.

I feel a flush of embarrassment – and anger – spread over my face. 'No, but I don't care,' I tell her stroppily.

She gives a sigh. 'Then perhaps it's lucky for you that others do. This will be your last chance, so I'm hoping you won't let me down.'

Since she didn't ask a question, I don't say anything,

but I don't like the fact that no one wants me here. It's horrible. I hate them all anyway.

'I don't think anyone's in any doubt that you have a great deal of potential,' she drones on, 'but we're not having much success in persuading you to show it in the right ways. Is it of no interest to you to do well, to come top of the class even, in subjects you like?'

'I don't want people calling me teacher's pet,' I tell her.

She heaves another sigh and shakes her head. 'For an intelligent girl that was a particularly stupid reply,' she informs me. 'I expect more of you.'

I feel my mouth go tight, but I'm too afraid to cheek her back, so I let the insult pass.

'You have some strong leadership qualities that are not currently being put to their best use. So, do you have any suggestions as to how we might change that?'

I'm startled, because she genuinely seems to be asking my advice. But then I think it must be a trick question, because teachers never ask our advice. She's obviously waiting for an answer though, and I don't want her calling me stupid again, so I give it some thought before I say, 'I think I would make a good prefect.' That would make everyone laugh, but I'm serious, I think I would, and to my amazement Miss Fisher's only starting to nod.

'I'm not going to argue with that,' she tells me, 'because you could well be right, and that answer was far more worthy of you than the nonsense about not wanting to be called teacher's pet. However, the position of prefect has to be earned with good behaviour and excellent marks, so I'm sure you'll agree it wouldn't be fair on those who work hard and who deserve to be recognised for their efforts, if we gave you a badge and put you in charge of a class. Do you have any other suggestions?'

I suppose her answer makes sense, but it wouldn't half show those stuck-up old cows who think they're it with all their gold stars and glowing reports if I did get to tell them what to do. I'd really love watching them suffer, but I suppose it's not going to happen, and since Miss Fisher's asked a question this time, and the answer is I don't have any other suggestions, I shake my head.

'For the moment neither do I,' she admits, 'but this is what I'm proposing we do while we try to come up with something. Instead of attending PE for the last period on Wednesday afternoons where Miss Perry tells me you're extremely unco-operative, I want you to report here to me so we can have a chat about how things are going with your other lessons.'

I immediately baulk, and really, *really* wish I had the guts to tell her to get lost, but I don't, so I can only purse my lips to let her know that I think it's a rubbish idea.

'Right, so that's settled,' she says, getting to her feet. 'I'll expect you for our first chat tomorrow afternoon at three o'clock. Don't be late.'

Regally dismissed, I traipse off out of her office and go to find Lainey and the others in the playground. I barely have time to tell them what happened before the bell goes for the end of break and we have to go different ways, because they're all in C group for maths and I'm still stuck in A. I really thought I'd have gone down at least one group this year, but I didn't, so I'll just have to stop answering the questions in tests, because it's not as if I pay attention in class, it's just that I've done a lot of the work before, at Red Maids.

I go to fetch my books from my locker, then shuffle off to the lesson, making sure I'm the last to arrive just to show Mrs Brain that I don't want to be there. She waits till I'm sitting down at the back, then taking out her chalk she starts to write on the board.

Bloody hell. It's only bloody logarithms. Well, I'm not listening to all that crap, so I take out a pencil and start doodling things in the back of my book.

I'm wondering if Mrs Brain's one of the teachers who wants to expel me. I've never had an especially big row with her, but she's given me a few punishment marks for messing around in class, and a detention once for locking her in the stationery cupboard. Anyway, I'm sure she doesn't like me, because nobody does, and frankly I couldn't care less. I don't want to be here anyway, except I suppose I'd miss Lainey and the others who are my only real friends now I don't go round with Mandy any more.

I had a note from Mandy after the night Kev kicked Lucky, asking me to meet her round by the Anchor, but I didn't bother to go. I've decided I'm not speaking to her again after that, and though I still love Kev I won't be speaking to him again either.

Or to Dad, after what he did.

He keeps going on that Gran wants to have a chat with me, but I know I'm in for a lecture so I'm trying not to go up and see her. I wonder if he told her what he did to himself. If he did I expect she blames me. Every time I think that, the screaming inside me starts up and it's horrible, frightening. It makes me want to run away and hide and never come out again. I know I was being cheeky and he was mad about Mum's ring, but he shouldn't have attacked himself like that. His face is still bruised and the cut on his mouth hasn't healed yet. I really hope he never does it again or he'll end up being carted off down Barrow Gurney to live with the loonies and I don't want him to leave us, I really, really don't.

I love my dad more than I love anyone else in the whole wide world.

He made us turn the whole house upside down at the weekend looking for the ring, just in case it was still there somewhere, but we didn't find it. I hid in my bedroom after, afraid that he might start punching himself again, but when I crept down to find out what he was doing he was sitting in the front room with his head in his hands. It frightened me to see him like that and I wanted to shout at him to stop, but I didn't let on I was there. Instead, I just crept out again and went to find Lucky.

'Why did you take the ring?' Gary whispered as I came into the dining room.

'Don't you start,' I snapped.

'It wasn't yours, so you were stealing.'

'I'll thump you if you don't shut up,' I seethed.

'And I'll thump you back.'

I didn't really want to have a fight, so I went back upstairs, taking Lucky with me, and lay on the bed. She hasn't been very well again lately, seeming all lifeless, and I'm worried it might have something to do with how hard Kev kicked her. She had a fit last night, which really scared me the way she fell over on her side, shaking and foaming at the mouth and looking like a raging wild beast. Dad pulled me away to stop me from being bitten, and when she finally calmed down he picked her up and carried her over to her basket. Gary and I sat with her for ages after, stroking her and telling her she mustn't worry that she made a mess, because no one was cross. In the end she managed to get up again, and when she pawed the back door to go out Dad came for a walk too. Fortunately, by the time we'd gone round the block a couple of times she seemed to be more her old self again.

I've just come in from school now and Gary's all upset because Lucky's had another fit.

'It frightened him,' Mrs Bees, our home help, tells me, 'but you'll be all right in a minute, won't you, my old love,' she says, patting his back.

Ignoring Gary I go straight to Lucky's basket, where she's looking all dopey and half asleep. She knows me straight away though, and tries to give me a lick.

'I think you'll have to take her to the vet,' Mrs Bees advises, coming to stand over us.

I'm trying with all my might not to cry, so I keep my head down as I manage to say, 'I don't know where one is.'

'Mm, no, nor me,' she sighs, 'but I expect we'll find someone who does. Or, I'll tell you what, let's go round the phone box and have a look in the Yellow Pages. I can give them a ring then and make an appointment, because I expect you'll need one.'

'I want to stay with Lucky,' I tell her.

'I'll come with you,' Gary offers.

By the time they get back Lucky's up on her feet again and having a drink. She even jumps up on Gary, and gives him a lick.

'They can't fit her in tonight,' Mrs Bees tells me, 'but they said you can take her tomorrow morning at half past ten.'

I know I'm supposed to be going to school, but Lucky's much more important, so I'll either take the day off, or I'll go in the afternoon provided the vet's given her something to make her better. Come to think of it, I have to go in the afternoon because Miss Fisher's expecting me for our first cosy chat.

'Can you come with me to the vet?' I ask Dad when he gets home.

'No, my love,' he replies. 'I can't take the time off at the moment.'

I look down at Lucky, and my eyes fill up with tears, even though she's looking all chirpy and happy. 'I don't think there's anything wrong with her really, do you?' I say. 'Perhaps I won't go.'

By the time we're ready for bed Lucky's had another fit, so I ask Dad if she can sleep with me. For once he says yes, and carries her basket upstairs while I take one step at a time with her, until she regains her balance and starts to sniff around my room, seeming happy to be there.

After Dad's turned the light out she creeps out of her basket and climbs on to the bed, so we snuggle up together to go to sleep. I really love her, and it's upsetting me a lot to think that she's not very well, but at least she doesn't seem too bad now.

During the night she has another fit and makes such a mess of my bed that I have to go and sleep in Gary's room, while he goes in with Dad. Lucky's allowed to stay upstairs, but out on the landing in case the same thing happens. When Dad's disappeared into his room I take Gary's eiderdown and go to lie down with Lucky to keep her warm.

It's morning now and Dad's just gone off to work. Lucky

didn't have any more fits in the night, but he said I should take her to the vet anyway, and he gave me five pounds in case I have to pay, because we don't think dogs are covered by the National Health. He also gave me some change for the bus fare, because the vet's down Speedwell which is too far to walk, with her not being well.

Dogs have to ride upstairs on the bus, so the conductor helps me take her up, and then she has another fit on the top deck with everyone watching. Nobody says anything though, except the conductor who pats my head and tells me not to worry, he won't charge me for the fare today.

I sit on the edge of a seat with Lucky on the floor in the gangway. A woman has to step over her in order to get past, and she mutters something about 'girls your age should be at school.'

I want to tell her to fuck off, but Lucky's struggling to her feet, so I ignore the woman and clasp Lucky round the face. 'Are you all right?' I whisper. 'We'll be there soon and the vet will make you better again.'

'Are you going to see Ralph Carson?' an old man asks.

Recognising the vet's name, I nod.

'He's a good bloke. I've known him for years. Me and the missus always took our cats to him. Wouldn't never go anywhere else.'

When it comes time to get off Lucky nearly drags me down the stairs, which makes me feel a lot better, because she's obviously not feeling so bad any more.

In the vet's waiting room there's a woman with a hamster in a cage, and a policeman with a great big Alsatian dog that has a bandage on its foot. I expect the policeman to ask me why I'm not at school, but he's reading a paper and doesn't seem to be taking much notice of anyone else. Lucky growls at the Alsatian, but it ignores her, so she settles down at my feet and goes to sleep.

After a few minutes an old lady comes out of the vet's office with a budgie in a cage, and the woman with the hamster is called in next. When she's finished the receptionist is just telling the policeman to go through when Lucky starts to have another fit.

'Oh dear, oh dear,' the receptionist says, coming round her desk. 'Poor little thing. She's epileptic, is she?'

I look at her blankly, not knowing what that is.

'Let them go next,' the policeman offers. 'I don't mind waiting.'

'I'll get Mr Carson,' the receptionist says.

When the vet comes out he squats down next to Lucky, putting a hand gently on her head as the fit starts to pass. 'There's a good girl,' he murmurs. 'That's all better now, is it? Yes, I think so. Shall we take her into my office?'

I watch him pick her up and follow them into the next room, where he lies her on his operating table, then closes the door.

'How long has she been having the fits?' he asks as he starts to examine her teeth and eyes.

'Just for a few days,' I reply.

'Has she had many?'

'About, um, six or seven.'

'I see.' He sticks something up her bum, then puts his stethoscope over her heart. When he's finished that, he checks her eyes again, and smiles as she tries to give him a lick. She's all groggy, the way she usually is after a fit.

'Someone kicked her last week,' I tell him. 'Do you think that might be what's caused it?'

He looks at me with his kind grey eyes. 'No, that's not what caused it,' he replies. 'Tell me, did you have her vaccinated after you got her?'

I don't know what he means, so I shake my head.

'Mm, I thought not. I'm afraid, my dear, that your dog has distemper.'

I've got no idea what that is, but my chest is going all tight, like it's a fist trying to clench. 'What's that?' I manage to ask.

'It's a virus that's a bit like measles, but it has a different effect on a dog.'

'She's going to be all right, is she?'

He shakes his head. 'I'm sorry, my dear. The best thing you can do for her now is let me put her to sleep.'

I feel like he's hit me, because I know exactly what that means, and I'm not going to let him do it. I look at Lucky. She's looking at me, and I start to cry. 'Please don't take her away,' I beg him. 'Please, please. I want her to stay with me.'

'There, there,' Mr Carson says, patting my head. 'Where's your mum? She should have come with you really.'

'She can't,' I sob, 'she's dead.'

'Oh dear, dear,' he murmurs. 'I'll tell you what, why don't we ask my secretary to make us a nice cup of tea, and then we'll decide the best thing to do?'

I'm at school now. I had to come in because I have to spend the last period with Miss Fisher, otherwise I'd have gone straight home. Or up Gran's, or down Dad's factory to wait for him to come out. Anywhere really, except here.

It's break time, and I'm sitting outside the office with Lainey and Tina and a few of the others, who are being really kind and comforting about Lucky. Some of them even cried, because they loved her too. The vet explained to me that she would only get worse and worse and it would be cruel to make her suffer, so I ought to let her go. I wanted to scream at him and hit him and tell him to leave her alone, but I was sobbing too hard for any words to come out. In the end, I gave her a great big kiss and told her I was going to wait outside while the vet gave her an injection to take away the pain. I wished he could give me one too so I could die with her. When he came out I wanted to run away – run and run and run and never, ever come back.

It wasn't until I got to school and took off my coat that I realised I still had the fiver Dad gave me scrunched up in my pocket. I expect he'll take it to the vet tomorrow to pay what we owe. It seems really wrong to think that we have to pay for Lucky to die.

I don't want Lucky to be dead. Please let her be there when I get home.

'Susan Lewis! Is that you?'

We all look up to see Mrs Baron, the dragon of a music teacher, thundering towards us. Everyone hates her, and most of us are scared of her, but I don't feel very scared of anyone today. In fact, I couldn't really care less who she is, or what she's got to say.

'On your feet, girl,' she snaps at me.

I stand up and rest my weight on one leg.

She's so angry that her face is twitching and I think her glasses might be starting to steam up. God knows what I'm supposed to have done, but it looks like she's about to tell me.

'Where were you this morning?' she demands. 'You were supposed to be in my lesson, and just for *you*, because *you* never stop going on about it, we were going to discuss *pop*, only you didn't bother to turn up. We all bend over backwards for you, my girl, and you don't damn well deserve it. You're selfish, arrogant, disobedient and disrespectful and I'm . . . '

'I didn't come in because my dog died,' I shout at her.

'Don't *lie!*' she shouts back, and she slaps me so hard across the face that I see stars.

Everyone gasps.

Then it goes quiet.

My fists are clenched, and without even thinking I bang one of them right into her. 'I hate you,' I scream, and before she can stop me I turn and run out of the building. I keep going, across the forecourt, down the drive towards the cookery rooms. The lane leading towards home is behind them, but Mrs Philpott must have seen me coming, because all of a sudden she's there, trying to catch hold of me.

'Susan, Susan, what is it?' she cries.

'Nothing. Let go of me,' I sob.

'Susan, stop!' she shouts, holding me hard. 'You have to tell me what's wrong.'

'It's Mrs Baron,' I choke. 'She called me a liar because I said my dog was dead and then she slapped me, so I punched her, but she deserved it.'

'Oh my goodness,' she mutters. 'Is your dog really dead?'

'Yes.'

'OK. OK,' and gathering me up in her arms she hugs me so tight I can hardly breathe. 'You'll be all right,' she tells me. 'We'll get this sorted out.'

'I want to go home.'

'No, you must come with me, we'll talk to Mrs Baron together.'

'I don't want to see that old bag.'

'Susan, please, do as I say, just this once.'

Because I haven't been very nice to her lately, and because she's still bothering to be nice to me anyway, I let her take me back up to the main building, where we find Mrs Baron and my friends all talking at once, trying to tell Miss Fisher what all the fuss was about.

'Miss Fisher, here's Susan,' Mrs Philpott shouts above the noise.

Miss Fisher turns round, and is just about to speak when Mrs Baron says, 'We should call the police and let them deal with that girl. She's nothing but . . . '

'*Mrs Baron* will you be quiet,' Miss Fisher barks.

All our eyes go round. None of us have ever heard a teacher get told off before.

'Susan, did you punch Mrs Baron?' Miss Fisher demands.

'Yes, miss, but she slapped me first and she called me a liar.'

'That's what we were trying to tell you,' Lainey shouts.

'All right, thank you, Lainey,' Miss Fisher says.

Lainey hasn't finished. 'Sue's dog had to be put to sleep this morning, and she's really upset, so . . . ' She stops as Miss Fisher turns to glower at her. 'I'm just saying,' she adds sulkily.

'Mrs Philpott, bring Susan into my office,' Miss Fisher

says. 'Mrs Baron, I'll speak to you later. The rest of you, off to class.'

When we're in Miss Fisher's office, she closes the door and turns to glare at me.

'Miss Fisher, Susan isn't lying,' Mrs Philpott tells her, which I can hardly believe, because for all she knows I could be. I'm not though, and thinking about Lucky makes my eyes well up with tears again.

'What happened, Susan?' Miss Fisher asks. 'Start from the beginning.'

I feel really stupid as I try to tell her, because I keep sobbing and can hardly get the words out, but somehow I manage to describe about Lucky and what the vet told me, and why I even bothered coming to school today.

'Dearie, dearie me,' she sighs, coming to pat my shoulder. 'I'm very sorry about your dog. They're very special creatures, so I understand how you're feeling, my dear. You can go home early today. I think that'll be for the best.'

'Am I in trouble?' I ask.

'For once, no,' she replies.

I look at Mrs Philpott, who seems nearly as surprised as I am. 'Who's at home?' she says.

'No one,' I answer and start to cry again, because Lucky won't be there.

'What time does your home help come?' Miss Fisher asks.

'Actually she might be there by the time I get back,' I say.

Mrs Philpott puts an arm round me as we walk back down to the cookery rooms. 'Listen to them,' she says, rolling her eyes at all the noise going on in her class. 'Will you be all right?'

'Yes, thank you,' I reply. I take a breath. 'I'm sorry if I've been a bit mean to you lately . . . '

'Oh, you haven't really,' she interrupts, 'but I've missed seeing you from time to time.'

'I wish you weren't leaving. I mean, I know you have to, but . . . '

'I'll write to you,' she promises. 'I'll tell you all about my new life and my new school, and when you write back you'll be able to tell me what's happening to you. You will write back, won't you?'

I nod again, and I think I might, but only if she writes first.

'Will you be all right getting home?' she asks.

'Yeah, I'll be fine,' and turning away I start walking along the lane. If only I could stop wishing Lucky was with me, bouncing around on her lead and trying to get into mischief the way she does. I wonder if she's in heaven. If she is Mum and Robert will be looking after her. I look up at the sky, but then I have to drop my head again because I can't stop crying.

Eddie

I've been thinking about our Susan all day, wondering how she got on at the vet's and feeling terrible for not going with her. The trouble is there's a real crack-down happening at work, they're watching us like hawks, especially those of us involved in the union, and I don't want to be getting on the wrong side of them any more than I already am.

It's ten past five now, and I'm at the chemist's in Staple Hill because I promised Florrie I'd pick up a prescription for her and drop it in on my way home. I'd rather not be late tonight, but I reminded the children this morning that I would be so I hope they haven't forgotten. I don't want to find them pacing up and down the street again, which has happened when I'm not home at my usual time.

I thank the pharmacist for the tablets and take the change after purchasing a tube of toothpaste, and as I tuck it in my pocket I start wondering how much change I'll get out of the fiver I gave Susan for the vet. We're a bit short again this week, what with one thing and another, but I suppose as long as Lucky's all right, that's all that matters.

I'm just going past the baker's when I think it might be nice to have a cake or some sponge rolls after our tea, and since they're usually selling them cheap at this time of day, I turn back to find out what's left. To my surprise I almost bump into Anne as she comes out of the door.

'Mr Lewis,' she cries, looking pleased to see me.

'Hello, Anne, how are you?' I ask, hoping I'm looking just as pleased to see her, because I am.

'Oh, not too bad. Just on your way home from work, are you? It's a bit out of your way up around here, isn't it?'

'I had to pick up a prescription for my mother-in-law,' I explain, holding up the bag for her to see. 'Have you been working today?'

'No. Actually, I'm not at the shop any more, so I'm glad I ran into you. I've had to give it up, I'm afraid.'

'Oh, I'm sorry to hear that.' A lot sorrier than I dare to admit, in case it embarrasses her. 'I hope everything's all right.'

'My mother had a stroke,' she tells me, 'so someone has to be at home to look after her.'

'Oh dear, that is bad news. When did it happen?'

'A couple of weeks ago. She came home from hospital yesterday, and I don't suppose she's too bad, considering, but I don't like to leave her for long. My brother's promised to help as much as he can, and my aunt, her sister, is only a few doors away, so at least I can still go out for a few hours now and again.'

'That's good, because it can be a tiring business looking after someone who's ill.' I'm trying very hard to think of the right thing to say, and what comes out next is, 'Did you ever get to see that film *Paint Your Wagon*?' Immediately I've said it I realise how rude it was to change the subject so abruptly, especially when we'd been discussing something so important. 'I'm sor—'

'No, I didn't,' she answers. 'Did you?'

'No, but if it's still on, would you like to go? I mean, with me?' The words are tripping out like they have a will of their own, and I can feel myself blushing like a flipping teenager, all down over my neck and up around my ears.

'I'd love to,' she says.

I start to beam, but luckily someone wants to get into the shop, so we have to step out of the way and I've managed to get the foolish look off my face by the time I ask, 'Are you on the telephone at home?'

'Yes, we are. Are you?'

I laugh. 'No, not us, but if you give me your number I can find out if the picture's still showing, and if it is I'll ring you up and let you know.'

'That'll be lovely. Have you got a pen or pencil?'

Did she but know it, that's like asking me if I've got blood in my veins. Promptly I produce my notebook and after I've written her number down, she says, 'It's in the telephone directory, just in case you lose it.'

'Oh, I won't,' I assure her. Then, 'Well, I suppose I'd better be getting along. The children will be wondering what's happened to me.'

'They're all right, are they?' she asks.

I think of the trouble with our Susan lately, and feel thankful that the cuts and bruises on my face have healed and no longer show. What on earth would a genteel lady like Anne make of the way I behaved that day? 'They're very well, thank you,' I tell her, keeping my smile in place. 'I wish we could say the same for Susan's dog, but she took her to the vet today so I expect everything'll be better by the time I get home.'

'I hope so,' she says. 'Don't forget to call, will you?'

'No, I won't,' and forgetting all about going in to pick up a cake, I walk off down the road feeling a spring in my step like I haven't felt in a long time.

When I get to Florrie's Eddress's brother, Tom, is there, and he kindly offers to give me a lift home which I jump at, even though it means taking him out of his way.

'What do you make of our mam these days?' he asks as we drive down over Pound Road. 'Does she seem all there to you?'

I'm slightly taken aback by the question. 'I can't say I've

noticed anything wrong,' I tell him. 'Why do you ask?'

'It's just a couple of things she's said. She was talking about Maurice the other day as though he was upstairs, and when I reminded her he was in New Zealand she didn't seem to know what I was on about.'

'Oh,' I say, starting to worry. 'Was she all right after?'

'She seemed to be, but our Gordon said he had a similar thing happen with her last week, when she started calling him Albert, which was our dad's name. If you ask me, I reckon she's starting to lose her marbles.'

'Let's hope not,' I reply. 'We don't want to have to put her in a home, I don't think she'd like that at all.'

'Not one bit,' he agrees. 'She can't come and live with us though, we haven't got the room. Anyway, we don't need to do anything for the moment, except keep an eye on her. You'll let me know if you notice anything, won't you? We're having a telephone installed next month, so you'll be able to ring us up, any time.'

'That's nice,' I say. 'Lots of people seem to be getting them put in now.'

'Are you going to?'

'No, we don't have any need for one. The phone box is just around the corner.'

We're at the top of Holly Green now, where he pulls up so I can walk through the lane to home. 'Thanks for the lift,' I say, opening the door.

'That's all right. Oh, by the way, I saw your stepmother up Kingswood the other day. Beat, is it?'

'That's right. How is she?' I feel a sharp pang of guilt that I have to ask him when I should know for myself, but I just haven't had time to get over there these past few weeks.

'She seemed all right. She asked me to say hello if I saw you, so I'm passing the message on.'

Dear, dear Beat. She's probably as lonely as can be in that house all on her own, so come what may I have to make some time to get over and see her.

To my relief, when I go round the corner into Greenways

there's no sign of Susan and Gary pacing the street, or of their white faces peering out of the window to see if I'm coming.

'Hello,' I call out, as I let myself in the back door, 'anybody home?'

The dining-room door opens and Gary comes into the kitchen.

'What's the matter, my love?' I say when I see his blood-shot eyes. 'You two haven't been fighting again, have you?'

He shakes his head and starts to cry. 'Lucky's dead,' he tells me, and as my heart sinks he tumbles into my arms.

'There, there,' I say, trying to comfort him. 'What happened? Where's our Susan?'

'She's upstairs in her bedroom. She won't let me in.'

Cursing myself for not going with her this morning, I settle him down with a jam sandwich and a cup of Ribena, and putting my own sadness about the dog aside, I go upstairs to knock on Susan's door.

'Can I come in?' I ask.

She doesn't answer, which is usually a sign that it's safe to proceed, so I push the door open and when I see her, huddled up on her bed, I want to pick her up the way I used to when she was a baby.

'What did the vet say?' I ask, going to sit next to her.

'She had distemper,' she answers, 'so he put her to sleep.'

'Oh dear, oh dear,' I murmur, giving her back a rub. I can hardly bear to think of what she had to go through all on her own. What must the vet have thought, a girl her age turning up with a mortally sick dog and without any sign of a parent? It would serve me right if he reported me to the authorities. 'How did you get back from the vet's?' I say.

'I walked.'

'All that way?'

'I kept looking out for a bus but one didn't come.'

'So you haven't been to school at all today?'

'Yes, I went in this afternoon, and something really horrible happened.'

Alarm sinks my heart to further depths.

'Miss Fisher says it's all right now though, it wasn't my fault, so I'm not in trouble.'

'Are you going to tell me what it was?'

Eventually she rolls on to her back, and when I see how broken up she is I scoop her up in my arms. 'It'll be all right,' I tell her as she starts to sob. 'She's gone to heaven now. Jesus will take care of her.'

'Why does Jesus always have to take away everyone I love?'

'I don't know, my darling, but I hope you love me, and I'm still here, aren't I?'

'And me,' Gary says from the door.

Susan gives a splutter of laughter, and next thing Gary's on the bed too and we're all having a hug.

'I'll tell you what,' I say, 'why don't we have some tea, and after we've watched a bit of telly we'll all sleep in my room tonight. Is that a good idea?'

'Yes,' Gary cheers.

I look at Susan, and drop a kiss on her forehead as she nods.

How could I ever have contemplated having her put away? Life's giving her enough knocks as it is, without me making it all a hundred times worse.

Chapter Twenty-Four

Susan

Lucky's been dead for almost two weeks now, and the house is so quiet without her bouncing around and barking every time she hears a noise that it's like she's there by not being there, if you know what I mean.

Dad misses her too.

'She could be a blinking nuisance,' he grumbled the other day, 'and half the time she was more trouble than she was worth, but we all loved her and she loved us, which is why we're feeling so lost without her.'

I wanted to ask if he thought she was with Mum and Robert, but I didn't. I keep telling myself she is, but what happens after you die is God's big secret that He doesn't share with anyone else. Religious people say you go to heaven, but they can't tell you where heaven is, or even if it really exists, and I'm not sure it does. I have to admit, it would be nice to know that there's somewhere better than here when you die, with no rules, or crime, or evil people going round killing innocent people, just happiness, sunshine and kindness all day long. I wonder if that would get a bit boring, everything always being the same. Who knows? Who cares even, because we're not going to find out anything for certain until God decides to let us in on what happens next. And too bad if you don't like it, because you'll be dead so there won't be anything you can do about it.

Dad's blaming himself for Lucky's death. He says he

should have thought about the vaccines when I first got her, but I should have too, so it's both our faults. Between us we've killed Lucky, which is a terrible, unforgivable thing to do.

Gary wants to get another dog, but I don't think we will, in case it ends up dying too.

We're up Gran's now, on a Saturday night, because Dad's gone out. He's never been out at night before, apart from up the union, so maybe that's where he is, I forgot to ask. He was wearing his best suit when we left the house, and he'd combed Brylcreem through his hair, making it all greasy and slick, and he'd splashed some Old Spice on his face which really stinks. I'd much rather have Brut, but being in the older generation he probably hasn't even heard of it.

Gary's in next door with our cousins, which is where I was until a few minutes ago, watching Wendy getting ready to go out. I wish I was her age so I could have my own money and go down the Top Rank to meet blokes every week the way she does. I still haven't seen Kev since the night he kicked Lucky, even though Mandy keeps sending notes saying that he wants to see me. 'Everyone keeps asking where you are,' she wrote in her last one, and I wondered who she meant by everyone, because hardly anyone speaks to her, apart from Rich, Kev, Larry and Clive, and they only want her for one thing. It's all they want me for too, I can see that now, and I feel ashamed and stupid for what I let them do. As far as I'm concerned they can all drop dead, because they're not worth even thinking about, and Kev'll be sorry when he finds out I've met someone else who's much nicer and better-looking than him.

I'm talking about Lainey's brother, Mike, who's dead cool – apart from his spots and curly hair. Lainey says he really likes me, and her mum agrees. She's really nice, Mrs Dickson, and ever so pretty. I wonder what she'd say if I actually started going out with Mike. He's seventeen and according to Lainey he's had loads of girlfriends that her mum hasn't liked much, but she likes me so that could work out really well. I could marry Mike and have Lainey as a sister-in-law and Mrs Dickson as a mother-in-law, and we could live in between our house and the Dicksons' so we'd all seem like one great big family.

Lainey's going to ask Mike this weekend if he'll go out with me.

I bet he says no.

'What's the matter, my old love?' Gran asks. 'You don't look very happy.'

I didn't realise she was awake because she was dozing when I came in, and I was so carried away in my thoughts I'd almost forgotten where I was.

'I'm all right,' I tell her.

'You don't look it. Your face is as long as a fiddle. You're not still missing your dog, are you?'

I turn my head away as tears sting my eyes. I know it's stupid, but I can't help it.

She sighs and shakes her head. 'What are we going to do with you?' she says.

'Nothing,' I answer.

She doesn't say any more, and nor do I, but I know she's watching me, and I'm afraid she's about to start giving me the lecture I've been trying to avoid since Dad said she wanted to have a chat with me. 'What about your old mum,' she asks in the end, 'are you still missing her too?'

Suddenly everything seems blurred and horrible and wrong and I don't think I'm going to be able to stop myself shouting, or running away, or crying, or I don't know what.

'Come on my love,' she says, holding out her arms, 'come and see your old gran.'

I know I'm too big for her lap, but I go anyway, and bury my face in her chest the way I used to when I was little.

'There, there,' she murmurs, rubbing my back. 'You have a good cry now, Granny's here to make it all better.'

I suddenly can't stop myself sobbing and sobbing until my chest is tearing apart and my eyes are on fire. I keep wishing she was Mum, but that's not very nice when she's being so lovely. I love her more than anything, but with all my heart I want Mummy to walk in the door now and tell me she really did go off with another family, but she doesn't want them any more, so she's come back to us. I know it would have been a really mean and cruel thing for her to do, but I'd forgive her if only she'd come back. I remember the time I saw her standing outside our house wearing her pink pyjamas. She was smiling and looking all proud, but actually she was already dead by then, so I couldn't really have seen her, it must have been a ghost. I'm afraid I might see her like that again, but at the same time I wish I could, because it's horrible never seeing her at all. I'd give anything in the world to make her come back, not only for me, but because I know it would make Dad happy again and I hate it when he looks sad. I've always loved him the best, above anything and anyone, even Mum (I think), but he's different now. He used to laugh all the time and swing us around and read us stories in funny voices that made Mum roll her eyes and tease him, until he chased her back down the stairs telling her he'd deal with her later.

I know I ought to try and take her place so he won't be sad any more, but really he'd rather have her and who can blame him? I'm no good at housework, or cooking, or bossing people around, the way she was. Well, I suppose I'm all right at bossing people around, but I bet Dad wouldn't have beat himself up if she was still here. I didn't manage to stop him doing that, and I know it was my fault, the same as it was my fault that I lost her ring, and that Lucky died, and it's my fault that everything's going wrong.

'Oh there, there, my old love,' Gran soothes. 'What a state you're getting yourself into. Don't tell me this is all about your mum?'

I try to nod, but I'm sobbing so hard that my head goes more from side to side than up and down. 'I don't – don't . . . Please don't . . . tell Dad,' I beg, 'or he'll – he'll get upset too.'

She clucks and tuts, and pats my back some more. 'You listen to your old gran now,' she says. 'Your lovely dad won't mind a bit that you've had a good cry, but if you want it to be our secret, I promise I won't say a word.'

There's a question I want to ask, but I'm half afraid to, because Gran is Mum's mum and I don't want to make her unhappy by talking about things that we shouldn't mention really.

'Come on, out with it,' Gran says, when I start to stammer the words.

'Do – do you . . . Gran, do you miss her too?' I ask. I cross my fingers very tightly, hoping she's going to say yes, because I don't want to be the only one who admits that I do.

'Oh, Susan, Susan, Susan,' Granny sighs. 'I miss your mother every minute of every day. Sometimes I picture her walking in that door and it seems so real I find myself waiting for her to say, "So how are you today, Mam? Legs still playing you up, I suppose. Let's have a nice cup of tea and then we'll rub in some cream."'

Even though I can see it makes her sad, I feel a bit better to know that she misses Mum too after all this time. I'm certain Dad does, but he never mentions her, and I don't talk about her to Gary because I think he might have forgotten who she is by now, and that's probably for the best. I wish I could forget too, but I don't really, because she was my mum and I really, really loved her, even though she died and left us, but it wasn't her fault. When God makes up His mind, there's nothing you can do, you have to go, even if you'd rather stay here.

For a long time Gran and I sit quietly in our cuddle, not saying anything until in the end I hear her starting to snore. I don't want to wake her up, so I go as gently as possible as I ease myself off her lap. She snuffles, and clacks her teeth, and then her head lolls to one side, but she continues to sleep.

I wonder what to do next. I'd like to watch telly, but I

expect the noise will wake her up, so in the end I decide to get a duster and polish the room. These days we use a spray at home called Pledge, which Mrs Bees our home help buys and Dad pays her back, but Gran still prefers the tins of creamy wax that she buys from the Kleen-eze man when he comes round the door selling his buckets and mops. It's more work, because you have to put it on with one rag, then buff it off with another, but the shine is lovely and the smell reminds me of when we used to come up here with Mum. She used to do Gran's housework then, sweeping the carpets, scrubbing the kitchen floor and rubbing Windolene into the windows.

It's nearly ten o'clock now and Dad's just come in looking very pleased with himself. 'Look what I brought,' he announces as he walks through the door.

Gary leaps up from the game of donkey we're playing and he's losing. 'Fish and chips,' he cries. 'Did you get me a Clark's pie?'

'Of course,' he says, 'and there's a fishcake for Susan, and a lovely piece of cod for your gran. Florrie, are you awake?'

'What? What?' she mumbles, her teeth nearly falling out as she starts to come round. 'What did you say?'

'Dad's brought some fish and chips,' I tell her.

She looks around the room, blinking behind her glasses as though she can't see, then she spots Dad and sounds surprised as she says, 'Eddie, there you are.'

'Here I am,' he replies jovially. 'Gary, go and get the plates, there's a good boy.'

'All right, but can I eat mine out of the paper?'

'If you like.' Dad puts his salt-and-vinegary parcel down on Gran's yellow and green checked tablecloth, and shrugs off his coat.

Gran's staring at the TV, even though it's not on. 'Eddie, tell our Tom to come out from behind there,' she says. 'I don't know what he's hiding from, but if the police are after him, I don't want them finding him here.'

I stop unwrapping the chips and look at Dad.

He gives me a wink, then goes to check behind the telly. 'He's not there, Florrie,' he tells her. 'He must have gone when you weren't looking.'

She nods and grunts, and takes off her glasses to give them a wipe with her pinny. 'Where have you been then?' she asks, putting them on again.

We're not very sure who she's talking to now, because she's looking at the sideboard, so Dad answers, saying, 'I've been to the pictures. Do you want to know what I saw?'

'Yes,' Gary cries, bringing in the plates.

'*Paint Your Wagon*,' he tells us. 'Have you heard of it, Florrie?'

She's messing about with her glasses again, and seems not to have heard. Then she says, 'The pictures, that's nice. What did you see?'

Gary starts to snigger, but Dad puts a finger over his lips and giving me another wink he asks, 'Are you hungry, Florrie? We've got some fish and chips for you here.'

'Oh, there's lovely,' she says. She gives her glasses another wipe and puts them back on. 'Where's our Susan? I'm sure she was here just now.'

'I'm here, Gran,' I tell her.

She finds me with her eyes and says, 'So you are.'

I'm not sure what's happening so I look at Dad, hoping he might be able to explain.

'Ssh,' he whispers, 'she's a bit confused, because she's only just woken up.'

I suppose that makes sense, because she's quite old so it might take her a while to come round, so I go to give her a kiss, then I help Dad to lay our supper out on to plates. I'm nearly bursting with a question to ask him, but I'm not sure if it's allowed. In the end I decide that I don't care if I get told off, I have to ask it. 'Who did you go to the pictures with, Dad?' I make it sound chatty and casual, even though I'm feeling very stiff inside.

'Oh, just a friend,' he answers. 'No one you know.'

Now I'm sure it's a woman, but I don't say any more

because if I'm right I don't actually want him to tell me. I just hope that whoever she is, he doesn't see her again, because he's my dad and he belongs to my mum and we don't want to share him with anyone else.

'Here we are,' he says, passing Gran a plate of cod and chips. 'And I brought you a bottle of stout,' he tells her, taking one from his pocket.

'Ah, just what the doctor ordered,' she replies. 'There's some lemon squash out in the pantry for you children, if you want some, and you can bring in the bottle opener when you come.'

Gary does that, because I don't want to let them talk without me being there in case there's something I ought to hear. They don't say anything though, until we start to eat our chips and Dad begins telling us all about the film. He even sings in a gravelly voice, '*I was born under a wandering star.*'

'Oh no!' Gary shouts, blocking his ears.

Gran chuckles and stuffs another piece of cod in her mouth.

I'm not feeling all that hungry, which is when it's really good to have a little brother, because he can scoff anything. Down my chips go, hardly touching the sides!

We play a game on the way home, running through the beams of the lamp posts and walking through the shadows. Run, walk. Run, walk. It gets us there quicker, and helps to keep us warm. I've got my hand in Dad's pocket, all tucked up in his hand so we always run together.

It's gone eleven by the time we go in the door so Dad sends Gary straight up to bed.

'You too, my love,' he tells me.

'Will you come in and say goodnight?' I want to ask him not to go to the pictures again, but I don't expect I will, because it'll sound silly and selfish and he'll only laugh and ask me what on earth I'm talking about.

'Of course,' he says. 'Don't forget to brush your teeth. I'll go and set the fire, ready for the morning.'

By the time he turns Gary's light out and comes in to me I'm all snuggled in under the covers.

'Tired?' he asks, going to make sure the curtains are properly pulled.

'A bit,' I reply.

He takes some clean pyjamas out of the airing cupboard for himself and sniffs them with a great big 'aaaaah' because they're lovely and fresh and warm.

'Dad?' I say, as he tucks his pyjamas under his arm. 'What's wrong with Gran? Why did she say Uncle Tom was hiding behind the telly?'

'Oh, sometimes old people do that,' he tells me, putting his pyjamas on my old doll's pram and coming to sit on my dressing-table stool. 'They see things that aren't there, or they get muddled up in their heads. It's nothing to worry about.'

'She's not going to die, is she?' I ask.

'My love, we all die one day,' he says, brushing back my hair, 'but I don't think your old gran's going anywhere just yet.'

I knew she wasn't really, but I had to be sure, and now I'm ready to go on to the next subject. Only I wait till he's turned out the light, and is about to close the door, before I say, 'Dad, I don't mind if you've got a girlfriend.' (I do, I *really, really* do, but I'm hoping he's going to laugh and say something like, 'Where on earth did you get that idea from? Of course I haven't got a girlfriend.')

'You've got an overactive imagination, my girl,' he tells me, 'now off to sleep with you,' and with that he goes off and leaves me in the dark.

Eddie

It's been a couple of weeks now since I went to the pictures with Anne. We had a marvellous time, eating choc ices in the interval and chatting all the way home about other films

421

we've seen and finding we agreed about most of them. We caught the bus from the Centre up to the Regal in Staple Hill, where I got off with her to see her home safely. She has a Georgian-style house, as she described it, detached, and set in amongst several trees so you can't quite see it all from outside the gates. She was kind enough to invite me in for a cup of tea, and I'd have liked to accept, but the time was getting on, and I still had to pick Susan and Gary up from their gran's to take them home.

'I've had a lovely time,' she said, as we shook hands. 'Thank you very much for taking me, but you really shouldn't have paid for everything, you know.'

'It was my pleasure,' I assured her.

'Well, my treat next time.' She gave a girlish little laugh. 'Listen to me sounding all modern and liberated,' she joked.

'It's a man's place to pay,' I told her seriously, 'and that's how it should be.'

Thinking about that now makes me feel absurd, because she's obviously got a lot more than I have, so I can't imagine how I think I'm ever going to be able to afford her sort of lifestyle. Still, a pound for two cinema tickets, a couple of sixpenny ice creams and a few bob for bus fares is manageable every now and then, should she be interested in seeing me again. I'm presuming she is, because of offering to make it her treat, but I haven't rung her since because I don't want her thinking I'm too eager, or that we're actually courting, because I'm not sure I'm ready for anything as serious as that yet.

Eddress has been on my mind more than ever since that night. I don't know if she's haunting me, or if it's guilt that's making me think about her so much. I keep wondering what she'd make of me having a fancy woman, if that's what you can call Anne, though I find it a rather indelicate phrase myself. It's almost certainly one Eddress would use, and I can't work out whether I think she'd be glad I have a friend, or angry with me for being unfaithful, even though nothing in the least untoward went on. And as for what's going on in our Susan's head . . . There's no hiding anything from that girl, I know that. 'Dad, I don't mind if you've got a girlfriend.' Pull the other one, is what went through my mind when she said it, because I could tell by the tone of her voice that there would probably be merry hell to pay if I admitted I did.

Still, there's no point worrying myself about that now. If I do take Anne out again it'll only be as friends, so there's no reason for Susan even to know about it, much less to start working herself up into a state over someone taking her mother's place in our lives.

Ever since the day I lost my mind and started hitting myself in front of her, I've been noticing a change in her. We don't seem to be having quite so many rows now, and she's not sneaking out at night any more. Certainly she's always there when I go to check; however, I'm not a big enough fool to start believing we're out of the woods with her yet. It'll take some time, but at least we seem to be on the right road.

I managed to have a chat with Florrie when I called in to see her earlier. She hasn't been herself at all lately, forgetting what she's saying mid-sentence, or who people are when she's known them all her life. She's started seeing things too, like strangers walking past the windows, and the table moving across the room on its own. She got very upset about that, Tom told me, but the next minute she was telling him to sit himself down while she put the kettle on and made a cup of tea.

Yesterday she was more like her old self, grumbling about Reggie and the weather, and wondering if one of her grandsons had stolen her pension, because she'd sent him up the post office to collect it and he hadn't come back yet. I'm happy to report that he turned up while I was there, handed over every last penny, gave her a kiss and was off again.

'So how's our Susan?' she asked me.

'Well, as a matter of fact, she doesn't seem too bad,' I told her. 'She still has far too much to say for herself, but I'm not quite as worried as I was before.'

She was nodding. 'That's good to hear,' she said. 'I

wondered if she had it all bottled up about her mam, and it seems she did. Still, she's had a good cry now, so it's out of her system. She'll probably be all right from here on.'

She was talking as though her chat with Susan had happened a day or two ago, instead of a couple of weeks, but time seems to be as unstable an element in her life these days as her memory.

'Do you think I should have a chat with her myself?' I asked, concerned to hear that Susan had been crying about her mother.

'No, no. I told her I wouldn't let on that she'd got upset, so best not to say anything.'

I couldn't argue with that, because I certainly don't want Susan to stop trusting her gran.

'Anyway, it doesn't do to be dwelling on these things,' Florrie said. 'Best to let sleeping dogs lie, is my motto. Of course, you have to deal with it if something crops up, but unless it does, it's not a good idea to go stoking up fires that are trying to burn themselves out.'

I must say I tend to agree with her, but I can't help being mindful of what Dr Leigh said, that our Susan's behaviour was a cry for help. I wonder if we're managing to start answering it at last. I hope so, and she seems happy enough at the moment, so let's be grateful for that.

I'm sitting in the front room now, savouring a drop of the port Albert Pitman brought over last week for Christmas. Susan and Gary are upstairs getting ready for bed, and arguing again by the sound of it. I'll go and sort them out in a minute. I might even remind them that Father Christmas won't be coming down our chimney tonight if they don't start behaving themselves. That'll make them groan and throw pillows at me as they remind me they've known for years that he doesn't exist. It hasn't stopped them putting their stockings out, though. There they are, hanging off the mantelpiece, held in place by a couple of Eddress's prized ornaments, because our Susan's decided we should have Christmas in the front room this year.

Thanks to our Nance I've got plenty to put in the stockings, chocolate pennies, tangerines, hazelnuts, dot-to-dot books, crossword puzzles, tights for our Susan and football socks for Gary. Last week we drove up Kingswood in our new Ford Zephyr to have a look round John James, the electrical shop, to see if we could find a radiogram for Susan. As luck would have it they had just what she was looking for, reconditioned, but in very good nick, and I must say it's a handsome piece of furniture, made of teak with built-in speakers each side and the facility to hold eight records at a time that drop down one by one to play. There's a seventy-eight rpm setting as well as the forty-five and thirty-three, so from time to time I'll be able to listen to some of the old classical pieces I've collected on His Master's Voice.

I take another sip of port and find myself thinking back over the Christmases we've spent in this house, most of them with Eddress – this will be the fourth without her. It makes my heart churn to realise how much time has gone by, and even now I still half expect her to come waltzing in through the door. We always used to treat ourselves to a glass of port on Christmas Eve before she was ill, usually after we'd finished sorting out the presents and stockings. I wonder what she'd make of the way I'm coping with the children on my own, or of the present I gave to Anne when I took her for a drink last Saturday night. More chocolates, a Dairy Box this time, and a copy of Edna O'Brien's *The Girl with Green Eyes*, because she mentioned the night we went to the pictures that she hadn't read it, but would like to. I gave her a card too, saying *Merry Christmas Anne, with best wishes from Eddie*. In the card she gave me she'd written *Wishing you all the best for Christmas and the coming year, Anne*. She had a present for me too, *The Oxford Companion to English Literature*, a marvellous book that I shall spend many contented hours browsing through.

I wonder if a day will ever come when she spends Christmas with us, or us with her in her lovely Georgian

425

house set back amongst the trees. I can't say it's something I feel comfortable giving a lot of thought to, because this is where we belong, in Eddress's home. Still, there's no doubt Anne is a very kind and proper person, with exemplary morals and a gentility of spirit that is most becoming. Not at all like Eddress with her raucous laughter and boisterous shenanigans. She filled up the house in a way that can probably never be repeated, but we're starting to manage without her, I think, if only just.

They say you can wait half your life for a miracle to come along, and then half a dozen might turn up at once. I'm sure I was on the receiving end the day I met Eddress, and now I'm hopeful that one or two more will come our way over time, turning me into a father my children can be proud of, and our Gary into a professional footballer, or whatever he wants to be.

As for our Susan, one of the biggest miracles of all wouldn't be if she ended up doing well for herself, though that indeed would be big and welcome, it would be that for once in my life where she's concerned, I could end up having the last word.

AUTHOR'S NOTE

It wouldn't be true to say that the troubled years were all behind us from the point at which I end this book, because I'm afraid they weren't. Much to my dad's dismay I left school at fifteen with no qualifications, nor much ambition to speak of, though plenty of grand ideas to be sure.

After a series of temporary office jobs around Bristol, at the age of eighteen I finally found myself at HTV West's which was when the beginnings of a serious career got under way. From there I moved to Thames Television in London, aged twenty-two, and after working for some years in the drama department I started to write my first book, *Cloudesley*, a children's fantasy adventure which has never been published.

As for my dad, I wish I could say that he went on to find happiness with Anne, but alas, after several months of 'friendship' she made the mistake of asking him to choose between her and his children, and alas, he made the mistake of choosing us. As far as I'm aware he never met anyone after that; certainly there's no mention of anyone in his diaries, nor did he speak of anyone to me. I was in my thirties before he got round to telling me about Anne. Contrary to what I've written, I have no actual recollection of her, but I have a fair idea of how, in my self-absorbed teenage years, I'd have viewed a rival for my dad's affections.

He remained passionately interested in literature, poetry, philosophy, engineering, the physical act of writing and politics, throughout his life. However, during the early eighties, at the age of fifty-four, he was made redundant from his job. It broke his heart to see what happened to the unions during that time, most particularly the NUM. Like so many, he never really seemed to recover from it. His depression was long and very difficult for us all, but Gary and I never stopped loving and caring for him, and when eventually he received the right medication he and I started to become real friends. We spent many long hours talking about his life, and Mum's, which is mainly how I was able to write *Just One More Day*, and this book too.

He died in 1990, going peacefully in his sleep, aged sixty-two, at a time when I'm sure he truly believed that his children no longer needed him. (This is what he'd told the doctor he would do after my mother died, and it appears to be what happened.) Gary was doing well in his job with a sign company, and was about to get married, and I was on the eve of having my third book published. Dad was very proud of my success, but was forever insisting I should keep my feet on the ground. I think his early rejection from a publisher was a blow that he couldn't bear to think of me having to suffer.

I could wish he'd hung on just a little longer to meet his grandchildren, because I know how much joy they'd have brought him, but I guess by then he'd had enough and was ready to go.

Whether he's with my mum now I have no idea, but I'd certainly like to think so, because I know in his heart it was what he waiting for.